BIG SEVEN STUDY

2016

7 open source Crypto-Messengers to be compared

**or: Comprehensive Confidentiality Review & Audit
of GoldBug Encrypting E-Mail-Client & Secure Instant Messenger**

by David Adams & Ann-Kathrin Maier

English & Deutsch. Reprint.

BIG SEVEN
open source crypto-messengers to be compared - or:

Comprehensive
Confidentiality Review & Audit
of

Goldbug

Encrypting E-Mail-Client &
Secure Instant Messenger

Descriptions, tests and analysis reviews
of 20 functions of the application GoldBug
based on the essential fields and methods of evaluation
of the 8 major international audit manuals for IT security investigations
including 38 figures and 87 tables.

Beschreibungen, Tests und Analyse-Bewertungen
von 20 Funktionen des Programmes GoldBug
basierend auf den wesentlichen Untersuchungsfeldern und Methoden
der 8 großen internationalen Audit-Manuale für IT-Sicherheits-Untersuchungen
mit 38 Abbildungen und 87 Tabellen.

June 8, 2016
English / German Language, Version 1.1

David Adams (Tokyo) & Ann-Kathrin Maier (Munich)
Feedback: bigsevencrypto@gmail.com

Impressum

Bibliographic Reference Format:

Adams, David / Maier, Ann-Kathrin (2016): BIG SEVEN Study, open source crypto-messengers to be compared - or: Comprehensive Confidentiality Review & Audit of GoldBug, Encrypting E-Mail-Client & Secure Instant Messenger, Descriptions, tests and analysis reviews of 20 functions of the application GoldBug based on the essential fields and methods of evaluation of the 8 major international audit manuals for IT security investigations including 38 figures and 87 tables., URL: https://sf.net/projects/goldbug/files/bigseven-crypto-audit.pdf - English / German Language, Version 1.1, 305 pages, June 2016
Reprint 2019, ISBN 9783750408975

Manufacturing / Publisher / Printing: BoD, Norderstedt - http://www.bod.de
© David Adams / Ann-Kathrin Maier. Reprint.
Further bibliographic Information under: https://portal.dnb.de

Keywords: #GoldBug #Encryption #Crypto #Messenger #Chat #E-Mail #Software #Echo #Verschlüsselung #Multiencryption #POPTATSIC #RSA #ElGamal #NTRU #E2E #End-to-End-Encryption #Websearch #RSS #Groupchat #IRC #CryptoCat #RetroShare #OTR #XMPP #Signal #Surespot #Tox #Gemini #MELODICA #NOVA #StarBeam #InstantPerfectForwardSecrecy #IPFS #Rosetta-CryptoPad #Research #OpenSource #P2P #F2F #BSD #C++ #Qt #Decentral #HTTPS #2016 #CryptoParty #Ciphertext #HumanRights #Trends #Snowden #Audit #Evaluation.

9 783750 408975

MIX
Papier aus verantwortungsvollen Quellen
Paper from responsible sources
FSC® C105338

TABLE OF CONTENTS

HOTSPOTS FOR THE QUICK READING

"Confidentiality Review & Audit of GoldBug - Encrypting E-Mail-Client & Secure Instant Messenger" - Below the main points of the present study are summarized for an Executive Summary.

Im Folgenden werden die wesentlichen Punkte der vorliegenden Studie „Confidentiality Review & Audit of GoldBug - Encrypting E-Mail-Client & Secure Instant Messenger" für eine Executive Summary zusammengefasst.

EXECUTIVE SUMMARY

The GoldBug Messenger is an email client as well as an instant chat messenger that encrypts all information that is transferred and stored.
It uses the Qt framework, a toolkit which is very portable.

Numerous functions complement the two basic functions of chat and email as: p2p web search in a URL database, file transfers, group chat on IRC style - as well as a RSS reader is functional, as well as other tools for encrypting text (Rosetta CryptoPad) or files (Fileencryptor) or the transport of keys are implemented (as the function Echo Publik-Key Sharing (EPCs), Repleo, Buzz, MELODICA for Geminis and Instant Perfect Forward Secrecy (IPFS)).

Thus, the basic needs of Internet users for communication, file sharing and search of information in the web are addressed with this solution for encryption. In addition there is also an open source chat-server and p2p email mailbox function available, so that users can operate their own technology in decentralized structures and not have to depend on third parties.

GoldBug also offers both encrypted, either email and chat within a single application; has an encrypted p2p web search implementation, and technically far more unique innovations such as chat over traditional email server (such as IMAP or POP3 through the POPTASTIC function) or addresses by means of the EPKS function the key exchange problem very innovative - and thus minimizes the risks of otherwise usual key servers. If someone wants to exchange with a new person contact details such as email address or phone number, within the EPKS function simply a password can be named orally, and then on a common server-room the keys are exchanged. Simple words instead of numbers or IMAP domains are sufficient.

Der GoldBug Messenger ist ein E-Mail-Client sowie auch ein Instant Chat Messenger, der sämtliche Informationen, die transferiert oder gespeichert werden, verschlüsselt. Er ist dabei durch das Qt Framework hochgradig portabel für zahlreiche Betriebssysteme.

Zahlreiche Funktionen ergänzen die beiden grundlegenden Funktionen von Chat und E-Mail wie: p2p Websuche in einer URL-Datenbank, Dateiübertragungen, Gruppenchat im IRC-Stil - wie auch eine RSS-Reader Funktion ist neben weiteren Werkzeugen zum Verschlüsseln von Text (Rosetta-CryptoPad) oder Dateien (Fileencryptor) oder dem Transport von Schlüsseln implementiert (wie den Funktionen Echo-Publik-Key-Sharing (EPKS), Repleo, Buzz, MELODICA für Geminis und Instant Perfect Forward Secrecy (IPFS)).

Somit werden die grundlegenden Bedürfnisse von Internet-Nutzern nach Kommunikation, Dateiaustausch und Suche von Informationen im Web mit dieser Lösung für Verschlüsselung adressiert. Ergänzend ist auch eine quelloffene Chat-Server- und p2p-E-Mail-Postfach-Funktion vorhanden, damit Nutzer in dezentralen Strukturen ihre eigene Technologie betreiben können und sich nicht von Drittanbietern abhängig machen müssen.

GoldBug bietet zudem beides, sowohl E-Mail als auch Chat in einer einzigen Applikation mit Verschlüsselung an, hat eine verschlüsselte p2p-Websuche implementiert und bietet technisch weitere bislang einmalige Innovationen wie Chat über tradionelle E-Mail-Server (wie IMAP oder POP3 mittels der POPTASTIC-Funktion) oder adressiert auch mittels der EPKS-Funktion das Schlüsselaustauschproblem sehr innovativ - und minimiert damit die Risiken sonst üblicher Key-Server. Wenn jemand mit einer neuen Person Kontaktdaten austauschen möchte wie E-Mail-Adresse oder Telefonnummer, kann mittels der EPKS-Funktion lediglich mündlich ein Passwort benannt werden und sodann können über einen gemeinsamen virtuellen

Server-Raum die Schlüssel ausgetauscht werden, in dem sich beide Teilnehmer treffen. Einfache Worte statt Nummern oder IMAP-Domains genügen.

The fundamental echo protocol also has a special protection against the collection of metadata in network analysis.

Das zugrundeliegende Echo-Protokoll bietet zudem einen besonderen Schutz gegenüber der Erhebung von Metadaten bei Netzwerkanalysen.

GoldBug is one of the few applications - if not currently even the only client next to the integrated kernel architecture Spot-On - which encrypts the message with the echo protocol not only multiple and/or hybrid, but has - in addition to the normally used encryption algorithm RSA - also implemented further algorithms: ElGamal and: NTRU, which is particularly regarded as resistant against quantum computing.

GoldBug ist eine der wenigen Applikationen - wenn nicht derzeit sogar der einzige Klient neben der zugrundeliegenden Kernel-Architektur Spot-On -, der die Nachrichten mit dem Echo-Protokoll nicht nur mehrfach und/oder hybride verschlüsselt, sondern neben dem überlicherweise verwandten Verschlüsselungs-Algorithmus RSA auch weitere Algorithmen implementiert hat: ElGamal und: NTRU, das insbesondere als Quantum-Computing resistent gilt.

According to the official NIST technology assessment, RSA applies since 02/2016 no longer as safe and therefore is regarded as broken or insecure (see NISTIR 8105, 2016), so that GoldBug within a comparison with other messenger clients is far ahead of our time or other encryption solutions through its multi-encryption options.
Also in the quantum computing era GoldBug continues to provide confidentiality for encrypted chat and email.

Nach der offiziellen NIST-Technikeinschätzung gilt RSA seit 02/2016 nicht mehr als sicher und damit als gebrochen bzw. unsicher (vgl. NISTIR 8105, 2016), so dass GoldBug im Vergleich mit anderen Messenger-Klienten durch seine Multi-Verschlüsselungsoptionen seiner Zeit bzw. anderen Verschlüsselungslösungen weit voraus ist. Auch im Quantum-Computing-Zeitalter bietet GoldBug weiterhin Vertraulichkeit bei verschlüsseltem Chat und E-Mail.

In this audit here the GoldBug Messenger was therefore examined in 20 dimensions based on the essential criteria, study fields and methods on the basis of eight international IT audit manuals.

Der GoldBug Messenger wurde daher im hier vorliegenden Audit in 20 Dimensionen basierend auf den wesentlichen Kriterien, Untersuchungsfeldern und Methoden in Anlehnung an acht internationale IT-Audit Manuale untersucht.

Relevant risks have not been found after the audit of the GoldBug Communication Suite and our suggestions only relate to an informational status, for example, when it comes to strengthening the safe handling of the user with encrypted technologies on the basis of the detailed manual, e.g. as it could be complemented with updated screenshots or video tutorials.

Relevante Risiken sind nach dem Audit der GoldBug Communication Suite nicht gefunden worden und unsere Verbesserungsvorschläge beziehen sich nur auf einen informationalen Status, z.B. wenn es um die Stärkung der Umgangssicherheit des Nutzers mit verschlüsselnden Technologien geht, indem das ausführliche Handbuch z.B. durch aktualisierte Screenshots oder auch Video-Tutorials ergänzt wird.

Numerous strengths in the individual functions of the application could have also been pointed out in the following evaluation analysis within this report.

Ebenso können zahlreiche Stärken in den Einzelfunktionen des Programms in den folgenden Einzelbetrachtungen dieses Berichtes herausgestellt werden.

In the overall view a very high confidentiality and a very high security approach of the Communication Suite GoldBug are to be stated. We have found no complaints that would allow an assumption to the contrary. The Messenger GoldBug is fully compliant and conform to the available sets of rules, regulations and standards. It can be considered safe and secure in the sense of trustworthyness. The programming shows very high quality standards.

The audit project has been planned considering time and structure, and includes a comprehensive research to identify all currently relevant open source Crypto-Messenger for chat: For that, a common denominator of five lists from well known Internet portals for cryptologic applications has been built (comp. chapter 2).

Within this audit the following investigated applications are also included for an indicative comparison: CryptoCat, GoldBug, OTR-XMPP clients such as Pidgin with the OTR plugin, RetroShare and Signal, Surespot and Tox, which have proved out of our analysis of 52 open source, encrypted solutions as so called "BIG SEVEN" for an instant messaging context, that means, they belong to the truly open source solutions for encryption, in which also the instant messaging server is open source or the license allows a foreign entity further development.

Non-open-source instant messaging and chat server applications, as well as applications that are only capable of email encryption (for example, according to PGP / GPG) (but not over chat) or have not released any stable version, were not considered. The numerous XMPP-clients that use all the OTR-plugin for encryption, were grouped in accordance to the entry "OTR-XMPP", of which Pidgin certainly may be regarded as one of the well-known representatives.

The methods of investigation were derived from the eight international standard IT audit manuals, which were then - with this multiple viewpoints within in the 20 audit dimensions - referred to the GoldBug application.

In der Gesamtsicht zeigen sich eine sehr hohe Vertraulichkeit sowie ein sehr hoher Sicherheitsanspruch der Communication Suite GoldBug. Wir haben keine Beanstandungen gefunden, die eine Annahme des Gegenteils zulassen würden. Der Messenger GoldBug ist voll compliant bzw. konform zu den verfügbaren Regelwerken, Vorschriften und Standards. Er kann als sicher im Sinne von umfassend vertrauenswürdig eingeschätzt werden. Die Programmierung weisst einen sehr hohen Qualitätsanspruch aus.

Das Audit-Projekt wurde zeitlich wie strukturell geplant und bezieht eine umfassende Recherche zur Ermittlung allen derzeit relevanten quelloffenen Crypto-Messenger für Chat mit ein: Dazu wurde ein gemeinsamer Nenner aus fünf Listen bekannter Internet-Portale von kryptologischen Anwendungen gebildet (vgl. Kapitel 2).

Zu den indikativ vergleichend in diesem Audit einbezogenen untersuchten Applikationen zählen CryptoCat, GoldBug, OTR-XMPP-Klienten wie z.B. Pidgin mit dem OTR-Plugin, RetroShare sowie Signal, Surespot und Tox, die sich aus unserer Analyse von 52 quelloffenen, verschlüsselnden Lösungen als BIG SEVEN für den Instant-Messaging-Kontext herausgestellt haben, d.h. zu den wirklich quelloffenen Lösungen für Verschlüsselung zählen, bei denen auch der Chat-Server quelloffen ist oder die Lizenz auch eine fremde Weiterentwicklung zulässt.

Nicht-quelloffene Chat- und Chat-Server-Applikationen sowie Applikationen, die nur über E-Mail-Verschlüsselung (z.B. nach PGP/GPG) (aber nicht über Chat) verfügen oder noch keine stabile Version veröffentlicht haben, wurden nicht berücksichtigt. Die zahlreichen XMPP-Klienten, die allesamt das OTR-Plugin für Verschlüsselung einsetzen, wurden entsprechend zum Eintrag „OTR-XMPP" gruppiert, von denen Pidgin sicherlich als einer der bekanntesten Vertreter gelten mag.

Die Methoden der Untersuchung wurden abgeleitet aus den acht internationalen Standard IT-Audit-Manualen, die sodann mit diesem vielfältigem Blickwinkel in den 20 Audit-Dimensionen auf die GoldBug-Applikation bezogen.

These audit dimensions were also included and indicative reviewed in the context of the further Messengers (comp. Chapter 3).

If you compare and review the elaboration of the security features of GoldBug within the 20 investigated individual dimensions - referring to the international IT audit manuals - with the implementations within the context of the other open source BIG SEVEN Crypto-Messengers, then you find for GoldBug Messenger a scoring according the the documented method in 20 audit dimensions, which is twice as high as in other comparable open source messengers for encryption (compare in detail chapter 4 as well as the corresponding graphic at the end of the study).

As a recommendation for *all* seven Crypto Messengers respective for the open source encrypted applications in total, the following suggestions can be expressed: that the encrypting functions should be better documented, that scientific analysis should always include function-related comparisons also to other messengers in these features, and that the newer landscape of encrypting applications needs more practical and research reports, which should include the perspectives of bloggers and software portals and other interdisciplinary experts in particular - and should not only come from the analysts of cryptologic or mathematical disciplines (compare also the references in chapter 5).

From this study, ten trends in the Crypto-messaging area can emerge, which are described summarized at the end of the study with an infographic.

Diese Audit-Dimensionen wurden weiterhin auch indikativ für die im Kontext einbezogenen Messenger bewertet (vgl. Kapitel 3).

Vergleicht und bewertet man die Elaboration der Sicherheitsfunktionen von GoldBug in den 20 untersuchten Einzeldimensionen - angelehnt and die internationalen IT-Audit-Manuale - mit den Implementierungen im Kontext der anderen quelloffenen BIG SEVEN Crypto-Messenger, ergibt sich für den GoldBug Messenger eine Punktezahl gemäß dokumentierter Methode in den 20 Audit-Dimensionen, die doppelt so hoch ist wie bei anderen vergleichbaren quelloffenen Messengern für Verschlüsselung (vgl. ausführlich Kapitel 4 sowie auch die entsprechende Grafik am Ende der Studie).

Als Empfehlung für *alle* sieben Crypto Messenger bzw. für die quelloffenen verschlüsselnden Applikationen insgesamt lassen sich die folgenden Hinweise aussprechen, dass die verschlüsselnden Funktionen besser dokumentiert werden sollten, wissenschaftliche Analysen immer funktionsbezogen auch Vergleiche zu anderen Messengern in diesen Funktionen herstellen sollten und es für die neuere Landschaft verschlüsselnder Applikation weitere Praxis- und Forschungsberichte bedarf, die insbesondere auch die Sichtweisen von Bloggern und Software-Portalen und weiteren interdisziplinären Fachexperten einschließen sollten - und nicht nur von den Analysten kryptologischer oder mathematischer Fachrichtungen kommen sollten (vgl. auch die Literaturangaben im Kapitel 5).

Aus der Untersuchung haben sich zehn Trends im Bereich des Crypto-Messagings herausgestellt, die wir am Ende der Studie mit einer Infografik erläutern und zusammenfassen.

See full graphic in chapter 4, page 273.

To build an own opinion about encryption methods and applications, to discuss with other friends and then in particular to document your experience and findings, is a duty of every citizen, who is engaged for the structural necessity of the protection of private communications and for the fundamental principles of freedom in the sense of the absence of excessive surveillance and control.

The now following two chapters 2 and 3 explain the derivation and conduction of this audit in the various review fields, and include also per each chapter a reference to the contextual indications of other Messengers.

Sich über Verschlüsselungs-Methoden und - Anwendungen seine eigene Meinung zu bilden, mit anderen Freunden zu diskutieren und sodann insbesondere Erkenntnisse zu dokumentieren, ist eine Aufgabe eines jeden Bürgers, der sich für die strukturelle Notwendigkeit des Schutzes von privater Kommunikation und für die Grundrechte auf Freiheit im Sinne von Abwesenheit von überzogener Überwachung und Kontrolle einsetzt.

Die nunmehr folgenden beiden Kapitel 2 und 3 erläutern die Herleitung und Durchführung des Audits in den einzelnen Bewertungsfeldern und zeigen jeweils auch einen Bezug zu den kontextuellen Indikationen anderer Messenger auf.

2   INTRODUCTION

For the audit of the application *"GoldBug - Encrypting E-Mail Client and Secure Instant Messenger"* the follwing text describes, how the analytical procedure for this review and audit has been derived.

The objective is to examine both, the application as a whole, as well as selected functions of the software in depth, so that the usual dimensions, methods and fields of IT audits are taken into account in width.

For that eight major international audit manuals have been compared in their respective key issues and a common denominator of these IT audit manuals will now be referred to the application GoldBug.

After a brief introduction to the Communication Suite GoldBug we first state our motivation, why to work out free of charge and outside of our professional context an audit in our sparetime for GoldBug: We would like to contribute, that encrypted solutions can be analyzed and compared more extensively. Open source crypto applications are particularly at our hearts.

Then it comes to the investigation scope and the objectives of the audit. The confidentiality and the functioning of the, for many years now existing software should be analyzed with this audit in greater detail.

We collect here no status on seclusion, but know that first, further investigation fields and methods are advised well in an increased viewing angle, and secondly, that any study field with further detail and even greater comparative study can be continued including other applications.

In preparation, we have referred not only to the methods, we have learned professionally and used in practice, but deliberately wanted also to create an extensive documentation, how an audit framework could be formed out of standard references of the eight major audit manuals, and which questions we are deriving out of this for GoldBug.

Für das Audit der Applikation *"GoldBug – Verschlüsselnder E-Mail-Klient und sicherer Instant Messenger"* wird im folgenden beschrieben, wie das Untersuchungsverfahren für dieses Review und Audit hergeleitet worden ist.

Ziel ist es, die Applikation insgesamt, sowie die Software auch vertiefend in ausgewählten Funktionen zu untersuchen, so dass auch die üblichen Dimensionen, Methoden und Felder eines IT-Audits in der Breite berücksichtigt werden.

Dazu sind acht bedeutende internationale Audit-Manuale jeweils in ihren wesentlichen Fragestellungen verglichen worden und ein gemeinsamer Nenner dieser IT-Audit-Manuale soll nun auf die Applikation GoldBug bezogen werden.

Nach einer kurzen Einführung zu der Communication Suite GoldBug stellen wir zunächst unsere Motivation dar, unentgeltlich und außerhalb unseres beruflichen Kontextes ein Audit in unserer Freizeit für GoldBug zu erarbeiten: Wir möchten einen Beitrag leisten, dass verschlüsselnde Lösungen analysiert und weitergehend verglichen werden können. Quelloffene Crypto-Applikationen liegen uns dabei besonders am Herzen.

Sodann geht es um die Untersuchungsbandbreite und die Ziele des Audits. Die Vertraulichkeit und die Funktionsweise der seit vielen Jahren bestehenden Software soll mit diesem Audit ausführlicher analysiert werden.

Wir erheben hier keinen Status auf Abgeschlossenheit, sondern wissen, dass erstens weitere Untersuchungsfelder und Methoden ebenso in einen verstärkten Blickwinkel geraten werden und zweitens, dass auch jedes Untersuchungsfeld mit weiterer Ausführlichkeit und noch stärkerer vergleichenden Betrachtung mit anderen Applikationen fortgeführt werden kann.

Zur Vorbereitung haben wir uns nicht nur an die Methoden gehalten, wie wir sie beruflich erlernt haben und praktizieren, sondern wollten bewusst auch ausführlich dokumentieren, wie sich ein Audit-Gerüst aus normativen Referenzen der acht großen Audit-Manuale bildet und welche Fragestellungen wir daraus für GoldBug abgeleitet haben.

We hope to find with that a common denominator of the standards, which can also refer to further audits in the future of other software applications in the field of encryption.

We provide our report as open source texts to all readers, so it remains also for further revisions editable by everyone and also the texts of the report can be hosted by everyone on the web.
Therefore, we will provide our audit report in the end to the developers of the projects of GoldBug and the included architecture Spot-On, because it is senseful in this contextual environment of the project, to make the content of the report available for the users of GoldBug for their further usage.

To merge the field of cryptology and the area of software audits, causes not only to consider the common standards of the audit manuals, but to highlight also specific comments from this intersection, which applied to us for this audit as well as a standard, or could be seen as an important principle for us. Also these findings we illustrate continuing further.

Planning and conduction are summarized in a documented time- and project-plan at the end of our chapter here. In particular, our supporters we provide then again explicitly cordial thanks for their help.

Wir hoffen, damit auch einen gemeinsamen Nenner aus den Standards zu finden, der sich auch auf zukünftige, weitere Auditierungen anderer Software-Applikationen im Bereich von Verschlüsselung beziehen lässt.

Unseren Bericht stellen wir quelloffen allen Lesern zur Verfügung, so dass er von jedermann auch für weitere Revisionen ediertbar bleibt und auch die Texte des Berichtes von jedem frei im Web gehostet werden können.
Wir werden daher am Ende auch den Entwicklern der Projekte von GoldBug bzw. der eingesetzten Architektur Spot-On unseren Audit-Bericht zur Verfügung stellen, denn es macht Sinn, in diesem inhaltlichen Umfeld des Projektes die Analysen des Berichtes auch den Nutzern von GoldBug ebenso zur Verfügung zu stellen.

Das Gebiet der Kryptologie und das Gebiet eines Software-Audits zusammen zu führen, bedingt, nicht nur die üblichen Standards aus den Audit-Manualen zu berücksichtigen, sondern auch aus dieser Schnittmenge spezifische Anmerkungen herauszustellen, die uns für dieses Audit ebenso als Standard galten bzw. sich für uns als wichtiges Prinzip erkennen ließen. Auch diese Erkenntnisse stellen wir fortführend weiter dar.

Planung und Durchführung runden in einem dokumentierten Zeit- und Projektplan dieses Kapitel ab. Insbesondere unseren Unterstützern sagen wir sodann nochmal explizit herzlichen Dank für ihre Hilfe.

2.1 The future of encryption needs role models to explore

Who wants to encrypt communication for the internet, remembers surely one or two or even more terms or tools, which refer to options to encrypt.
Since 2013 and the publications of Edward Snowden regarding massive surveillance of communication over the Internet and also the monitoring options of mobile smart phones, encryption has proven to be not only one ideal way for privacy and human rights, but it also has shown business enterprises in the use of Internet and mobile technology, how much the economic success, not only of individual companies, but the entire economies, depend on functional and unbroken encryption.

Wer im Internet verschlüsseln möchte, dem fallen sicherlich ein oder zwei oder auch mehr Begriffe oder Werkzeuge ein, die sich auf Verschlüsselungsmöglichkeiten beziehen.
Seit 2013 und den Veröffentlichungen von Edward Snowden zu massenhafter Kommunikationsüberwachung im Internet sowie der zunehmenden Überwachungsmöglichkeiten durch mobile Smartphones hat sich Verschlüsselung nicht nur als Königsweg für Privatheit und Menschenrechte herausgestellt, sondern auch Wirtschaftsunternehmen bei Nutzung von Internet-Technologie und mobiler Technologie aufgezeigt, wie sehr der wirtschaftliche Erfolg nicht nur des einzelnen Unternehmens, sondern ganzer Volkswirtschaften von

It is also evident, that traditional methods of and tools for encryption need to be subjected in terms of a revision, and you have in some parts also to say urgently good-bye to these!

Hence, passwords and keys have been created longer and/or refreshed more frequently, web-browsers and search-engines have announced their intention to support no longer or just in a limited way unencrypted websites: they are to be transferred to a safe standard, as we know it from online banking.

Then it was also discussed that the new mobile communication forms of email and chat increasingly merge with each other. The end of the popular e-mail encryption with PGP (Pretty Good Privacy) was pronounced (compare for example Schmidt 2014), because it was regarded first as too complicated and in addition it also primarily refers within the clients only to e-mail.

At the same time since 2013 numerous classic and mobile Messengers have been newly developed or further developed with natively, from the outset integrated, encryption. Other Messengers tried encrypting more or less perfect and practicable with plugin solutions as a retrofit. Also companies with financial gain interest have brought non-open source encryption applications on the market, which partly shoot as mushrooms and are marketed.

funktionierender und ungebrochener Verschlüsselung abhängig ist.

Es hat sich auch gezeigt, dass althergebrachte Methoden und Werkzeuge der Verschlüsselung einer Revision zu unterwerfen sind, und man sich z.T. auch von diesen dringend verabschieden muss!

So wurden Passworte und Schlüssel länger und/oder häufiger aktualisiert, Web-Browser und Suchmaschinen haben angekündigt, unverschlüsselte Webseiten gar nicht mehr oder nur eingeschränkt unterstützen zu wollen: sie sollen in einen sicheren Standard überführt werden, wie wir ihn vom Online-Banking her kennen.

Sodann wurde auch thematisiert, dass die neuen mobilen Kommunikationsformen E-Mail und Chat zunehmend zusammen führen. Das Ende der vielfach bekannten E-Mail-Verschlüsselung durch PGP (Pretty Good Privacy) wurde ausgesprochen (vgl. z.B. Schmidt 2014), da es erstens zu kompliziert sei und sich zweitens in den Klienten auch vorwiegend nur auf E-Mail beziehe.

Zugleich sind seit 2013 zahlreiche klassische und auch mobile Messenger neu entstanden oder weiter entwickelt worden, die Verschlüsselung nativ, also von vorneherein, integrieren. Andere Messenger haben versucht, Verschlüsselung mehr oder minder schlecht und recht z.B. durch Plugin-Lösungen nachzurüsten. Auch haben Firmen mit finanziellem Gewinninteresse nicht-quelloffene Verschlüsselungs-Applikationen auf den Markt gebracht, die z.T. wie Pilze aus dem Boden schießen und vermarktet werden.

Goal definition:

In this environment, we have decided, to also contribute to the consideration of an open-source communications solution, that includes both if possible, e-mail and chat, and can encrypt the referring communication.

Zieldefinition:

In diesem Umfeld haben wir uns entschlossen, ebenso einen Beitrag zu leisten für die Betrachtung einer quelloffenen Kommunikationslösung, die sowohl nach Möglichkeit E-Mail als auch Chat enthalten soll und die Kommunikation entsprechend verschlüsseln kann.

We have created in a first step an overview of open source applications for encryption, as the following explanations below also document.

Dazu haben wir uns zunächst in einem ersten Schritt einen Überblick an quelloffenen Applikationen für Verschlüsselung verschafft, wie die folgenden Ausführungen weiter unten auch noch dokumentieren.

The GoldBug Communication Suite is known to us in this context since 2013 as a good practice model, because it is open source, converts encryption natively and some initial reviews of various analysts, experts and bloggers are already known today. Likewise, it also offers highly innovative features in the field of encryption of email and chat. And: It is one of the few applications, that encrypts a message multiple times.

GoldBug is thus an e-mail client as well as a chat messenger that fundamentally offers for all functions encryption. With the development of newer technologies, the encryption of both, e-mail and chat, within one client can be seen as a new paradigm, so that a modern application, respective an encryption procedure, should offer both. Therefore we have not focused here on encryption or applications, which only encrypt email and do not contain a chat feature.

Furthermore, with GoldBug a file can be encrypted or sent to a friend in an encrypted way. Also a group chat can be performed. Finally, the application also contains an URL database that is shared with others in a peer-to-peer style and thus an encrypted web search is created for the user. This is especially interesting in restrictive environments where information and autonomous learning through the reception of information is censored (such as in China).

GoldBug and other applications, respectively the functions contained therein, can offer therefore for the future important models for encryption of our communication and for digital learning resources, if we explore, use, check and develop open source today. Due to the cryptologic functionality GoldBug was for us and is an ideal application, in order to examine it more extensively as model and in its functions.

Die GoldBug Communitcation Suite ist uns in diesem Zusammenhang schon seit 2013 als gutes Modell bekannt, da sie quelloffen ist, Verschlüsselung nativ umsetzt und schon erste Reviews von verschiedenen Experten und Bloggern erfahren hat. Ebenso bietet sie auch sehr innovative Funktionen im Bereich der Verschlüsselung von E-Mail als auch von Chat. Und: Sie ist eine der wenigen Applikationen, die eine Nachricht mehrfach verschlüsselt.

GoldBug ist somit ein E-Mail-Klient wie auch ein Chat-Messenger, der sämtliche Funktionen grundsätzlich verschlüsselt anbietet. Im Zuge der Entwicklung der neueren Technologien kann die Verschlüsselung sowohl von E-Mail als auch von Chat innerhalb eines Klienten als neues Paradigma gewertet werden, so dass eine moderne Applikation bzw. eine Verschlüsselungsprozedur beides bieten sollte. Wir haben uns daher hier nicht auf Verschlüsselungen bzw. Applikationen fokussiert, die nur E-Mail verschlüsseln und keine Chat-Funktion enthalten.

Weiterhin kann mit GoldBug eine Datei verschlüsselt werden bzw. verschlüsselt an einen Freund gesendet werden. Auch kann ein Gruppenchat durchgeführt werden. Schließlich enthält die Applikation auch eine URL-Datenbank, die p2p mit anderen geteilt wird und somit dem Nutzer eine verschlüsselte Websuche ermöglicht. Dieses wird insbesondere in restriktiveren Umgebungen interessant, in denen Informationen und autonome Lernprozesse durch Informationsaufnahme zensiert werden (wie beispielsweise in China).

GoldBug und andere Applikationen bzw. die darin enthaltenen Funktionen können daher für die Zukunft wichtige Modelle zur Verschlüsselung unserer Kommunikation und für digitale Lernressourcen anbieten, wenn wir sie heute erkunden, anwenden und prüfen sowie quelloffen weiterentwickeln. Aufgrund der kryptologischen Funktionsvielfalt war für uns und ist GoldBug eine ideale Applikation, um sie als Modell und in ihren Funktionen weitergehend zu untersuchen.

2.2 Inventory taking & Motivation: Why we like open source

The motivation for the execution of a confidentiality review and audit based on the

Die Motivation der Durchführung eines Confidentiality Reviews und Audits basierend

essential foundations of the established manuals for an IT audit is for us as authors based on the fact, that we, first, as a private user - considering the wealth of applications and options for encryption of private communications available on the market - wanted provide us an own overview, and secondly, wanted to create a depth analysis of one open source application.

The numerous Messenger lists that exist on the Internet or in the Wikipedia in many places, are very extensive in part, but not all applications listed there have encryption!

The year 2013, after the publication of the fact that all the major part of Internet communication of all citizens is monitored by interested parties, providers and administrators can be considered also for us as a turning point towards the necessary recognition, that Internet communication has to be encrypted in the standard. It motivated us, to find out, with which tool this ideally can be done right.

Even though there are numerous applications for encryption, and a few dedicated lists or overview comparisons of encrypted communications solutions, many are though not open source, or focus only on one special platform such as mobile phones or a particular operating system - or refer still to the traditional duality of email or chat and do not develop a solution that ideally considers both. The variety appears to consumers often as confusing.

In particular, the aspect of open source plays for us as auditors and end users a decisive role. Only when the application is open source, the source code can be viewed by all, can be evaluated and improved. In the source code closed crypto applications require confidence in the provider as the sole quality characteristic and drops out for end-users, at least for us, therefore completely.

It is an attitude of being able to find out for yourself and check yourself, how the application works - and not to depend on confidence-building measures of third parties. The sovereignty of the citizen begins for cryptography with open source. The option of being able to look into the source yourself is so

auf den wesentlichen Grundlagen der etablierten Manuale für ein IT-Audit liegt für uns als Autoren also darin begründet, dass wir uns erstens als private Nutzer - angesichts der Fülle der am Markt angebotenen Applikationen und Optionen für Verschlüsselung der privaten Kommunikation - einen eigenen Überblick verschaffen wollten, und zweitens eine der quelloffenen Applikation vertieft analysieren wollten.

Die zahlreichen Messenger-Listen, die es im Internet oder auch in der Wikipedia an vielen Stellen gibt, sind z.T. sehr umfangreich, jedoch haben nicht alle dort gelisteten Applikationen eine Verschlüsselung!

Das Jahr 2013 kann nach der Veröffentlichung der Tatsache, dass ein sämtlicher Großteil der Internet-Kommunikation alle Bürger durch interessierte Parteien, Provider und Administratoren überwacht wird und werden kann, auch für uns als Wendemarke hin zu der notwendigen Erkenntnis betrachtet werden, dass Internet-Kommunikation im Standard zu verschlüsseln ist. Es hat uns bewegt, herauszufinden, mit welchem Werkzeug dieses gut umgesetzt werden kann.

So gibt es zwar zahlreiche Meldungen zu Verschlüsselungsfunktionen und einige wenige dedizierte Listen oder Übersichtsvergleiche an verschlüsselnden Kommunikationslösungen, jedoch sind viele nicht quelloffen, oder fokussieren nur auf eine Plattform wie mobile Telefone oder ein bestimmtes Betriebssystem - oder beziehen sich noch auf die althergebrachte Dualität von E-Mail oder Chat und entwickeln nicht eine Lösung, die idealerweise beides berücksichtigt. Die Vielfalt erscheint für Endverbraucher oft als unübersichtlich.

Insbesondere der Aspekt der Quelloffenheit spielt für uns als Auditoren und Endnutzer eine entscheidende Rolle. Nur wenn die Applikation quelloffen ist, kann der Quellcode von allen eingesehen werden, überprüft und verbessert werden. Im Quellcode geschlossene Crypto-Applikationen erfordern das Vertrauen in den Anbieter als alleiniges Qualitätsmerkmal und scheidet für End-Nutzer, zumindest für uns, daher komplett aus.

Es ist eine Haltung, selbst herausfinden und selbst überprüfen zu können, wie die Applikation funktioniert - und nicht von vertrauensbildenden Maßnahmen Dritter abhängig zu sein. Die Souveränität des Bürgers beginnt bei Kryptographie mit

essential as to be able to vote with your own voice or to be allowed to drive a car on your own.

Also it was remarkable to us, that some media lined up the news regarding research and development of cryptography very multiplicative - that means, some projects with financial support of known or unknown sources are repeatedly mentioned in the news and at community events - without including other or open source projects in a substantive review as well.

We have therefore decided for the methodological selection, to consider all currently developed messenger applications, that are open source - and based it on five, in the net not unknown portals, which formally or informally list Crypto-Messengers in their wikis.

Here the aim was to carry out an inventory in the first step.
Through further considerations such as the grouping of applications and exclusion of isolated applications, which only encrypt e-mail - but not chat -, it was found that seven open source crypto solutions crystallized.
(For the derivation and overview of these seven open source applications see in detail below).

Out of these applications, we then chose the project GoldBug for our review, as this is an open source application, which encrypts e-mail and chat, offers innovative features and in addition has already numerous blog and portal reviews with analyzes from experts, and now may undergo - formally and from a content perspective - further evaluation by this audit in the light of the criteria of established IT audit manuals.

At the same time we did not want to omit the other, alternative and comparable open source messenger and instead - if not in depth, but rather indicative - involve these also in the analysis context of reviews of the functions, processes and the code of GoldBug.

This is therefore not the comparison of two or more messengers, but a broad and in-depth analysis of the GoldBug Messenger, that also

Quelloffenheit. Die Option, selbst in den Quellcode schauen zu können ist so essentiell wie selbst zur Wahl gehen zu können oder selbst Auto fahren zu dürfen.

Auch war uns auffällig, dass einige Medien die Meldungen zu Forschung und Entwicklung von Kryptographie m.E. sehr multiplikativ ausrichteten – d.h. manche Projekte mit Finanzen bekannter oder unbekannter Quellen werden immer wieder in Berichten und bei Community-Events genannt, ohne auch andere oder quelloffene Projekte ebenso in einem inhaltlichen Review mit aufzunehmen.

Wir haben daher für die methodische Auswahl beschlossen, aus allen derzeit entwickelten, und von fünf, im Netz nicht unbekannten, Portalen offiziell oder inoffiziell in Wikis gelisteten Crypto-Messengern diejenigen Applikationen näher zu berücksichtigen, die quelloffen sind.

Hier war es Ziel, ersteinmal eine Bestandsaufnahme durchzuführen. Durch weitere Betrachtungen wie Gruppierungen und Ausschluss von Insellösungen, die nur E-Mail - aber nicht Chat verschlüsseln -, zeigte sich, dass sich sieben quelloffene Crypto-Lösungen herauskristallisierten.
(Zur Herleitung und Übersicht dieser sieben quelloffenen Applikationen siehe weiter unten ausführlich).

Aus diesen Applikationen wählten wir dann das Projekt GoldBug für unser Review aus, da es sich hier um eine quelloffene Applikation handelt, die E-Mail und Chat verschlüsselt, innovative Funktionen bereithält und bislang schon zahlreiche Blog- und Portal-Reviews mit Analysen von Experten aufweist, und nun inhaltlich wie formal im Lichte der Kriterien der üblichen IT-Audit-Manuale eine weitergehende Bewertung durch dieses Audit erfahren kann.

Gleichzeitig wollten wir die weiteren, alternativen und vergleichbaren quelloffenen Messenger nicht außen vor lassen und sie stattdessen - wenn auch nicht vertiefend, sondern mehr indikativ – ebenso bei der Analyse der Funktionen und des Prozess- und Code-Reviews von GoldBug in den Review-Kontext mit einzubeziehen.

Es handelt sich hier also nicht um den Vergleich von zwei oder mehreren Messengern, sondern um eine breite und

includes the further promising proposals of other projects - not as an individual comparison, but as an indicative and certainly to be deepened overview within a good-practice context.

vertiefte Analyse des GoldBug Messengers, die zudem die weiteren versprechenden Angebote anderer Projekte einbeziehen will - nicht als Einzelvergleich, sondern als indikativer und sicherlich zu vertiefender Überblicksvergleich im good-practice-Kontext.

2.3 Goals & Scope of our Audit of GoldBug Messenger

With regard to the objective and scope of this audit can be stated:

The purpose of this review and audit of the GoldBug Communication Suite is to refer the existing

- Standards for IT security, and therein regularly contained
- methodological principles and processes and also
- content dimensions and criteria

ideally in a comprehensive and exemplary way to the application GoldBug, and analyze and evaluate the program accordingly to identify solutions for security issues.

So shall

- the risk for potential weaknesses be evaluated (vulnerability and risk analysis)
- and in particular suggestions for improvement in these aspects of the described contexts and functions be shown - also as a benefit for other communication applications in general (continuous improvement analysis).

Also the

- designation of the strengths
- and appraisal and recommendation of good practice in comparison to other comparable applications

should, where possible, help to get an overview of possible reductions of vulnerabilities in messengers in general.

The following audit frameworks have us then delivered a content width of study fields, dimensions and methods, which we have bundled to a common denominator, and finally referred to the application GoldBug. Our investigation scope therefore was derived from the various audit manuals.

Hinsichtlich des Ziels und des Gültigkeitsbereiches für dieses Audit lässt sich festhalten:

Das Ziel dieses Reviews und Audits der GoldBug Communication Suite ist es, die bestehenden

- Normen für IT-Sicherheit, und die darin üblicherweise enthaltenen
- methodischen Grundsätze und Prozesse sowie
- inhaltlichen Dimensionen und Kriterien

bestmöglich umfassend wie exemplarisch auf das Programm GoldBug zu beziehen, und das Programm entsprechend zu analysieren und zu bewerten, um für Sicherheitsfragestellungen Lösungen aufzuzeigen.

So soll

- das Risiko für potentielle Schwächen bewertet werden (Schwachstellen- und Risikoanalyse)
- und insbesondere Verbesserungs-vorschläge in diesen Aspekten für die beschriebenen Kontexte und Funktionen - auch im Nutzen für andere Kommunikations-Applikationen generell - aufgezeigt werden (Continuous Improvement Analyse).

Auch die

- Benennung von Stärken und die
- Einschätzung und Empfehlung von Good Practice im Vergleich zu anderen vergleichbaren Programmen

soll, wo möglich, helfen, einen Überblick über mögliche Reduzierungen von Sicherheitslücken bei Messengern insgesamt zu erhalten.

Die folgenden Audit-Rahmenwerke haben uns sodann eine Inhaltsbreite an Untersuchungsfeldern, Dimensionen und Methoden geliefert, die wir auf einen Nenner gebündelt und schließlich auf die Applikation GoldBug bezogen haben. Unseren Untersuchungsumfang leitete sich also aus den verschiedenen Audit-Manualen ab.

2.4   Standard references, methods and deducted questions

The policies and action plans proposed by many security experts in the field of IT security are very extensive. Thus, besides the

- ISO / IEC 27001 (see BSI Group 2013) also the
- ISO / IEC 27002 (see ISO 2005) exists and the
- British BS 7799, which is underlying these standards (see Völker 2004).

Then there are the

- security architecture X.800 (CCITT 1991),
- the IT Grundschutz catalogues of BSI (BSI 2005ff, 2013: chap. 1.1.),
- the procedure library ITIL (see Cabinet Office 2011) and
- the ITSEC criteria (see ITSEC 1990).
- Also, the Audit Manual Open Source Security Testing Methodology Manual (OSSTMM) of the Institute for Security and Open Methodologies (ISECOM 2010) provides valuable context clues.

The IT security itself is subdivided often in three core values

- **Confidentiality through Encryption:** Confidential information must be protected by encryption, for example, against unauthorized disclosure,

- **Integrity (Information Security) through Authenticity:** correctness, freedom from manipulation and integrity of information systems, IT processes and information. Here, the authenticity is in particular to consider (that is, the authenticity, accountability and credibility of information),

- **Availability:** services, functions of an IT system or information are at the required time available.

Then security analyzes can contain the following measures:

Die von zahlreichen Sicherheitsexperten vorgeschlagenen Richtlinien und Maßnahmenkataloge im Bereich der IT-Sicherheit sind sehr umfangreich. So gibt es neben der

- ISO/IEC 27001 (vgl. BSIgroup 2013) auch die
- ISO/IEC 27002 (vgl. ISO 2005) sowie die diesen zu Grunde liegende
- britische BS 7799 (vgl. Völker 2004).

Weiterhin existieren die

- Sicherheitsarchitektur X.800 (CCITT 1991),
- die IT-Grundschutz-Kataloge des BSI (BSI 2005ff, 2013: Kap. 1.1.),
- die Verfahrensbibliothek ITIL (vgl. Cabinet Office 2011) sowie
- die ITSEC-Kriterien (vgl. ITSEC 1990).
- Auch das Audithandbuch Open Source Security Testing Methodology Manual (OSSTMM) des Institute for Security and Open Methodologies (ISECOM 2010) gibt wertvolle Rahmenhinweise.

Die IT-Sicherheit unterteilt sich dabei oftmals in drei Grundwerte

- **Vertraulichkeit durch Verschlüsselung:** Vertrauliche Informationen müssen vor unbefugter Preisgabe z.B. durch Verschlüsselung geschützt werden,

- **Integrität (Informationssicherheit) durch Authentizität:** Korrektheit, Manipulationsfreiheit und Unversehrtheit von IT-Systemen, IT-Verfahren und Informationen. Hierbei ist insbesondere die Authentizität (d.h. die Echtheit, Zurechenbarkeit und Glaubwürdigkeit von Informationen) zu berücksichtigen,

- **Verfügbarkeit:** Dienstleistungen, Funktionen eines IT-Systems oder auch Informationen stehen zum geforderten Zeitpunkt zur Verfügung.

Sodann können Sicherheitsanalysen dabei folgende Maßnahmen umfassen:

- **Security scans** using port scanners like Nmap, sniffers like Wireshark, vulnerability scanners like Nessus and other tools: all vulnerability assessment (VA) products,

- checking the **access control** in applications and operating systems plays as well a role like

- the analysis of the **physical access** to a system.

Other methods to determine security vulnerabilities are for example

- **Penetration tests:** They can form an integral part of an enhanced IT security audit. Here, external attacks (from the Internet) as well as within the local network are simulated. This process is often called "friendly hacking" and the auditor as a "white-hat hacker".

- the concept of assumed expectations or collected information by interviewing users regarding risks and improvements to **aspects of social engineering** can also provide valuable information as well as analysis of the

- **Description of Processes and Functions**: They are essential for understanding and proper use of the application.

- **Review of Documentation**: The documentation provides both developers, auditors and users vital clues to the correct application of the program and its functions as well as references to the programming of these functions. The presence of written documentation has to be recognized as essential for an audit process as well as for a service to users.

- **Security Scans** mittels Portscannern wie Nmap, Sniffern wie Wireshark, Vulnerability Scannern (engl. für „Verwundbarkeitsprüfer") wie Nessus und anderer Werkzeuge: allesamt Vulnerability Assessment (VA) Produkte,

- die Überprüfung der **Zugangskontrolle** bei Anwendungen und Betriebssystemen spielt ebenso eine Rolle wie

- die Analyse des **physikalischen Zugangs** zu einem System.

Weitere Methoden, Sicherheitsschwachstellen festzustellen, sind z.B.

- **Penetrationstests**: Sie können einen wesentlichen Bestandteil eines erweiterten IT-Sicherheitsaudits darstellen. Hierbei werden Angriffe von außen (aus dem Internet) als auch von innerhalb des eigenen Netzwerkes simuliert. Dieser Vorgang wird häufig auch als „Friendly Hacking" und der Auditor als White-Hat-Hacker bezeichnet,

- die Konzeption von angenommenen Erwartungshaltungen oder durch Befragung von Nutzern gesammelte Informationen hinsichtlich Risiken und Verbesserungen zu **Aspekten von Social Engineering** können ebenso wertvolle Hinweise liefern wie auch Analysen der

- **Prozess- und Funktionsbeschreibungen:** Sie sind entscheidend für das Verständnis und die richtige Anwendung der Applikation.

- **Durchsicht der Dokumentation:** Die Dokumentation bietet sowohl für Entwickler, Auditoren als auch Nutzer entscheidende Hinweise auf die richtige Anwendung des Programms und seiner Funktionen wie auch Hinweise auf die Programmierung der Funktionen. Das Vorhandensein schriftlicher Dokumentation ist entscheidend für einen Auditprozess als auch als Service für die Nutzer zu verstehen.

- **Involvement of other audit reports of other communication programs:** it makes sense for an audit to get an understanding of the solutions available at the market and to have an overview of good practice - also to clarify or to generate this understanding. Only in the context of the knowledge - for example, how other applications administer their chat server, manage friends lists or implement methods for forward secrecy - the "State of the Art" can be understood and the extent and quality of the implementation of functions can be traced.

- **Data Analysis:** Statistical analysis of the data, or the examination of the data with different tools should generally be considered as methods in the IT sector. In regard to encryption this can for example be related to the ciphertext or as well to the plain text - as well it can be referred to other statistical tests for encrypted or to be encrypted data - or to be stored or to be transferred data.

- **search engine queries:** It is to examine, how confidential and sensitive data can be possibly spotted unnoticed by search engine queries. The range of so-called "security nuggets" ranges generally from private information like credit card numbers, social security numbers and passwords, and files stored like internal auditing reports, password hashes or log files via insecure open services such as OWA, VPN and RDP to the disclosure of numerous exploits and vulnerabilities of related websites (Nessus, sniffers).

- **Einbezug anderer Audit-Berichte von anderen Kommunikationsprogrammen:** Es macht Sinn, für ein Audit ein Markt- oder Überblicks-Verständnis von Good Practice zu haben und auch zu verdeutlichen bzw. zu erzeugen. Nur im Zusammenhang der Kenntnisse - wie andere Applikationen beispielsweise ihre Chatserver administrieren, Freundeslisten verwalten oder Methoden für Forward Secrecy implementieren - kann der „State of the Art" nachvollzogen und der Umfang und die Qualität einer Funktionsimplementierung nachvollzogen werden.

- **Data Analysis:** Statistische Analysen der Daten oder die Untersuchung der Daten mit verschiedenen Tools gehören im IT-Bereich grundsätzlich als Methoden berücksichtigt. Verschlüsselung kann sich dieses z.B. auf den Ciphertext oder aber auch auf den Einbezug des Plaintextes beziehen - wie auch auf weitere statistische Untersuchungen der zu verschlüsselnden, verschlüsselten, zu transferierenden oder zu speichernden Daten.

- **Suchmaschinenabfragen:** Es ist zu untersuchen, in wie weit vertrauliche und sensible Daten ggf. mit Suchmaschinenabfragen unbemerkt erspäht werden können. Die Bandbreite der sogenannten „Security Nuggets" (engl. für „Sicherheitsbrocken") reicht dabei generell von privaten Informationen wie Kreditkartennummern, Sozialversicherungsnummern und Passwörtern sowie abgelegten Dateien wie internen Auditing-Berichten, Passwort-Hashes oder Logdateien über unsichere offene Dienste wie OWA, VPN und RDP bis zur Offenlegung zahlreicher Exploits und Schwachstellen der betreffenden Websites (Nessus, Sniffer).

The Audit Manual Open Source Security Testing Methodology Manual (OSSTMM) of the Institute for Security and Open Methodologies (ISECOM) differs according to the possible attacks then five categories of security interaction, also called channels (Herzog 2008):

- **physical interaction**

- Telecommunications (**analog communication**)

- data networks (**packet communication**)

- **wireless interaction**

- **human interaction**

From the good practice we know that
- **default settings** at hardly configured routers, firewalls, web servers, etc.
- and especially simple, unencrypted and / or default **passwords** (according to factory setting)
include the most common vulnerabilities (compare e.g. McClure 2008).

In order to meet the objectives and dimensions of investigation of these individual manuals, this audit combined analysis of data and relevant documentations with code reviews and analysis of the main functions of the application GoldBug;

These distinctive features, methods and criteria of the above-mentioned IT audit manuals should find all a use case. Thus it was sought in the application GoldBug for functions and test possibilities to apply this range of audit methods with the given functions and code.

As follows, therefore the audit dimension (first column) can be assigned to a core feature in the Messenger GoldBug (second column), and thirdly, formulate a question that should convey in this respect of audit methodology and core function our research question to the application.

Das Audithandbuch Open Source Security Testing Methodology Manual (OSSTMM) des Institute for Security and Open Methodologies (ISECOM) unterscheidet entsprechend der möglichen Angriffsmöglichkeiten sodann noch fünf Kategorien der Sicherheitsinteraktion, auch Kanäle genannt (Herzog 2008):

- **physikalische Interaktion**

- Telekommunikation (**analoge Kommunikation**)

- Datennetzwerke (**Paketkommunikation**)

- **drahtlose Interaktion**

- **menschliche Interaktion**

Aus der guten Praxis heraus weiß man, dass
- Vorgabeeinstellungen (**default settings**) bei kaum konfigurierten Routern, Firewalls, Webservern etc.
- sowie insbesondere einfache, unverschlüsselte und/oder voreingestellte **Passwörter** (laut Fabrikseinstellung)
zu den häufigsten Sicherheitslücken zählen (vgl. z.B. McClure 2008).

Um entsprechend die Ziele und Untersuchungsbereiche der einzelnen Manuale einzubeziehen, hat dieses Audit Analysen von Daten und relevanten Dokumentationen kombiniert mit Code-Analysen und Analysen zu den wesentlichen Funktionen der Applikation GoldBug:

Diese entscheidenden Merkmale, Methoden und Kriterien der obengenannten IT-Audit-Manuale sollen alle eine Anwendung finden. Es wurde dazu in der Applikation GoldBug nach Funktionen und Testmöglichkeiten gesucht, diese Bandbreite an Audit-Methoden mit den gegebenen Funktionen und Code auch anzuwenden.

Wie folgt lassen sich daher die Audit-Dimension (erste Spalte) zu einer Kern-Funktion im Messenger GoldBug zuordnen (zweite Spalte) sowie drittens auch eine Fragestellung formulieren, die in dieser Beziehung von Audit-Methode und Kern-Funktion der Applikation unsere Forschungsfragestellung vermitteln soll.

Table 01: Referring of methodical audit-dimensions to functions of the programm GoldBug, each with a question for research

Audit-Method / Audit-Dimension	To be related function in GoldBug	Question for a test & an investigation	#
Confidentiality through encryption / Vertraulichkeit durch Verschlüsselung	Multi-Encryption / Multi-Verschlüsselung	How can confidentiality be generated by hybrid or multi-encryption? / Wie lässt sich Vertraulichkeit durch hybride oder Multi-Verschlüsselung herstellen?	3.01
Integrity (information security) through authenticity / Integrität (Informationssicherheit) durch Authentizität	Authenticated E-Mails / Authentifizierte E-Mails	How is authenticity implemented in the e-mail function in order to ensure information security? / Wie wird Authentizität bei der E-Mail-Funktion umgesetzt, um Informationssicherheit zu gewährleisten?	3.02
Availability / Verfügbarkeit	P2P-HTTPS	How is the connection availability ensured over a P2P-HTTPS network connection? / Wie ist die Verfügbarkeit der Verbindung in einem P2P-HTTPS Verbindungsnetz gewährleistet?	3.03
Security Scan	Transferred Ciphertext / Transferierter Ciphertext	How can a proof of a transfer of ciphertext and not of plaintext be provided? / Wie kann ein Nachweis des Transfers von Ciphertext und nicht von Plaintext erbracht werden?	3.04
Access Control / Zugangskontrolle	Login into the App (Method) / Login in die App (Methode)	What are the security features of the two provided login methods and wherein they differ? What security aspects does the built-in virtual keyboard offer? / Was sind die Sicherheitsmerkmale der beiden angebotenen Login-Methoden und worin unterscheiden sich sie sich? Welche Sicherheit bietet die integrierte virtuelle Tastatur?	3.05
Acces to the system / Zugangs zum System	Encrypted databases / Verschlüsselte Datenbanken	Can an upload of the installation files contribute to an easier access to weaken the encryption? / Kann ein Upload der Installationsdateien zu einem leichteren Zugang zur Schwächung der Verschlüsselung beitragen?	3.06
Penetrationtest / Penetrationstest	Account-Firewall	Is the account function for networking nodes as a firewall stable respectively penetrable? / Ist die Account-Funktion zur Vernetzung von Knotenpunkten als Firewall penetrierbar?	3.07
Durchsicht der Dokumentation / Review of the documentation	Usermanual at wikibooks / Handbuch bei Wikibooks	Covers the manual the essential features of the application? / Deckt das Handbuch die wesentlichen Funktionen des Programmes ab?	3.08

Involvement of further audit reports of other communication applications / Einbezug weiterer Audit-Berichte von anderen Kommunikationsprogramm en	Comparisons with other open source applications / Vergleiche mit anderen open source Programmen	What other applications perform a similar function, and how is this comparable in various respects as according to their audit reports? / Welche weiteren Programme erfüllen eine ähnliche Funktion und wie sind dieses vergleichbar in verschiedener Hinsicht z.B. nach deren Audit-Berichten?	3.09
Descriptions of processes and functions / Prozess- und Funktionsbeschreibungen	The example of the data transfer / Am Beispiel der Dateiübertragung	How can the data transmission described as process, analyze and possibly improve considering the Magnet URI standard? / Wie lässt sich die Dateiübertragung als Prozess beschreiben, analysieren und ggf. verbessern unter Berücksichtigung des Magnet-URI-Standards?	3.10
Descriptions of processes and functions / Prozess- und Funktionsbeschreibungen	POPTASTIC E-Mail-Client	How can the process POPTASTIC be explained, analyzed and, if necessary improved in addition to the echo protocol? / Wie lässt sich der POPTASTIC Prozess erläutern, analysieren und ggf. verbessern als Ergänzung zum Echo-Protokoll?	3.11
Data Analysis / Daten Analyse	Encryption Process / Entschlüsselungs-Prozess	How can the decryption process be explained, analyzed and improved, if necessary? / Wie lässt sich der Entschlüsselungs-Prozess erläutern, analysieren und ggf. verbessern?	3.12
Security Nuggets / Suchmaschinenabfragen	Key Handling	Comparison of the safety of keys and their transmission respectively providing keys by conventional methods e.g. a key server / Vergleich der Sicherheit von Schlüsseln und ihrer Übertragung bzw. Zur-Verfügung-Stellung mit üblichen Verfahren z.B. eines Key-Servers	3.13
Physical Interaction / physikalische Interaktion	GUI-Kernel-Interaction	How is the communication of the kernel with the user interface protected? / Wie wird die Kommunikation des Kernels mit der Benutzeroberfläche abgesichert?	3.14
Analog Communication / analoge Kommunikation	Gemini, Goldbug & Forward Secrecy, Nova	How do analog (for example oral) communication or transmission of a symmetric key by the user create more security and what risks can arise here? / Wie kann analoge (z.B. mündliche) Kommunikation bzw. Übermittlung eines symmetrischen Schlüssels durch die Nutzer zu mehr Sicherheit beitragen und welche Risiken können dabei entstehen?	3.15

Packet Communication / Paketkommunikation	Adaptive Echo-Test	How are data packets forwarded in a setting of the adaptive echo? Test of the security of the exclusion of a node from the receipt of data packets. / Wie werdend die Datenpakete in einem Setting des Adaptiven Echos weitergeleitet? Test der Sicherheit des Ausschlusses eines Knotenpunktes vom Erhalt der Datenpackete.	3.16
Wireless interaction / drahtlose Interaktion	Bluetooth Listener	Considers the wireless echo-communication via Bluetooth security aspects? / Berücksichtigt die drahtlose Echo-Kommunikation über Bluetooth Sicherheitsaspekte?	3.17
Menschliche Interaktion / Social Engineering	SMP: Socialist-Millionaire-Protocol	What scenarios are conceivable in a social engineering attack on the Socialist Millionaire Protocol (SMP)? / Welche Szenarien sind denkbar bei einem Social-Engineering-Angriff auf das Socialist Millionaire Protocol (SMP)?	3.18
Default Settings	Default Crypto values for key generation / Default Crypto Werte für eine Schlüsselerstellung	Do the default values for key generation correspond to current security standards? / Entsprechen die voreingestellten Werte für die Schlüsselgenerierung den aktuellen Sicherheitsstandards?	3.19
Passwords / Passwörter	Account-Password / Account-Passwort	Are password-provided accounts securely protected in its firewall function against connecting a user who does not have the account password? / Sind mit Passworten versehene Accounts in ihrer Firewall Funktion sicher geschützt vor dem Verbinden eines Nutzers, der nicht über das Account-Passwort verfügt?	3.20
Files / Dateien	Delivered Files / Dateien der Installation	Are the files correct and from which library are they referring from? / Sind die Dateien der Installation in Ordnung und von welcher Bibliothek entstammen sie?	3.21

Source: Own referencing.

The research questions raised have been comprehensively and deepened analyzed and evaluated and are summarized on the following pages with their analyzes and assessments.

In each section a further detailed scientific study would be possible as documentation.

Even the wording of the text-chapters tries to address the summaries in each case also to a reader, who wants to learn more extensively in the field of software programming and cryptography.

Die aufgeworfenen Forschungsfragen sind umfassend und vertieft analysiert und bewertet worden und werden auf den folgenden Seiten mit ihren Analysen und Beurteilungen zusammenfassend dargestellt. In jeder einzelnen Sektion wäre weitergehend eine ausführliche wissenschaftliche Untersuchung als Dokumentation möglich. Auch wird sprachlich versucht, die Zusammenfassungen jeweils auch an einen Leser zu adressieren, der im Bereich der Software-Programmierung und Kryptologie weitergehend lernen möchte.

The aim of the audit is also to pick up on different audit methods and apply them as examples for the selected application: Every possible viewing angle of an audit method should be applied to the GoldBug Messenger, than just to look through all the functions of the application with only one point of view.

Furthermore, an audit shall always give suggestions to the reader, how to update the found research areas and issues in their own studies in depth (and at a later point of time).

Ziel des Audits ist es auch, verschiedende Audit-Methoden aufzugreifen und sie exemplarisch für die gewählte Applikation anzuwenden: Es soll also jeglich möglicher Blickwinkel einer Audit-Methode auf den GoldBug Messenger angewendet werden, als lediglich nur mit einem Blickwinkel alle Funktionen der Applikation durchzusehen.
Weiterhin soll ein Audit für den Leser auch immer Anregungen geben, die vorgefundenen Forschungsbereiche und Fragestellungen ggf. in eigenen Studien vertiefend (und zu einem späteren Zeitpunkt ggf. aktualisierend) selbst fortzuführen.

2.5 Context embedding: Why other Messengers than my well known Messenger?

The investigations in this broad consideration of methods and numerous functions and processes of GoldBug should also consider the diverse, now available additional encryption applications in terms of a context of comparable applications and in terms of an exchange community of "Good Practice".

Five greater blogs can be found on the Internet with lists of encrypting applications (Messenger):

Die Untersuchungen in dieser breiten Berücksichtigung von Methoden und zahlreichen Funktionen und Prozessen von GoldBug soll auch die inzwischen vielfältig erhältlichen weiteren Verschlüsselungs-Applikationen hinsichtlich eines Kontextes vergleichbarer Applikationen und einer Austausch-Community von „Good Practice" berücksichtigen.
Im Internet lassen sich fünf größere Blogs mit Listen an Verschlüsselungsapplikationen (Messenger) finden:

- The portal *"You broke the internet"* (YBTI) published a list of more than three dozen encrypting communication tools. 12 of these are open-source applications. The focus of the filter criteria of this portal is here based on e-mail clients, and encryption and anonymization basics (see YBTI 2014). The first editing of this list took place in February, 2014.

- Das Portal *"You broke the internet"* (YBTI) veröffentlichte eine Liste von über drei Dutzend verschlüsselnder Kommunikationswerkzeuge. 12 sind davon quelloffene Applikationen. Der Schwerpunkt der Filterkriterien dieses Portals liegt hier auf E-Mail-Klienten sowie Verschlüsselungs- und Anonymisierungsgrundlagen (siehe YBTI 2014).
Die erste Edierung dieser Liste erfolgte im Februar 2014.

- The German study-group *"Arbeitskreis Vorratsdatenspeicherung"* (AKV) and the Alliance *"Freedom Not Fear"* lists in its Wiki - which can be *extended* by any Internet user - more than 20 communication tools for encryption, of which 12 applications are open source. It is thus a corresponding wiki-list, which is a comprehensive edition by the community connected to the study-group "Arbeitskreis".
Here is value placed on key criteria

- Der deutsche *"Arbeitskreis Vorratsdatenspeicherung"* (AKV) bzw. mit dem Bündnis *"Freiheit statt Angst"* listet in seinem Wiki, das von jedem Internetnutzer erweitert werden kann, über 20 verschlüsselnde Kommunikationswerkzeuge, von denen 12 Applikationen quelloffen sind. Es ist somit eine entsprechende Wiki-Liste, die eine umfassende Edierung aus der dem Arbeitskreis angeschlossenen Community darstellt.

like: open source - namely the application software as well as the chat server software -, furthermore, if (manual editable) end-to-end encryption is implemented and also the criterion of encryption type and method is underlined. The first editing of this list took place in May, 2014.

- Peter Eckersley of the EFF listed in his list more than 30 communication tools for encryption, of which only 12 are open source. As essential criteria are in the foreground, that the application is open source, that an end-to-end encryption with Forward Secrecy is implemented, and a security audit has been conducted. Unfortunately, the audit reports are not linked and also only a few open source applications are mentioned. The first editing of this list took place in November, 2014.

- Blogger Peng Zhong expanded his list of tools, intended to limit surveillance, within the portal *"Prism Break"* (PB) since June 2013 continuously. This list also includes encryption tools, 18 are open source. Many of these applications, however, are specified as a separate entry for each operating system, so that, for example, PGP is considered individually as OpenPGP and as GNUPG for each operating system such as Android, Windows, Mac, Linux. In the following they are listed here as a cluster, because they are tools or plug-ins, that do not constitute an own private e-mail client, and also reflect chat only occasionally.

- Also Schneier Blog (SB) has published a list, which we will discuss in detail later.

It turns out that, firstly, many brand names differentiate, because they refer to only one operating system, and secondly, many applications use the same protocol respectively the same encryption method:

Hier wird auf wesentliche Kriterien Wert gelegt wie: Quelloffenheit - und zwar der Applikationssoftware wie auch der Chat-Server Software -, weiterhin ob (manuell definierbare) Ende-zu-Ende Verschlüsselung implementiert ist und auch das Kriterium der Verschlüsselungs-Art bzw. Methode wird herausgestellt. Die erste Edierung dieser Liste erfolgte im Mai 2014.

- Peter Eckersley von der *EFF* listet in seiner Liste über 30 verschlüsselnde Kommunikationswerkzeuge, von denen nur 12 quelloffen sind. Als wesentliche Kriterien sind hier im Vordergrund, dass die Applikation quelloffen ist, dass eine Ende-zu-Ende-Verschlüsselung mit Forward Secrecy möglich ist und ggf. ein Security Audit stattgefunden hat. Leider sind die Audit-Reporte nicht verlinkt und es sind auch nur wenige quelloffene Applikationen benannt. Die erste Edierung dieser Liste erfolgte im November 2014.

- Der Blogger Peng Zhong erweitert seine Liste an Werkzeugen, die Überwachung eingrenzen sollen, im Portal *"Prism-Break"* (PB) seit Juni 2013 kontinuierlich. Darunter sind auch Verschlüsselungswerkzeuge, von denen 18 quelloffen sind. Viele dieser Applikationen sind jedoch spezifiziert als eigener Eintrag für ein jedes Betriebssystem, so dass man beispielsweise PGP als OpenPGP und auch als GNUPG für Betriebssysteme wie Android, Windows, Mac, Linux jeweils einzeln zählt. Sie werden hier im Folgenden gruppiert gelistet, da es sich um Werkzeuge bzw. Plugins handelt, die keinen eigenen E-Mail-Clienten darstellen und auch Chat nur bedingt abbilden.

- Ebenso hat *"SchneierBlog"* (SB) eine Liste veröffentlicht, auf die wir später noch detailliert eingehen.

Es zeigt sich, dass erstens viele Marken-Namen sich differenzieren, weil sie sich auf jeweils nur ein Betriebssystem beziehen und zweitens viele Applikationen dasselbe Protokoll bzw. dieselbe Verschlüsselungs-Methode benutzen:

If we sort all available open source messaging tools and eliminate duplicates from all five lists,

- group XMPP clients and
- PGP tools and
- tools, that require an underlying rooting network like Tor, Gnunet or I2P,

this results in the following summary overview of open-source Crypto-Messenger.

Some applications also

- have no release available, so they are in the planning stage or
- are in code-parts then not open source (e.g. for the chat server) or
- open source applications are under a proprietary license so that a fork or an own development of the existing code base is not allowed.

Within this audit, those Messengers should be included as an extended context that

- substantially provide both, chat, as well as possibly e-mail messaging: this means to allow chat or messaging also to offline friends (marked in the table with "Reference 1" chat encryption is not present, such as in some PGP tools) and
- are completely open source (that means also the chat server ("Reference 2a": open source nature of the IM server or certificate server is not the case, such as in Telegram) or
- are not using a proprietary license ("Reference 2b": proprietary license is the case, such as in Silent Phone & Silentext) and
- have published first binary release or are judged as "productive" by the developer or a functioning test server is given ("Reference 3": No productive binary release available or no test server infrastructure exists, is the case for example at Briar or Pond and Jericho Comms).

Sortiert man alle damit erhältlichen Open Source Messaging Tools und eliminiert die Doubletten aus allen fünf Listen,

- gruppiert XMPP-Klienten und
- PGP-Tools sowie
- Tools, die ein unterliegendes Rooting-Netzwerk wie Tor, GnuNet oder I2P benötigen,

ergibt sich folgende zusammenfassende Übersicht an quelloffenen Crypto-Messengern. Einige Applikationen haben auch noch

- kein Release verfügbar, befinden sich also im Planungsstadium oder
- sind in Code-Teilen dann doch nicht quelloffen (wie für den Chat-Server) oder
- oder quelloffene Applikationen stehen unter einer proprietären Lizenz, die einen Fork oder eine eigene Weiterentwicklung der bestehenden Code Basis nicht erlauben.

Innerhalb dieses Audits sollen die Messenger als erweiterter Kontext einbezogen werden, die

- im wesentlichen vorrangig sowohl Chat-, als auch ggf. E-Mail-Messaging vorsehen, d.h. also Chat- bzw. Messaging auch zu Offline-Freunden ermöglichen (in der folgenden Tabelle mit „Reference 1" gekennzeichnet: Chat-Verschlüsselung ist nicht vorhanden, wie z.B. bei einigen PGP-Tools) sowie
- vollständig quelloffen sind (d.h. auch beim Chat-Server („Reference 2a": Quelloffenheit des Chat-Servers oder des Zertifikat-Servers ist nicht gegeben, wie z.B. bei Telegram) bzw.
- keine proprietäre Lizenz verwenden („Reference 2b": proprietäre Lizenz ist der Fall, wie z.B. bei Silentphone & Silentext) und auch ein
- erstes Binary-Release veröffentlicht haben bzw. vom Entwickler selbst auch als „produktiv einsetzbar" beurteilt werden bzw. ein funktionierender Test-Server vorhanden ist („Reference 3": Kein produktives Binary Release vorhanden oder keine Test-Server-Infrastruktur vorhanden, ist der Fall z.B. bei Briar oder Pond sowie Jericho Comms).

As additional notes it should be mentioned that the Messenger TextSecure was another name for today's Messenger Signal. And: that Telegram is labled in some portals as open source, though the Chat server is not open source. Furthermore, that programs like Threema and others are in the media often mentioned, but are also not open source and therefore do not constitute a serious open source alternative and can not be considered further here, because the research-context is intended to refer to only complete open source messenger.

Als ergänzende Hinweise seien genannt, dass der Messenger Textsecure eine andere Bezeichnung für den heutigen Messenger Signal war. Und: dass Telegram in manchen Portalen als quelloffen bezeichnet wird, ob schon der Chat-Server nicht quelloffen ist. Ferner, dass Programme wie Threema und weitere in den Medien gerne genannt werden, jedoch ebenso nicht quelloffen sind und daher keine erntszunehmende open source Alternative darstellen und hier nicht weiter berücksichtigt werden können, da sich der Untersuchungs-Kontext auf ausschließlich vollständig quelloffene Messenger beziehen soll.

Table 02: 38 Open Source Crypto-Applications & -Tools out of several Blog-Portals

	(OPEN SOURCE) APPLICATION	BLOG-PORTALS e.g.:					SOURCE / COMMENTS URL / Reason for no further consideration as context within this audit:
		YBTI	AKV	EFF	PB	SB	
1	BitChat					☑	https://github.com/TechnitiumSoftware/BitChatClient - - Reference 2a (Server)
2	BitMail	☑	☑			☑	http://bitmail.sf.net - Reference 1 (no chat available).
3	Bitmessage	☑				☑	https://github.com/Bitmessage/PyBitmessage - Reference 1.
4	Briar	☑				☑	https://code.briarproject.org/akwizgran/briar - Reference 3 (not productive).
5	**CryptoCat**		☑	☑	☑	☑	https://github.com/cryptocat/cryptocat
6	Folpy		☑				https://bitbucket.org/folpy/folpy - Reference 1.
7	**GoldBug**	☑	☑			☑	**http://goldbug.sf.net/** Security Review Audit within this study
8	GPG for E-Mail						
	APG				☑	☑	http://www.thialfihar.org/projects/apg/ Reference 1.
	Enigmail				☑	☑	https://www.enigmail.net Reference 1.
	GNU Privacy Guard				☑	☑	https://www.gnupg.org/ Reference 1.
	GPG for Android				☑	☑	https://github.com/guardianproject/gnupg-for-android Reference 1.
	Gpg4win			☑	☑	☑	http://www.gpg4win.de Reference 1.
	GPGTools/Suite				☑	☑	https://gpgtools.org/ Reference 1.
	Mailvelope	☑		☑	☑	☑	https://github.com/mailvelope/mailvelope - Reference 1.
	OpenKeychain				☑	☑	https://www.openkeychain.org Reference 1.
	+ 19 other E-Mail-Apps & Plugins of SB-Portal-List					☑	See Footnote 1: Due to often Beta or Plugin status counted as one entry.
17	Jericho Comms					☑	http://joshua-m-david.github.io/jerichoencryption Reference 3.
18	Mailpile	☑				☑	https://github.com/mailpile/Mailpile Reference 1.
19	**OTR & XMPP**						
	OTR & Adium				☑	☑	https://otr.cypherpunks.ca/
	OTR & BitlBee-Plug in IRC					☑	http://bitlbee.org
	OTR & Bombus					☑	http://bombus-im.org
	OTR & Coccinella					☑	http://coccinella.im
	OTR & Gajim				☑	☑	http://gajim.org
	OTR & Kadu					☑	http://kadu.im
	OTR & Kontalk					☑	http://kontalk.org
	OTR & Kopete					☑	http://kopete.kde.org
	OTR & MCabber					☑	http://mcabber.com
	OTR & Monal					☑	http://monal.im

		YBTI	AKV	EFF	PB	SB	
	OTR & Pidgin			☑	☑	☑	https://otr.cypherpunks.ca/
	OTR & Profanity Console					☑	http://profanity.im
	OTR & Psi / Psi-Plus				☑	☑	https://otr.cypherpunks.ca/
	OTR & TKabber					☑	http://tkabber.jabber.ru
	ChatSecure		☑	☑	☑	☑	https://github.com/guardianproject/ChatSecureAndroid
	Conversations				☑	☑	https://github.com/siacs/Conversations
	FireFloo QXMPP		☑			☑	http://firefloo.sf.net/ Qt-XMPP-Chat-Client, no E-Mail-Function.
	Jitsi Ostel			☑	☑	☑	https://jitsi.org/
	SecuXabber		☑			☑	http://sourceforge.net/projects/secuxabber/
	Xabber				☑	☑	http://www.xabber.com/
39	Pond	☑				☑	https://pond.imperialviolet.org – Reference 3
40	**RetroShare**	☑	☑	☑	☑	☑	http://retroshare.sf.net/
41	RoutingNet-Overlays						
	Cables	☑				☑	https://github.com/mkdesu/cables Reference 1.
	Freemail	☑				☑	https://freenetproject.org/documentation.html#freemail - Reference 1.
	I2P-Bote	☑				☑	http://i2pbote.i2p.us/ Reference 1.
	Secushare	☑				☑	http://secushare.org/ Reference 1.
	Ricochet				☑	☑	https://ricochet.im/ Reference 1.
	TorChat					☑	http://github.com/prof7bit/TorChat Reference 1.
47	**Signal**		☑	☑		☑	https://github.com/WhisperSystems/Signal-Android
48	Silent Phone & Text			☑		☑	https://github.com/SilentCircle/silent-text-android - Reference 2b (License)
49	Spot-on		☑			☑	http://spot-on.sf.net Alternative GUI for GoldBug.
50	**SureSpot**		☑	☑		☑	https://github.com/surespot
51	Telegram		☑	☑		☑	https://github.com/telegramdesktop/tdesktop - Reference 2a (Server)
52	**Tox**		☑		☑	☑	https://github.com/lrungentoo/toxcore

Listed entries of all common available entries	YBTI	AKV	EFF	PB	SB
	12/52	13/52	11/52	20/52	51/52
	= 23 %	= 25 %	= 21 %	= 38 %	= 98 %

It appears from the overview that bloggers often designate only 1/4 or maximum just over a third of all available encrypting and privacy enabling communication tools for encryption for chat and e-mail in the year, 2014. The analysis in Schneier Blog (SB) based on a scientific collection (2016) achieved nearly a full survey for the chat messengers.

The portal YBTI highlights at the end of their list, that their list goes back to a draft of the development group "Open Technology Fund", that also brings out its own secure application,

Es zeigt sich aus der Übersicht, dass Blogger oftmals nur 1/4 oder maximal etwas mehr als ein 1/3 aller verfügbaren verschlüsselnden und Privatsphäre ermöglichenden Kommunikationswerkzeuge für Chat und E-Mail im Jahr 2014 benennen. Die Analyse im Schneier Blog (SB) basierend auf einer wissenschaftlichen Sammlung (2016) erreicht nahezu eine Vollerhebung für die Chat-Messenger.

Das Portal YBTI hebt am Ende ihrer Liste hervor, dass ihre Liste zurückgehe auf einen Entwurf der Entwicklergruppe "Open Technology Fund", die auch eine eigene

so YBTI enlarged the list by their own development (since the original creator for some reason had no interest in enlarging the list or in giving full transparency). That means possibly that any list creator has "some biased views on the topic, as everyone prefers to maintain their own version of these lists" (YBTI 2014).

As a recommendation from the YBTI index and their published critical remark can therefore be deduced, that further bloggers should also carry out comparative overviews from their own perspective, but

- leave non-open source crypto solutions disregarded
- include comparisons with a reference to all the currently existing open source applications in order to involve in none fact of a limited perspective, a "biased view".

Turning now to the 52 listed Messenger of five known blogs, so remain - after sorting out

- not open source applications
- grouping of brands and operating systems,
- E-mail tools, that support no presence chat
- as well as tools, that require complicated to install routing networks (not necessarily with an increase of encryption) -

only a handful relevant open source Crypto-Messenger.

From the above overview thus seven open source communications applications result, that have the feature "chat" and open source encryption:

sichere Applikation herausbringen, so dass YBTI die Liste selbst weiterentwickelt habe (da der ursprüngliche Ersteller aus bestimmten Gründen kein Interesse an Listenerweiterung bzw. an der Bereitstellung vollständiger Transparenz hatte). Somit habe ggf. jeder Listensersteller "some biased views on the topic, so everyone prefers to maintain his own version of these lists" (YBTI 2014).

Als Empfehlung aus der YBTI-Übersicht und dort veröffentlichten kritischen Anmerkung lässt sich daher ableiten, dass weitere Blogger ebenso Vergleichsübersichten aus ihrer Sicht erstellen sollten, die jedoch

- nicht-quelloffene Crypto-Lösungen unberücksichtigt lassen und
- Vergleiche mit einem Verweis auf sämtliche derzeit vorhandenen quelloffenen Applikationen einbinden, um sich bei keinem Tatbestand einer beschränkten Sichtweise, eines „biased views", zu involvieren.

Betrachtet man nun die 52 gelisteten Messenger aus fünf bekannten Blogs, so bleiben - nach einer Aussortierung von

- nicht quelloffenen Applikationen und einer
- Gruppierung von Marken und Betriebsystemen sowie
- E-Mail-Tools, die keinen Präsenz-Chat unterstützen
- als auch von Werkzeugen, die ein kompliziert zu installierendes Routing-netzwerk erfordern (das nicht zwin-gend die Verschlüsselung erhöht) -

nur eine Handvoll an relevanten quelloffenen Crypto-Messengern übrig.

Aus obiger Übersicht ergeben sich somit sieben quelloffene Kommunikations-programme, die das Merkmal „Chat" und quelloffene Verschlüsselung aufweisen:

BIG SEVEN CRYPTO MESSENGER FOR CHAT
(open source)

- Cryptocat
- GoldBug
- OTR+XMPP
- RetroShare
- Signal
- SureSpot
- Tox

These we will call **BIG SEVEN** and reference each indicatively to the audit of a GoldBug function.

Diese wollen wir als **BIG SEVEN** bezeichnen und jeweils zu dem Audit einer GoldBug Funktion indikativ miteinander referenzieren.

If this is now subsequently examined whether the applications are developed by volunteer programmers (and not by a company with economic interests) and if they run not only on mobile applications (but classically are also on a laptop or desktop PC as an independent client operational) remain not many comparable applications left: CryptoCat, GoldBug, OTRinXMPP, RetroShare and Tox.

In February 2016 published Bruce Schneier in his blog (Portal SchneierBlog: "SB") a study collection - already carried out in 1999 at the George Washington University - and identified then 856 encryption tools worldwide, that affect both: software as well as hardware, and: proprietary and open source applications. Among these are in the first revision level 67 open source <u>chat</u> applications (Message-SW-Free-OS), 23 open-source <u>e-mail</u> applications (mail SW-Free-OS), and 8 open source applications (multi-SW-free OS), which are marked with the type of "multi" and <u>unspecified relate to chat and email</u>.
Amoung these GoldBug Messenger is also listed.

All other above mentioned 52 applications of the other portals are also included in this list of the SB-Portal (except for Folpy).

The list in Version 1.0 is a first draft with the goal, to identify the countries of the companies or projects, and to show, that national political cryptography regulations are absurd, because many projects exist in other countries and are also even open source. The list contained in this release still numerous errors, so Tox.im and Tox.Chat was (like Briar and Ricochet) listed as a duplicate, some applications are referred to as "Free", although they are not open source, many applications are not encrypting, and can implement this only over a plugin for encryption. Others are browser or cloud applications, where the key is possibly not in the user's hand.

Some applications are also characterized as a chat application, but they are misclassified (conversions tools) or purely a transport encryption is available - but no dedicated Messenger. Some applications have been published to date still in beta, or in an experimental status, or neither the release nor the source code is given (for example, Hemlis). Some applications have published no more releases for many years. Some other well-known applications such as "Alliancep2p", or Veteran`s Messenger "Waste" or "Antsp2p" are not included in this list,

Wenn man dieses nun noch danach untersucht, ob sie auch von ehrenamtlichen Entwicklern (und eben nicht durch ein Unternehmen mit wirtschaftlichen Interessen) entwickelt werden und ob sie nicht nur auf mobilen Applikationen laufen (sondern klassischerweise auch auf einem Laptop oder Desktop-PC als eigenständiger Klient einsatzfähig sind) bleiben nicht viele vergleichbare Applikationen übrig: CryptoCat, GoldBug, OTRinXMPP, RetroShare und Tox.

Im Feburar 2016 veröffentlichte Bruce Schneier in seinem Blog (Portal SchneierBlog: "SB") eine bereits in 1999 an der George Washington University durchgeführte Studiensammlung mit sodann 856 weltweit identifizierten Verschlüsselungswerkzeugen, die sowohl Software wie auch Hardware als auch proprietäre und quelloffene Applikationen betreffen. Darunter sind in dem ersten Revisionstand 67 quelloffene <u>Chat-Applikationen</u> (Message-SW-Free-OS), 23 quelloffene <u>E-Mail-Applikationen</u> (Mail-SW-Free-OS), sowie 8 quelloffene Applikationen (Multi-SW-Free-OS), die mit dem Typ "multi" gekennzeichnet sind und sich unspezifiziert auf <u>Chat und E-Mail</u> beziehen. Darunter ist auch der GoldBug Messenger gelistet.

Alle anderen oben genannten 52 Applikationen der anderen Portale sind (bis auf Folpy) ebenso in dieser Liste des SB-Portals enthalten.

Die Liste ist in Version 1.0 ein erster Entwurf, mit dem Ziel, die Länder der Firmen oder Projekte zu identifizieren, und damit zu zeigen, dass nationale politische Kryptologie-Regelungen unsinnig sind, da zahlreiche Projekte auch in anderen Ländern und quelloffen bestehen. Die Liste enthielt in dieser Version noch zahlreiche Fehler, so wurde Tox.im und Tox.Chat (wie auch Briar und auch Ricochet) als Doublette geführt, einige Applikationen sind als "Free" bezeichnet, obwohl sie nicht quelloffen sind, zahlreiche Applikationen sind nicht verschlüsselnd, sondern können dieses nur über eine Plugin-Verschlüsselung umsetzen. Andere sind Browser- oder Cloud-Applikationen, bei denen der Schlüssel ggf. nicht in Hand des Nutzers liegt.
Einige Applikationen sind auch als Chat-Applikation gekennzeichnet, die jedoch falsch eingeordnet sind (Conversions-Werkzeuge) oder lediglich eine Transportverschlüsselung vorhanden ist - aber kein dedizierter Messenger. Einige Applikationen sind bis dato noch im Beta- oder experimentellen Status oder wenn im Release noch im Quellcode veröffentlicht worden (z.B. Hemlis). Einige Applikationen haben schon seit vielen Jahren keine Versionen mehr veröffentlicht. Einige andere in der Fachwelt bekannte Applikationen wie z.B. Alliance-

and also not in the lists of the other portals. We have therefore these three apps also not added to the portal lists comparison. Email clients and plugins (category Mail-SW-Free-OS) have been designated due to the "Reference 1" as above stated (Chat option missing). According to the following footnote 01, all these applications from the list in the SB-Portal have been examined for consideration in the above overview, and comments were added.

p2p, oder die Urgesteine "Waste Messenger" oder AntsP2P sind in dieser Liste und auch den anderen Listen z.B. gar nicht enthalten. Wir haben diese drei daher auch dem Portal-Listen-Vergleich nicht hinzugefügt. E-Mail-Klienten und -Plugins (Kategorie Mail-SW-Free-OS) sind mit der "Reference 1" wie oben vermerkt bezeichnet worden. Entsprechend der folgenden Fußnote 01 wurden alle genannten Applikationen aus der Liste im SB-Portal für die Berücksichtigung im obiger Übersicht geprüft und mit Kommentaren versehen.

Footnote 01: Survey of Encryption Products (Chat / E-Mail / Multi) - SB-Portal-List

Category	# of Apps listed / # of Apps identified as open source for chat or e-mail & considered in table above		Comments / Not considered due to beta or plugin status etc.
Chat & E-Mail (Multi-SW-Free-OS)	8 / 5	GoldBug, GPG Suite, Gpg4win, Jitsi, Retroshare.	Applications not in the status to be considered as open source and with stable release for this category: Kontact (Kontact is the integrated Personal Info Manager of KDE and supports email via KMail, which is not natively encrypted), MECrypt (Mobile Mobile Encryption App by T-Systems, not open source), Secret Space Encryptor (Password Manager file and text encryption, but no Chat or Email, though the category "multi" applies with this.
Chat (Message-SW-Free-OS)	67 / 30	Adium, APG, BitMessage, Briar, ChatSecure, Coccinella, CryptoCat, Gajim, BitChat, BitlBee, Bombus, Jericho Comms, Kadu, Kontalk, Kopete, (Libre)Signal (clone issue #127), MCabber, Monal, OTR Message Encryption (plugin referring to XMPP, Pidgin, Pond, Profanity, PSI/ Psi+, Ricochet, Signal, Xabber, Spot-On Communications Suite (GoldBug Kernel Development), Tkabber, TorChat, Tox-Chat.	Applications not in the status to be considered as open source and with stable release for this category: CenoCipher (Ciphertext-Conversion-Tool, not an own Chat or E-Mail Client), Confusion (Ciphertext--Conversion-Tool, not an own Chat or E-Mail Client), Crypho (Not open source, business purpose, free for individuals), Diaspora (no user-to-user encryption, just transport-encryption), End-to-End (Ciphertext-Conversion-Tool as Browser-Plugin), Etherpad (no user-to-user encryption, just transport-encryption), Friendica (no user-to-user encryption, just transport-encryption), Hemlis (not released & stopped), HexChat (IRC chat only with Encryption Cipher-plugin "FishLim" 2004, Webpage has gone: http://fish.sekure.us/), Hydan (Steganography Conversion tool, no messaging), IRC w/Blowfish (Cipher only and no URL for Own Client given), Jabber.org (Foundation Website, not own Client), Jiffy (experimental client release only, Jiffy (server code not released since 2013), Kleeq (outdated code, no binary release given), m2 circles Messenger (no open source code given), Mumble (no user-to-user encryption, just transport-encryption), Nxtty Crypto Messenger (in Bitcoin paid service with no open source server core), okTurtles Browser Extension (in experimental development, no stable release), OneTime (commandline conversion tool, not a messenger client), OnionShare (file sharing client, not messaging client), Paranoia Text Encryption for iOS & PC (Ciphertext-Conversion-Tool, not an own Chat or E-Mail Client), Pastebin (not a messenger with encryption), Peerio (cloud-based, not open source), Petmail ("nothing works yet", no stable release), Ploggy (experimental "prototype" status, no stable release), PuTTY (not a messenger), Ring (DHT Voip with only experimental text chat only on Linux), SafePad (conversion tool, not a messenger client), SafeSlinger (conversion tool, not a messenger client), SecureCom (fork based on old brand), ShadowCash (digital currency system), SMSSecure (Signal fork with SMS), Sneakertext (still experimental develpment status), Tinfoil Chat CEV (encryption plugin for Pidgin over TOR, not an own Messenger), Tor Messenger (based on Instantbird still in beta), Trsst (still in aplpha, no stable release), Twister (beta software), vim (beta, paused due to family), Vuvuzela (based on ideas taken from the echo-protocol, incorporating also TOR and still in first beta release with several bugs: Forward Secrecy missing, no groupchat and servers do not start gracefully: #7, #4, #3).
E-Mail (Mail-SW-Free-OS)	23 / 4	23 Encryption solutions are provided by SB, four solutions are also cosidered by the other 4 Blog-Post-Lists: EnigMail, GnuPG, Mailvelope, OpenKeychain. Compare „Reference 1": No Chat is given in these Apps.	Compare „Reference 1": No Chat is given in these Apps. Mostly clients, which require a plugin for encryption, or a plugin still under development for encryption. Also routing plugins are not providing necessarily encryption: Bitmask Encrypted Email, Claws-Mail, Confidant Mail, Darkmail, Evolution, K-9 Mail, Mymail-crypt, OmniMix, OnionMail, OpenMailbox, PEP Plugin Project, Pixelated, Rugged Inbox, Scramble, Sylpheed, TorBirdy, Tutanota, Whiteout Mail. This shows, that the Lists of the Portals YBTI, AKV, EFF, & PB miss each over 20 E-Mail-Clients preparing in beta or with plugins for encryption, as shown in the List of SB-Portal.

Source: Schneier et al. 2016 (v.1.0) with own further referencing and comments.

If you analyse as in the following table the code uploads in purely quantitative terms (so-called "commits") to each of these BIG SEVEN projects, so arises for each project a lead committer, which accompanied most commits within a development team.

Analysiert man wie in der folgenden Tabelle rein quantitativ die Code-Uploads (sog. "Commits") zu diesen einzelnen BIG SEVEN Projekten, so stellt sich für jedes Projekt ein Lead-Committer heraus, der die meisten Commits innerhalb eines Entwicklerteams beifügt.

Tabelle 03: Group of the „Big SEVEN" - to be compared open source Crypto-Messengers

e.g. APPLIKATION	Main Committer	Last time activity of the Main Committer	average # of commits per Year	Win	Mac	Linux	Mobile
Cryptocat	arlolra	Contributions in the last year 673 total Feb 8, 2015 – Feb 8, 2016	673	☑	☑	☑	☑
GoldBug	Spot-On	Contributions in the last year 2,445 total Feb 8, 2015 – Feb 8, 2016	2.445	☑	☑	☑	TBD
OTR+XMPP	goldberg	N/A	N/A	☑	☑	☑	☑
RetroShare	csoler	Contributions in the given time: 498 total Aug 1, 2015 – Feb 8, 2016 (191 days)	951	☑	☑	☑	TBD
Signal	moxie0	Contributions in the last year 986 total Feb 8, 2015 – Feb 8, 2016	986	Browser based	Browser based	Browser based	☑
SureSpot	2fours	Contributions in the last year 31 total Feb 8, 2015 – Feb 8, 2016	31	TBD	TBD	TBD	☑
Tox	irungentoo	Contributions in the last year 946 total Feb 8, 2015 – Feb 8, 2016	946	☑	☑	☑	☑

Source: GitHub statistic function.

These frequencies of the annual contributions of each main developer are also very limited in significance and only to use indicative, since it can not be clear whether someone contributes code in larger tranches, how much projects they support and if also a financing or leisure activity stands behind. Someone who implements the code contributions both, professionally and as a paid programmer, possibly have more posts than when someone contributes this in his spare time only.

Diese Häufigkeiten der jährlichen Beiträge eines jeweiligen Haupt-Entwicklers sind jedoch auch nur sehr bedingt aussagekräftig und lediglich indikativ zu nutzen, da nicht deutlich werden kann, ob jemand Code in größeren Tranchen beiträgt, wieviel Projekte er unterstützt und ob zudem auch eine Finanzierung oder Freizeitbeschäftigung dahinter steht. Jemand, der die Code-Beiträge beruflich und als bezahlter Programmierer umsetzt, wird ggf. mehr Beiträge haben, als wenn jemand dieses ausschließlich in seiner Freizeit einbringt.

It is here therefore only indicative apparent, that SureSpot has deployed no large code activity in the last time period. Also OTR (as well as CryptoCat) code developments are on the back burner respectively the commits are not hosted at Github and remain therefore only estimate in the statistical analyzes. OTR is considered for many years as established and has though not implemented many development perspectives yet.

Es wird hier also nur indikativ deutlich, dass Surespot keine grosse Code-Aktivität in der letzen Zeit entfaltet hat. Auch OTR (wie auch Cryptocat) Code-Entwicklungen auf Sparflamme beifügen bzw. die Commits nicht bei Github gehostet werden und die statistischen Analysen daher nur abzuschätzen bleiben. OTR gilt seit vielen Jahren als etabliert und hat dennoch viele Entwicklungsperspektiven noch nicht umgesetzt.

Signal and Surespot have so far also only mobile applications, respectively allows the browser implementation at Signal indeed a

Signal und Surespot sind bislang zudem nur mobile Applikationen bzw. ermöglicht die Browser-Implementierung bei Signal zwar eine

---

function of the Messenger then on all operating systems, but remains absolutely dependent on a mobile furnished account. A fast browser implementation without own clients to develop for each operating system - that is also reflected then in less code contributions.

Also the qualitative analysis considers not, if anyone has developed a significant innovation, or exchanges with their code commit only a single graphic. And the consideration only of the main developer also hides the additional contributions from the project team, if given.

We have decided to document this analysis, yet to show, that background analyzes should be thought out varied and we at least indicative wish from this analysis, that, e.g., the Surespot development does not fall asleep, and OTR with XMPP as well also is leaving the achieved comfort zone to develop XMPP solutions, that lie beyond plugin risks, missing file transfers & group chats in OTR, and the lack of options at enhanced asynchronous respectively ephemeral keys.

Further, for example, show the team commits e.g. at Retroshare approximately 11 users with more than 5 commits (https://github.com/ csoler / Retroshare / graphs / contributors).
In Tox there are 41 users with more than 5 contributions and 147 contributors altogether only for the Tox-Core (https://github.com/ irungentoo / toxcore / graphs / contributors).
While it can be assumed that a small team of developers can coordinate the team better, and also quality reviews of the code are better coordinated, for RetroShare one can already speak of an extended team, so the code possibly has numerous styles of personal code writings and hence vulnerabilities or coordinating necessities can reveal.

In contrast, the development of Tox can be indicative rather called `promiscuous pool´: everyone may at times install something in the code, which can contribute to high vulnerability and a high need for code reviews.

However, these remain under mostly, when quality management does not come out of a hand of a smaller or in reviews specialized team.

Funktion des Messengers sodann auf allen Betriebssystemen, ist jedoch weiterhin von einem mobil eingerichteten Account zwingend abhängig. Eine schnelle Browser-Implementierung ohne eigene Klienten für jedes Betriebssystem zu entwickeln - schlägt sich also auch in weniger Code-Beiträgen nieder.

Auch bleibt bei der qualitativen Analyse außen vor, ob jemand eine wesentliche Neuerung entwickelt hat, oder mit seinem Code-Commit nur eine Grafik austauscht. Und die Betrachtung nur des Hauptentwicklers blendet auch die weiteren Kontributionen aus dem Projektteam, sofern vorhanden, aus.

Wir haben uns entschieden, diese Analyse dennoch zu dokumentieren, um zu zeigen, dass Hintergrundanalysen vielfältig durchdacht sein sollten und wir uns zumindest indikativ aus dieser Analyse wünschen, dass z.B. die Surespot-Entwicklung nicht einschläft, und OTR mit XMPP auch ebenso die erreichte Komfort-Zone verlässt, um für XMPP Lösungen zu entwickeln, die jenseits von Plugin-Risiko, fehlendem Dateitransfer & Gruppenchat bei OTR und fehlenden Optionen bei erweiterten asynchronen bzw. ephemeralen Schlüsseln liegen.

Ferner zeigen z.B. die Team-Commits z.B. bei RetroShare ca. 11 Nutzer mit mehr als 5 Commits an (https://github.com/ csoler/ RetroShare/ graphs/ contributors). Bei Tox sind es 41 Nutzer mit mehr als 5 Beiträgen und 147 Contributoren insgesamt nur für den Tox-Core (https://github.com/ irungentoo/ toxcore/ graphs/ contributors).
Während anzunehmen ist, das ein kleines Entwicklerteam sich besser koordiniert und auch Qualitäts-Reviews des Codes besser aufeinander abstimmen kann, kann bei RetroShare schon von einem erweiterten Team gesprochen werden, so dass der Code ggf. zahlreiche Handschriften und damit auch Anfälligkeit oder Koordinierungs-notwendigkeiten aufzeigen kann.

Bei Tox hingegen kann die Entwicklung indikativ eher als `promiskuitiver Pfuhl´ bezeichnet werden: jeder darf mal etwas einbauen, was zu einer hohen Sicherheitsanfälligkeit und hohen Notwendigkeit an Code-Reviews beitragen kann. Diese unterbleiben jedoch meistens, wenn Qualitätsmanagement nicht aus Hand eines kleineren oder nur auf Reviews spezialisierten Teams kommt.

As a result of this research, the wish or the request remains on the multipliers and accompanying community members of the developers, that portals with listings about Crypto-Messengers remove the closed-source applications and develop (or add) especially in detail written reviews in their list of open-source applications - or at least link the existing literature references and audit reports properly.

Ideally there are in the near future portals for Crypto that provide information exclusively on open-source programs for encrypted messaging. Again, the information policy can not be left to only a handful of players, but requires instead analysis and knowledge exchanges of many people. Bloggers should fulfill the encountered state of a lack of transparency for the particular source-open solutions for encrypted communication with light.

In regard to further or future developers the wish remains, to support the teams of the existing source-open applications, or - having read this - to develop their own new source-open applications. It also remains to be hoped, that developers come from numerous nations and countries - to reserve the development of Crypto-Apps not only to few nations (see also Schneier et al. 2016).

We cordially recommend auditors, as well as students and scholars, to read more comparative and deeper about these BIG SEVEN applications and/or compare the different functions in particular qualitatively in regard of their relevance for specific problems and issues.

Im Ergebnis dieser Recherche bleibt der Wunsch bzw. die Aufforderung auch an die Multiplikatoren und begleitende Community der Entwickler, dass Portale mit Listungen über Crypto-Messenger die closed-source Applikationen entfernen und bei der Listung von open-source Applikationen insbesondere ausführlich geschriebene Reviews erarbeiten und hinzufügen - oder zumindest die bestehenden Literaturangaben und Audit-Reporte fachgerecht verlinken.

Idealerweise gibt es in naher Zukunft Crypto-Portale, die ausschließlich über quelloffene Programme zur verschlüsselten Nachrichtenübermittlung informieren. Auch hier kann die Informationspolitik nicht nur einer Handvoll an Akteuren überlassen werden, sondern bedarf Analysen und Wissensvermittlungen zahlreicher Personen. Auch Blogger sollten den vorgefundenen Zustand an fehlender Transparenz für insbesondere die quell-offenen Lösungen für verschlüsselte Kommunikation mit Licht erfüllen.

Hinsichtlich weiterer oder zukünftiger Entwickler bleibt zu wünschen, dass sie die Teams der bestehenden quell-offenen Applikationen unterstützen, oder in Kenntnis dieser, eigene neue Applikationen quell-offen entwickeln. Auch bleibt zu hoffen, dass Entwickler aus zahlreichen Nationen und Ländern entstammen, um die Entwicklung der Crypto-Apps nicht nur wenigen Nationen vorzubehalten (vgl. a. Schneier et.al. 2016).

Auditoren, wie auch Studierenden und Wissenschaftlern empfehlen wir kollegial, sich vergleichend und vertiefend mit diesen BIG SEVEN Applikationen auseinander zu setzen und/oder die unterschiedlichen Funktionen insbesondere qualitativ in ihrer Relevanz für bestimmte Probleme und Fragestellungen zu vergleichen.

2.6   References to our further core audit principles

The audit process was thus carried out as described above with regard to international audit standards and, in particular, specific IT-standards, guidelines and principles in order to achieve a comprehensive picture from as many angles.

Der Audit-Prozess wurde somit unter Berücksichtigung internationaler Audit-Standards sowie insbesondere spezifischer IT-Normen, Richtlinien und Prinzipien wie oben beschrieben durchgeführt, um ein möglichst umfassendes Bild aus möglichst vielen Blickwinkeln zu erreichen.

The assessments and conclusions are based on both, the established process models and content areas, as well as on the basis of a comprehensive employment, analyzing and comparing created within these topics - like they were found at the time of conducting the audit.

This is not to be understood as a completed process and standard, but should explicitly postulate further research and research needs, in which the following principles of an audit should find a reflection:

- **Timeliness:** Only when the processes and programming is continuous inspected in regard to their potential susceptibility to faults and weaknesses, but as well with regard to the continuation of the analysis of the found strengths, or by comparative functional analysis with similar applications an updated frame can be continued.

- **Source openness:** It requires an explicit reference in the audit of encrypted programs, how the handling of open source has to be understood. E.g. programs, offering an open source application, but not considering the IM server as open source, have to be regarded as critical. An auditor should take an own position to the paradigm of the need of the open source nature within cryptologic applications.

- **Elaborateness:** Audit processes should be oriented to certain minimum standard. The recent audit processes of encrypting software often vary greatly in quality, in the scope and effectiveness and also experience in the media reception often differing perceptions. Because of the need of special knowledge on the one hand and to be able to read programming code and then on the other hand to also have knowledge of encryption procedures, many users even trust the shortest statements of formal confirmation. Individual commitment as an auditor, e.g. for quality, scale and

Die Einschätzungen und Schlussfolgerungen sind auf Basis sowohl der etablierten Vorgehensmodelle und Inhaltsbereiche als auch auf Basis einer umfangreichen Beschäftigung mit, Analyse von und Vergleichen innerhalb dieser Themenstellungen entstanden - wie sie zum Zeitpunkt der Durchführung des Audits vorgefunden wurden.
Dieses ist nicht als abgeschlossener Prozess und Standard zu verstehen, sondern soll explizit weiteren Untersuchungs- und Forschungsbedarf postulieren, bei dem die folgenden Prinzipien eines Audits eine Reflexion finden sollten:

- **Aktualität:** Nur wenn die Prozesse und Programmierungen kontinuierliche untersucht werden hinsichtlich möglicher Fehleranfälligkeit und Schwächen, aber auch hinsichtlich der Fortschreibung der Analyse der gefundenen Stärken, oder durch vergleichende Funktions-Analysen mit ähnlichen Applikationen, kann ein aktualisierteres Bild fortgesetzt werden.

- **Quelloffenheit:** Es bedarf eines ausdrücklichen Hinweises im Audit von verschlüsselnden Programmen, wie der Umgang mit Quelloffenheit zu verstehen ist. Programme z.B., die eine quelloffene Applikation bereit stellen, jedoch den Chat-Server nicht darunter fassen, sind als kritisch zu betrachten. Ein Auditor sollte zum Paradigma der Quelloffenheit von kryptologischen Applikationen Stellung beziehen.

- **Ausführlichkeit:** Audit-Prozesse sollten sich an einen gewissen Mindestmaß-Standard orientieren. Die bisherigen Audit-Prozesse von verschlüsselnder Software variieren oftmals sehr stark in der Qualität, im Umfang und der Effektivität und erleben auch in der medialen Rezeption differierende Wahrnehmung. Aufgrund der z.T. erforderlichen Spezialkenntnisse zum einen, Programmiercode lesen zu können, sowie sodann auch noch Kenntnisse in Verschlüsselungs-prozeduren zu haben, vertrauen viele Anwender selbst den kürzesten

effectiveness, is thus to be assessed reflexively for yourself and to be documented within the audit.

- **The financial context:** Further transparency is needed to clarify whether the software has been developed commercially and whether the audit was funded commercially (paid Audit). It makes a difference whether it is a private hobby / community project or whether a commercial company is behind it.

- **Scientific referencing of learning perspectives:** Each audit should describe the findings in detail within the context and also highlight progress and development needs constructively. An auditor is not the parent of the program, but at least he or she is in a role of a mentor, if the auditor is regarded as part of a PDCA learning circle (PDCA = Plan-Do-Check-Act). There should be next to the description of the detected vulnerabilities also a description of the innovative opportunities and the development of the potentials.

- **Literature-inclusion:** A reader should not rely solely on the results of one review, but also judge according to a loop of a management system (e.g. PDCA, see above), to ensure, that the development team or the reviewer was and is prepared to carry out further analysis, and also in the development and review process is open to learnings and to consider notes of others. A list of references should be accompanied in each case of an audit.

- **Inclusion of user manuals & documentation:** Further a check should be done, whether there are manuals and technical documentations, and, if these are expanded.

Aussagen formaler Bestätigung. Das eigene Engagement als Auditor, also Qualität, Umfang und Effektivität, ist somit weitergehend reflexiv für sich selbst einzuschätzen und im Audit zu dokumentieren.

- **Finanzieller Hintergrund:** Weiterhin ist Transparenz erforderlich, um zu verdeutlichen, ob die Software kommerziell entwickelt wurde und ob auch das Audit kommerziell gefördert wurde (bezahltes Audit). Es ist ein Unterschied, ob es sich um ein privates Hobby/Community-Projekt handelt oder ob ein Wirtschaftsunternehmen dahinter steht.

- **Wissenschaftliche Referenzierung von Lernperspektiven:** Jedes Audit sollte die Fundstellen ausführlich im Kontext beschreiben und auch Fort- und Entwicklungsbedarf konstruktiv aufzeigen. Ein Auditor wird nicht zum Elternteil des Programmes, so aber doch zu einem Paten, wenn er sich selbst als Teil eines PCDA-Lern-Zirkels einbringt (PDCA = Plan-Do-Check-Act). Es sollte neben der Beschreibung der gefundenen Schwachstellen auch eine Beschreibung der innovativen Entwicklungsmöglichkeiten und des Ausbaus der Potentiale geben.

- **Literatur-Einbezug:** Ein Leser sollte sich nicht nur auf die Ergebnisse eines Reviews verlassen, sondern auch entsprechend dem Regelkreis eines Management-Systems (z.B. PDCA, s.o.) beurteilen, ob das Entwicklerteam oder der Reviewer bereit war und ist, weitere Analysen durchzuführen und auch im Entwicklungs- und Überprüfungsprozess offen ist, zu lernen und Hinweise anderer aufzunehmen. Eine Literaturliste sollte in jedem Fall einem Audit begefügt sein.

- **Einbezug von Nutzermanualen & Dokumentationen:** Es sollte weiterhin eine Überprüfung vorgenommen werden, ob Manuale und technische Dokumentationen vorliegen und ausgebaut werden.

- **Identify references to innovations:** Applications that allow both, messaging to offline and online contacts, so considering chat and e-mail in one application - as it is also the case with GoldBug - should be tested with high priority (criterion of presence chats in addition to the e-mail function). The auditor should also highlight the references to innovations and underpin further research and development needs.

- **Referenzen zu Innovationen aufzeigen:** Applikationen, die sowohl Messaging zu Offline- und Online-Kontakten ermöglichen, also Chat und E-Mail in einer Applikation berücksichtigen - wie es bei GoldBug ebenso der Fall ist – sollten vordringlich getestet werden (Kriterium des Presence-Chats neben der E-Mail-Funktion). Der Auditor sollte daher auch die Referenzen zu Innovationen aufzeigen und weiteren Forschungs- und Entwicklungsbedarf herausstellen.

This **list of audit principles for crypto applications** describes - beyond the methods of technical analysis - particularly core values, that should be taken into account, and auditors from our point of view should reflect in their reports.

Diese **Liste an Audit-Prinzipien für Crypto-Applikationen** beschreibt - jenseits der Methoden zur technischen Analyse - insbesondere Kernwerte, die ein Auditor aus unserer Sicht in seinem Bericht berücksichtigen und reflektieren sollte.

Figure 01: Eight Principles of a Crypto-IT-Audit

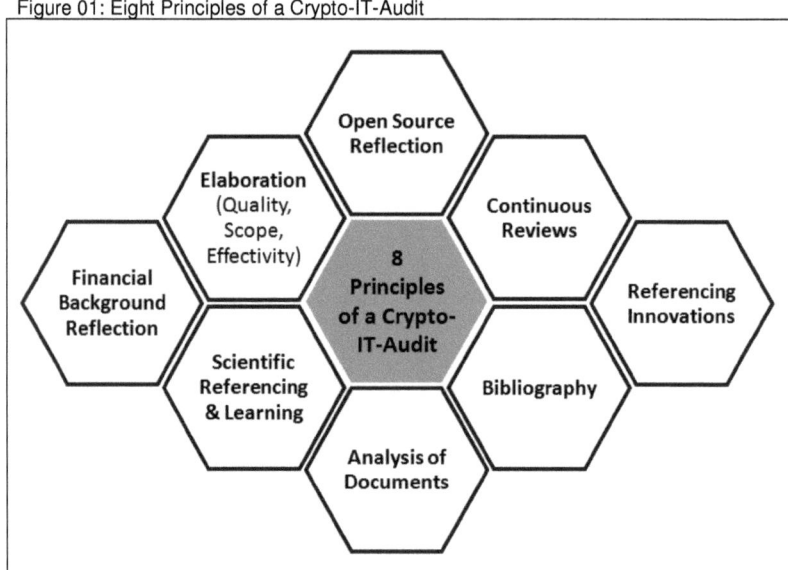

Source: Own presentation.

In summary, according to a self-reflection of an auditor therefore as well for this audit can be stated:

The present review audit study is a private audit without influence from commercial or financial interests and checks the open source program GoldBug, which is implemented according to the website of the developers also without any financial impact of third parties as a hobby spare time project.

The conduction of this audit and the present documentation was made therefore by the two authors, who made this financially independent and in leisure without the use of their membership of a professional audit institution.

As mentioned before also this audit of GoldBug is based in knowledge and in consideration of the numerous derivatives of the above-mentioned audit-standards, -rules and -principles. Numerous analyzes and investigations have been made accordingly, like the following 21 areas of investigation in the next chapter 3 will show subsequently and will address all these eight IT-Auditor-principles.

2.7 Planning, Support, Conduction & further Hosting

We have created our analyzes as mentioned without authority and financial backgrounds or promotions. At the same time we provide the texts of our study under open source license and therefore they are free of copyright available. So any user or blogger and each portal may refer to this study and is able to continue this.
We will make this study subsequently available as well for the GoldBug project e.g. for hosting / downloading. So particularly the users of the application have these reviews and analyzes as information available.

The conduction of the audit we have provided with a project management plan to coordinate the individual steps and the inclusion of additional testers and machines.

The individual audit steps can be documented in a schedule as follows:

Die einzelnen Audit-Schritte lassen sich in einem Zeitplan wie folgt dokumentieren:

Audit Key Steps of GoldBug v.2.7 / v.2.8 / v.2.9

Planning completed	*August 2015*
Comparison of Audit manuals completed	*September 2015*
Field research for open source Crypto-Messengers completed	*September 2015*
Structuring Audit Methods to main features of GoldBug Messenger	*November 2015*
Research in these features, testing, code review, evaluation	*November / December 2015*
Comparison to Big-7-Crypto-Messengers completed	*December 2015 / February 2016*
Final report completed	*March 2016*
Translation to English & German Language	*April / May 2016*
Release of the Report	*June 2016*

Acknowledgments

Danksagung

The two authors responsible for this audit would like to thank cordially those individuals, who contributed to this study, and particularly, friends who provided testing and comments as part of this audit.
Thanks also to the GoldBug project, that agreed in course of completion of our research to establish an URL as an archiving download option for our report.

Die beiden für dieses Audit verantwortlichen Auditoren möchten denjenigen herzlich danken, die zu dem Gelingen dieser Studie beigetragen haben und insbesondere den Freunden, die an unseren Tests teilgenommenn haben und ihre Kommentare und Bewertungen dazu beisteuerten.
Dank geht auch an das GoldBug-Projekt, dass sich im Zuge des Abschlusses unserer Forschung bereiterklärte, eine URL als archivierende Download-Möglichkeit für unseren Bericht einzurichten.

3   FINDINGS AND RECOMMENDATIONS

The following sections of this chapter 3 contain the individual examinations and assessments of the previously in Chapter 2 executed central research methods and areas as joint investigation consensus from the various audit manuals as they are referred to the features in GoldBug Messenger.

Die folgenden Abschnitte dieses Kapitels 3 enthalten die einzelnen Untersuchungen und Beurteilungen der zuvor in Kapitel 2 ausgeführten zentralen Untersuchungsmethoden und Bereiche als gemeinsamer Untersuchungskonsens aus den verschiedenen Audit-Manualen, wie sie auf die Funktionen im Messenger GoldBug bezogen worden sind.

After a brief derivation, content and processes of the referring GoldBug function are described, subsequently a procedure for our assessment is presented, then the results of our investigations are summarized - which always contain a code review, but not in every chapter a code quote respectively a snapshot is included.

Es werden jeweils nach einer kurzen Herleitung die Inhalte und Prozesse der jeweiligen GoldBug-Funktion beschrieben, sodann ein Vorgehen für unser Assessment dargestellt, die Ergebnisse unserer Untersuchungen zusammengefasst, die auch immer ein Code-Review enthielten, jedoch nicht in jedem Kapitel ein Code-Zitat bzw. Snapshot einbinden.

Afterwards, the various findings are presented.

Sodann werden auch die verschiedenen Findings dargestellt.

We provide the audit issues with the security considerations in a relevant practical case, where one can illustrate the findings - potential risks and suggestions for improvement as well as the client's strengths - and general considerations in a handy example: Good Practice Insights.

Dabei stellen wir die Audit-Thematik mit den Sicherheitsüberlegungen auch in einem jeweiligen Anwendungsfall vor, an dem man die Findings - potentielle Risiken und auch Verbesserungsvorschläge sowie auch die Stärken des Klienten - sowie generelle Überlegungen an einem praktischen Beispiel verdeutlichen kann: Good Practice Insights.

Finally, it is also about embedding the content of the section with an indicative, contextual comparison among the in chapter 2 recognized seven major open source messenger applications with encryption (BIG SEVEN).

Schließlich geht es auch um die Einbettung der Inhalte des Abschnittes mit einem indikativen, kontextuellen Vergleich unter den in Kapitel 2 erkannten sieben wesentlichen quelloffenen Messenger Applikationen mit Verschlüsselung (BIG SEVEN).

3.1 Confidentiality through Multi-Encryption

In order to achieve confidentiality over the Internet, various methods can be used.

If a text has been encrypted once, why not encrypt this one more time? Or a file to be sent, can, before it will be sent, as well be encrypted - and here again there are various possibilities, the encrypted file can be sent through an encrypted channel (or possibly even within a non-encrypted one). This designates **multi-encryption**: Chipertext is again converted into ciphertext.

As widely known and briefly summarized here for beginning readers - fundamentally we can differ symmetric keys from asymmetric keys:

- In case you use a symmetric key, a jointly shared, secret password is known only to the two participants, which exchange messages. The password should consist out of at least 32 randomly distributed characters - including upper and lower case, numbers and special characters.

- In asymmetrical encryption, a public key and a private key for each user is used. Both parties must exchange their public keys. The public key of the communication partner is then used to encrypt the message, and private and public keys are then used in combination after the transfer of the encoded message in order to decrypt the encrypted message at the side of the receiver. This works by mathematical operations and is based on the prime factoring, which would take for sufficiently large keys - even using fast computers - many years to complete, if you do not know the private key.

Um Vertraulichkeit im Internet zu erreichen, können verschiedene Methoden angewandt werden.

Wenn ein Text einmal verschlüsselt wurde, warum sollte man diesen nicht ein weiteres Mal verschlüsseln? Oder eine Datei, die gesandt werden soll, kann, bevor sie versandt wird, ebenso verschlüsselt worden sein – und auch hier bestehen wieder verschiedene Möglichkeiten, die verschlüsselte Datei durch einen verschlüsselten Kanal zu senden (oder ggf. auch durch einen unverschlüsselten). Dieses bezeichnet **Multi-Verschlüsselung**: Chipertext wird nochmals in Ciphertext gewandelt.

So lassen sich - wie vielfach bekannt und hier für einen Erstleser kurz zusammengefasst - grundlegend symmetrische Schlüssel unterscheiden von asymmetrischen Schlüsseln:

- Bei einem symmetrischen Schlüssel handelt es sich um ein gemeinsam geteiltes, geheimes Passwort, das nur den beiden Teilnehmern an dem Nachrichtenaustausch bekannt ist. Es sollte mindestens 32 zufällig verteilte Zeichen inklusive Klein- und Großschreibung, Zahlen und Sonderzeichen umfassen.

- Bei der asymmetrischen Verschlüsselung wird ein öffentlicher und ein privater Schlüssel für jeden Teilnehmer genutzt. Beide Teilnehmer müssen ihren öffentlichen Schlüssel tauschen. Der öffentliche Schlüssel des Kommunikationspartners wird sodann genutzt, um die Nachricht zu verschlüsseln und private und öffentliche Schlüssel werden dann nach Transfer der verschlüsselten Botschaft im Zusammenspiel genutzt, um die verschlüsselte Nachricht auf Empfängerseite zu entschlüsseln. Dieses funktioniert durch mathematische Operationen und basiert auf der Primfaktor-Zerlegung, die bei hinreichend großen Schlüsseln selbst unter Einsatz von schnellen Computern viele Jahre in Anspruch nehmen würde, wenn man den privaten Schlüssel nicht kennt.

It is a common standard in cryptography, that symmetric keys are transmitted under use of other encrypted channels. The same applies to temporary, so-called ephemeral keys (which can be symmetric as well as a-symmetric keys).

Es ist dabei ein gängiger Standard in der Kryptographie, dass symmetrische Schlüssel übertragen werden unter Nutzung von anderen verschlüsselten Kanälen. Gleiches gilt für temporäre, also sogenannte ephemerale Schlüssel (die sowohl symmetrisch wie auch asymmetrische Schlüssel sein können).

The GoldBug Messenger combines the established, and standardized methods of encryption into a smart process. So new temporary keys are optionally prepared by asymmetric keys or symmetric keys, and the new communication can be run either with complementary asymmetric encryption as well as with pure symmetric encryption.

Der GoldBug Messenger verbindet die etablierten und standardisierten Methoden der Verschlüsselung zu einem smarten Prozess. So werden neue temporäre Schlüssel wahlweise durch asymmetrische Schlüssel oder auch symmetrische Schlüssel hergestellt und die neue Kommunikation kann wahlweise mit ergänzender asymmetrischer Verschlüsselung wie auch nur mit purer symmetrischer Verschlüsselung laufen.

Under hybrid encryption it is now understood to have a combination of asymmetric and symmetric encryption. Here, a random symmetric key is created, which is called session key. With this session key the data to be protected is encrypted symmetrically. Afterwards the session key is asymmetrically encrypted using the recipient's public key. This approach solves the key distribution problem and sustains also the speed advantage of the symmetric encryption.

Unter **hybrider Verschlüsselung** versteht man nun eine Kombination aus asymmetrischer Verschlüsselung und symmetrischer Verschlüsselung. Dabei wird ein zufälliger symmetrischer Schlüssel erstellt, der Session-Key genannt wird. Mit diesem Session-Key werden die zu schützenden Daten symmetrisch verschlüsselt. Anschließend wird der Session-Key asymmetrisch mit dem öffentlichen Schlüssel des Empfängers verschlüsselt. Dieses Vorgehen löst das Schlüsselverteilungsproblem und erhält dabei auch den Geschwindigkeitsvorteil der symmetrischen Verschlüsselung.

3.1.1 Inventory taking, structural analysis and descriptions of the functions

The encryption in GoldBug - making use of established encryption libraries like OpenSSL and libgcrypt - applies multiple encryption and hybrid encryption, which can be graphically depict as a capsule:

Die Verschlüsselung in GoldBug unter Nutzung von etablierten Verschlüsselungsbibliotheken wie libgcrypt und OpenSSL wendet mehrfache Verschlüsselung und auch hybride Verschlüsselung an, die sich graphisch wie eine Kapsel wie folgt abbilden lässt:

Figure 02: GoldBug – Encrypted Message Format within the Echo-Protocol

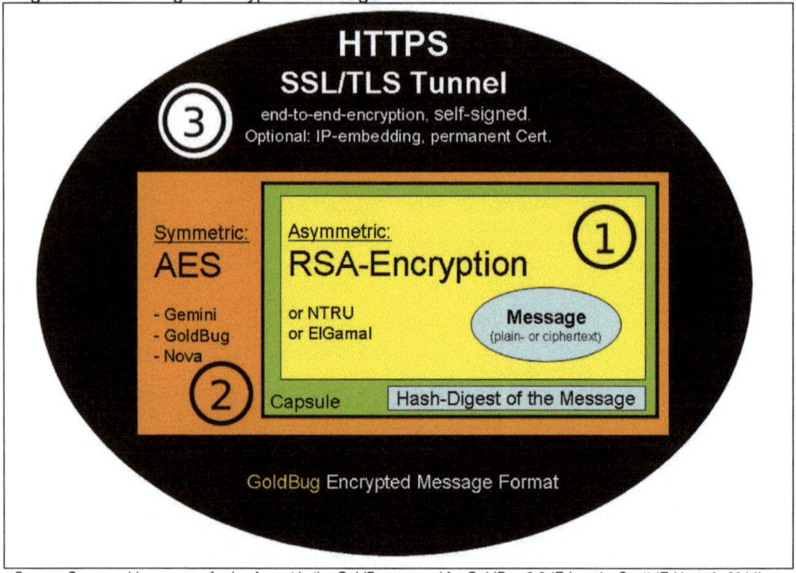

Source: Own graphic, comp. referring format in the GoldBug manual for GoldBug 2.8 (Edwards, Scott (Ed.) et al., 2014)

The figure shows from inside to outside the process of how the encrypted capsule is formed in the context of Echo Protocol:

Die Abbildung zeigt von innen nach außen den Prozess, wie die verschlüsselte Kapsel im Rahmen des Echo Protokolls gebildet wird:

First layer of the encryption:
The ciphertext of the original readable message is hashed, and subsequently the symmetric keys are encrypted via the asymmetric key - e.g. deploying the algorithm RSA.

Erste Ebene der Verschlüsselung:
Die Nachricht wird verschlüsselt und der Ciphertext der Nachricht wird gehashed und sodann können mit dem asymmetrischen Schlüssel (z.B. des Algorithmus RSA) auch die symmetrischen Schlüssel verschlüsselt werden.

In an intermediate step the ciphertext, and the hash digest of the ciphertext are combined into a capsule, and packed together.
It follows the approach: Encrypt-then-MAC. In order for the receiver to verify that the ciphertext has not been tampered with, the digest is computed before the ciphertext is decrypted.

In einem Zwischenschritt werden also der verschlüsselte Text und der Hash-Digest der Nachricht in eine Kapsel gebündelt und zusammen gepackt.
Es folgt dem Paradigma: Encrypt-then-MAC. Um dem Empfänger zu beweisen, dass der Ciphertext nicht verfälscht wurde, wird der Hash-Digest zuerst gebildet, bevor der Ciphertext entschlüsselt wird.

Third layer of the encryption:
Then, this capsule is transmitted via a secure SSL/TLS connection to the communication partner.

Dritte Ebene der Verschlüsselung:
Sodann kann diese Kapsel über ein gesicherte SSL/TLS-Verbindung zum Kommunikations-partner übertragen werden.

Second layer of encryption:
Optionally it is still possible, therefore to

Zweite Ebene der Verschlüsselung:
Optional besteht noch die Möglichkeit, die

encrypt the capsule of the first layer in addition with an AES-256, - comparable to a commonly shared, 32-character long symmetric password. Hybrid Encryption is then added to multiple encryption.

GoldBug has implemented a hybrid system for authenticity and confidentiality.

Keys for encryption can usually be secured with other keys, called signatures. Then in particular there is evidence that the used keys for encryption belong to an authenticated person.

When signatures are added to the actual encryption, the process, which has been shown above simplified and vividly illustrated, has to be enhanced accordingly in a technical explanation:

One portion of the system generates per-message authentication and encryption keys. These two keys are used for authenticating and encapsulating data. The two keys are encapsulated via the public-key portion of the system.

The application also provides a mechanism for distributing session-like keys for data encapsulation. Again, the keys are encapsulated via the public-key system. An additional mechanism allows the distribution of session-like keys via previously-established private keys.

Digital signatures are optionally applied to the data.

As an example, please consider the following message:

$E_{Public\ Key}$(Encryption Key || Hash Key) || $E_{Encryption\ Key}$(Data) || $H_{Hash\ Key}$ ($E_{Public\ Key}$(Encryption Key || Hash Key) || $E_{Encryption\ Key}$(Data)).

The private-key authentication and encryption mechanism is identical to the procedure more deeply discussed in the encrypted and authenticated containers section of the projectr documentation of the source code (Project documentation Spot-On 2013).

Kapsel der ersten Ebene zusätzlich mit einem AES-256, also vergleichbar mit einem gemeinsam geteilten, 32-Zeichen langem Passwort symmetrisch zu verschlüsseln. Hybride Verschlüsselung wird sodann zur Mehrfach-Verschlüsselung ergänzt.

GoldBug hat somit ein hybrides System für die Authentizität und Vertraulichkeit implementiert.

Schlüssel für Verschlüsselung können üblicherweise mit weiteren Schlüsseln, sogenannten Signaturen, abgesichert werden. Dann kann insbesondere nachgewiesen werden, dass die genutzten Schlüssel zur Verschlüsselung von einer authentifizierten Person kommen.

Kommen Signaturen zur eigentlichen Verschlüsselung hinzu, ist der oben vereinfacht und anschaulich dargestellte Prozess dementsprechend in einer technischen Erläuterung zu erweitern:

Ein Teil des Systems erzeugt pro Nachricht Authentifizierungs- und Verschlüsselungs-Schlüssel. Diese beiden Schlüssel werden für die Authentifizierung und das "Einkapseln" von Daten verwendet. Die zwei Schlüssel sind wiederum über den Public-Key-Teil des Systems eingekapselt.

Die Anwendung bietet auch einen Mechanismus zur Verteilung von sitzungsbasierten Schlüsseln für die Datenkapselung. Das heißt, dass die Schlüssel über das Public-Key-System eingekapselt werden. Ein zusätzlicher Mechanismus ermöglicht die Verteilung der sitzungsbasierten Schlüssel über zuvor festgelegte private Schlüssel.

Digitale Signaturen werden ebenso wahlweise auf die Daten angewendet.

Als ein Beispiel, sei das Format der folgenden Nachricht vergegenwärtigt:

$E_{Public\ Key}$(Encryption Key || Hash Key) || $E_{Encryption\ Key}$(Data) || $H_{Hash\ Key}$ ($E_{Public\ Key}$(Encryption Key || Hash Key) || $E_{Encryption\ Key}$(Data)).

Der Mechanismus zur Authentifikation und zur Verschlüsselung ist identisch, wie es im weiteren Abschnitt für das Verfahren bei den verschlüsselten und authentifizierten Container in der Projektdokumentation des Quellcodes vertiefend erörtert wird (Project Documentation Spot-On 2013).

3.1.2   Selected method for studying and function reference

As method of investigation should first be worked quite fundamentally here, that means to determine from the known information and the source code, how the encryption works in principle respectively is implemented procedurally. It involves an analysis of whether the encryption process is transparent and understandable.

Als Methode der Untersuchung soll hier zunächst ganz grundlegend gearbeitet werden, aus den bekannten Informationen und dem Quell-Code zu ermitteln, wie die Verschlüsselung prinzipiell funktioniert bzw. prozessural umgesetzt wird. Es geht um eine Analyse, ob der Prozess der Verschlüsselung transparent nachvollziehbar ist.

It's not about - and that can an audit in this way also not afford - whether an encryption layer discloses another layer of encryption by various decoding attempts. The aim of our review is not to try to break the RSA encryption. (For example, here is therefore only referred to the appropriate tests, for example, using the "Adaptive chosen-ciphertext attack (abbreviated as CCA2)" (compare further the authors: Bleichenbacher 1998, Fujisaki et al. 2004, Cramer 2004, Hofheinz 2007) as well as the NIST publication by Chen et al. 2016).

Es geht nicht darum – und dass kann ein Audit in dieser Form auch nicht leisten – ob eine Verschlüsselungsschicht eine andere Verschlüsselungsschicht offenbart durch verschiedene Dekodierungsversuche. Ziel unseres Reviews ist nicht, zu versuchen, die RSA-Verschlüsselung zu brechen. (Hier sei daher z.B nur auf die entsprechenden Versuche z.B. mit der Methode „Adaptive chosen-ciphertext attack (abgekürzt als CCA2)" hingewiesen (z.B. weitergehend bei den Autoren: Bleichenbacher 1998, Fujisaki et al. 2004, Cramer 2004, Hofheinz 2007) sowie auf die NIST-Veröffentlichung von Chen et al. 2016).

The basic principles should be here clarified and understood, in order to assess whether the encryption complies with the standard principles of software libraries used, and these have to be judged accordingly.

Die grundlegenden Prinzipien sollen hier verdeutlicht und nachvollzogen werden, um beurteilen zu können, ob die Verschlüsselung den Standardprinzipien der genutzten Bibliotheken entspricht und diese entsprechend zu werten sind.

3.1.3.   Conduction and findings of the examinations

Based on our code-review the individual sections of the functions of the encryption process are clearly structured, integrate the used libraries and are accordingly related to each other.

Ausgehend von unserem Code-Review sind die einzelnen Funktionsabschnitte des Verschlüsselungsprozesses klar gegliedert, binden die genutzten Bibliotheken ein und sind dementsprechend aufeinander bezogen.

The relevant programming can be found in the file: spot-on-crypt.cc. Because the process consists of several steps and references in the source code, here only a selected code passage should be inserted: the hash-digest-comparison; and then furthermore pointed to the inspection in the mentioned references.

Die relevanten Programmierungen finden sich in der Datei: spot-on-crypt.cc. Da der Prozess mehrere Schritte und Verweise im Quellcode umfasst, soll hier nur eine ausgewählte Code-Passage eingefügt werden: der Hash-Digest-Vergleich, und weiterhin auf die Durchsicht in den genannten Referenzen verwiesen werden.

As a result of our review we can state to have found respectively identified no particular disorders and that we were able to validate the mapping of the individual process steps for the

Im Ergebnis unserer Durchsicht können wir festhalten, keine besonderen Auffälligkeiten festgestellt bzw. ermittelt zu haben und die Abbildung der einzelnen Prozess-Schritte zur

encapsulation of the message.

It's not just about the illustration of the process in machine language, but also about getting the idea behind the encrypted capsule, when the user applies this encrypting Messenger:

If the hash of the ciphertext, which is converted from ciphertext by my client´s deposited keys, is identical with the supplied hash-digest of the original ciphertext, then an indicator is given, that I have the cipher converted properly (with any of my (from friends) available keys) - and a human beeing can read this as well.

The conversion process is - also in its process sequence - clear to understand, when reading the source code.

Verkapselung der Nachricht nachvollziehen konnten.

Weiterhin geht es auch nicht nur um die Abbildung des Prozesses in Maschinensprache, sondern auch um das Nachvollziehen der Idee, die hinter der verschlüsselten Kapsel steckt, wenn der Anwender diesen verschlüsselnden Messenger anwendet:

Wenn der Hash des Textes, der von Ciphertext durch die in meinem Klienten hinterlegten Schlüssel umgewandelt wird, identisch mit dem mitgelieferten Hash-Digest der Originalnachricht ist, dann ist ein Indikator gegeben, dass ich den Ciphertext (mit irgendeinem meiner (von Freunden) verfügbaren Schlüssel) richtig umgewandelt habe - und ein Mensch diesen auch lesen kann.

Der Umwandlungsprozess ist beim Lesen des Quellcodes ebenso in seiner Prozessfolge deutlich nachzuvollziehen.

Figure 03: Source Code for the Hash Comparision memcmp in spot-on-crypt.cc

```
bool spoton_crypt::memcmp(const QByteArray &bytes1,
                          const QByteArray &bytes2)
{
  QByteArray a;
  QByteArray b;
  int length = qMax(bytes1.length(), bytes2.length());
  int rc = 0;

  a = bytes1.leftJustified(length, 0);
  b = bytes2.leftJustified(length, 0);

  /*
  ** x ^ y returns zero if x and y are identical.
  */

  for(int i = 0; i < length; i++)
    {
      std::bitset<CHAR_BIT * sizeof(unsigned long)> ba1
        (static_cast<unsigned long> (a.at(i)));
      std::bitset<CHAR_BIT * sizeof(unsigned long)> ba2
        (static_cast<unsigned long> (b.at(i)));

      for(size_t j = 0; j < ba1.size(); j++)
        rc |= ba1[j] ^ ba2[j];
    }

  return rc == 0; /*
             ** Return true if bytes1 and bytes2 are identical or
             ** if both bytes1 and bytes2 are empty.
             ** Perhaps this final comparison can be enhanced.
             */
}
```

```
QByteArray spoton_crypt::decryptedAfterAuthenticated(const QByteArray
&data,
                                                      bool *ok)
{
  if(data.isEmpty())
    {
      if(ok)
        *ok = false;

      return QByteArray();
    }

  unsigned int length = gcry_md_get_algo_dlen(m_hashAlgorithm);

  if(length == 0)
    {
      if(ok)
        *ok = false;

      spoton_misc::logError
        ("spoton_crypt::decryptedAfterAuthenticated(): "
         "gcry_md_get_algo_dlen() failure.");
      return QByteArray();
    }

  if(data.mid(static_cast<int> (length)).isEmpty())
    {
      if(ok)
        *ok = false;

      return QByteArray();
    }

  QByteArray computedHash(keyedHash(data.mid(static_cast<int> (length)),
                                    ok));
  QByteArray hash(data.mid(0, static_cast<int> (length)));

  if(!computedHash.isEmpty() && !hash.isEmpty() && memcmp(computedHash,
                                                          hash))
    return decrypted(data.mid(static_cast<int> (length)), ok);
  else
    {
      if(ok)
        *ok = false;

      return QByteArray();
    }
}
```

Source: spot-on-crypt.cc - of GoldBug 2.9

3.1.4.   Evaluation of the results with regard to weaknesses, risks, potentials for improvements and strengths

With regard to the code implementation there are no findings from our side. The strength of the protocol lays in the multiple respectively hybrid encryption, and in an intelligent hash comparison to detect a message addressed to the own person: a human being can read it - when the hash comparison is consistent.

As shown below at the types for the so called "Calling" (compare Pure Forward Secrecy for e-mail or in chat: Calling with Forward Secrecy), it is also possible, to systematically "play" with the use of symmetric and/or asymmetric encryption, (e.g.

- first encrypt multiple, then encrypt hybrid, and respectively vice versa
- first encrypt symmetric and then encrypt asymmetric and vice versa, respectively
- alternating from asymmetric encryption to pure symmetric encryption).

This optionality is given in the encapsulation of the echo protocol in the version of the examined application 2.8 (2015) and 2.9 (2016) for additional symmetric encryption during chat in particular by means of a so-called Gemini-Call (using an AES-256): That means, with a call in a chat an AES is as symmetric encryption always added to the asymmetric encryption (compare layer 2 in the graphic above).

Mind you, it is not about the development of a proprietary algorithm or a homemade encryption, instead only about the procedural application of existing standards from the existing crypto libraries. As with the Mac-then-Encrypt or Encrypt-then-Mac procedure one can define with a call, respectively with multi-encryption, whether first an asymmetric, and then a symmetric encryption is performed (or vice versa) or whether ephemeral (temporary) new keys are then transferred through existing symmetric or asymmetric channels.

Hinsichtlich der Code-Implementierung gibt es keine Findings unsererseits. Die Stärke des Protokolls liegt in der mehrfachen bzw. hybriden Verschlüsselung und eines intelligenten Hash-Vergleiches, um eine ggf. an einen selbst adressierte Nachricht zu erkennen: indem ein Mensch sie lesen kann, wenn der Hash-Vergleich stimmig ist.

Wie weiter unten bei den Arten des sog. "Calling" noch zu sehen sein wird (vgl. Pure Forward Secrecy beim E-Mail oder beim Chat: Calling mit Forward Secrecy), besteht auch die Möglichkeit, mit der Anwendung von symmetrischer und/oder asymmetrischer Verschlüsselung systematisch zu „spielen" (z.B.

- erst mehrfach verschlüsselt, dann hybrid verschlüsselt und vice versa bzw.
- erst symmetrisch verschlüsselt und dann asymmetrisch verschlüsselt und vice versa, bzw.
- Wechsel von asymmetrischer Verschlüsselung auf pure symmetrische Verschlüsselung).

Diese Optionalität ist bei der Verkapselung des Echo-Protokolls in der Version der untersuchten Applikation 2.8 (2015) bzw. 2.9 (2016) für die zusätzliche symmetrische Verschlüsselung beim Chat insbesondere mittels eines sogenannten Gemini-Calls (unter Nutzung eines AES-256) gegeben: D.h. bei einem Call im Chat wird ein AES als symmetrische Verschlüsselung immer in die asymmetrische Verschlüsselung mit einbezogen (vgl. Ebene 2 in obiger Grafik). Wohlgemerkt es geht es dabei nicht um die Entwicklung eines eigenen Algorithmus oder einer hausgemachten Verschlüsselung, sondern nur um die prozessurale Anwendung der bestehenden Standards aus den vorhandenen Crypto-Bibliotheken. Wie bei der Mac-then-hash oder Hash-then-Mac Prozedur kann man beim Call bzw. der Multi-Verschlüsselung definieren, ob erst eine asymmetrische und dann eine symmetrische Verschlüsselung erfolgt (oder umgekehrt) oder ob ephemerale (temporäre) neue Schlüssel sodann durch bestehende asymmetrische oder symmetrische Kanäle transferiert werden.

GoldBug can therefore be considered not only as the founder and pioneer of the age of a modern client-side hybrid and/or multi-encryption and their numerous variations. With the echo protocol - which refers to the incorporated architecture of the Spot-On kernel since 2011 - this crypto-network-concept can be considered as the first theoretical and practical elaboration in an application, which introduced the paradigm of **crypto-keys as network-address** (instead of the previous IP-addresses), and thus indicates avoidant against metadata analysis.

GoldBug kann daher nicht nur als Begründer und Pioneer des Zeitalters einer modernen klientenseitigen hybriden und/oder Multi-Verschlüsselung und deren zahlreichen Variationen betrachtet werden. Mit dem Echo-Protokoll – das sich auf die zugrundegelegte Architektur des Spot-On-Kernels seit 2013 bezieht – kann dieses Crypto-Netzwerk-Konzept als erste theoretische wie praktische Ausarbeitung in einer Applikation betrachtet werden, die das Paradigma der **Crypto-Keys als Netzwerkadresse** (anstelle von bisherigen IP-Adressen) vorstellte und sich damit vermeidend gegenüber Metadaten-Analysen zeigt.

Table 05: Description of findings 3.01

#	Area	Description of the finding	Valuation Severity Category / Difficulty Level / Innovation & Improvement Class / Strength Dimension
	Weakness / Schwäche	./.	./.
	Risk / Risiko	./.	./.
3.01.4.A	Potential for Improvement / Verbesserungspotential	./.	./.
3.01.4.B	Strength / Stärke	The strength of the hyrid encryption lays in the several layers of encryption, which makes it harder to get to the core of the capsule: the original message.	High

3.1.5. Appraisal of good practices in comparison with other similar applications

The encryption process of each application by the seven to be compared open source messengers is different in each case.

The multiple packing of a text in a new encryption process as multi-encryption respectively as hybrid-encryption, that uses both, asymmetric and symmetric methods, and identifies the proper decryption via the hash digest of the message, can so far be found only in the GoldBug client.

Der Verschlüsselungsprozess einer jeder Applikation von den sieben zu vergleichenden quelloffenen Messengern ist jeweils unterschiedlich.

Das mehrfache Einpacken eines Textes in einem neuen Verschlüsselungsprozess als Multiverschlüsselung bzw. als hybride Verschlüsselung, die sowohl asymmetrische und auch symmetrische Verfahren einsetzt und die richtige Entschlüsselung über den Hash-Digest der Nachricht identifiziert, lässt sich bislang nur beim GoldBug Klienten finden.

Table 06: Indicative BIG SEVEN context references 3.01

Logo	Application	Comments
	Cryptocat	No usage of hybrid or multi-encryption.
	GoldBug	Usage of multi layers of encryaption: Hybrid Encryption. Different methods for encryption, e.g. asymmetric and symmetric encryption.
	OTR+XMPP	Usage of sessionbased keys within the OTR process.
	RetroShare	No usage of hybrid or multi-encryption.
	Signal	Usage of ephemeral keys transferred over the messenger.
	SureSpot	No usage of hybrid or multi-encryption.
	Tox	No usage of hybrid or multi-encryption.

At the same time, today also in other applications newer development approaches show up to protect the encrypted message through multiple keys and various encryption methods.

This opens up another area of research, to carry out this comparison in the appropriate level of detail in the next few years again, to compare the then current status regarding multiple or hybrid encryption of message texts in these or newly arrived open source applications.

GoldBug has presented an excellent model, how hybrid- respectively multi-encryption can be implemented, and will certainly influence the other Messengers with only one layer of encryption in their further development.

Gleichzeitig zeigen sich heute auch bei den weiteren Applikationen erste neuere Entwicklungsansätze, die verschlüsselte Nachricht durch mehrere Schlüssel sowie verschiedene Verschlüsselungsmethoden abzusichern.

Dieses eröffnet ein weiteres Forschungsfeld, in den nächsten Jahren diesen Vergleich im entsprechenden Detailierungsgrad erneut durchzuführen, um den dann aktuellen Stand hinsichtlich mehrfacher bzw. hybrider Verschlüsselung von Nachrichtentexten bei diesen oder auch neu hinzukommenden quelloffenen Applikationen zu vergleichen.

GoldBug hat ein excellentes Modell vorgelegt, wie hybride bzw. Multi-Verschlüsselung umgesetzt werden kann und wird sicherlich auch die anderen Messenger mit nur einer Verschlüsselungsschicht in ihrer weiteren Entwicklung beeinflussen.

For example, after the term of "Calling" for a to be manufactured end-to-end encryption was established by GoldBug and the underlying architecture Spot-On since mid-2013 (compare for detail as well section 3.15), subsequently other research papers have applied the to GoldBug / Spot-On referring **Concept of Calling in Cryptology** (see Spot-On Project Documentation 2013) for the preparation of a (a)symmetrical, possibly ephemeral (temporary) end-to-end encryption (e.g. as van den Hooff / Lazar / et. al 2015 in their Paper "Scalable Private Messaging Resistant to Traffic Analysis", which plagiarized without referencing the aspects of the echo protocol in part, and in particular for the Crypto-Calling: "When receiving a call via the protocol, the recipient needs to identify who is calling, based on the caller's public key", as cited, MIT-CSAIL 2015).

Nachdem beispielsweise der Begriff des Callings für eine herzustellende Ende-zu-Ende Verschlüsselung durch GoldBug und die zugrundegelegte Architektur Spot-On seit Mitte 2013 etabliert wurde (vgl. ausführlicher auch Abschnitt 3.15), haben sodann auch andere Forschungspapiere den auf GoldBug/Spot-On zurückgehenden Begriff des Callings in der Kryptologie (siehe Spot-On Projekt-Dokumentation 2013) für die Herstellung einer (a)symmetrischen, ggf. ephemeralen (temporären) Ende-zu-Ende-Verschlüsselung angewandt (wie z.B. van den Hooff / Lazar / et. al 2015 in ihrem Papier „Scalable Private Messaging Resistant to Traffic Analysis", das die Aspekte des Echo-Protokolls z.T. und insbesondere für das Crypto-Calling ohne Referenzierungen plagiarisiert: „When receiving a call via the protocol, the recipient needs to identify who is calling, based on the caller's public key", aaO MIT-CSAIL 2015).

Also the draft of "Matrix" of Erik Johnston (08/2014) contains backings to the Echo protocol, also if not in the same manner and coding environment. Furthermore also the draft of the "noise" detailed specifications of Trevor Perrin (2016) (first Github code-commit 08/2014 and the website domain creation and registration according to Whois was on 2016-04-01) overtook the idea of the Super-Echo Modus of the echo protocol from many years before.

Ferner enthält auch der „Matrix"-Entwurf von Johnston (08/2014) Anlehnungen an das Echo-Protokoll, wenn auch nicht in gleicher Art und Programmier-Umgebung. Auch der Entwurf der "Noise" Spezifikationen von Trevor Perrin (erster GitHub Code-Commit war in 08/2014 und die Domain Erstellung folgte laut Whois Erstellung und Registrierung erst am 04.01.2016) übernahm die Idee des Super-Echo Modus des Echo-Protokolls, das viele Jahre zuvor veröffentlicht wurde.

The Echo-Protocol represents so far the `Original Noise of the Matrix´ and is the inventor of both, `cryptographic routing´ and the term `calling in cryptography´ for instant renewable end-to-end encryption.

Das Echo-Protokoll stellt somit das `Original des Geräuschpegels, des Noise, in der Matrix´ dar und ist der Innovator des cryptographischen Routings als auch des Begriffes des "Calls" in der Kryptographie für sofortig erneuerbare Ende-zu-Ende Verschlüsselung.

Table 07: Good Practice Insight # 01

Good Practice Insight # 01	
with GoldBug Multi-Encrypting Communication Suite	
Case	If RSA could no longer be considered as secure e.g. due to quantum computing, would multi-encryption then be a solution? Wenn RSA z.B. aufgrund von Quantum-Computing nicht mehr als sicher gilt, kann Multi-Encryption dann eine Lösung sein?
Solution	GoldBug encrypts not only multiple, but also hybrid: symmetric and asymmetric encryption is combined. Also, you can renew different levels of encryption at any time instant. GoldBug verschlüsselt nicht nur mehrfach, sondern auch hybride: symmetrische und asymmetrische Verschlüsselung wird kombiniert. Zudem kann man verschiedene Ebenen der Verschlüsselung jederzeit instant erneuern.

Source: Own Case.

3.2   Integrity & Security of Information through Authenticity

The integrity and security of information respectively data transmitted is marked in particular by authentication.

In information security authenticity refers to the characteristics of the originality, accountability and trustworthiness. The verification of an alleged characteristic is called authentication (compare as well Shirey 1987). Through authentication of data origin is proven that data can be assigned to the claimed sender, which can be reached by digital signatures.

As can be demonstrated with the problem of Byzantine generals, one can examine many questions about the authenticity of information: The adjective Byzantine refers to the problem of Byzantine generals. In this scenario, several generals, who do not trust each other, raided Byzantium and send messages to each other. Therefore algorithms for secure transmission and verification of these messages are needed, because the sender or an entire message can be forged by another, messages can be intercepted by trapped couriers or can be replaced by fake notifications.

It is thus a problem of agreement to resolve, which is that the commanders must decide unanimously whether to attack an enemy army or not. The problem is complicated by the spatial separation of the commanders; so they need to send couriers back and forth. Then there is the possibility that among the generals traitors can be located, which can send a deliberately misleading information to the other generals (compare Dolev 1982).

The further publication with solutions to the problem of the Byzantine generals then is referred back to Lamport, Shostak and Pease in 1982 (ibid). They led back the problem to a "commanders and lieutenant" problem, where all loyal lieutenants must act in harmony and must match its actions with the orders of the

Die Integrität und Sicherheit von Informationen bzw. übermittelten Daten wird insbesondere durch Authentifizierung geprägt.

In der Informationssicherheit bezeichnet Authentizität die Eigenschaften der Echtheit, Überprüfbarkeit und Vertrauenswürdigkeit. Die Überprüfung einer behaupteten Eigenschaft wird als Authentifikation bezeichnet (vgl. auch Shirey 1987). Durch Authentifikation des Datenursprungs wird nachgewiesen, dass Daten einem angegebenen Sender zugeordnet werden können, was durch digitale Signaturen ermöglicht werden kann.

Wie anhand des Problems der byzantinischen Generäle aufgezeigt werden kann, kann man viele Fragestellungen zur Authentizität von Informationen untersuchen: Das Adjektiv byzantinisch bezieht sich auf das Problem der byzantinischen Generäle. Bei diesem Szenario belagern mehrere Generäle, die sich gegenseitig nicht vertrauen, Byzanz und lassen sich Mitteilungen zukommen. Gesucht sind daher Algorithmen zur sicheren Übertragung und Verifikation dieser Mitteilungen, da der Absender oder eine ganze Mitteilung von einem anderen gefälscht sein kann, Mitteilungen durch abgefangene Boten verloren gehen oder durch gefälschte Mitteilungen ersetzt werden können.

Es ist somit ein Problem der Übereinkunft zu lösen, welches darin besteht, dass die Heerführer einstimmig beschließen müssen, ob sie eine feindliche Armee angreifen sollen oder nicht. Kompliziert wird das Problem durch die räumliche Trennung der Befehlshaber; sie müssen also Boten hin- und herschicken. Dazu kommt die Möglichkeit, dass sich unter den Generälen Verräter befinden können, die an die anderen Generäle absichtlich irreführende Informationen schicken können (vgl. Dolev 1982).

Die weitere Veröffentlichung mit Lösungen zum Problem der byzantinischen Generäle geht sodann auf Lamport, Shostak und Pease im Jahr 1982 zurück (aaO). Sie führten das Problem auf ein „Befehlshaber und Leutnant"-Problem zurück, wobei alle loyalen Leutnants in Einklang handeln müssen und ihre Aktionen

commander, if he is loyal.

mit den Befehlen des Befehlshabers übereinstimmen müssen, wenn dieser loyal ist.

An illustrated solution considers the scenario, in which messages are faked. As long as the proportion of traitorous generals is less than one third, this solution should be tolerant in regard of a Byzantine fault.

Eine erläuterte Lösung beachtet das Szenario, bei dem Nachrichten gefälscht werden. Solange der Anteil der verräterischen Generäle kleiner als ein Drittel ist, sei diese Lösung tolerant gegenüber einem byzantinischen Fehler.

A second solution requires non-counterfeit-able signatures - what is now achieved in modern computer systems through public-key cryptography.

Eine zweite Lösung benötigt nicht fälschbare Signaturen – was heute in modernen Computersystemen durch Public-Key-Kryptographie erreicht wird.

The authentication characteristic is thus the characteristic, with which a user can be authenticated by a protected system.

Das Authentifizierungsmerkmal ist also das Merkmal, mit dem ein Benutzer von einem geschützten System authentifiziert werden kann.

This feature can be referred to knowledge (password, PIN, parole), to possession (key, card) or on an attribute (biometric feature such as voice, iris image, fingerprint) or an original signature - or beeing a combination of these features.

Dieses Merkmal kann auf Wissen (Passwort, PIN, Parole), auf Besitz (Schlüssel, Karte) oder auf einer Eigenschaft (biometrisches Merkmal z.B. Stimme, Irisbild, Fingerabdruck) oder Original-Unterschrift basieren oder auf einer Kombination dieser Merkmale.

Dynamic authentication is possible when the operational context is included. Then, the authentication factors are recognized by itself in a predetermined explicit context.

Dynamische Authentifizierung wird möglich, wenn der operationelle Kontext einbezogen wird. Dann gelten die Authentifizierungsmerkmale (engl. authentication factors) allein in einem zuvor bestimmten explizit erkannten Kontext.

In cryptography, the authenticity of a message is created by digital signatures.

In der Kryptographie wird die Authenizität einer Nachricht über digitale Signaturen hergestellt.

A digital signature, as well digital signature method, is an asymmetric cryptosystem, in which a transmitter calculates with a secret signature key (the private key) a value in regard to a digital message (that is for any data), which is also called digital signature.

Eine digitale Signatur, auch digitales Signaturverfahren, ist ein asymmetrisches Kryptosystem, bei dem ein Sender mit Hilfe eines geheimen Signaturschlüssels (dem Private Key) zu einer digitalen Nachricht (d. h. zu beliebigen Daten) einen Wert berechnet, der ebenfalls digitale Signatur genannt wird.

This value allows anyone using the public verification key (the public key) to check the non-deniable authorship and integrity of the message. To assign a signature generated with a signature key to a person, the corresponding verification key of this person must be assigned unambiguously.

Dieser Wert ermöglicht es jedem, mit Hilfe des öffentlichen Verifikationsschlüssels (dem Public Key) die nichtabstreitbare Urheberschaft und Integrität der Nachricht zu prüfen. Um eine mit einem Signaturschlüssel erstellte Signatur einer Person zuordnen zu können, muss der zugehörige Verifikationsschlüssel dieser Person zweifelsfrei zugeordnet sein.

For the data to be signed and the private signature key, the signature is computed by a unique computational rule.

Aus den zu signierenden Daten und dem privaten Signaturschlüssel wird durch eine eindeutige Rechenvorschrift die Signatur berechnet.

Different data have thus lead to almost certainly to a different signature, and the signature must result to another value for each key.

In deterministic digital signature process, the digital signature is uniquely defined by the message and the key.

In probabilistic digital signature process random values in the signature calculation are integrated, so that the digital signature of a message and a key can have many different values.

For a digital signature therefore the private key usually is not applied directly to the message, but their hash value using a hash function (such as SHA-256) calculated from the message. To prevent attacks, this hash function must be collision-resistant, that means, it must be practically impossible to find two different messages, whose hash value is identical.

Since in the RSA signature method - the digital signature method most commonly used - the operations used are almost identical to the RSA encryption, is sometimes spoken in the creation of a digital signature of the "encryption" or "decoding" of the hash value (compare also Wikipedia).

This terminology, however, is inappropriate, since a signature creation syntactically is something other than an encryption or decryption.

For most digital signature schemes (e.g. as for DSA) this equation therefore does not apply. There in the verification, the ("encrypted") hash value is not reconstructed from the signature.

Verschiedene Daten müssen also mit an Sicherheit grenzender Wahrscheinlichkeit zu einer anderen Signatur führen, und die Signatur muss für jeden Schlüssel einen anderen Wert ergeben.

Bei deterministischen digitalen Signaturverfahren ist die digitale Signatur durch die Nachricht und den Schlüssel eindeutig festgelegt. Bei probabilistischen digitalen Signaturverfahren gehen Zufallswerte in die Signaturberechnung ein, so dass die digitale Signatur zu einer Nachricht und einem Schlüssel viele verschiedene Werte annehmen kann.

Bei einer digitalen Signatur wird also der private Schlüssel in der Regel nicht direkt auf die Nachricht angewendet, sondern auf deren Hash-Wert, der mittels einer Hashfunktion (wie z.B. SHA-256) aus der Nachricht berechnet wird. Um Angriffe zu verhindern, muss diese Hashfunktion kollisionsresistent sein, d.h. es muss praktisch unmöglich sein, zwei unterschiedliche Nachrichten zu finden, deren Hash-Wert identisch ist.

Da beim RSA-Signaturverfahren, dem am häufigsten verwendeten digitalen Signaturverfahren, die eingesetzten Operationen fast identisch zu denen der RSA-Verschlüsselung sind, wird bei der Erstellung einer digitalen Signatur gelegentlich von der „Verschlüsselung" oder „Entschlüsselung" des Hashwertes gesprochen (vgl. a. Wikipedia).

Diese Terminologie ist jedoch unpassend, da eine Signaturerstellung syntaktisch etwas anderes ist als eine Ver- oder Entschlüsselung. Bei den meisten digitalen Signaturverfahren (z.B. bei DSA) trifft diese Gleichsetzung deshalb nicht zu. Dort wird bei der Verifikation keineswegs der („verschlüsselte") Hashwert aus der Signatur rekonstruiert.

3.2.1 Inventory taking, structural analysis and descriptions of the functions

GoldBug encrypts the various possible messages not only - that it is a chat message, a group chat posting or an email, or sending a file or some URLs -, but can also optionally add a digital signature. So the message or file package is uniquely referred to a particular sender or encryption key.

GoldBug verschlüsselt die vielfältigen möglichen Nachrichten nicht nur, sei es eine Chat-Message, ein Gruppen-Chat-Posting oder auch eine E-Mail oder der Versand einer Datei oder von URLs, sondern kann optional auch eine digitale Signatur hinzufügen. So ist die Nachricht bzw. das Dateipacket einem bestimmten Absender bzw. Schlüssel zur Verschlüsselung eindeutig zuzuordnen.

This function is embedded in GoldBug optionally, that means the user also has the option to send an e-mail without a digital signature.

Diese Funktion ist in GoldBug optional eingebettet, d.h. der Nutzer hat auch die Möglichkeit, eine E-Mail ohne digitale Signatur zu senden.

In the options of GoldBug can be controlled very decidedly whether a function should include signatures or not, for example, E-mail:

In den Optionen von GoldBug kann sehr dezidiert geregelt werden, ob eine Funktion Signaturen einbinden soll oder nicht, z.B. für E-Mail:

- Reject Letters without signatures
- Sign Letters.

- Reject Letters without signatures
- Sign Letters.

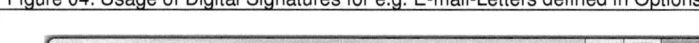

Figure 04: Usage of Digital Signatures for e.g. E-mail-Letters defined in Options

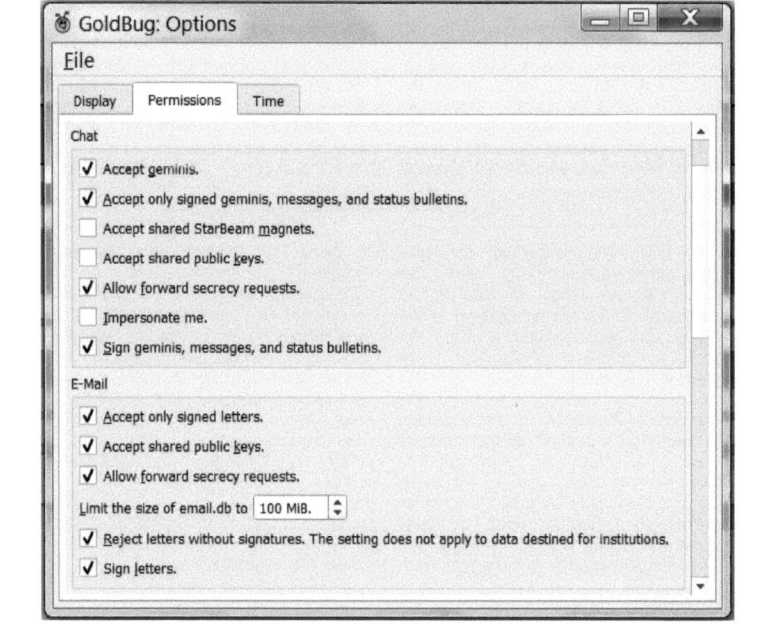

Source: Screenshot of Goldbug Options 2.9

Correspondingly, the receiver of the message has the option, to not allow e-mails in their e-mail inbox, when they were sent without a signature.

Entsprechend hat auch der Empfänger der Nachricht die Möglichkeit, E-Mails gar nicht in sein E-Mail-Postfach zu lassen, wenn sie ohne Signatur gesandt wurden.

Alone this architecture or option wealth shows, that information security and integrity through the use of authentication considers a high status in the Messenger GoldBug.

Alleine diese Architektur bzw. Optionsfülle zeigt auf, dass die Informationssicherheit und Integrität durch die Anwendung von Authentifizierungen einen hohen Stellenwert im Messenger GoldBug geniesst.

3.2.2   Selected method for studying and function reference

To investigate this, we will conduct a corresponding practical test: Two GoldBug instances were interconnected, and tested the e-mail function in different variations.

Um dieses zu untersuchen werden wir einen entsprechenden Praxistest durchführen: Es wurden zwei GoldBug-Instanzen miteinander verbunden, und die E-Mail-Funktion in verschiedenen Variationen ausgetestet.

Once was the instance of Alice examined with and without signature when sending e-mails, as well as the receipt of e-mails with and without signatures was approved.

Einmal wurde die Instanz von Alice mit und ohne Signatur beim Versand von E-Mails untersucht, sowie auch der Empfang von E-Mails mit und ohne Signaturen zugelassen.

The same has been created for the node of Bob.

Gleiches wurde für den Node von Bob erstellt.

3.2.3   Conduction and findings of the examinations

The following combinations have therefore result in our practical tests of the e-mail function with and without digital signatures:

Folgende Kombinationen haben sich daher in unseren Praxistests der E-Mail-Funktion mit und ohne digitale Signaturen ergeben:

Table 08: GoldBug Authentification Matrix for Digital Signatures

GoldBug Authentication Matrix for Digital Signatures	Alice allows receiving E-Mails without Signature	Alice requests receiving E-Mails with Signature	Bob allows receiving E-Mails without Signature	Bob requests receiving E-Mails with Signature
Alice sends E-Mails with Signature			Transfer OK	Transfer OK
Alice sends E-Mails without Signature			Transfer OK	**NO E-Mail shown**
Bob sends E-Mails with Signature	Transfer OK	Transfer OK		
Bob sends E-Mails without Signature	Transfer OK	**NO-E-Mail shown**		

Source: Own table.

In our tests, we were able for all above-mentioned cases to confirm correct operation of the reception and transmission of e-mails with or without digital signature.

In unseren Tests konnten wir für alle o.g. Fälle die Richtigkeit der Funktionsweise des Empfangs und des Sendens von E-Mails mit und ohne digitaler Signatur bestätigen.

Also the following cases important to information integrity were confirmed:

Auch die folgenden für Informationsintegrität wichtigen Fälle wurden bestätigt:

- Alice expects an e-mail signature, but Bob does not send a signature: The e-

- Alice erwartet eine E-Mail-Signatur, Bob sendet jedoch keine: Die E-Mail

mail will not be delivered or displayed.

- Bob expects an e-mail signature, but Alice does not send a signature: The e-mail will not be delivered or displayed.

GoldBug allows further during key generation also to define the entities for digital signatures manually.

wird nicht zugestellt bzw. angezeigt.

- Bob erwartet eine E-Mail-Signatur, Alice sendet jedoch keine: Die E-Mail wird nicht zugestellt bzw. angezeigt.

GoldBug ermöglicht weiterhin bei der Schlüsselgeneration auch die Entitäten für die digitalen Signaturen manuell zu definieren.

3.2.4 Evaluation of the results with regard to weaknesses, risks, potentials for improvements and strengths

Our evaluation due to the practical test shows no reason weaknesses or risks to assume. Also in the code review, we found no irregularities.

Unsere Evaluation durch den Praxistest zeigt keinen Grund, Schwächen oder Risiken anzunehmen. Auch im Code-Review haben wir keine Auffälligkeiten gefunden.

Table 09: Description of findings 3.02

#	Area	Description of the finding	Valuation Severity Category / Difficulty Level / Innovation & Improvement Class / Strength Dimension
	Weakness / Schwäche	./.	./.
	Risk / Risiko	./.	./.
	Potential for Improvement / Verbesserungspotential	./.	./.
	Strength / Stärke	./.	./.

GCM is not supported in digital signatures, because the Spot-On kernel and the corresponding user interface also refers to compilations, that might include an older version of the library gcrypt - even if the latest version is always distributed in the releases.

GCM wird bei den digitalen Signaturen nicht unterstützt, da sich der Spot-On-Kernel und die entsprechende Benutzeroberfläche auch auf Kompilierungen bezieht, die eine ältere Version der Bibliothek gcrypt einbeziehen könnten – auch wenn die jeweils aktuellste Version in den Releases distribuiert wird.

3.2.5 Appraisal of good practices in comparison with other similar applications

The manual switching on or off of signatures for each individual function is not possible in any other messenger. Also the manual selection of the specifications in the creation of signatures is not existing in any other messenger.

Das manuelle Hinzu- oder Abschalten von Signaturen jeweils für einzelne Funktionen ist in keinem anderen Messenger möglich. Auch die manuelle Wahl der Vorgaben bei der Erstellung der Signaturen ist in keinem anderen Messenger vorhanden.

Table 10: Indicative BIG SEVEN context references 3.02

Logo	Application	Comments
	Cryptocat	Has no option to send messages with or without digital signatures.
	GoldBug	Offers the choice to use or not use digital signatures. Offers also the choice which dedicated digital signature should be generated.
	OTR+XMPP	Has no option to send with or without digital signatures.
	RetroShare	Has no option to send messages with or without digital signatures.
	Signal	Has no option to send messages with or without digital signatures.
	SureSpot	Has no option to send messages with or without digital signatures.
	Tox	Has no option to send messages with or without digital signatures.

Table 11: Good Practice Insight #02

Good Practice Insight # 02	
with GoldBug Multi-Encrypting Communication Suite	
Case	I want to use a modern P2P e-mail system to make me more independent of central e-mail providers: How do I know that an email is actually from my friend?
	Ich möchte ein modernes P2P-E-Mail-System nutzen, um mich von zentralen E-Mail-Anbietern mehr unabhängig zu machen: Wie kann ich dann feststellen, dass eine E-Mail tatsächlich auch von meinem Freund ist?
Solution	GoldBug offers optional digital signatures for each email - this refers to both, POP3/IMAP E-Mail, as well as for the integrated P2P e-mail-system. So authenticity is ensured. Also, on every email a password can be placed - a so-called "GoldBug" - so that only the authenticated recipients are able to open the email.
	GoldBug bietet optional digitale Signaturen für jedes E-Mail an, sei es über POP3/IMAP oder im P2P E-Mail-System. Somit wird Authentizität sichergestellt. Ebenso kann auf jedes E-Mail eine Password – ein sogenanntes „GoldBug" – gesetzt werden, damit kann nur der authentifizierte Empfänger die E-Mail öffnen.

Source: Own Case.

3.3　Availability: Decentral P2P - HTTPS

An audit should as well assess the availability of the IT infrastructure respectively the services and also the continuity and peculiarities in the administrative service.
Included should be here also the feedback from administrators and experts, who mediate this as a multiplier of technology to others. So it's not just about the technical availability of one wire, of one encryption, a connection or a server, but also about the support that others can give and want to give, and about the basic ease of the learning about the usage of this technique from the perspective of supporters. How is the availability of technology and social support to assess?

Ein Audit sollte ebenso die Verfügbarkeit der IT-Infrastruktur bzw. des Services und auch die Kontinuität sowie Besonderheiten in der administrativen Betreuung beurteilen. Einbezogen werden soll dabei also auch das Feedback der Administratoren und Fachexperten, die als Multiplikator der Technik diese anderen vermitteln. Es geht also nicht nur um die technische Verfügbarkeit einer Leitung, einer Verschlüsselung, einer Verbindung oder eines Servers, sondern auch um die Unterstützung, die andere geben können und wollen sowie um die grundsätzliche Leichtigkeit der Erlernbarkeit der Anwendung dieser Technik aus Sicht von Unterstützern.
Wie ist die Verfügbarkeit von Technik und sozialer Unterstützung zu beurteilen?

3.3.1　Inventory taking, structural analysis and descriptions of the functions

In GoldBug Messenger is basically a decentralized architecture used.
This means that each user is able to set up with simple means an own chat server.

This not only strategically crucial that each user can set up their own IT infrastructure and services, and therefore decentralized structures can be available as an alternative in the context of potential attacks by surveillances entities of central structures and approaches.

Also in the context of cryptological to be assessed processes, it is critical, that the technology does not make a potential attacker the data and metadata of the user so easily accessible through e.g. decentralized infrastructure options.
GoldBug uses therefore an architecture that is based on the hard blockable HTTPS protocol, when a client addresses to a listener or chat server. This only needs to be accessible from the port and can be created either way, on the web (for example, through the ports 80, 8080, or 443, or 4710) as well as by another user at home (with any port or default 4710). If necessary, therefore a simple port forwarding on the router at home is required.

Beim GoldBug Messenger handelt es sich grundsätzlich um eine dezentrale Architektur.
D.h. jeder Nutzer ist mit einfachen Mitteln in der Lage, einen eigenen Chat-Server aufzusetzen.

Dieses ist nicht nur strategisch entscheidend, dass jeder Nutzer seine eigene IT-Infrastruktur und Dienste aufsetzen kann, und somit vor dem Hintergrund von potentiellen Angriffen von Überwachern zentraler Strukturen und Zugängen auch dezentrale Strukturen als Alternative bereitstehen können.

Auch vor dem Hintergrund kryptologisch zu beurteilender Prozesse ist es entscheidend, dass die Technik einem potentiellen Angreifer die Daten und Metadaten des Nutzers z.B. durch dezentrale Infrastrukturoptionen nicht so leicht zugänglich macht.
GoldBug setzt daher auf eine Architektur, die auf das schwer blockbare HTTPS-Protokoll aufsetzt, wenn ein Client sich an einen Listener bzw. Chat-Server adressiert. Dieser muss lediglich vom Port erreichbar sein und kann sowohl im Web (z.B. über die Ports 80, 8080 oder 443 oder 4710) als auch bei einem anderen Nutzer zuhause (mit beliebigem Port bzw. default 4710) erstellt werden. Ggf. ist dazu lediglich eine Portweiterleitung zu Hause am Router erforderlich.

By the decentralized structure thus very easy growing peer-to-peer networks or decentralized server services can be created to establish the service for an own team.

The stability of the kernel is just as crucial as the HTTPS connection and thirdly the presence of a chat-server or connectivity solution, which is supported in the community or by your own circle of friends.

Furthermore, there is also over the below (in Chapter 3.10) described POPTASTIC function - that is, to operate the encrypted chats as well as secure e-mail via a POP3 or IMAP server - an option, with which this stability of the services is given by further professional e-mail mailbox providers (in addition to a p2p embodiment of the email-function or - communication via a dedicated server or via the project-server given by GoldBug).

Finally, the complementary networking option exists, that server administrators connect among each other, to connect various remote chat servers and their users together.

In a fifth option the possibility also exists to design the entire system for a local group via a Bluetooth listener. Here no cable or internet is used, but an administrator just opens a Bluetooth listener and within the about 25 meters the present users e.g. of a Lan- or Crypto-Party or in a lecture auditorium of the school or university can connect wirelessly to the service and communicate with each other, share files, or contribute p2p to the URL Web search.

Durch die dezentrale Struktur können somit sehr einfach wachsende peer-to-peer Netze oder dezentrale Serverangebote geschaffen werden, um den Service für ein eigenes Team zu erstellen.

Die Stabilität des Kernels ist dabei ebenso von entscheidender Bedeutung wie der HTTPS-Verbindungsaufbau und drittens das Vorhandensein von einer in der Community oder für den eigenen Freundeskreis getragenen Chat-Server- bzw. Verbindungslösung.

Weiterhin besteht auch über die weiter unten (in Kapitel 3.10) beschriebene POPTASTIC-Funktion - d.h. den verschlüsselten Chat wie auch sicheres E-Mail über einen POP3 bzw. IMAP Server zu betreiben - eine Möglichkeit, mit der hier eine Stabilität des Services durch weitere professionelle E-Mail-Postfach-Anbieter gegeben ist (zusätzlich zu einer p2p Ausgestaltung der E-Mail-Funktion bzw. - Kommunikation mittels eines eigenen Servers oder dem projektseitig vorgegebenen Server).

Schließlich besteht auch die ergänzende Vernetzungsoption, dass sich Server-Administratoren untereinander miteinander vernetzen, um verschiedene dezentrale Chat-Server und deren Nutzer miteinander zu verbinden.

In einer fünften Option besteht auch die Möglichkeit, das gesamte System für eine lokale Gruppe über einen Bluetooth-Listener zu gestalten. Hier wird kein Kabel oder Internet genutzt, sondern ein Administrator eröffnet einen Bluetooth-Listener und die im Umkreis von ca. 25 Metern vorhandenen Nutzer z.B. einer Lan- oder Crypto-Party oder in einem Vorlesungs-Auditorium der Schule oder Universität können sich per Funk an den Service verbinden und untereinander kommunizieren und Dateien tauschen, oder p2p zur URL-Websuche beitragen.

3.3.2 Selected method for studying and function reference

For this portion of the assessment is to be investigated, how a user, who uses the software for the first time, connects to a server. For this, the software on the three operating systems Linux (Ubuntu), Windows and MAC OS X is downloaded respectively compiled and

Für diesen Abschnitt des Assessments soll untersucht werden, wie ein Nutzer, der die Software das erste Mal nutzt, sich zu einem Server verbindet. Dazu wird die Software auf den drei Betriebssystemen Linux (Ubuntu), Windows und MAC OS X heruntergeladen

provided with the necessary installation files. Then should be examined, whether in each system a stable connection to the available chat-project-server can be established. The method consists in the comparative embodiment of the processes on different operating systems in order to test whether the stability of the application for different users is the same performance and can be judged as "stable availability".

The details of the test chat server provided by the project will be loaded automatically during installation out of the file "spot-on neighbors.txt" and then used in the client for a connection. This server will be provided by the project for scientific test purposes. Although experienced users can and shall build their own server, two first-time users, who want to use the application without much effort, are dependent on the reliable availability respectively especially the proper functioning of the import of these server details.

The project server data is therefore not stored in the source code, but are loaded initially at startup out of of the above-mentioned file.

It is a text-file, that is located in the path, in which the binaries are also to be found, and which by everyone can be viewed with in regard to the stored server details (server address and port)

Thus, the initially to be loaded chat server can be adjusted individually e.g. in a re-distribution of the installation-zip to a group of friends, because the initial project server has not been defined in the source code.

bzw. kompiliert und mit den notwendigen Installationsdateien versehen. Sodann soll untersucht werden, ob in jedem System eine stabile Verbindung zu dem projektseitig vorhanden Chat-Server hergestellt werden kann. Die Methode besteht also in der vergleichenden Ausführung der Prozesse auf verschiedenen Betriebssystemen, um zu testen, ob die Stabilität der Anwendung für unterschiedliche Nutzer jeweils gleich performant ist und als „stabile Verfügbarkeit" beurteilt werden kann.

Die seitens des Projektes als Test-Server bereitgestellte Chat-Server-Angaben werden bei Installation automatisch aus der Datei „spot-on-neighbors.txt" geladen und sodann im Klienten für eine Verbindung genutzt. Dieser Server wird seitens des Projektes für wiss. Testzwecke zur Verfügung gestellt. Auch wenn erfahrenere Nutzer ihren eigenen Server errichten können und sollen, sind zwei Erstnutzer, die die Applikation ohne größeren Aufwand nutzen wollen, auf die zuverlässige Verfügbarkeit bzw. insbesondere die ordnungsgemäße Funktion des Imports dieser Serverdetails angewiesen.

Die Projektserverdaten sind daher nicht im Quellcode hinterlegt, sondern werden beim erstmaligen Programmstart aus der o.g. Datei eingeladen. Es ist eine Text-Datei, die sich im Pfad befindet, in dem auch die Binärdateien zu finden sind, und die von jedem hinsichtlich der hinterlegten Serverdetails (Serveradresse und Port) eingesehen werden kann.

Somit kann z.B. bei einer Re-Distribuierung des Installationszips an einen Freundeskreis auch der jeweils bei Erstinstallation zu ladende Chat-Server den dezentralen Gebenheiten individuell angepasst werden, weil der initiale Projektserver nicht im Quellcode hinterlegt ist.

Figure 05: Neighbor connection to the project server

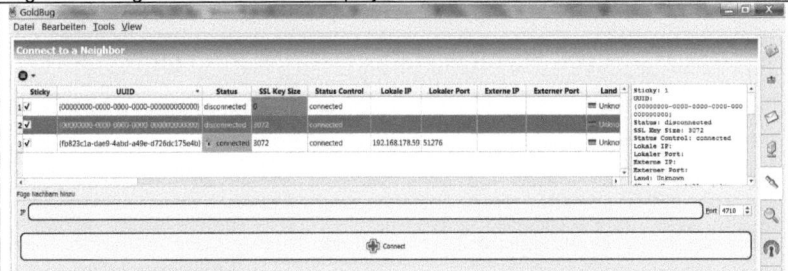

Source: Own screenshot of GoldBug.

3.3.3 Conduction and findings of the examinations

To carry out this assessment it is therefore intended, to install the software on Windows with the installation zip, on the operating system MAC OS X via the DMG installation file and on Linux Ubuntu over the existing Debian package.

As well on the Windows system, as well on the MAC OS X system and even under Ubuntu Linux, the file with the server details is included in the respective installation file.

After installing the application, after key generation and kernel activation, the connection with the project chat server is in the tab "neighbors" shown.

Both, the data for a IPv4-connection, and also IPv6-connection are available there. So that means that in the presence of the project server, the installation procedure for a connectivity indicates no deviations: that functionality is given on all tested operating systems.

The availability of the project server was given at any time and can be enriched with appropriate, additional servers from friends or for the own institution.

Also by the availability of listeners for IPV4 and IPV6 the security of the availability of an existing server as well as the scaling to more, other servers can be confirmed.

Thanks to the architecture and the integration of the server details not through the source

Zur Durchführung dieses Assessments ist daher vorgesehen, die Software auf Windows mit dem Installations-Zip, auf dem Betriebssystem MAC OS X über die DMG-Installationsdatei sowie auf Linux-Ubuntu die Installation über das vorhandene Debian Packet vorzunehmen.

Sowohl auf dem Windows System wie auch auf dem MAC OS X System und auch unter Ubuntu-Linux ist die Datei mit den Server-Details in der jeweiligen Installationsdatei enthalten.

Nach der Installation der Applikation sowie der Schlüsselgenerierung und der Kernelaktivierung zeigt sich die Verbindung zum Projekt-Chat-Server im Tabulator „Nachbarn".

Sowohl die Verbindungsdaten für eine IPV4-, als auch IPV6-Verbindung sind dort vorhanden. Das bedeutet also, dass bei Vorhandensein des Projektservers die Installationsprozedur für eine Konnektivität keine Abweichungen zeigt: die Funktionalität ist auf allen getesteten Betriebssystemen gegeben.

Die Verfügbarkeit des Projektservers war jederzeit gegeben und kann mit entsprechenden, weiteren Servern aus dem Freundeskreis oder für die eigene Institution angereichert werden.

Auch durch die Verfügbarkeit von Listenern für IPV4 und IPV6 kann die Sicherheit der Verfügbarkeit eines bestehenden Servers sowie auch die Skalierung auf weitere, andere Server bestätigt werden.

Durch die Architektur der Einbindung der Serverdetails nicht durch den Quellcode,

code, but by an installation file, the initial server can always be adapted without the application having to recompile.
(Compare for example the encrypted application CSpace by Tachyon Technologies, that had programmed in an Indian server service.
After turning off the server, the program was not only as a service no longer available, but also the use of all installers was made impossible - until the application - but again not the chat server - was documented as open source after many years without the service).

Therefore it can be stated an excellent result from the investigation of the program GoldBug on three different operating systems for the here examined process architecture, server availability, possibility of remote provisioning of servers and easy addition of chat servers by friends.
Even without the chat server provided by the project, the architecture also can be made available decentrally in an easy way and without modifications in the source code.

sondern durch eine Installationsdatei, kann der Erst-Server jederzeit angepasst werden ohne die Applikation neu kompilieren zu müssen.
(Vgl. z.B. das verschlüsselnde Programm CSpace von Tachyon Technologies, dass einen indischen Server-Dienst einprogrammiert hatte.
Nach Abschaltung des Servers stand das Programm nicht nur als Service nicht mehr zur Verfügung, sondern auch die Nutzung aller Installations-Dateien wurde unmöglich gemacht - bis die Applikation, wiederum jedoch nicht der Chat-Server, nach vielen Jahren ohne Service quelloffen dokumentiert wurde).

Für die hier untersuchte Prozess-Architektur, Server-Verfügbarkeit, Möglichkeit der dezentralen Bereitstellung von Servern und einfachen Hinzufügung von Chat-Servern aus dem Freundeskreis kann daher ein excellentes Ergebnis aus der Untersuchung des Programmes GoldBug auf drei verschiedenen Betriebssystemen festgehalten werden.
Auch ohne den projektseitig vorgegebenen Chatserver kann die Architektur auch dezentral einfach und ohne Anpassungen im Quellcode verfügbar gemacht werden.

3.3.4. Evaluation of the results with regard to weaknesses, risks, potentials for improvements and strengths

The strength of the examined application GoldBug lies in its option, that not only each user can create a decentralized listener, but the chat server can also be created very easily.

Die Stärke der untersuchten Applikation GoldBug liegt in ihrer Option, dass nicht nur jeder Nutzer einen dezentralen Listener erstellen kann, sondern sich der Chat-Server auch sehr einfach erstellen lässt.

Besides the ease of use, it is an additional plus, that the server software is already integrated in the application GoldBug.

Neben der einfachen Handhabung ist es ein zusätzlicher Pluspunkt, dass auch die Server-Software bereits in dem Programm GoldBug integriert ist.

Table 12: Description of findings 3.03

#	Area	Description of the finding	Valuation Severity Category / Difficulty Level / Innovation & Improvement Class / Strength Dimension
	Weakness / Schwäche	./.	./.
	Risk / Risiko	./.	./.
3.03.4.A	Potential for Improvement / Verbesserungspotential	Decentral servers are possible for local teams even over Bluetooth.	Informational
3.03.4.B	Strength / Stärke	Server Software in the client: Already integrated and easy to set up.	High

3.3.5 Appraisal of good practices in comparison with other similar applications

Comparing this with the difficult and mostly only by experts executable installing of a XMPP chat server, it is obvious, that for XMPP servers custom software and detailed administration skills must be available, however, also these chat clients permit the addition of decentralized chat servers.

CryptoCat permits as well server alternatives. However, the server software also relates as well to server software installable only with expertise.

RetroShare is substantially comparable with GoldBug concerning the availability and decentralization of chat servers, but when you first install RetroShare, it is required from the user to add a neighbor with a key, search the friend in the DHT and then trying to connect. If the friend, however, has not set up a listener port, the initial connection is not or only partially functioning.

Vergleich man dieses mit der schwierigen und meist nur von Fachexperten ausführbaren Installation eines XMPP-Chat Servers, zeigt sich, dass bei XMPP Server eigene Software und detaillierte Administrationskenntnisse verfügbar sein müssen, gleichwohl wenn diese Chat-Clienten auch die Hinzufügung von dezentralen Chat-Servern zulassen.

CryptoCat lässt ebenso Serveralternativen zu. Sie Server-Software bezieht sich jedoch auch ebenso auf nur mit Fachkenntnissen installierbare Server-Software.

RetroShare ist mit GoldBug hinsichtlich der Verfügbarkeit und Dezentralität von Chat-Servern im Wesentlichen vergleichbar, jedoch bei der Erstinstallation erfordert RetroShare vom Nutzer, einen Nachbarn per Schlüssel hinzuzufügen, diesen im DHT zu suchen und sodann zu verbinden. Wenn der Freund jedoch keinen Listener-Port eingerichtet hat, funktioniert die Erstverbindung nicht oder nur eingeschränkt.

Table 13: Indicative BIG SEVEN context references 3.03

Logo	Application	Comments
	Cryptocat	Central Server since many years, availability given.
	GoldBug	Both, decentral and central model since many years, a project test server is given and stable. Fast availability of connections.
	OTR+XMPP	Decentral services, availability depending on server admins.
	RetroShare	Decentral service, uses a DHT, no central server. DHT availability depending on configuration and environment.
	Signal	Central Server, stable, no decental servers. Many recommendations to use this central server availability.
	SureSpot	Central Server, stable & available.
	Tox	Usage of a DHT. Connection process depending on configuration and environment. Stun-Process and connection-process might take a time to connect.

Although Tox offers different user interfaces, the kernel as well as the chat server software in use by the user is rather slight.

Signal and SureSpot use essentially a central IM server, which also can not be installed from a user so easily without further modifications - if this would be even desired by the two projects at all.

As an improvement and outlook is thus in summary to realize that further from the community provided server may of course correspondingly increase the connectivity of users among each other.

As a recommendation can be therefore expressed, that the IM servers of the examined application are possibly preferable in regard to a XMPP chat server, because XMPP servers are not designed for exclusive encrypted traffic like a GoldBug chat server.

Moreover GoldBug communication servers are much easier to administer and contain also an email server: IMAP and POP3 server can be replaced easily and in a decentral way.

A note to the messenger Signal with its central server architecture is that in both, in the mobile version and in the desktop version, first, it is always necessarily to conduct a telephone number verification via SMS and thus also an identity check, and - secondly, even more astonishing, is that at the same time on the mobile version all the contacts of the user are uploaded.
Here is as well (as in Whatsapp) a comprehensive database by the supplier created, according to the pattern: who-knows-who.
Anyone wishing to use the desktop version, must have necessarily previously registered with their phone under the disclosure of their full contact list.
After public discussion in the field of cryptology, that backdoors in open source programming can be built only with difficulty into the encryption (Nakashima 2015), and that a ban on encryption would not only cripple the economy and the financial sector of each country, but rather has to be considered as a nonsense, like "mathematics to ban" (Wales

Auch wenn Tox verschiedene Benutzeroberflächen anbietet, ist der Kernel wie auch die Chat-Server-Software in der Anwendung durch die Nutzer eher gering ausgeprägt.

Signal und Surespot nutzen im Wesentlichen einen zentralen Chat-Server, der auch nicht ohne weitere Modifikationen von einem Nutzer so einfach installiert werden kann – wenn dieses von den beiden Projekten überhaupt gewollt wäre.

Als Verbesserung und Ausblick ist somit zusammenfassend zu erkennen, dass weitere aus der Community bereitgestellte Server die Verbindungsmöglichkeiten der Nutzer untereinander natürlich entsprechend erhöhen können.

Als Empfehlung kann daher ausgesprochen werden, dass die Chat-Server der untersuchten Applikation einem XMPP-Chat-Server ggf. vorzuziehen sind, da XMPP-Server nicht wie ein GoldBug-Chat-Server für ausschließlichen verschlüsselten Datenverkehr ausgelegt sind.

Zudem sind GoldBug-Kommunikations-Server wesentlich einfacher zu administrieren und beinhalten auch einen E-Mail-Server: IMAP und POP3 Server können einfach und dezentral ersetzt werden.

Ein Hinweis zum Messenger Signal mit seiner zentralen Server-Architektur ist, dass sowohl in der mobilen Version als auch in der Desktop Version erstens immer zwingend eine Telefon-Nummern-Prüfung per SMS und damit auch eine Identitätsprüfung erfolgt, und - was zweitens mehr noch zu wundern gibt, ist, dass zugleich über die mobile Version sämtliche Kontakte des Nutzers hochgeladen werden.
Hier entsteht beim Anbieter ebenso (wie in Whatsapp) eine umfassende Datenbank nach dem Muster: Wer-kennt-wen.
Auch wer die Desktop Version nutzen will, muss sich vorher zwingend mit seinem Telefon und der Preisgabe seiner vollständigen Kontaktliste angemeldet haben.
Nachdem im Bereich der Kryptologie öffentlich diskutiert wurde, dass Hintertüren bei open source Programmierungen nur schwer in die Verschlüsselung eingebaut werden können (Nakashima 2015), und, dass auch ein Verbot der Verschlüsselung nicht nur die Wirtschaft und den Finanzsektor eines jeden Landes lahmlegen würde, sondern auch ein Unsinn ist,

2015), the strategy does not seem to be to look at encryption, but to save the meta data of the social networks and to collect and to save all contacts of the users.

That the friends list or telephone list of Apple and Android phones now also may be uploaded by any application. or also by the providers of the operating system, demonstrates a possible, to be assumed, underlying strategy: `We can not get into the crypto, so it is for us more essential, to record, with whom you communicate. What you have to communicate, we possibly can ask for or get to know over other ways. It is important for us to know your network - with whom you communicate.´
For this, one have not even to break Crypto.

The change of paradigm from breaking crypto towards of bulk copying of private social contacts of users seems obvious.

It is a procedure, that will be implemented not only by the non-open source and non-encrypted Messenger "Whatsapp", but procedurally also by the encrypted messenger "Signal" - and therefore one can only warn against clients like these:
E.g. compared to SureSpot, in which although the user sends also its public key to a central server, the user's friend must be notified in this Messenger still manually about the own nickname.
This indicates for SureSpot that there contact lists are not matched respectively uploaded via automatic access to your own phone, to save, to collect and to analyze these - for business and, if applicable, governmental access.

For this important analysis area, to be able to operate an own chat server for a permanent availability of the service - which is the topic of this assessment chapter -, are therefore RetroShare, GoldBug or XMPP-OTR and Tox the defintitive preferable Crypto-Messenger clients. In the end remain concerning the simpler manageability of an own server GoldBug, and, with inclusion of a DHT, respectively RetroShare and Tox left.

"wie die Mathematik zu verbieten" (Wales 2015), scheint die Strategie nicht mehr zu sein, die Verschlüsselung zu betrachten, sondern die Metadaten der Sozialen Netzwerke und alle Kontakte der Nutzer zu sammeln und zu speichern.

Dass die Freundesliste oder Telefonliste der Apple- und Android-Telefone von mittlerweile jeglicher Applikation oder auch von den Anbietern des Betriebssystems hochgeladen werden können, kann auch eine mögliche, anzunehmende, dahinterstehende Strategie zeigen: `Wir kommen an die Crypto nicht heran, daher ist es für uns umso wesentlicher zu erfahren, mit wem Du kommunizierst. Was Du kommuniziert hast, kann man ggf. auch erfragen oder durch andere Wege erfahren. Wichtig ist für uns, Dein Netzwerk zu kennen, mit wem Du kommunizierst´.
Dazu muss man nichtmal Crypto brechen.

Der Paradigmenwechsel vom Brechen der Crypto hin zum massenweisen Kopieren der privaten sozialen Kontakte der Nutzer scheint offensichtlich.

Es ist eine Vorgehensweise, die nicht nur vom nicht-quelloffenen und nicht-verschlüsselnden Messenger „Whatsapp" umgesetzt wird, sondern prozedural auch vom verschlüsselnden Messenger „Signal" - und lässt daher vor Klienten wie diesen nur warnen: Z.B. im Vergleich zu SureSpot, bei dem der Nutzer zwar auch seinen öffentlichen Schlüssel zu einem zentralen Server sendet, muss der Nutzer bei diesem Messenger dem Freund seinen Nicknamen noch manuell mitteilen.
Das deutet bei SureSpot darauf hin, dass dort die Kontaktlisten nicht per automatischem Zugriff auf das eigene Telefon abgeglichen bzw. hochgeladen werden, um diese massenhaft für unternehmerischen und ggf. staatlichen Zugriff zu speichern, zu sammeln bzw. zu analysieren.

Für diesen wichtigen Analyse-Bereich, eigene Chat Server betreiben zu können für eine dauerhafte Verfügbarkeit des Services - um die es in diesem Assessment-Teil geht - sind also RetroShare, Goldbug oder XMPP-OTR sowie Tox die defintitiv vorzuziehenden Crypto-Messenger Klienten. Bzw. hinsichtlich der einfacheren Administrierbarkeit der Server bleiben GoldBug, bzw. RetroShare und Tox mit Einbezug eines DHTs übrig.

Therefore these are crucial questions e.g. to the Messenger Signal,

1. firstly, why not allow independent, decentralized server and
2. secondly, why the contacts of the user are completely uploaded each time you install - and why with this process they are stolen and
3. thirdly, why not contact options via this Messenger are possible without to announce the own phone number to others or to the central service. Aside from the ultimate
4. fourth question, why the user can not use manually definable symmetrical end-to-end passwords together with their chat friend.

Es sind daher entscheidende Fragen an z.B. den Messenger Signal,

1. erstens, warum keine unabhängigen, dezentralen Server ermöglicht werden und
2. zweitens, warum bei jeder Installation die Kontaktdaten des Nutzers komplett hochgeladen und damit gestohlen werden werden und
3. drittens, warum keine Kontaktmöglichkeit über den Messenger möglich ist, ohne anderen oder dem zentralen Service die eigene Telefonnummer bekannt zu geben. Von der entscheidenden
4. vierten Frage, warum der Nutzer kein manuell definierbares symmetrisches Ende-zu-Ende Passwort gemeinsam mit seinem Chatfreund nutzen kann, mal abgesehen.

Meanwhile, it is also reported that the Messenger Whatsapp, associated with Facebook, wants to introduce, an end-to-end encryption.
The protocols of the Signal application respectively their developers should support it: this can also be seen as a strategic market agreement to prevent a supposedly encrypting Messenger to the date unencrypting Messenger takes pride of place:
Indeed, both Messenger are unanimous into their technical processes about wanting to get hold of all the metadata of the social network of a user and to record it massively. ("These applications stores your messages, content and contacts", compare Jacobs 2016).

Inzwischen wird auch berichtet, dass der Messenger Whatsapp, zugehörig zu Facebook, eine Ende-zu-Ende Verschlüsselung einführen möchte.
Die Protokolle der Signal-Applikation bzw. deren Entwickler sollen dabei unterstützen: dieses kann auch als eine strategische Marktabsprache gewertet werden, damit nicht ein vermeintlich verschlüsselnder Messenger den bislang unverschlüsselten Messenger den Rang abläuft:
Tatsächlich sind sich beide Messenger in ihren technischen Prozessen darüber einig, an die Metadaten des Sozialen Netzwerkes eines Nutzers herankommen und massenhaft speichern zu wollen. ("Diese Applikationen laden Deine Nachrichten, Inhalte and Kontakte hoch", vgl. Jacobs 2016).

Facebook has quickly recognized the strategic importance of Whatsapp, when it has purchased this Messenger for an unlikely excessive sum of USD 19 billion (Albergotti 2014).

Facebook hat schnell die strategische Bedeutung von Whatsapp erkannt, als es diesen Messenger für eine unwahrscheinlich überhöhte Summe von 19 Milliarden USD gekauft hat (Albergotti 2014).

The state can not save all the communications, data and metadata of the people, it needs companies for it. These may generate earnings from the government within demand cases as well, if they give out data (or it is only about to have the power, to be able to look it up).

Der Staat kann die Kommunikation, Daten und Metadaten der Menschen nicht selbst speichern, er braucht Unternehmen dafür. Diese mögen in Nachfragefällen vom Staat ggf. daran verdienen, wenn sie Daten preis geben (oder es ist lediglich die Macht mit ihnen, dieses nachschauen zu können).

The monopolization processes are certainly obvious:
The objective seems then to push large masses of users to a few or just two large

Die Monopolisierungsprozesse sind jedenfalls offensichtlich:
Ziel scheint also das Lotzen grosser Massen an Nutzern zu wenigen oder zwei grossen

cooperating Messenger services, that know the friends lists of all the participants and so the metadata "who-knows-who" can be evaluated, if necessary at any time. Facebook and Whatsapp Messenger of the same company of the operator Mark Zuckerberg have 800,000,000 plus 900,000,000 = 1.700 billion users - while the world has only 7.125 billion inhabitants (compare Wikipedia in 2013).

A messenger provider has thus approx 1/4 of the world population under his wing - a "giant" (Kannenberg 2016). And despite other own statements (Marcus 2015) now both Messenger merge their functions increasingly together (Santos 2016).

Thus the paradigm of pseudonyms is transferred for Facebook not only into the rule of real names coercion, but rather extended in an identity card certified identity, because cell phone numbers are only granted upon identity verification. And with the linking of Facebook with Whatsapp the real names coercion is introduced not only through the back door, but also identity checked by means of the identity card!

The vision to uniformly use the number of the social security card as phone number and chat ID respectively email address and therefore to make every citizen identifiable and thus controllable with each utterance is therefore not far away.

The idea of a crypto network rather than an IP network is transferred to a lifetime valid and federally registered citizens numbers, which any communication packet and any friend contact will be unprotected against accesses?

Beneficial for the deal could also be the reasons, why the project Signal and its company Open Whisper Systems has received also greater financial investments from various sources (Knight Foundation 2014) and shall develop end-to-end encryption in cooperation with Whatsapp (Floemer 2016): analysis of friends lists and the pushing of users to a central monopoly supplier could be to be regarded with more priority - than the breaking of cryptography.

Whatever the development status of these "verified end-to-end encryption" (Floemer

kooperierenden Messenger Diensten zu sein, die die Freundeslisten aller Teilnehmer kennen und so die Metadaten "wer-kennt-wen" jederzeit im Bedarfsfalle auswerten können. Facebook und Whatsapp Messenger derselben Unternehmung des Betreibers Mark Zuckerberg haben 800.000.000 plus 900.000.000 = 1.700 Milliarden Nutzer - die Welt hat dabei nur 7,125 Milliarden Einwohner (vgl. Wikipedia für 2013).

Ein Messenger-Anbieter hat damit rd. 1/4 der Weltbevölkerung unter seine Fittiche - ein "Gigant" (Kannenberg 2016). Und legt trotz anderer eigener Bekundungen (Marcus 2015) nunmehr auch beide Messenger zunehmend zusammen (Santos 2016).

Damit wird das Pradigma der Pseudonyme bei Facebook nicht nur in die Regel des Klarnamenszwangs überführt, sondern noch erweitert in eine Personalausweis-geprüfte Identität, denn Handynummern werden nur gegen Identitätsprüfung ausgegeben. Und mit der Verknüpfung von Facebook mit Whatsapp ist der Klarnamenzwang nicht nur durch die Hintertüre eingeführt, sondern auch mittels des Personalausweises identitätsgeprüft!

Die Vision, die Nummer des Sozialversicherungsausweises einheitlich als Telefonnummer und Chat-ID bzw. Emailadresse zu nutzen und damit jeden Bürger mit jeder sprachlichen Äußerung identifizierbar und damit kontrollierbar zu machen, ist somit nicht mehr weit.

Die Idee eines Crypto-Netzwerkes anstelle eines IP-Netzwerkes wird überführt in lebenslang geltende und staatlich registrierte Bürgernummern, deren jegliches Kommunikationspacket und jeglicher Freundes-Kontakt vor Zugriffen ungeschützt sein wird?

Dem Deal zuträglich könnten auch Gründe sein, warum das Projekt Signal und dessen Unternehmen Openwhispersystems auch größere Finanzspitzen von verschiedenen Seiten erhalten hat (Knight Foundation 2014) und auch in Kooperation die Ende-zu-Ende Verschlüsselung von Whatsapp mit entwickeln soll (Floemer 2016): Die Analyse von Freundeslisten und das Lotsen der Nutzer zu einem zentralen Monopolanbieter könnte prioritärer zu sehen sein als das Brechen von Kryptographie.

Wie immer der Entwickungsstand dieser „verifizierten Ende-zu-Ende-Verschlüsselung"

2016) out of this cooperation might look like: it will remain the further questions for this client,

5. if the processes of the authentication could also correspond to the Socialist Millionaire Protokol and also,
6. if the paradigm of deniability - the deniability of the communication from the past (compare OTR) - will be made possible by ephemeral keys - and,
7. if it is an end-to-end encryption, which safeguards users consistently from user to user - and not only from user to a central server.

In the case of Whatsapp no one can verify it more accurate, because it is not an open source messenger, and therefore can not and should not be considered here in greater detail. The portal Heise Security referred encryption into Whatsapp therefore as a "gesture" (Scherschel 2015). As mentioned, the issue of registration of lists of friends is strategically more significant than the entire crypto debate!

Meanwhile Whatsapp has released the end-to-end encryption. It is prozessural as constructed in Telegram (see also chapter 3.09.5 and the criticism of it respectively Whatsapp 2016).

It is true, encrypted communication is given (compare e.g. Scherschel 2016th), nevertheless arise questions: Who all gets a key? Can the symmetrical end-to-end key also be created and inserted manually by the user? How strong the key is protected, with which the temporary key is transmitted?

It remains - as with Telegram - to continue to suspect, that WhatsApp has a possibility of picking up the symmetric key; the symmetric key can not be defined and edited manually by the user and third, the transfer of the symmetric key is possibly not sufficiently protected - and especially the user cannot use oral agreement as a method to transfer the key.

Encryption will now be standard as in Telegram, but more out of the necessity to let no other Messenger come up - and because it is not open source, this monoculture is no safe

(Floemer 2016) aus dieser Kooperation aussehen mag: es werden auch für diesen Klienten die weiteren Fragen bleiben,

5. ob die Prozesse der Authentifizierung auch der eines Socialist-Millionaire-Protokols entsprechen werden und auch,
6. ob das Paradigma der Deniability - die Abstreitbarkeit der Kommunikation aus der Vergangenheit (vgl. OTR) - durch ephemerale Keys ermöglicht werden soll - sowie,
7. ob es um eine Ende-zu-Ende Verschlüsselung geht, die die Nutzer durchgängig von Nutzer zu Nutzer und nicht nur von Nutzer zu zentralem Server absichern.

Im Falle von Whatsapp wird es keiner genauer nachprüfen können, da es kein open source Messenger ist und daher hier auch nicht weiter betrachtet werden kann und soll. Das Portal Heise Security bezeichnet Verschlüsselung in Whatsapp daher als "Geste" (Scherschel 2015). Wie genannt, ist das Thema der Erfassung der Freundeslisten ein strategisch bedeutsameres als die gesamte Crypto-Debatte!

Inzwischen hat Whatsapp die Ende-zu-Ende Verschlüsselung veröffentlicht. Sie ist prozessural wie die von Telegram aufgebaut (vgl. auch Kapitel 3.09.5 und die Kritik daran bzw. Whatsapp 2016).

Es ist richtig, verschlüsselt wird die Kommunikation (vgl. z.B. a. Scherschel 2016), dennoch entstehen die Fragen: Er hat alles einen Schlüssel? Können die symmetrischen Ende-Zu-Ende Schlüssel auch durch den Nutzer manuell erstellt und insertiert werden? Wie stark wird der Schlüssel geschützt, mit dem der temporäre Schlüssel übertragen wird?

Es bleibt wie bei Telegram weiterhin zu vermuten, dass WhatsApp eine Möglichkeit des Abgreifens der symmetrischen Schlüssel hat, die symmetrischen Schlüssel können nicht durch den Nutzer manuell definiert und ediert werden und drittens ist auch die Übertragung der symmetrischen Schlüssel ggf nicht ausreichend geschützt - bzw. kann der Nutzer keine mündliche Absprache als Übertragungsweg nutzen.

Verschlüsselung wird zwar Standard wie bei Telegram, aber mehr aus der Notwendigkeit heraus, keine anderen Messenger aufkommen zu lassen und da es nicht open source ist,

solution against open source and verifiable alternatives!

The security expert Fabian Scherschel (2016) summarizes: "A certain residual risk remains, of course:.. WhatsApp is not open source .. Users therefore can never be sure that their service provider imputes no malicious app, which undermines the encryption. In addition WhatsApp-server still collect metadata "- that means: who is communicating with whom.

The same questions therefore exist ongoing within this (audit)context for the interdependent Signal Messenger, and here are enlightened user decisively, which can not be fooled for an U a X.

Furthermore, the actors are to be asked, which should trigger a marketing hype for the Messenger Signal: the manufacturer of Signal, OpenWhisperSystems, sets currently two prominent activists and two prominent scientists of the Crypto-area to the front page of the website with the phrases: Use only these monoculture, use this every day, it is the first choice and has great programming, that brings tears even in the face of experts. What kind of a message is that to the user: `Do not think about it and leave the review to the experts, - you enjoy instead unquestioningly exclusively our products?´

("Use anything by Open Whisper Systems." Edward Snowden, Whistleblower and privacy advocate / "Signal is the most scalable encryption tool we have. It is free and peer reviewed. I encourage people to use it everyday." Laura Poitras, Oscar winning filmmaker and journalist) / "I am regularly impressed with the thought and care put into both the security and the usability of this app. It's my first choice for an encrypted conversation." Bruce Schneier, internationally renowned security technologist / "After reading the code, I literally discovered a line of drool running down my face. It's really nice." Matt Green, Cryptographer, Johns Hopkins University, cited according to Website, 2015).

We have learned in science to always designate an alternative, science should conduct especially comparisons and thirdly prove objective facts, not tearful outbursts.

bleibt diese Monokultur keine sichere Lösung gegenüber quelloffenen und nachprüfbaren Alternativen!

Der Sicherheits-Experte Fabian Scherschel (2016) fasst zusammen: "Ein gewisses Restrisiko bleibt natürlich: WhatsApp ist .. nicht quelloffen. Nutzer können sich also nie ganz sicher sein, dass ihnen der Dienstanbieter keine manipulierte App unterschiebt, welche die Verschlüsselung untergräbt. Außerdem sammeln WhatsApps Server nach wie vor Metadaten" - also wer kommuniziert mit wem.

Gleiche Fragen bestehen daher in diesem (Audit-)Kontext weiterhin auch für den interdependenten Signal Messenger, und hier sind aufgeklärte Nutzer entscheidend, die sich nicht ein X für ein U vormachen lassen.

Ferner sind auch die Akteure zu fragen, die für Signal einen Marketing Hype auslösen sollen: Die Webseite des Signal-Herstellers Openwhispersystems bringt die derzeit beiden prominenten Aktivisten und zwei prominente Wissenschafter des Crypto-Fachgebietes auf die Web-Frontseite mit den Phrasen: Nutze nur diese Monokultur, nutze diese täglich, sie ist erste Wahl und so toll programmiert, dass sie den Experten die Tränen ins Gesicht bringen. Was ist das für eine Botschaft an den Nutzer: `Denke nicht drüber nach und überlasse den Experten die Durchsicht - erfreue Dich stattdessen unhinterfragt ausschließlich an unseren Produkten?´

("Use anything by Open Whisper Systems." Edward Snowden, Whistleblower and privacy advocate / "Signal is the most scalable encryption tool we have. It is free and peer reviewed. I encourage people to use it everyday." Laura Poitras, Oscar winning filmmaker and journalist) / "I am regularly impressed with the thought and care put into both the security and the usability of this app. It's my first choice for an encrypted conversation." Bruce Schneier, internationally renowned security technologist / "After reading the code, I literally discovered a line of drool running down my face. It's really nice." Matt Green, Cryptographer, Johns Hopkins University, zitiert nach Webseite, 2015).

Wir haben in der Wissenschaft gelernt, immer auch eine Alternative zu benennen, Wissenschaft soll insbesondere vergleichen und drittens objektive Fakten herausstellen,

nicht tränenreiche Gefühlsausbrüche.

It is not clear, why the above analysis of the practice of mass picking up of private contact lists and the intended establishment of a centralized monoculture of chat servers does not arise in those minds, which from the public so far are seen as lawyers or even as experts for users of encrypted communications solutions.

Es ist unverständlich, warum obige Analyse an der Praxis des massenhaften Abgreifens von privaten Kontaktlisten und der beabsichtigten Etablierung einer zentralistischen Monokultur an Chat-Servern nicht auch in denen Geistern entsteht, die von der Öffentlichkeit bislang als Advokaten oder gar als Experten für die Nutzer von verschlüsselten Kommunikationslösungen gesehen werden.

Should the assumed goal of not controlling of the speech contents, but rather of the social contacts and metadata also be found in the judgment of the thought processes of the users, would be subsequently to wonder, whether the four multipliers have been promoted for their statements financially or with other bonuses?

Sollte sich das zu vermutende Ziel der Kontrolle nicht der Gesprächsinhalte, sondern der sozialen Kontake und Metadaten auch im Urteil der Gedankengänge der Nutzer wiederfinden, wäre folgerichtig zu fragen, ob die vier Multiplikatoren für Ihre Aussagen finanziell oder mit anderen Boni gefördert worden sind?

A statement thereto has been especially so far not been presented by Edward Snowden, if he was promoted for his mono-culture advertising financially by Signal from Open Whisper Systems or has possibly got in his case implicitly promised mitigation of sentence, e.g. by continuing to assist that his former employer can understand the social networks of each user through agreements with intermediary companies?

Eine Aussage dazu ist insbesondere von Edward Snowden bislang nicht präsentiert worden, ob er für seine Monokultur-Werbung finanziell seitens Signal von Openwhisperssystems gefördert wurde oder ggf. auch in seinem Fall implizit Strafmilderung staatlicherseits zugesichert bekommen hat, z.B. in dem er weiterhin mithilft, dass sein bisheriger Arbeitgeber die sozialen Geflechte eines jeden Nutzers über Absprachen mit intermediären Firmen nachvollziehen kann?

Especially since it was reported within the research for this analysis, that Edward Snowden was asked to give his comparative technical expertise for several different messenger. He has chosen for specific reasons, that may lie not only in a technical analysis, for a mono propaganda.

Zumal in den Recherchen zu dieser Analyse berichtet wurde, dass Edward Snowden angefragt wurde, für mehrere verschiedene Messenger seine vergleichende fachliche Expertise abzugeben. Er hat sich aus bestimmten Gründen, die nicht nur in einer fachlichen Analyse liegen können, für eine Mono-Propaganda entschieden.

Otherwise remain overlooked, that the Messenger without metadata attack opportunities are only CryptoCat (with decentral server), GoldBug due to the utilized Echo protocol and RetroShare operated over the Tor network (seen apart from as susceptible to be designated graph chain: OTR-XMPP-Tor-XMPPSERVER-Tor-XMPP-OTR, with consideration of the Tor network as the more observable, the more Tor nodes are into one's control).

Andernfalls bliebe übersehen, dass die Messenger ohne Metadaten-Angriffs-möglichkeiten lediglich CryptoCat (mit dezentralem Server), GoldBug aufgrund des Echo-Protokolls, und RetroShare betrieben über das Tor-Netzwerk, sind (von der als anfällig zu bezeichnenden Graphenkette mal abgesehen: OTR-XMPP-Tor-XMPPSERVER-Tor-XMPP-OTR, wobei das Tor Netzwerk als umso beobachtbarer gilt, je mehr Tor-Knotenpunkte in der eigenen Kontrolle sind).

This leads then not only to the provided technical or strategic issues, but ultimately also moves an entire community, which sets a

Dieses führt somit nicht nur zu den gestellten fachlichen oder strategischen Fragen, sondern bewegt letztlich auch eine ganze Community,

focus on a necessary comprehensive review of the acting persons and experts in the public.

First critical analyses are in the rise already: There are complains about the central server model of these mobile messengers (Öberg 2016, Kumar 2016). And: Also with the in the meanwhile established end-to-end encryption (compare for Whatsapp the chapter before) the - in case of closed source non-answerable trust question - still remains, if the encryption key, which is not able to be defined manually by the user, can be tapped at the central server. And: in the end also the metadata will always be revealing (Teicke 2016). Furthermore a group of security researchers has pointed out still more central questions in regard of the security of the Whatsapp end-to-end encryption (Bolluyt 2016, Postive Technologies 2016, Fadilpašić 2016).

Also exist especially in the legal sense some problems, which depend on the SMS-authentification respectively on the upload of all friend-contacts from the phone of the user: "Especially this is (- at least -) according to the EU law forbidden: Who wants to forward Data of third persons, has in Europe to get the agreement of the persons, who own the data. If someone has saved 200 contacts with phone numbers and mail addresses in his contact book, then he would require exact 200 written declarations of agreement, before the Whatsapp application could be established on the smartphone" – says Peter Burgstaller, Chairman for IT and IP-Law at the faculty for Informatic, Communication and Media of the Fachhochschule in Hagenberg (cit. acc. to Könau 2016).

That is "why every Whatsapp-user can sue every other Whats-user at the data protection authority. Should now also consumer protection agencies sue Whatsapp, could this mean the end for this service in Europe", summarizes IT-Laywer Christian Solmecke the legal situation. So why are consumer protection organizations and agencies in charge for data security still sleeping?

Considering this background, even at network meetings within the IT community it is to recommend not to get the supposedly established "Heros" and "luminaries" a request for giving a presentation, but in particular the little alternatives and young scientists. And, a contribution should be given also to

die die handelnden Aktvisten und Experten in notwendige umfassende Betrachtung stellen.

Erste kritische Analysen entstehen bereits: So wird das zentralistische Chat-Server-Modell der mobilen Messenger beklagt (Öberg 2016, Kumar 2016). Und: Auch bei einer eingeführten Ende-zu-Ende Verschlüsselung (vgl. für Whatsapp den Abschnitt zu vor) bleibt immer die bei closed source unbeantwortbare Vertrauensfrage, ob der Schlüssel, der nicht durch den Nutzer selbst manuell definiert werden kann, am zentralen Server abgegeriffen werden kann. Und: schließlich sind auch die Metadaten jederzeit offen gelegt (Teicke 2016). Weiterhin haben Sicherheitsforscher weitere zentrale Sicherheitsfragen bei der Whatsapp Ende-zu-Ende Verschlüsselung herausgestellt (Bolluyt 2016, Postive Technologies 2016, Fadilpašić 2016).

Es bestehen insbesondere auch rechtliche Probleme, die sich mit der SMS-Authentifizierung bzw. dem Upload aller Freundeskontakte vom Telefon des Nutzers ergeben: "Genau dieses ist nach europäischem Recht verboten: Wer Daten Dritter weitergeben will, benötigt in der EU zuvor die Genehmigung dessen, dem die Daten gehören. Wenn jemand 200 Telefonnummern und Mailadressen in seinem Kontaktspeicher hat, bräuchte er also exakt 200 schriftliche Einverständniserklärungen, ehe er die Whatsapp-App auf seinem Smartphone einrichten darf." - so Peter Burgstaller, Professor für IT- und IP-Recht an der Fakultät für Informatik, Kommunikation und Medien der Fachhochschule in Hagenberg (vgl. Könau 2016).

Daher "könne deshalb eigentlich jeder Whatsapp-Nutzer jeden anderen Whatsapp-Nutzer bei der Datenschutzbehörde anzeigen. Sollten nun auch Verbraucherschützer gegen Whatsapp klagen, könnte das das Aus für den Dienst in Europa bedeuten" fasst IT-Anwalt Christian Solmecke zusammen (vgl. ebda). Warum also schlafen Verbraucher- und Datenschützer hier noch?

Vor diesem Hintergrund ist auch bei Netzwerktreffen innerhalb der IT-Community zu empfehlen, nicht immer die vermeintlich etablierten "Heros" und "Koryphäen" um einen Vortrag anzufragen (die mehr Marketing statt Analysen anbieten), sondern insbesondere die kleinen Alternativen und

"criticizing nest aspersers" - which would be a term from the perspective of focused activists and participants more unmatured from technology and life experienced.

(Compare in this regard also Levin 2014, who received personal accusations, when he announced, that many Tor servers, Tor activists, Tor operators and Tor developers are sponsored by governmental money donations, in order to be able to control the exit nodes. The thesis of Tor as honeypot community was then thought a step too far).

Many technology enthusiasts show therefore, that it is often difficult to say goodbye to a technology tool, with which they have learned and have grown up with, respectively it is hard to perceive alternatives for testing and learning. Even if it is just for activists with high ideals difficult, to move the thinking in the round head in a different direction, if an erosion of the role models and community multipliers should be questioned, idealizations from technical tools or their representatives should be (well as in religion) avoided - regardless of whether they have dreadlocks, keen on visiting for free and are present on each cat fair, or live in exile.

Tools should not be a religious question and coexistence is widely regarded as the learning objective for unilaterally focused activists. Currently, the user community is looking for secure communication solutions: These search and discovery processes should not be done strategically under monoculture propaganda (as with the bloggers for Signal) nor under denunciation of other clients (as with the developers from CryptoCat, see below).

Only in the common technical comparing and questioning of technical solutions based on defined criteria and a mutually supportive community of developers, there can be several, encrypting communication solutions.

Among the criteria of a technical comparison belong firstly source openness and secondly, the assessment of the decentralization of the server infrastructure to avoid the collection of metadata and thirdly, the manual definability of

Nachwuchswissenschaftler. Und auch den - aus Sicht der fokussierten Aktivisten und noch nicht aus Technik- und Lebenserfahrung gereiften Teilnehmern - "nestbeschmutzenden Kritikern" sollte ein Beitrag verliehen werden (Vgl. in dieser Hinsicht auch Levin 2014, der persönliche Anschuldigungen erhielt, als er mitteilte, dass zahlreiche Tor-Server, Tor-Aktivisten, Tor-Betreiber und Tor-Entwickler durch staatliche Geldzuwendungen gefördert werden, um die Exitnodes kontrollieren zu können. Die These von Tor als Honeypot war der Community dann doch einen Schritt zu weit gedacht).

Vielen Technik-Begeisterten fällt es somit oftmals schwer, von dem Technik-Tool, mit dem die gelernt haben und gross geworden sind, Abschied zu nehmen bzw. Alternativen wahrzunehmen, auszutesten und zu erlernen. Auch wenn es gerade Aktivisten mit hohen Idealen schwer fallen mag, das Denken im runden Kopf in eine andere Richtung zu bewegen, wenn eine Erosion der Vorbilder und Community-Multiplikatoren zu hinterfragen ist, Idealisierungen von technischen Werkzeugen oder deren Vertreter sind wie auch in der Religion zu vermeiden - egal ob sie Dreadlocks haben, gerne kostenfrei vorbeischauen und auf jeder Katzenkirmes präsent sind, oder im Exil leben.

Werkzeuge sollten nicht zu einer religiösen Frage werden und Coexistenz gilt vielfach als das Lernziel für einseitig fokussierte Aktivisten. Derzeit sucht die Nutzergemeinde nach sicheren Kommunikationslösungen: Diese Such- und Findungsprozesse sollten jedoch nicht strategisch unter Monokultur-Propaganda (wie bei den Bloggern für Signal) noch unter Denunziation anderer Klienten (wie bei den Entwicklern von Cryptocat, s.u.) erfolgen.

Nur im gemeinsamen fachlichen Vergleichen und Hinterfragen von technischen Lösungen anhand definierter Kriterien sowie einer sich gegenseitig unterstützenden Entwicklergemeinde kann es verschiedene, verschlüsselnde Kommunikationslösungen geben.

Zu den Kriterien eines technischen Vergleichs gehören allen voran erstens Quelloffenheit und zweitens die Beurteilung der Dezentralität der Server-Infastuktur zur Vermeidung der Erhebung von Metadaten sowie drittens die

encryption values, or in particular of end-to-end encrypted symmetric passwords.

manuelle Definierbarkeit von Verschlüsselungswerten bzw. insbesondere des Ende-zu-Ende verschlüsselnden symmetrischen Passwortes.

However, from these contextual analysis of the latest developments of further clients a fourth paradigm can be derived: Everyone, who writes about encrypted applications, should include at least two more applications into a technical comparison.

Aus diesen kontextuellen Analysen der neuesten Entwicklungen weiterer Klienten lässt sich jedoch noch ein viertes Paradigma ableiten: Jeder, der über verschlüsselnde Applikationen schreibt, sollte mindestens zwei weitere Applikationen in einen technischen Vergleich einbeziehen.

Otherwise, the attribution of the idea of subjectivity, of a bias and a strategic promotion due to suspect reasons (e.g. for monoculture of a centrality or for the culture of the mass capturing of metadata or the concealment of financiers and their interests) cannot be kept any longer in distance and is highly topical.

Andernfalls ist die Attribuierung der Idee von Subjektivität, eines Bias sowie einer strategischen Promotion aufgrund zu vermutender Gründe (z.B. für die Monokultur einer Zentralität oder für die Kultur der Massen-Erfassung von Metadaten oder zur Verschleierung von Financiers und ihren Interessen) nicht weiter auf Distanz zu halten und hochaktuell.

The comparison of open source and encrypting Messengers should be a topic for each blogger and active user in the internet.

Der Vergleich von quelloffenen und verschlüsselnden Messengern sollte daher zu einem Thema für einen jeden Blogger und im Internet aktiven Nutzer werden.

Table 14: Good Practice Insight # 03

Good Practice Insight # 03
with GoldBug Multi-Encrypting Communication Suite

Case	On my site I can not use other messengers like Pidgin or Retroshare because of port restrictions. What options remain, to communicate with friends? An meinem Ort kann ich aufgrund von restriktiven Portbeschränkungen andere Messenger wie Pidgin oder RetroShare nicht nutzen. Welche Optionen bleiben, um mit Freunden zu kommunizieren?
One Solution	GoldBug uses the HTTPS protocol. If the Web is accessible with a browser, GoldBug can also be used at any time. A chat server with a corresponding port is subsequently at any time reachable. Installing GoldBug requires no admin rights and can be portably operated out of a path or from a stick. GoldBug nutzt das HTTPS-Protokol. Sofern das Web mit einem Browser erreichbar ist, kann GoldBug auch jederzeit eingesetzt werden. Ein Chat-Webserver mit entsprechendem Port ist sodann jederzeit ereichbar. Die Installation von GoldBug erfordert keine Admin-Rechte und kann portabel von einem Pfad oder Stick aus betrieben werden.

Source: Own Case.

3.4 Security Scan of the transferred Ciphertexts

The scan of the transferred data is also another regular action to find out any irregularities, respectively also to prove, that except ciphertext no readable plaintext was transferred.

Der Scan der transferierten Daten ist ebenso eine weitere reguläre Maßnahme, um eventuelle Auffälligkeiten heraus zu finden bzw. auch nachzuweisen, dass außer Ciphertext kein lesbarer Plaintext transferiert wurde.

To view the transferred content, not even have to be used the most frequently used tool Wireshark, like we have done in the investigation of the GUI-kernel-interaction (compare Section 3.14).

Um sich die transferierten Inhalte anzuschauen, muss nicht mal das wohl vielgenutzte Werkzeug Wireshark eingesetzt werden, wie wir es bei der Untersuchung der GUI-Kernel Interaktion gemacht haben (vgl. Abschnitt 3.14).

For the monitoring of the transferred data of the connection between two instances of GoldBug over the Internet thereby a simple Web browser is sufficient, which is set to the local host.

Für das Monitoring der transferierten Daten der Verbindung zweier Instanzen von GoldBug über das Internet genügt dabei ein einfacher Web-Browser, der auf den Localhost eingestellt wird.

The aim is to examine the information sent over an Internet connection regarding the integrity of encryption and to scan the ciphertext.

Ziel ist es, die über eine Internetverbindung übersandte Information auf Vollständigkeit der Verschlüsselung hin zu untersuchen und den Ciphertext zu scannen.

3.4.1 Inventory taking, structural analysis and descriptions of the functions

The data sent by GoldBug can be easily viewed by any user. For this purpose it is not necessary to use special tools: In the user-manual it is described, how to utilize a simple browser.

Die von GoldBug gesandten Daten können von jedem Nutzer ganz einfach eingesehen werden. Dazu ist es nicht erforderlich, Spezialwerkzeuge zu nutzen: Im Handbuch wird die Nutzung eines einfachen Browser beschrieben.

Normally two GoldBug clients build their connection with a self-signed TLS/SSL certificate via a HTTP connection. That means, HTTP is configured as a HTTP-S.

Normalerweise bauen zwei GoldBug-Klienten ihre Verbindung mit einem selbstsignierten TLS/SSL Zertifikat über eine HTTP-Verbindung auf. D.h. HTTP ist als HTTP-S ausgestaltet.

Since this can then only connect clients like GoldBug with a corresponding key, the sent ciphertext can not be viewed in a Web browser.

Da dieses sodann nur Klienten wie GoldBug mit einem entsprechenden Schlüssel verbinden lässt, kann der gesandte Ciphertext nicht in einem Webbrowser angezeigt werden.

If, however, we dispense of the additional layer of encryption of the HTTPS channel, the still persistent encryption within the message capsule can be displayed in a web browser.

Wenn jedoch auf die zusätzliche Verschlüsselungsschicht des HTTPS-Kanals verzichtet wird, kann die weiterhin bestehende Verschlüsselung innerhalb der Nachrichtenkapsel auch in einem Webbrowser angezeigt werden.

For this purpose only the listener of the GoldBug node must be set up via HTTP.

Dazu muss lediglich der Listener der GoldBug Instanz mittels HTTP eingerichtet werden.

Then in the browser via HTTP on localhost also the corresponding port is entered. In the following the browser shows subsequently the transferred ciphertext.

Sodann wird im Browser mittels HTTP über localhost auch der entsprechende Port eingegeben. Fortfolgend zeigt der Browser sodann den transferierten Ciphertext an.

Figure 06: Encrypted Message of GoldBug shown in a web browser

Source: Own screenshot of GoldBug and Webbrowser.

3.4.2 Selected method for studying and function reference

As method to view the transferred information of a GoldBug client, should thus a scan be used. Using a browser and a listener configured within GoldBug to HTTP this was viewed and recorded.

Als Methode, die aus einem GoldBug Klienten transferierte Informationen anzusehen, soll somit ein Scan genutzt werden. Mittels eines Browsers und einem in GoldBug auf HTTP konfigurierten Listener wurde dieses eingesehen und aufgezeichnet.

3.4.3 Conduction and findings of the examinations

For the conduction we have used different standard browsers like Firefox and also the Dooble Web browser. The screenshot shows the IRON web browser, which we used instead of Firefox (it is a fork of Chrome and exempt from certain tracking code that otherwise affect private information, compare IRON browser project).

Zur Durchführung haben wir verschiedene handelsübliche Browser wie Firefox und auch den Dooble Web Browser eingesetzt. Der Screenshot zeigt den IRON Web-Browser, den wir statt Firefox nutzten (er ist ein Fork von Chrome und von bestimmten Tracking-Codes befreit, die sonst private Informationen tangieren, vgl. IRON Browser Projekt).

As a result, we can say that even in the absence of HTTPS encryption only ciphertext (the message capsule) was sent by the established channel to another peer of GoldBug. The figure above shows the structure of the transmitted content as an example.

Im Ergebnis können wir festhalten, dass selbst bei fehlender HTTPS Verschlüsselung durch den zum anderen Peer aufgebauten Kanal von GoldBug ausschließlich Ciphertext gesandt wurde (die Nachrichtenkapsel). Die Abbildung weiter oben zeigt die Struktur der übermittelten Inhalte exemplarisch auf.

3.4.4 Evaluation of the results with regard to weaknesses, risks, potentials for improvements and strengths

Weaknesses or risks were not detected as a result of this investigation, also potentials were not seen according to the investigations for this topic in the specific application. The strength is certainly the additional encryption layer that is built up through the HTTPS channel.

Schwächen oder Risiken wurden aufgrund dieser Untersuchung nicht festgestellt, auch weitere Potentiale wurden nach der Beschäftigung mit diesem Themenbereich im konkreten Anwendungsfall nicht gesehen. Die Stärke liegt sicherlich in der zusätzlichen Verschlüsselungsebene, die durch den HTTPS-Kanal aufgebaut wird.

Thus, one can apply GoldBug anytime even in more restrictive environments (such as specific country or corporate firewalls) - and possibly other messengers not, like OTR-XMPP (e.g. Pidgin) or Retroshare due to specified protocols and ports.

Somit kann man in restriktiveren Umgebungen (wie bestimmten Länder- oder Firmen-Firewalls) GoldBug jederzeit anwenden und andere Messenger wie OTR-XMPP (z.B. Pidgin) - oder auch RetroShare aufgrund spezifizierter Protokolle und Ports ggf. auch nicht.

GoldBug is therefore because of the universality of the HTTP protocol always to prefer - like it is basically to create always an accessible website for the blind or like students of the newer generation learn right from the start as a standard, that new Underground stations are basically to be provided with features for the orientation of the blind.

GoldBug ist daher aufgrund der Universalität des HTTP-Protokolls jederzeit zu bevorzugen – wie bei Vorhandensein der Möglichkeiten grundsätzlich auch immer eine barrierefreie Webseite zu erstellen ist oder Studierende der neuen Generation von vorneherein als Standard lernen, dass neu zu bauende Bahnhöfe grundsätzlich mit Merkmalen zur Orientierung für Blinde zu versehen sind.

Table 15: Description of findings 3.04

#	Area	Description of the finding	Valuation Severity Category / Difficulty Level / Innovation & Improvement Class / Strength Dimension
	Weakness / Schwäche	./.	./.
	Risk / Risiko	./.	./.
	Potential for Improvement / Verbesserungspotential	./.	./.
3.04.4.A	Strength / Stärke	Additional layer of encryption over HTTPS channel provided.	High

3.4.5 Appraisal of good practices in comparison with other similar applications

All mentioned, comparable open source applications send ciphertext over the Internet. Feature in particular for GoldBug is to use the HTTPS protocol, and the establishment of this additional encrypting, secure channel for the existing ciphertext.

The ciphertext of the other applications is also dependent on key size, the selected algorithm and the architecture of the application.

This can not only comparative, but should especially be investigated in depth in the process and within the respective architecture elsewhere.
Although each app sends at the end ciphertext, this must also be seen in conjunction with the relevant crypto-specifications in each application.

Alle genannten, vergleichbaren quelloffenen Applikationen senden Ciphertext über das Internet. Merkmal inbesondere bei GoldBug ist die Nutzung des HTTPS-Protokolls sowie die Errichtung dieses zusätzlich verschlüsselnden, sicheren Kanals für den bestehenden Ciphertext.

Der Ciphertext der anderen Applikationen ist auch von Schlüsselgröße, gewähltem Algorithmus sowie der Architektur der Applikation abhängig.

Dieses kann nicht nur vergleichend, sondern sollte insbesondere im Prozess und innerhalb der jeweiligen Architektur an anderer Stelle vertiefend untersucht werden.
Auch wenn am Ende jeder Ciphertext sendet, muss dieses auch im Zusammenhang mit den bei jeder Applikation relevanten Crypto-Spezifikationen gesehen werden.

Table 16: Indicative BIG SEVEN context references 3.04

Logo	Application	Comments
	Cryptocat	Sends out ciphertext, further investigation is needed as an addition to the given audit reports.
	GoldBug	Sends out ciphertext, uses additionally the http protocol and secures it with TLS/SSL.
	OTR+XMPP	Sends out ciphertext, further investigation is needed as an addition to the given audit reports for OTR and several clients. The cooperation of host and plugin has to be considered for security analyzes.
	RetroShare	Sends out ciphertext, further investigation is needed.
	Signal	Sends out ciphertext, further investigation is needed.
	SureSpot	Sends out ciphertext, further investigation is needed.
	Tox	Sends out ciphertext, further investigation is needed.

Table 17: Good Practice Insights #04

	Good Practice Insight # 04	
	with GoldBug Multi-Encrypting Communication Suite	
Case	I want to protect my communications and everything leaving my laptop, either e-mail, chat or a file transfer should be encrypted.	
	Ich möchte meine Kommunikation schützen und alles, was meinen Laptop verlässt, sei es E-Mail, Chat oder auch ein Dateitransfer, soll verschlüsselt werden.	
Solution	GoldBug sends either chat, and emails, as well as transferred files encrypted. The transmission takes place as ciphertext, which is transmitted like a website with the HTTPS protocol.	
	GoldBug sendet sowohl Chat, als auch E-Mails, als auch transferierte Dateien verschlüsselt. Die Übertragung erfolgt als Ciphertext, der als eine Webseite im HTTPS-Protokoll übertragen wird.	

Source: Own Case.

3.5   Access-Control: Login into the Application (Method)

The entry of a password for starting an application is extremely crucial. With this, for example, the encrypted containers will be released and loaded into the temporary RAM memory to enable the necessary decryption e.g. through the private asymmetric key.

Die Eingabe eines Passwortes für den Start einer Applikation ist äußerst entscheidend. Damit werden z.b. die verschlüsselten Container freigegeben bzw. in den temporären RAM-Speicher geladen, um die notwendigen Entschlüsselungen z.b. durch den privaten asymmetrischen Schlüssel zu ermöglichen.

3.5.1   Inventory taking, structural analysis and descriptions of the functions

The GoldBug Messenger maintains basically all user data in an encrypted way. If someone would remove the hard drive; on which the installation is saved, and look at the files, no relevant user data would be revealed. In particular, of course, no data will be published, which would give you clues about the components necessary for encryption.

Der GoldBug Messenger hält grundsätzlich alle Nutzerdaten in verschlüsselter Weise vor. Wenn jemand die Festplatte, auf der die Installation gespeichert ist, ausbauen würde und sich die Dateien anschaut, würden keine relevanten Nutzerdaten preisgegeben. Insbesondere werden natürlich auch keine Daten veröffentlicht, die Hinweise auf die zur Verschlüsselung notwendigen Bestandteile geben würden.

To enable the necessary cryptographic components, a master password is required, that must be entered at the start of the application.

Zur Freigabe der notwendigen kryptographischen Bestandteile ist ein Masterpasswort erforderlich, dass zum Start der Applikation eingegeben werden muss.

This password is not used as it is defined, but it is converted via a hash function in a new password string - so that a much longer passphrase is generated, in which in addition also further random characters - known as cryptographic salt - are added.

Dieses Passwort wird nicht genutzt, wie es definiert ist, sondern es wird über eine Hashfunktion in einen neuen Passwortstring gewandelt - so dass eine wesentlich längere Passphrase generiert wird, in der zudem auch Zufallswerte durch das sog. kryptographische Salz, also weitere Zufallszeichen, hinzufügt werden.

Furthermore, there are in principle two methods for GoldBug login provided: Once you can define and enter a passphrase, also there is the possibility to define a question and answer phrase.

Weiterhin bestehen in GoldBug grundsätzlich zwei Methoden zum Login bereit: Einmal kann man eine Passphrase definieren und eingeben, ebenso besteht die Möglichkeit, eine Frage- und Antwort-Phrase zu definieren.

Both methods do not save the password itself on the hard disk, but only the generated hash values; and, in the question-answer method more random values are additionally supplemented further (compare the user manual for the technical process).

Beide Methoden speichern nicht das Passwort selbst auf der Festplatte, sondern nur die generierten Hashwerte, und, bei der Frage-Antwort-Methode werden zusätzlich nochmals weitere Zufallswerte ergänzt (vgl. das Benutzerhandbuch für den technischen Prozess).

By maintaining both login methods, a potential attacker it is made further more difficult, as

Durch das Vorhalten beider Login-Methoden wird es einem potentiellen Angreifer weiterhin

they do not know, which of the two methods has been used by the user.

schwerer gemacht, indem dieser nicht weiß, welche der beiden Methoden vom Anwender genutzt wurde.

Thirdly - and this is here the assessment to be subjected function - the user can use for the input of his password respective his Q and A phrases also a virtual keyboard.

Drittens schließlich – und das ist die hier dem Assessment zu unterwerfende Funktion – kann der Nutzer die Eingaben seines Passwortes bzw. seiner Frage- und Antwort-Phrasen auch mit einer virtuellen Tastatur umsetzen.

Figure 07: Virtual keyboard of the GoldBug application

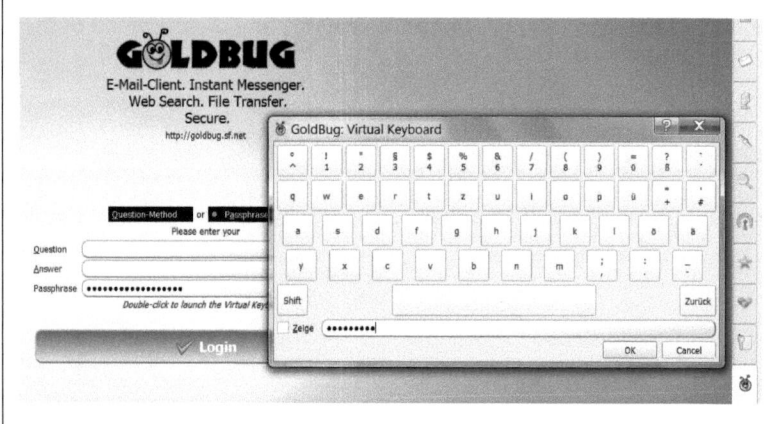

Source: Screenshot of Goldbug

For example, it is conceivable, that an attacker has installed on the machine of the user a key logger or might sniff in real time the keystrokes. Then, with access to the system, they could copy the installation of the software and find the login password via a keyboard log and control the application.

Beispielsweise wäre es denkbar, dass ein Angreifer auf der Maschine des Nutzers einen Key-Logger installiert hat oder in Echtzeit die Tastatureingaben mitschneiden kann. Sodann könnte er bei Zugriff auf das System die Installation der Softwarte kopieren und über einen Keyboard-Log das Login-Passwort erfahren und die Applikation fremdsteuern.

"If you encrypt end-to-end, the attacker is forced to use specific monitoring (rather than mass surveillance), for example, by bugging keyboards", confirms the American scientist James Bamford (2015).

"Wenn Sie Ende-zu-Ende verschlüsseln, zwingt das Angreifer dazu, spezifische Überwachung einzusetzen (statt Massenüberwachung), zum Beispiel, indem sie Tastaturen verwanzen", bestätigt der amerikanischer Wissenschaftler James Bamford (2015).

Since this therefore with functioning encryption often is the only realistic target for a third party, the users should enter their passphrase to open up the application possibly always with the Virtual Keyboard (VK)!

Da dieses also bei funktionierender Verschlüsselung meistens die einzig realistische Angriffsfläche für Dritte ist, sollte der Nutzer seine Passphrase zur Öffnung der Applikation ggf. immer mit dem Virtuellen Keyboard (VK) eingeben!

For this purpose just the mouse is used and no keylogger can track any keystrokes, because the mouse only generates a "click".

The virtual keyboard is part of the application, and not a plugin or a predetermined part out of the operating system. Comparing it with a virtual keyboard on a mobile operating system, one would also point out, that the keyboard should come out of the application, because it remains independent of the operating system. The virtual keyboard of an operating system could record inputs unnoticed, so that a virtual keyboard of an application - if it exists - is preferable.

Hierzu wird lediglich die Maus genutzt und kein Key-Logger kann irgendwelche Tastatureingaben mit verfolgen, denn die Maus generiert lediglich einen „Klick".

Die virtuelle Tastatur ist Bestandteil der Applikation, und nicht ein Plugin oder vorgegebener Bestandteil aus dem Betriebssystem heraus. Vergleicht man es mit einer virtuellen Tastatur auf einem mobilen Betriebssystem, wäre hier auch herauszustellen, dass die Tastatur aus der Applikation heraus kommen sollte, denn sie bleibt dann unabhängig von dem Betriebssystem. Auch die virtuelle Tastatur eines Betriebssystem könnte Eingaben unbemerkt aufzeichnen, so dass eine virtuelle Tastatur einer Applikation – sofern vorhanden – zu bevorzugen ist.

3.5.2 Selected method for studying and function reference

The selected examination is intended to refer to the operation of the virtual keyboard in GoldBug. The question consists in two aspects: first, could a key logger record the input of the virtual keyboard, and second, works the virtual keyboard also in different operating systems and languages versions?

The research method of this example is to show, that access to the system and application should be a key element of an audit. As explained above, this examination is especially for encrypted applications a linchpin, to complicate for attackers the possibility of obtaining an attack on the security of the entire application.

Die gewählte Untersuchung soll sich auf die Funktionsweise des virtuellen Keyboards in GoldBug beziehen. Die Fragestellung besteht in zweierlei Hinsicht: erstens, könnte ein Key-Logger die Eingaben der virtuellen Tastatur aufzeichnen und zweitens, funktioniert die virtuelle Tastatur auch in unterschiedlichen Betriebssystemen und Sprachen-Versionen?

Die Untersuchungsmethode an diesem Beispiel soll zeigen, dass der Zugang zum System bzw. Programm ein wesentliches Element eines jeden Audits sein sollte. Wie oben erläutert, stellt diese Untersuchung insbesondere für verschlüsselnde Applikationen ein Dreh- und Angelpunkt dar, um Angreifern die Möglichkeit zu erschweren, einen Angriff auf die Sicherheit der gesamten Applikation zu erwirken.

3.5.3 Conduction and findings of the examinations

Ad 1: We have installed a keylogger on a Windows system. In order not to promote keylogger tools, the concrete used tool should not be further specified here. Then the virtual keyboard of the application was used. The results showed, that the key-logger could not record keyboard characters when entering the passphrase by the virtual keyboard.

Ad 1: Wir haben einen Key-Logger auf einem Windows System installiert. Um Key-Logger-Werkzeuge nicht weiter zu promoten, soll hier das konkret genutzte Tool nicht weiter spezifiziert werden. Sodann wurde die virtuelle Tastatur der Applikation genutzt. Im Ergebnis zeigte sich, dass der Key-Logger bei Eingabe der Passphrase durch die virtuelle Tastatur keine Tastaturzeichen aufzeichnen konnte.

Ad 2: Further, a GoldBug installation was created with the language files on a German operating system and the log-in process using the virtual keyboard was performed, which led to the correct result. Then, the application has been closed and we deleted at the file level in the installation path "/translations" the German language file "german.qm". Then, the application has been started again and the language switched automatically to English as a default language version (because the German translation file was no longer present). Now the password has been entered also via the virtual keyboard and also the application opened accordingly.

This test shows clearly that the support for international language characters has been implemented correctly according UTF-8.

Ad 2: Weiterhin wurde eine GoldBug Installation mit den Sprachdateien auf einem deutschsprachigen Betriebssystem erstellt und der Einlog-Prozess mit der virtuellen Tastatur durchgeführt, die zu einem korrekten Ergebnis führte. Sodann wurde die Applikation geschlossen und auf der Dateiebene der Installation im Pfad „/Translations" die deutsche Sprachdatei "german.qm" gelöscht. Sodann wurde die Applikation neu gestartet und die Sprache schaltete automatisch auf Englisch als vorgegebene Sprachversion um. (Da ja die deutsche Übersetzungsdatei nicht mehr vorhanden war). Nun wurde das Passwort ebenso über die virtuelle Tastatur eingegeben und auch hier öffnete sich die Applikation entsprechend.

Dieser Test zeigt deutlich, dass auch die Unterstützung für internationale Sprachzeichen entsprechend UTF-8 korrekt implementiert wurde.

3.5.4 Evaluation of the results with regard to weaknesses, risks, potentials for improvements and strengths

The implementation of the login process can be regarded within the GoldBug application as extremely mature: First, there are two methods to define the login, further is - regardless of the method chosen - not used the selected password, but a longer passphrase is generated, which is derived by a hash function, and provided with additional random values.

Then there is the possibility to enter the passphrase without specifying a keyboard by the hardware or the operating system: The GoldBug application provides its own virtual keyboard.

Die Implementierung des Login-Prozesses kann im Programm GoldBug als äußerst ausgereift betrachtet werden: Zum einen bestehen zwei Methoden, um den Login zu definieren, weiterhin wird – unabhängig von der gewählten Methode – nicht das gewählte Passwort genutzt, sondern durch die Hashfunktion eine längere und mit weiteren Zufallswerten versehene, abgeleitete Passphrase generiert. Sodann besteht die Möglichkeit, die Passphrase ohne Vorgabe einer Tastatur seitens der Hardware oder des Betriebssystem umzusetzen: Die GoldBug Applikation stellt dafür eine eigene virtuelle Tastatur zur Verfügung.

If you compile the application for a Windows-10-tablet or laptop with touch screen, which can execute a Win32 executable, it can be seen, that the virtual keyboard is freely movable as a pop-up window and not as by the operating system given virtual keyboard attached at the bottom of the screen.

Kompiliert man die Applikation für ein Windows-10-Tablet bzw. Laptop mit Touch-Screen, das eine Win32-Exe ausführen lässt, zeigt sich, dass die virtuelle Tastatur als Pop-Up-Fenster frei beweglich ist und sich nicht wie die vom Betriebssystem vorgegebene virtuelle Tastatur an den unteren Rand des Bildschirms angegliedert.

This is merely a layout or habituation question, to find besides the virtual keyboard of the tablet also the in the application predefined virtual keyboard.

Dieses ist lediglich eine Layout- oder Gewöhnungsfrage, neben der virtuellen Tablet-Tastatur auch die seitens der Applikation vorgegebene virtuelle Tastatur vorzufinden.

Table 18: Description of findings 3.05

#	Area	Description of the finding	Valuation Severity Category / Difficulty Level / Innovation & Improvement Class / Strength Dimension
	Weakness / Schwäche	./.	./.
	Risk / Risiko	./.	./.
	Potential for Improvement / Verbesserungspotential	./.	./.
	Strength / Stärke	./.	./.

The following method can be also recommended as an improvement of logins: The usage of a file as a key file to generate the password for login from the derived hash of the file. However, this process makes only sense, if the file is not on the system - since an attacker would rehash all files on the disk and then try the thousands of trials. Since an USB dongle with a key file as login would be not as practical as one in the head stored password, should this recommendation not be indicated as a finding, but only be addressed briefly here.

Als Verbesserungspotential des Logins kann auch folgende Methode empfohlen werden: Die Nutzung einer Datei als Key-File, um aus dem abgeleiteten Hash der Datei das Passwort für den Login zu generieren. Dieser Prozess macht jedoch nur Sinn, wenn die Datei nicht auf dem System liegt - denn ein Angreifer würde alle Dateien der Festplatte hashen und dann die mehreren tausend Versuche durchprobieren. Da ein USB-Dongle mit einem Key-File jedoch als Login nicht praktikabler als ein im Kopf gespeichertes Passwort ist, soll dieses Empfehlung nicht als Finding vermerkt werden, sondern nur hier kurz angesprochen werden.

3.5.5. Appraisal of good practices in comparison with other similar applications

Comparing the ability to record the password for the other six open source messengers, it is clear, that none of the below mentioned other comparable applications offers a virtual keyboard on the application side.

Vergleicht man die Möglichkeit, das Passwort bei den anderen sechs quelloffenen Messengern mitzuloggen, so zeigt sich, dass keine der genannten weiteren vergleichbaren Applikationen eine virtuelle Tastatur applikationsseitig anbietet.

Although CryptoCat works as a browser plug-in, a key logging would also be possible here (also for a planned Desktop version). RetroShare even offers the possibility, that the user stores the login password. This can certainly be a user decision, which takes place more or less at own risk without warning at the login procedure. However, the application can then be executed by any other attacker directly, when an unauthorized copy of the installation has been made.

Auch wenn CryptoCat als Browser-Plugin funktioniert, wäre auch hier ein Key-Loggen gegeben (ebenso für eine geplante Desktop-Version). RetroShare bietet sogar die Möglichkeit, dass der Nutzer das Login-Passwort abspeichert. Dieses ist sicherlich dann eine Nutzerentscheidung, die mehr oder weniger ohne Vorwarnung seitens des Login-Prozesses auf eigenes Risiko erfolgt, jedoch ist die Applikation sodann bei einer unbefugten Kopie der Installation von jedem anderen direkt ausführbar.

Authentication measures, such as the Socialist-Millionaire-Protocol (SMP), get therefore a decisive role as complementary verifying the authenticity of the other person with manually entered passwords.

Authentifizierungsmaßnahmen, wie das Socialist-Millionaire-Protokoll (SMP), bekommen daher als ergänzende Verifizierung der Authentizität des Gegenübers mit manuell einzugebenden Passworten eine entscheidende Rolle.

This is so far only given at OTR-XMPP clients, which procedures of logins - for example, through various methods and the addition of cryptographic salt - are not subject of this investigation. First, such an investigation would turn out - considering the high variety of OTR-XMPP clients - possibly as `divers´ and furthermore study an architecture at the applications, which is not aligned with encryption:

The encrypting element (OTR) is introduced only through a plug-in variant with these clients. It therefore concerns only the transfer of the message - but not whether the plugin hosting client (the XMPP-chat-application) stored the texts obtained possibly again in plain text after decoding in the local databases of the XMPP-cient.

The OTR usage is no guarantee, that the chat client stores the buddy list or received messages on the hard disk encrypted, and also does not provide information about whether a login into the chat application can easily be eavesdropped or which login-key-strength lies behind it.

Thus, OTR is a plug-in solution, which is to be assessed as critical in conjunction with a host: Java, for example, was as a plug removed from browsers and abandoned (Dalibor 2016) and crypto solutions are seen as a plugin in the browser as extremely critical (compare Ptacek 2011, Arcieri 2013). The encryption with the plugin OTR in an XMPP-host thus says nothing about a login, which was to examine in this section, and its security standard for the Messenger host.

GoldBug uses with a password with a minimum length of 16 characters and the underlying conversion using the hash function in consideration of cryptologic salt an excellent procedure to secure the login. The virtual keyboard for entering the password is an ideal additional protection as a supplement.

Dieses ist bislang nur bei OTR-XMPP Klienten gegeben, deren Prozeduren des Logins - z.B. über verschiedene Methoden und der Hinzufügung von kryptographischen Salzes - nicht Gegenstand dieser Untersuchung sind. Eine solche Untersuchung würde bei der Vielzahl an OTR-XMPP Klienten erstens ggf. divers ausfallen und weiterhin eine Architektur bei den Applikationen untersuchen, die nicht auf Verschlüsselung ausgerichtet ist:

Das verschlüsselnde Element (OTR) wird bei diesen Klienten nur durch eine Plugin-Variante eingebracht. Es betrifft somit nur den Transfer der Nachricht - nicht aber, ob der das Plugin hostende Klient (die XMPP-Chat-Applikation) die erhaltenen Texte ggf. nach der Decodierung auch wieder im Plaintext in den lokalen Datenbanken im XMPP-Klienten abgespeichert.

Die OTR Nutzung ist keine Garantie dafür, dass der Chat-Klient die Freundesliste oder erhaltende Nachrichten auf der Festplatte verschlüsselt ablegt und trifft auch keine Aussage darüber, ob ein Login in die Chat-Applikation leicht abgegriffen werden kann oder welche Login-Schlüssel-Stärke dahinter steckt.

Somit bleibt OTR eine Plugin-Lösung, die als kritisch im Zusammenspiel mit einem Host zu bewerten ist: Java z.B. wurde als Plugin aus Browsern entfernt und aufgegeben (Dalibor 2016) und auch Crypto-Lösungen werden als Plugin im Browser als äußerst kritisch gesehen (vgl. Ptacek 2011, Arcieri 2013). Die Verschlüsselung mit dem Plugin OTR in einem XMPP-Host sagt somit auch nichts über ein Login, das in diesem Abschnitt zu untersuchen war, und dessen Sicherheitsstandard für den Messenger-Host aus.

GoldBug nutzt mit einem Passwort mit einer Länge von mindestens 16 Zeichen und der dahinterstehende Umwandlung mittels der Hashfunktion unter der Berücksichtigung von kryptologischem Salz eine exzellente Prozedur zur Absicherung des Logins. Die virtuelle Tastatur zur Eingabe des Passwortes stellt eine ideale weitere Absicherung als Ergänzung dar.

Table 19: Indicative BIG SEVEN context references 3.05

Logo	Application	Comments
	Cryptocat	No virtual keyboard given. CryptoCat is a browser-plugin.
	GoldBug	High requirements for the password-length, two different login-methods, consideration of cryptographic hash-functions, existence of a virtual keyboard, which is independently given from the application.
	OTR+XMPP	No virtual keyboard given.
	RetroShare	No virtual keyboard given. Emerging risik due to the decision oft he user to use the option to save the login-password for an auto-login process. No awareness notification to the user in this process.
	Signal	No virtual keyboard given. Does not meets the standard of 16 characters for a minimum requirement regarding the password length.
	SureSpot	No virtual keyboard given.
	Tox	No virtual keyboard given.

As further research consists the investigation of the minimum requirements of the password length in each application as well as the strength and method of the hash and other cryptographic functions, which will be considered in the login process for the comparable applications.

It is desirable that also other applications consider different login method and a virtual keyboard in the future, since the protection of access to the own system plays an increasingly important role, if online connections, certain operating systems and hardware components are not tustworthy, to not copy the password entries and handing it over to third parties.

Compare also the discussion in the San Bernardino case where the login password should be unlocked of the phone of a Murderer by Apple: Because after 10 times incorrect entering the login password, all user data on the phone will be deleted.

Als weiterer Forschungsbedarf besteht für die vergleichbaren Applikationen die Untersuchung der jeweiligen Mindestanforderungen der Passwortlängen in jeder Applikation sowie die Stärke und Methode der Hash- und weiteren kryptologischen Funktionen, die im Login-Prozess Berücksichtigung finden.

Wünschenswert ist, dass auch andere Applikationen verschiedene Login-Methode sowie eine virtuelle Tastatur in Zukunft berücksichtigen, da der Schutz des Zugangs zum eigenen System eine zunehmend wichtiger werdende Rolle spielt, wenn Online-Verbindungen, bestimmten Betriebssystemen und auch Hardware-Komponenten nicht mehr vertraut werden kann, die Passwort-Eingaben nicht zu kopieren und Dritten auszuhändigen.

Vergleiche dazu auch die Diskussionen im San Bernardino Fall, bei dem das Login-Passwort zum Telefon eines Mörders seitens Apple entsperrt werden solle: Denn nach 10-maliger falscher Eingabe des Login-Passwortes werden sämtliche Nutzerdaten auf dem Telefon gelöscht.

But Apple refused to the FBI, to change this lock in future phone production, as this could be a gateway then for anyone. The user therefore also spoke of a future #FBIOS - not of Apple's "iOS", but an operating system, that will be programmed with a governmental monitoring institution. (Https://en.wikipedia.org/wiki/ FBI_v._Apple & https://en.wikipedia.org / wiki / 2015_San_Bernardino_attack).

The monitoring of a telephone during operation and of data, stored in the cloud by the operating system vendors, is another risk aspect, that needs to be differentiated in the context of access to systems.

In addition to protecting the own login passwords therefore hardware and software is also to be investigated regarding possibly inserted so-called "source telecommunication surveillance" (in German language abbreviated as: Q-TKÜ), that means, to take the recording, where it is entered: at the interface of the user in plaintext. Due to the technical possibilities of the "listening in real time" (Simonite 2015) and usage of operating systems or (any) apps for that, encryption is to be regarded now as a human rights issue, when everyone can be a subject of monitored online communications and this is a mass phenomenon (compare also Amnesty International 2016):

If everyone is potentially monitored, and their communication is structurally always recorded, everyone should not only secure the own system and application access with passwords, but also encrypt the online transfer of their communication - with a manually and together with the communication partner secretly defined end-to-end password.

Again, the end-to-end encryption does not mean to follow an automatic process, but manually typing the symmetrical password, which consists out of 32 random characters. And this also applies to login passwords with regard to access to the application.

Privacy advocates and security experts recommend regional hardware and the use of an open source operating system, so a Linux

Apple weigerte sich jedoch gegenüber dem FBI, diese Sperre bei der zukünftigen Telefonproduktion auszuhebeln, da dieses dann zu einem Einfallstor für jedermann werden könne. Die Nutzer sprachen daher auch von einem zukünftigen #FBIOS - also nicht von Apples "iOS", sondern einem Betriebssystem, das von einer staatlichen Überwachungsinstitution mit-programmiert werde. (https://en.wikipedia.org/wiki/ FBI_v._Apple & https://en.wikipedia.org /wiki/ 2015_San_Bernardino_attack).

Die Überwachung eines Telefons im laufenden Betrieb und der in der Cloud hinterlegten Daten durch den Betriebssystem-Anbieter ist dabei ein weiterer Risikoaspekt, der im Zusammenhang von Zugängen zu Systemen zu differenzieren ist.

Neben dem Schutz der eigenen Login-Passworte ist daher Hard- und Software auch hinsichtlich möglicherweise eingesetzter sogenannter Quellen-Telekommunikations-überwachung (Q-TKÜ) zu untersuchen. Aufgrund der technischen Möglichkeiten des "Abhörens in Echtzeit" (Simonite 2015) und der Nutzung von Betriebssystemen und (beliebigen) Apps dafür, ist Verschlüsselung inzwischen als Menschenrechtsthema zu betrachten, wenn die Überwachung der Online-Kommunikation jeden betreffen kann und ein Massenphänomen darstellt (vgl. auch Amnesty International 2016):

Wenn jeder potentiell überwacht, bzw. seine Kommunikation strukturell immer aufgezeichnet wird, sollte jeder nicht nur seine System- und Applikations-Zugänge mit Passworten sichern, sondern auch den Online-Transfer seiner Kommunikation verschlüsseln - mit einem manuell und gemeinsam mit dem Kommunikationspartner im Geheimen definierten Ende-zu-Ende Passwort.

Nochmals: Ende-zu-Ende Verschlüsselung bedeutet nicht, einen automatischen Prozess zu folgen, sondern das symmetrische Passwort bestehend aus 32 zufälligen Zeichen manuell einzutippen. Und dieses gilt auch für Login-Passworte hinsichtlich des Zugangs zur Applikation.

Datenschützer und Sicherheitsexperten empfehlen daher auch regionale Hardware sowie den Einsatz eines quelloffenen

system. The three action measures in the age after Snowden thus are:

Betriebsystems, also ein Linux-System. Die drei Handlungsmaßnahmen im Zeitalter nach Snowden heissen somit:

1. Encrypt your online communication,

2. Keep your passwords secret and

3. Learn and use the Linux operating system, as this guarantees even with the random number generators, which play an essential role in the encryption process, a transparent process.

1. Verschlüssele Deine Online-Kommunikation,

2. Halte Deine Passworte geheim und

3. Lerne und nutze Linux als Betriebsystem, denn dieses garantiert auch bei den Zufallszahlengeneratoren, die im Verschlüsselungsprozess eine wesentliche Rolle spielen, einen transparenten Prozess.

Table 20: Good Practice Insights #05

Good Practice Insight # 05	
with GoldBug Multi-Encrypting Communication Suite	
Case	My laptop has been stolen yesterday. How can I prevent in the future, that others use my communications instances? *Mir wurde gestern das Laptop gestohlen. Wie kann ich zukünftig verhindern, dass meine Kommunikations-Instanzen von anderen genutzt werden?*
Solution	It is crucial to equip the login in the communications application with a password. GoldBug uses a 16-character long password that is then converted into an even longer hash string. Furthermore GoldBug offers two different login methods, to make it extremely difficult for attackers to log into your communication application. *Entscheidend ist, den Login in die Kommunikationsapplikation mit einem Passwort zu versehen. GoldBug nutzt ein 16-Zeichen langes Passwort, dass dann in einen noch längeren Hash-String gewandelt wird. Zudem bietet GoldBug zwei verschiedene Login-Methoden an, um es Angreifern äußerst schwierig zu machen, sich in Dein Kommunikations-Programm einzuloggen.*

Source: Own Case.

3.6   Access to the system: Encrypted Databases

The access to the IT system will develop in the future as one of the largest gateways to infiltrate encrypted environments. It is therefore not so much about breaking the math behind the encryption, it will prove to be access-proof with the right algorithms and with multi-encryption - but the access to the hardware, to the storage of passwords and private keys, or even the unnoticed install of keyboard loggers, will be exploited as potential weaknesses, as already explained for the login password in the section above.

Thus, it is crucial for encrypting applications, that, when the hardware is lost, no one can get data and identifications out of the encrypted application.

Particularly in the mobile operating systems for tablets and phones it has been clarified, that operators like Google, Apple or Microsoft - if encryption out of the data is available - have full access to all data on the phone - because these operating systems most fundamentally must be operated with an Internet connection to the manufacturer.

Three quarters of phone users of the operating system Android do not encrypt their hardware (2014). Although newer versions should allow encryption for the mobile operating system, it is not excluded, that the provider retains still an access key for it or that the password entries can be tapped in addition.

Therefore, a "Crypto-War" should not be based on the question, whether we encrypt or not, but better on which operating system the user data is better encrypted and stronger protected against access by suppliers and third party: Apple, Windows, Android or Linux. The division of society in digital security arises, when citizens were not able to learn the secure Linux and encryption.

Therefore, it is important to store the personal data also in encrypted containers - on the

Der Zugang zum IT-System wird sich in Zukunft zu einer der größten Einfallstore entwickeln, um verschlüsselte Umgebungen zu infiltrieren. Es geht somit nicht mehr so sehr um das Brechen der Mathematik hinter der Verschlüsselung, sie wird sich mit entsprechenden Algorithmen und mit Multiverschlüsselung als zugangssicher erweisen – sondern der Zugang zur Hardware, zu der Speicherung der Passworte und zu den privaten Schlüsseln oder gar das unbemerkte Installieren von Tastatur-Loggern werden als mögliche Schwachstellen ausgenutzt werden, wie im Abschnitt zuvor schon für das Login-Passwort erläutert.

Somit ist es für eine verschlüsselnde Applikation entscheidend, dass bei Verlust der Hardware niemand an die Daten und Identifikationen der verschlüsselnden Applikation heran kann.

Insbesondere bei den mobilen Betriebssystemen für Tablets und Telefonen wurde verdeutlicht, dass die Betreiber wie Google, Apple oder Microsoft – wenn eine Verschlüsselung der Daten vorliegt – uneingeschränkten Zugang zu allen Daten auf dem Telefon haben - da diese Betriebssysteme meistens grundlegend mit einer Internetverbindung zum Hersteller betrieben werden müssen.

So verschlüsseln Dreiviertel der Telefonbenutzer des Betriebssystems Android ihre Hardware nicht (2014). Auch wenn neuere Versionen eine Verschlüsselung des mobilen Betriebssystems ermöglichen sollte, ist nicht auszuschließen, dass der Anbieter einen Zugriffsschlüssel dazu behält oder die Passworteingaben wiederum abgreifen kann.

Ein "Crypto-War" sollte daher nicht auf die Frage bezogen sein, ob wir verschlüsseln oder nicht, sondern besser darauf, welches Betriebssystem die Nutzerdaten besser verschüsselt und vor Zugriffen von Anbietern und Dritter stärker schützt: Apple, Windows, Android oder Linux. Die Spaltung der Gesellschaft bei digitaler Sicherheit entsteht, wenn Bürger das sichere Linux und Verschlüsselung nicht erlernen konnten.

Daher ist es wichtig, die persönlichen Daten ebenso in verschlüsselten Containern

mobile system as also on a laptop or desktop.

Thus, not only the research field of the storage in and encryption of data in databases such as SQLite or PostgreSQL and further is opened, but also the search in encrypted databases will remain an interesting field of research as a perspective.

abzulegen – auf dem mobilen System wie ebenso auf einem Laptop oder Desktop. Damit eröffnet sich nicht nur das Forschungsfeld der Ablage in und Verschlüsselung von Daten in Datenbanken wie SQLite oder PostgreSQL und weiteren, sondern auch die Suche in verschlüsselten Datenbeständen wird perspektivistisch ein interessantes Forschungsfeld bleiben.

3.6.1 Inventory taking, structural analysis and descriptions of the functions

GoldBug Messenger installs itself such that any use of data and as far as possible the initialization information is stored encrypted.

Hereinafter, the storage and filing of transferred and to be transferred user data is intended to be explored in depth and assessed: The data in GoldBug is stored in encrypted SQL databases. These are individual files, that can indeed be viewed with a SQL-browser, but then only contain ciphertext. Content is thereby protected.

GoldBug Messenger installiert sich dergestalt, dass jegliche Nutzungsdaten und weitestmöglich auch die Initialisierungsinformationen verschlüsselt abgelegt sind.

Im Folgenden sollen die Speicherung und Ablage der transferierten und zu transferierenden Nutzungsdaten vertieft betrachtet und beurteilt werden: Die Daten werden bei GoldBug in verschlüsselten SQL-Datenbanken abgelegt. Es handelt sich um einzelne Dateien, die mit einem SQL-Browser zwar eingesehen werden können, aber sodann ausschließlich Ciphertext enthalten. Die Inhalte werden somit geschützt.

Encrypted and authenticated Containers:

Relevant data, that the application retains locally, is stored in encrypted and authenticated containers. CBC and CTS encryption modes are used with a variety of block ciphers. Encryption and authentication occur as follows:

1. If the size of the original data is less than the specified cipher's block size, the original data is re-sized such that its new size is identical to the cipher's block size. A zero-byte pad is applied.

2. Append the size of the original data to the original container.

3. Encrypt the augmented data via the selected cipher and specified mode.

4. Compute a keyed-hash of the encrypted container.

Verschlüsselte und authentifizierte Container:

Relevante Daten, die die Applikation lokal speichert, werden in verschlüsselten und authentifizierten Containern abgelegt. Die Verschlüsselungs-Modi CBC und CTS werden mit verschiedenen Block Ciphern genutzt. Verschlüsselung und Authentifizierung erfolgt wie folgt:

1. Wenn die Größe der Original-Daten geringer ist als die spezifizierte Blockgröße der Cipher, dann werden die Original-Daten vergrößert bzw. angereichert dergestalt, dass die neue Größe identisch mit der Block-Größe der Cipher ist. Ein Zero-Byte-Pad wird also angewandt.

2. Die Größe der Original-Daten wird dem originalen Container zugewiesen.

3. Die so vergrößerten Daten werden mit der gewählten Cipher und dem spezifizierten Modus verschlüsselt.

5. Ein keyed-Hash vom verschlüsselten Container wird erstellt.

4. Concatenate the hash output with the encrypted data, H_{Hash} $_{Key}(E_{Encryption}$ $_{Key}(Data \parallel Size(Data))) \parallel E_{Encryption}$ $_{Key}(Data \parallel Size(Data))$.

6. Der Hash-Output wird mit den verschlüsselten Daten wie folgt verknüpft: H_{Hash} $_{Key}(E_{Encryption}$ $_{Key}(Data \parallel Size(Data))) \parallel E_{Encryption}$ $_{Key}(Data \parallel Size(Data))$.

The architecture of GoldBug also includes a mechanism for re-encoding data, if new authentication and encryption keys are desired (also compare the project documentation in the source code, 2014).

Die Architektur von GoldBug inkludiert ebenso einen Mechanismus zum erneuten encodieren der Daten, wenn neue Schlüssel für die Authentifizierung und Verschlüsselung gewünscht sind (vgl. auch die Projektdokumentation im Quellcode, 2014).

3.6.2   Selected method for studying and function reference

As method for the investigation of the databases should be sought the access with appropriate tools into these databases, to check, whether there usage-content is available, which is not encrypted.

Als Methode zur Untersuchung der Datenbanken soll die Einsicht mit entsprechenden Werkzeugen in diese Datenbanken erwirkt werden, um zu prüfen, ob dort Nutzungs-Inhalte vorhanden sind, die nicht verschlüsselt sind.

While chat will be exchanged directly from the kernel to the user interface, it is, for example, for e-mail, required, to store received and sent e-mails on the hard disk. Because here we have to consider a greater amount of data and longer retention periods, especially the file "email.db" should be analyzed within this assessment.
The file is located in the sub-path of the GoldBug communicator: ./spoton/email.db.

Während der Chat direkt vom Kernel in die Benutzeroberfläche gesendet wird, ist es z.B. beim E-Mail erforderlich, empfangene und gesandte E-Mails auf der Festplatte zu speichern. Da es sich hier um eine beachtliche Datenmenge und auch längere Speicherzeiträume handeln kann, soll in diesem Assessment besonders die Datei „email.db" analysiert werden.
Die Datei befindet sich im Unterpfad des GoldBug-Communicators: ./spoton/email.db.

As tool a helper application is here considered, so that each reader can repeat this test at any time. The Mozilla Web Browser Firefox offers an addon plugin, which allows to introspect SQL databases: SQL Browser. With that tool we looked into the encrypted file email.db.

Als Werkzeug kommt hier eine Hilfsapplikation in Betracht, damit jeder Leser diese Überprüfung jederzeit wiederholen kann. Der Mozilla Web Browser Firefox bietet ein Addon-Plugin an, mit dem man SQL-Datenbanken einsehen kann: den SQL-Browser. Damit schauten wir uns die verschlüsselte Datei email.db an.

3.6.3   Conduction and findings of the examinations

The SQL tool we have installed within the version 3.8.11.1 of the Firefox browser with the Gecko engine version 42.0.
By setting up and using the POPTASTIC email function an e-mail inbox has been loaded into the GoldBug client, so that the file "email.db" has itself increased accordingly on disk level.

Das SQL-Werkzeug haben wir in der Version 3.8.11.1 im Firefox-Browser mit der Gecko Engine-Version 42.0 installiert.
Durch Einrichtung und Nutzung der POPTASTIC-E-Mail-Funktion ist ein E-Mail-Postfach in den GoldBug Klienten geladen worden, so dass sich die Datei „email.db" auf der Festplatten-Ebene entsprechend vergrößert hat.

The file has been then opened within the SQL Browser (compare Figure).

It is found as a result, that the tables are only filled in the file structure with ciphertext. There is no user data, which is not encrypted.

The code review for opening the database and in turn also encrypting the database (by the application) shows a clean implementation of the process.

Die Datei ist sodann in dem SQL-Browser geöffnet worden (vgl. Abbildung).

Es zeigt sich im Ergebnis, dass die Tabellen in der Dateistruktur lediglich mit Ciphertext gefüllt sind. Es gibt keinerlei Nutzerdaten, die nicht verschlüsselt sind.

Der Code-Review für die Öffnung der Datenbank und wiederum auch Verschlüsselung der Datenbank (durch die Applikation) zeigt eine saubere Implementierung des Prozesses.

Figure 08: Database email.db with ciphertext

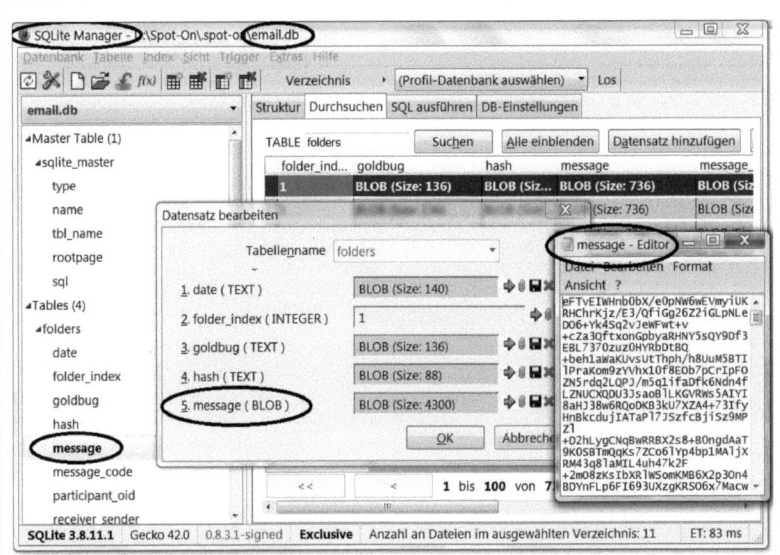

Source: Own screenshot of SQL Browser.

Outook: This section refers to an evaluation of the encryption function of the e-mail database. The application GoldBug has furthermore within other databases also a search functionality - for example, in the "URL.db, within which the data for the p2p URL website search is stored.

This shows, as at the beginning already explained, further research needs how a

Ausblick: Der vorliegende Abschnitt bezieht sich auf eine Evaluation der Verschlüsselungsfunktion der E-Mail-Datenbank. Die Applikation GoldBug verfügt darüber hinaus in anderen Datenbanken auch eine Such-Funktionalität - beispielsweise in der „URL.db, in der die Daten für die p2p URL-Webseitensuche abgelegt sind.

Hier zeigt sich wie Eingangs schon erläutert weitergehender Forschungsbedarf, zu

search in chipertext can be successfully designed. This field of research offers additional theoretical questions for universities, as that this issue could be further developed theoretically within a review process. The audit process therefore relates to the encryption of information to be deposited within SQL databases, as it was practically examined for both, email.db and for urls.db.

erläutern, wie eine Suche im Chipertext erfolgreich gestaltet werden kann. Dieses Forschungsfeld bietet weitere theoretische Fragestellungen für Universitäten an, als dass dieses Thema in einem Review-Prozess weiter theoretisch entwickelt werden könnte. Der Audit-Prozess bezieht sich daher auf die Verschlüsselung von abzulegenden Informationen in SQL-Datenbanken, wie es sowohl für die email.db als auch für die urls.db praktisch untersucht wurde.

3.6.4 Evaluation of the results with regard to weaknesses, risks, potentials for improvements and strengths

Risks and weaknesses have not been found while conducting the analysis of the storage of the encrypted e-mails in the database SQLite. It is an advanced implementation and also an adequate claim, to deposit all relevant user data only encrypted on the hard disk.

Risiken und Schwächen sind für die Analyse der Ablage der verschlüsselten E-Mails in der Datenbank SQLite nicht gefunden worden. Es ist eine fortschrittliche Implementierung und auch ein adäquater Anspruch, alle abzulegenden relevanten Nutzerdaten auf der Festplatte ausschließlich verschlüsselt zu speichern.

One of the strengths of the application is, that this is done automatically and without major installation effort for the user, certainly also by the adaptive configurability of the implemented SQLite databases, in addition to PostgreSQL.

Eine Stärke der Applikation ist, dass dieses automatisch und ohne größeren Installationsaufwand für den Nutzer geschieht, sicherlich auch durch die sich anpassende Gestaltbarkeit der implementierten SQLite Datenbanken, neben PostgreSQL.

Table 21: Description of findings 3.06

#	Area	Description of the finding	Valuation Severity Category / Difficulty Level / Innovation & Improvement Class / Strength Dimension
	Weakness / Schwäche	./.	./.
	Risk / Risiko	./.	./.
	Potential for Improvement / Verbesserungspotential	./.	./.
	Strength / Stärke	./.	./.

3.6.5 Appraisal of good practices in comparison with other similar applications

The encryption of user data should be a fundamental issue for the further open source Crypto-Messengers. An analysis was already deepening extended within another previous chapter with regard to the data of the login, which needs special protection.

Die Verschlüsselung von Nutzerdaten – die in einem weiteren vorherigen Untersuchungsabschnitt auch um eine Analyse der besonders zu schützenden Daten des Logins schon vertiefend erweitert wurde – sollte ein grundsätzliches Thema auch für die weiteren quelloffenen Crypto-Messenger sein.

Not all further here involved, open-source Messengers consider in their documentation in an elaborated way their options of the encryption of data, which is to be stored on the hardware.	Nicht alle anderen hier einbezogenen, quell-offenen Messenger gehen in ihrer Dokumentation ausführlich auf ihre Optionen der Verschlüsselung der auf der Hardware zu speichernden Daten ein.

Table 22: Indicative BIG SEVEN context references 3.06

Logo	Application	Comments
	Cryptocat	No sufficient information about encrypting the saved data and applied databases in the documentation.
	GoldBug	GoldBug encrypts the saved data and has a technical specification about the process. Compatibilitiy to SQlite and PostGres databases.
	OTR+XMPP	No sufficient information about encrypting the saved data´, depending on the chosen client, no common standard for the different clients.
	RetroShare	Retroshare encrypts the saved data, e.g. of partial files.
	Signal	No sufficient information about encrypting the saved data and applied databases in the documentation.
	SureSpot	No sufficient information about encrypting the saved data and applied databases in the documentation.
	Tox	No sufficient information about encrypting the saved data and applied databases in the documentation.

The aim of this section is not to analyze the code base of the further Messengers, but to pick and indicatively to involve within each study context the existing information from the projects - here: regarding encrypted storage of the user data on the hard disk.	Ziel dieses Abschnittes ist es nicht, die Code-Basis der weiteren Messenger zu analysieren, sondern die seitens der Projekte vorhandenen Informationen in dem jeweiligen Untersuchungskontext – hier: verschlüsselte Speicherung der Nutzungsdaten auf der Festplatte – aufzugreifen und indikativ einzubeziehen.
It is evident from the documentations, that only sparse information is given from the further to be compared Messengers - how data is stored: encrypted and to what extent.	Es zeigt sich somit in den Dokumentationen, dass darüber, wie die weiteren, zu vergleichenden Messenger ihre Daten ablegen – verschlüsselt und in welchem Umfang –, nur spärlich Informationen dargestellt werden.
The search function in an encrypted database has to be assessed besides GoldBug in the client RetroShare as more advanced or at least in a richer perspective than in the other clients.	Die Suchfunktion in einer verschlüsselten Datenbank ist neben Goldbug im Klienten RetroShare fortgeschrittener bzw. zumindest perspektivenreicher als bei den anderen Klienten einzuschätzen.

The raising of consciousness not only in terms of enhanced documentation in general, but at this point of the encrypted storage of data in particular, therefore can be attributed to all clients. It provides in particular for students an ideal research area for further comparative study.

Die Bewußtseinsförderung nicht nur allgemein, sondern in diesem Punkt der verschlüsselten Ablage von Daten insbesondere, kann daher insgesamt noch mehr Aufmerksamkeit von allen Klienten zugemessen werden. Es bietet insbesondere auch für Studierende ein ideales Forschungsfeld für eine weitergehende vergleichende Studie.

Table 23: Good Practice Insights #06

Good Practice Insight # 06	
with GoldBug Multi-Encrypting Communication Suite	
Case	I've sold my old hard disk, there was still a GoldBug installation on the hard drive. Can now the buyer read my communication?
	Ich habe meine alte Festplatte verkauft, es war noch eine GoldBug-Installation auf der Festplatte. Kann der Käufer nun meine Kommunikation auslesen?
Solution	No. Compared to numerous other programs is at GoldBug all personal data, that is written to the hard disk, stored in encrypted databases. Even the search of the data in the operation is carried out in the encrypted data indexes.
	Nein, gegenüber zahlreichen anderen Programmen werden bei GoldBug alle persönlichen Daten, die auf die Festplatte geschrieben werden, in verschlüsselten Datenbanken abgelegt. Auch die Suche der Daten im Betrieb erfolgt in den verschlüsselten Datenbeständen.

Source: Own Case.

3.7   Penetrationtest: Account-Firewall

The connection to a neighbor should be on the on hand for a new user or tester of the software easy to manufacture. This is given in GoldBug clients by a predetermined project server connecting each participant. Later, then everyone within his circle of friends also should have the option to build an own chat-, e-mail- or URL-server. The contribution of each user to create a custom listener for his friends is to be understood in the sense of creating a decentralized network.

In addition to the simple creation of a stable connection to a neighbor, it is on the other hand also about, when someone offers a connection through an account on their server, that here the connection is only available to those, who are authorized to connect.

For that, in GoldBug clients will be offered the option for an established listener, to create an account for a specific user.
An account is characterized by a username and a password. Regarding the password design the connection to the network for users of this important element is investigated in more detail in the last chapter evaluation (3.20).

It should firstly go in the sense of the previously described contents in terms of accessing the system about the blocking of connection attempts, that may be exercised by users without appropriate account access.

Die Verbindung zu einem Nachbarn soll zum einen für einen neuen Nutzer oder Tester der Software einfach herzustellen zu sein. Dieses ist im GoldBug Klienten gegeben, indem ein projektseitig vorgegebener Server die Teilnehmer verbindet. Später sodann kann ein jeder in seinem Freundeskreis auch einen eigenen Chat-, E-Mail oder URL-Server errichten. Der Beitrag eines jeden Nutzers, für seine Freunde einen eigenen Listener zu erstellen, ist auch im Sinne der Erstellung eines dezentralen Netzwerkes zu verstehen.

Neben der einfachen Erstellung einer stabilen Verbindung mit einem Nachbarn geht es aber zum anderen auch darum, wenn jemand eine Verbindung über einen Account auf seinem Server anbietet, dass hier die Verbindung auch nur denjenigen zur Verfügung steht, die berechtigt sind, sich zu verbinden.

Dazu wird im GoldBug Klienten für erstellte Listener die Option angeboten, einen Account für einen spezifischen Nutzer zu erstellen. Ein Account kennzeichnet sich durch einen Nutzernamen und ein Passwort. Hinsichtlich der Passwortgestaltung für Accounts wird dieses wichtige Element der Verbindung zum Netzwerk noch ausführlicher im letzten Evaluierungskapitel (3.20) untersucht.

Hier soll es zunächst im Sinne auch der zuvor ausgeführten Inhalte hinsichtlich eines Zugangs zum System um die Blockung von Verbindungsversuchen gehen, die von Nutzern ohne passende Account-Zugänge ausgeübt werden könnten.

3.7.1   Inventory taking, structural analysis and descriptions of the functions

If a listener as a chat server was created in the client GoldBug and was changed to account-based formats, then the account functions as a firewall. Only for users with the appropriate account name and password, it is possible to connect.

Wenn im Klienten GoldBug ein Listener als Chat Server erstellt wurde und auf account-basierte Zugänge umgestellt wurde, dann wirkt die Account-Funktion wie eine Firewall. Nur Nutzern mit entsprechendem Account-Namen und -Passwort wird ermöglicht, sich zu verbinden.

The Accounts procedure is as follows:

1. Binding endpoints are responsible for defining account information. During the account-creation process, an account may be designated for one-time use. Account names and account passwords each require at least 32 bytes of data.

2. After a network connection is established, a binding endpoint notifies the peer with an authentication request. The binding endpoint will terminate the connection if the peer has not identified itself within a fifteen-second window.

3. After receiving the authentication request, the peer responds to the binding endpoint. The peer submits the following information: $H_{Hash\ Key}(Salt\ ||\ Time)\ ||\ Salt$, where the Hash Key is a concatenation of the account name and the account password. The SHA-512 hash algorithm is presently used to generate the hash output. The Time variable has a resolution of minutes. The peer retains the salt value.

4. The binding endpoint receives the peer's information. Subsequently, it computes $H_{Hash\ Key}(Salt\ ||\ Time)$ for all of the accounts that it possesses. If it does not discover an account, it increments Time by one minute and performs an additional search. If an account is discovered, the binding endpoint creates a message similar to the message created by the peer in the previous step and submits the information to the peer. The authenticated information is recorded. After a period of approximately 120 seconds, the information is destroyed.

Die Abweisung von nicht berechtigten Verbindungsversuchen und Nutzern ohne Berechtigung lässt sich als Prozess wie folgt beschreiben:

1. Bindende Endpunkte sind verantwortlich für die Definition der Account Informationen. Während des Erstellungsprozesses für einen Account, kann der Account für eine Einmal-Nutzung markiert werden. Sowohl Account-Namen wie auch Account-Passworte erfordern wenigstens 32 Zeichen.

2. Nachdem eine Netzwerkverbindung etabliert ist, informiert ein bindender Endpunkt den Peer über seine Authentifizierungsanfrage. Der bindende Endpunkt wird die Verbindung unverzüglich beenden, wenn der Peer sich selbst nicht innerhalb eines Zeitfensters von fünfzehn Sekunden identifiziert hat.

3. Nachdem die Authentifizierungs-Anfrage erhalten wurde, antwortet der Peer zum bindenden Endpunkt. Der Peer übermittelt die folgenden Informationen: $H_{Hash\ Key}(Salt\ ||\ Time)\ ||$ Salt, wobei der Hash Key eine Verknüpfung aus dem Account-Namen und dem Account-Passwort ist. Derzeit wird der SHA-512 Hash Algorithmus genutzt, um das Hash Ergebnis zu berechnen. Die Zeit-Variable hat eine Auflösung von Minuten. Der Peer sichert den Wert für das Salz.

4. Der bindende Endpunkt erhält die Informationen von dem Peer. Folgerichtig wird für alle verfügbaren Accounts die folgende Operation ausgeführt: $H_{Hash\ Key}(Salt\ ||\ Time)$. Wenn damit kein Account entdeckt werden kann, wird der Zeitfaktor um eine Minute verlängert und führt eine zweite Suche durch. Wenn ein Account gefunden wurde, zu dem die Werte passen, erstellt der bindende Endpunkt eine ähnliche Nachricht, wie sie der Peer im vorherigen Schritt erstellt hat, und sendet diese Information an den Peer. Die authentifizierende Information wird gespeichert. Nach einer Zeitperiode von näherungsweise 120 Sekunden wird die Information gelöscht.

5. The peer receives the binding endpoint's information and performs a similar validation process, including the analysis of the binding endpoint's salt. The two salt values must be distinct. The peer will terminate the connection if the binding endpoint has not identified itself within a fifteen-second window.

6. Der Peer erhält die vom bindenden Endpunkt gesandte Information und führt einen ähnlichen Validierungsprozess durch, einschließlich der Analyse des kryptoloischen Salzes des bindenden Endpunkts. Beide Salz-Werte müssen eindeutig sein. Der Peer wird die Verbindung weiterhin abwerfen, wenn der bindende Endpunkt sich diesbezüglich nicht innerhalb eines fünfzehn Sekunden-Fensters identifiziert hat.

3.7.2 Selected method for studying and function reference

As method here should be created a practical verification of the firewall, which is implemented by an account. Can anyone else connect to a listener, as the one, who has the account information?

Als Methode soll hier eine praktische Überprüfung der durch einen Account errichteten Firewall umgesetzt werden. Kann jemand anderes zu einem Listener verbinden, als derjenige, der über die Account-Informationen verfügt?

If a connection to the listener on the specified port is possible, so to say to break unauthorized into the system, should be checked with a penetration test. Thus the penetration test determines the sensitivity of the system to be tested against such attacks.

Ob eine Verbindung zum Listener am definierten Port möglich ist, quasi unautorisiert in das System einzudringen, ist mit einem Penetrationstest zu überprüfen. Der Penetrationstest ermittelt somit die Empfindlichkeit des zu testenden Systems gegen derartige Angriffe.

The term penetration test is sometimes used mistaken for an automatic vulnerability scan. While this is done mostly automatically, it requires in a real penetration test manual preparation in the form of sighting of the test piece, plan the test methods and objectives, selecting the necessary tools and finally the implementation. The security scan again differs from vulnerability scanning through the manual verification of the test results.

Der Begriff Penetrationstest wird gelegentlich auch fälschlich für einen automatischen Vulnerability Scan (vulnerability engl. und fachsprachlich für Schwachstelle) verwendet. Während dieser weitgehend automatisch abläuft, bedarf es bei einem echten Penetrationstest manueller Vorbereitung in Form von Sichtung des Prüflings, Planung der Testverfahren und Ziele, Auswahl der notwendigen Werkzeuge und schließlich die Durchführung. Der Security Scan wiederum unterscheidet sich vom Schwachstellen Scan durch die manuelle Verifikation der Testergebnisse.

The penetration testing can be supported by various software products. These include port scanners as Nmap, Vulnerability Scanner as Nessus, sniffer like Wireshark, packet generators as HPing 2/3 or Mausezahn and password crackers as John the Ripper. In addition, increasingly are more tools available, that are designed specifically for security testing, often due to the verifiability of the source code from the open source segment and tailored to very specific test areas: ARP0c

Die Durchführung von Penetrationstests kann durch verschiedene Softwareprodukte unterstützt werden. Dazu zählen etwa Portscanner wie Nmap, Vulnerability Scanner wie Nessus, Sniffer wie Wireshark, Paketgeneratoren wie HPing 2/3 oder Mausezahn und Passwortcracker wie John the Ripper. Zudem stehen zunehmend mehr Werkzeuge zur Verfügung, die speziell für Sicherheitstests entwickelt wurden, häufig aufgrund der Überprüfbarkeit des Quellcodes

for example is a link Interceptor, another example of such a special tool is Egressor, to check the configuration of Internet point-to-point routers (compare also Wikipedia).

The German Federal Office for Information Security (BSI, as quoted) has developed a classification schema, how to describe a test. Essentially six different aspects are considered as: information base, assertiveness, scope, approach, technique, starting point. Based on these criteria an individual test then can be put together with an administrator.

Our penetration test of an account in the program GoldBug should therefore be carried out as a further empirical part of our review.

aus dem Open-Source Bereich stammen und auf sehr spezielle Testbereiche zugeschnitten sind: ARP0c ist beispielsweise ein Verbindungs-Interceptor, ein weiteres Beispiel eines solchen Spezialwerkzeugs ist Egressor zur Überprüfung der Konfiguration von Internet Punkt-zu-Punkt Routern (vgl. auch Wikipedia).

Das deutsche Bundesamt für Sicherheit in der Informationstechnik (BSI, aaO) hat ein Klassifikationsschema entwickelt, anhand dessen sich ein Test beschreiben lässt. Im Wesentlichen werden sechs verschiedene Aspekte betrachtet wie: Informationsbasis, Durchsetzungsstärke, Umfang, Vorgehensweise, Technik, Ausgangspunkt. Anhand dieser Kriterien kann dann zusammen mit dem Administrator ein individueller Test zusammengestellt werden.

Unser Penetrationstest eines Accounts im Programm GoldBug soll somit als weiterer empirischer Teil unseres Reviews durchgeführt werden.

Figure 09: GoldBug – Account Firewall for Accounts and IP-Addresses

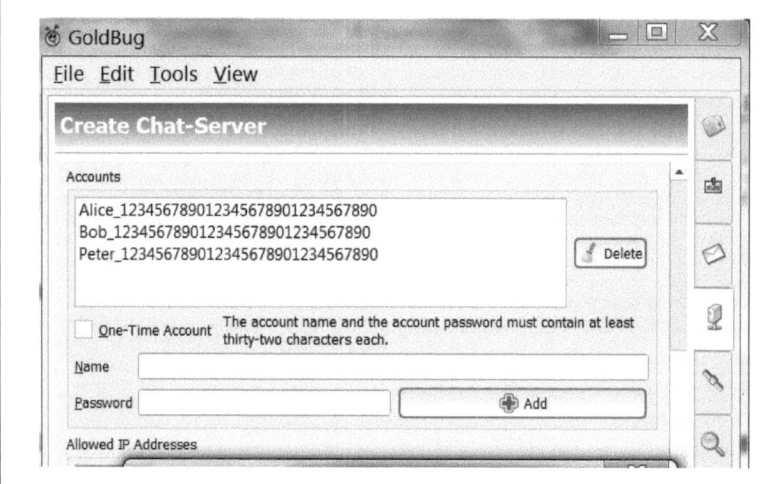

Source: Own Screenshot of Goldbug

3.7.3   Conduction and findings of the examinations

To perform a connection to the account-based listener within GoldBug, we first looked at the processes in the user interface as well as the

Zur Durchführung einer Verbindung mit dem account-basierten Listener in GoldBug haben wir uns zunächst die Prozesse in der

programming within the code base (compare Section 3.20).

It was then first tried to establish a connection with an account, of which we knew the account name and password. The connection succeeded.

Further attempts with the wrong account information were not successful. Even with a port scanner it failed to address the system using the account-based listener default port, such that a communication of a user might have worked.

The corresponding protocol of the TLS connection also provides further reassurance, that no such unauthorized connection can be established.

The same procedure was also performed with a GoldBug client, which did not connect via the HTTPS protocol, but only had a HTTP configuration. Again, it did not succeed to connect without account details.

The account firewall has successfully kept state against the here attempted connection tries.

Benutzeroberfläche angeschaut und ebenso auch die Programmierung in der Code Basis (vgl. auch Abschnitt 3.20).

Es wurde sodann zunächst mit einem Account versucht, zu verbinden, bei dem Accountname und Passwort bekannt waren. Die Verbindung gelang.

Weitere Versuche, mit falschen Account-Daten gelangen nicht. Auch mit einem Portscanner gelang es nicht, das System über den accountbasierten Listener am Standard-Port zu adressieren dergestalt, dass eine Nachrichtenübermittlung eines Nutzers hätte funktionieren können.

Das entsprechende Protokoll der TLS-Verbindung sorgt auch zusätzlich dafür, dass keine entsprechende unbefugte Verbindung aufgebaut werden kann.

Die gleiche Prozedur wurde ebenso mit einem GoldBug Klienten durchgeführt, der nicht über das HTTPS Protokoll verband, sondern lediglich über eine HTTP Konfiguration verfügte. Auch hier gelang eine Verbindung ohne Account-Details nicht.

Die Account-Firwall hat den hier umgesetzten Verbindungsversuchen erfolgreich Stand gehalten.

3.7.4 Evaluation of the results with regard to weaknesses, risks, potentials for improvements and strengths

With regard to the account function to prevent unauthorized connections, there are from our tests no weaknesses or risks to describe. Also, in the code review no objection has to be pointed out.

Hinsichtlich mit der Account Funktion, unberechtigte Verbindungen abzuhalten, gibt es aus unserem Praxistest keine Schwächen oder Risiken zu beschreiben. Auch der Code-Review gibt keine Beanstandung.

Table 24: Description of findings 3.07

#	Area	Description of the finding	Valuation Severity Category / Difficulty Level / Innovation & Improvement Class / Strength Dimension
	Weakness / Schwäche	./.	./.
	Risk / Risiko	./.	./.
	Potential for Improvement / Verbesserungspotential	./.	./.
	Strength / Stärke	Authorization concept, that is not linked to a key	Informational

Potential improvements were not identified. The strength of the implemented account function is in an authorization concept, that is not linked to a key that encrypts the message (compare Retroshare).

Verbesserungspotentiale wurden nicht identifiziert. Die Stärke der implementierten Account-Funktion liegt in einem Berechtigungskonzept, das nicht an einen Schlüssel geknüpft ist, der die Nachrichten verschlüsselt (vgl. RetroShare).

3.8.5 Appraisal of good practices in comparison with other similar applications

Compared to the other messengers it turns out, that they can not be aligned on a P2P structure. They are all client-server based using an account, so that connection attempts from unauthorized peers can not arise, if they are not to be understood as a direct attack.

Im Vergleich zu den anderen Messengern zeigt sich, dass diese nicht auf eine P2P Struktur ausgerichtet werden können. Sie sind alle Client-Server basiert mittels eines Accounts, so dass Verbindungsversuche von nicht authorisierten Peers gar nicht entstehen können, wenn sie nicht als ein direkter Angriff zu verstehen sind.

Only the two clients Retroshare and Tox rely on a DHT, in which numerous IP connections in addition to the account-based connection to the host or clients used occur.

Lediglich die beiden Klienten RetroShare und Tox setzen auf einen DHT, bei dem zahlreiche IP-Verbindungen neben der accountbasierten Verbindung mit dem Host bzw. genutzten Klienten auftreten.

Table 25: Indicative BIG SEVEN context references 3.07

Logo	Application	Comments
	Cryptocat	Password based login, no option to run the application in a p2p network.
	GoldBug	P2P and F2F Modus. Server and Client, and also Client-Client-Modus. Web-of-Trust over accounted Listeners - independent from encryption key. Works as firewall for connection-attempts without authorization.
	OTR+XMPP	Account based architecture. No option to run the application in a p2p network.
	RetroShare	DHT Usage with stun-technology and NAT hole punching for DHT-Peer-Connections. Firewall build upon a Web-of-Trust architecture tied to the encryption key.
	Signal	Password based login, no option to run the application in a p2p network.
	SureSpot	Password based login, no option to run the application in a p2p network.
	Tox	DHT Usage with stun-technology and NAT hole punching for DHT-Peer-Connections.

Table 26: Good Practice Insights #07

Good Practice Insight # 07	
with GoldBug Multi-Encrypting Communication Suite	
Case	I run a chat server for friends, who use GoldBug. I want only these friends and no one else to use my server. Ich betreibe einen Chat-Server für Freunde, die GoldBug benutzen. Ich möchte, dass nur diese Freunde und niemand anderes meinen Server nutzt.
Solution	GoldBug has the function, to create a chat server, integrated into each client. A so-called listener can be made in the P2P-Modus for all users, or using the account function in the F2F mode only for friends. Friends will receive then a username and password to log in. GoldBug hat die Funktion, einen Chat-Server zu erstellen zu können, in jedem Klienten integriert. Ein sogenannter Listener kann im P2P-Modus für alle, oder auch im F2F-Modus nur für Freunde erstellt werden mittels der Account-Funktion. Freunde erhalten dann einen Benutzernamen und ein Passwort, um sich einzuloggen.

Source: Own Case.

3.8 Assessment of the Documentation: Usermanuals e.g. hosted at Wikibooks

Further up the function was addressed by the example of another application, with which it can be convenient for users, to store in the installation path of the application the password to login into the application permanently (in plain text). Now, if an attacker uploads a copy of the installation, or otherwise can tap it as is, any certainty about the application and the private key used has gone.

Weiter oben wurde am Beispiel einer anderen Applikation die Funktion angesprochen, mit der es für Nutzer bequem sein kann, das Passwort zum Login in die Applikation dauerhaft im Installationspfad der Applikation (im Plaintext) zu speichern. Wenn nun ein Angreifer eine Kopie der Installation hoch lädt, kopiert oder sonst wie abgreifen kann, ist jegliche Sicherheit über die Applikation sowie der verwendeten privaten Schlüssel dahin.

It is therefore important, as this example shows, to educate users on how to use the functions and document functionalities within manuals and handbooks.

Wichtig ist es daher, wie dieses Beispiel zeigt, die Nutzer über den Gebrauch der Funktionen aufzuklären und Funktionsweisen in Manualen und Handbüchern zu dokumentieren.

Likewise, almost all presented at the beginning IT-assessment-manuals require in each assessment a study of the existing documentation and operating instructions of a software.

Ebenso erfordern fast alle zu Beginn vorgestellten IT-Assessment-Manuale in jedem Assessment eine Untersuchung der vorhandenen Dokumentationen und Gebrauchsanweisungen zu einer Software.

Furthermore, an essential element in particular the DIN-certifications is to evaluate, how far consciousness (the awareness) of users is promoted to deal with the particular system or an organizational, prozessural or electronically illustrated IT-context.

Weiterhin ist ein wesentliches Element insbesondere der DIN-Zertifizierungen, zu evaluieren, inwieweit das Bewußtsein (die Awareness) der Nutzer gefördert wird, sich mit dem jeweiligen System oder einem organisational, prozessural bzw. elektronisch abgebildeten IT-Kontext zu beschäftigen.

Therefore, the user-manual for GoldBug within this assessment section should be examined in detail.

Daher soll auch das Benutzer-Handbuch zu GoldBug in diesem Assessment-Abschnitt eingehend untersucht werden.

3.8.1 Inventory taking, structural analysis and descriptions of the functions

GoldBug is an application, that has to this open source project so far English and German-language documentaries because of the voluntary contributions. The documentation is given in many ways:

GoldBug ist eine Applikation, die aufgrund der freiwilligen Kontributionen zu diesem quelloffenen Projekt bislang über englische und deutschsprachige Dokumentationen verfügt. Die Dokumentationen sind in vielerlei Hinsicht gegeben:

- The most extensive documentation consists within the source code of Spot-On itself. The code is not only written within machine language, but also contains many readable comments and advice on how certain

- Die umfangreichste Dokumentation besteht in dem Quellcode von Spot-On selbst. Er ist nicht nur in Maschinensprache geschrieben, sondern enthält auch viele lesbare Kommentare und Hinweise, wie

functions or next steps are to be understood.

- There is also a technical documentation in the source repository to the cryptologic, mathematical and programming-language-oriented processes and functions. This is attached at any installation of GoldBug Messenger next to the source code. So anyone, who downloads the installation files, obtained at the same time the source code and its documentation supplied.

- For the project are in addition to the technical project documentation also two user manuals for the end-users given. These are open source and editable within the "Wikibooks"-project of the Wikipedia placed and also on the homepage of GoldBug Messenger available - and include (in the single-column layout) about 50 manuscript pages of reading material to get deeper read within the cryptologic functions of GoldBug.

Both, the English-language as well as the German-language user manual are current. Since the manual was written in German, and the English translation seems to possibly represent an automated translation (by google) and at present time a not yet fully proofread version, should the analysis related to the current, very comprehensive and detailed user manual within German language.

The German-language user guide, which serves as the basis for further analysis within this assessment, is found in the path "/documents" of each installation file from GoldBug in current status and at Wikibooks:

bestimmte Funktionen oder nächste Schritte zu verstehen sind.

- Ebenso gibt es eine technische Dokumentation im Source-Repositorium zu den kryptologischen, mathematischen und Programmiersprache-orientierten Prozessen und Funktionen. Diese ist neben dem Quellcode auch jeder Installation des GoldBug Messengers beigefügt. Wer sich also die Installationsdateien herunterlädt, erhält zugleich auch den Quellcode und dessen Dokumentation mitgeliefert.

- Projektseitig liegen zusätzlich zu der technischen Projektdokumentation auch zwei Benutzer Handbücher für den End-Nutzer vor. Diese sind quelloffen und edierbar bei dem „Wikibooks"-Projekt der Wikipedia hinterlegt, als auch auf der Homepage des GoldBug Messengers verfügbar und umfassen (im einspaltigen Ausdruck) über 50 Manuskript-Seiten Lesestoff, um sich in die kryptologischen Funktionen von GoldBug tiefergehend einzulesen.

Sowohl das englischsprachige, wie auch das deutschsprachige Benutzerhandbuch sind aktuell. Da das Handbuch in deutscher Sprache verfasst wurde, und die englische Übersetzung ggf. auch eine (durch Google-Übersetzer) automatisierte und zum heutigen Zeitpunkt noch nicht vollends lektorierte Fassung darzustellen scheint, soll die Analyse auf das aktuelle, sehr umfangreiche und detailgenaue Benutzermanual in deutscher Sprache bezogen werden.

Das deutschsprachige Benutzerhandbuch, das zur weiteren Analyse in diesem Assessment zugrunde gelegt werden soll, findet sich in dem Pfad "/documents" einer jeden Installationsdatei von GoldBug im aktuellen Stand beigelegt sowie bei Wikibooks:

Figure 09: GoldBug – Handbook and User-Manual of GoldBug Messenger

Source: https://de.wikibooks.org/wiki/Goldbug

Due to the ongoing development of the software, the English as well as the extensive German user manual is considered as "work in progress".	Aufgrund der voranschreitenden Software-Entwicklung ist das englische wie auch das umfangreichere deutsche Benutzermanual als „Work in Progress" zu betrachten.

3.8.2 Selected method for studying and function reference

Because the application Goldbug not only offers encrypted chat, but also secure e-mail within a full functioning e-mail client, and besides that also file-transfer, plus Web search within a URL database - besides numerous options for each end-to-end encryption - , the manual should be checked, to see, if it provides a complete overview within the essential main features of the application. As well as: If the information relevant for the encryption functions is also explained extensively in detail.	Da die Applikation Goldbug nicht nur verschlüsselten Chat anbietet, sondern auch sicheres E-Mail innerhalb eines voll funktionswertigen E-Mail-Klienten und darüber hinaus auch File-Transfer, sowie Web-Suche in einer URL-Datenbank – neben zahlreichen Optionen zur jeweiligen Ende-zu-Ende Verschlüsselung – anbietet, soll das Handbuch dahingehend überprüft werden, ob es einen vollständigen Überblick in den wesentlichen Haupt-Funktionen des Programms bietet. Sowie: Ob die für die Verschlüsselung relevanten Funktionen auch im Detail ausführlich erläutert sind.

3.8.3 Conduction and findings of the examinations

The German user manual has been printed thereto corresponding to the Wikibooks-text once in a one line respectively one column layout and came up with more than 50 pages.	Das deutsche Benutzerhandbuch wurde dazu entsprechend dem Wikibooks-Text einmal einzeilig bzw. einspaltig ausgedruckt und kam dabei auf über 50 Seiten.

We then counted the lines and figures per main function to analyze a quantitiative distribution:

Sodann wurden die Zeilen und Abbildungen pro Haupt-Funktion gezählt, um eine quantitiative Verteilung zu analysieren:

Table 27: Allocation of function, number of pages & screenshots in the manual

Function & Key of GoldBug Application	Key Type	Number of pages in the Manual	Number of Figures & Screenshots in the Manual
Chat	a-symmetric	pages 18-24 & 42-44 = 12	6
E-Mail	a-symmetric	25-29 = 4	3
Poptastic	a-symmetric	30-32 = 3	1
URLs	a-symmetric	39-41 = 3	5
Rosetta	a-symmetric	45-46 = 2	1
Magnet for StarBeam-File-Transfer	symmetric	34-38 = 4	4
Magnet for Groupchat	symmetric	33 = 1	1

Source: own overview.

The quantitative analysis shows, that the essential functions for each key are described in the User Manual in detail and the features are also iluustrated for the user by numerous pictures and screenshots.

Die quantitative Auswertung zeigt, dass die wesentlichen Funktionen für jeden Key ausführlich im Benutzermanual beschrieben sind und auch durch zahlreiche Abbildungen und Screenshots dem Nutzer die Funktionen verdeutlichen werden.

For a qualitative analysis, the individual sections were read accordingly and rated from the content:

Für eine qualitative Analyse wurden die einzelnen Abschnitte entsprechend gelesen und inhaltlich bewertet:

There is no significant functional section, which may be referred to the substantive examination as incomprehensible or qualitatively poor. Rather, a good reader guidance and derived explanation of the functions is given in many places, so that it can also be understood well by a user without in-depth technical skills.

Es gibt keinen wesentlichen Funktionsabschnitt, der nach der inhaltlichen Prüfung als unverständlich oder qualitativ dürftig bezeichnet werden kann. Vielmehr ist an vielen Stellen eine gute Leserführung und hergeleitete Erklärung der Funktionen gegeben, so dass sie auch ein Nutzer ohne vertiefte Fachkenntnise gut verstehen kann.

The comparison with the English manual on the other hand looks a little incomplete, it is yet to provide further translation respectively proofreading work in some sections of the original German document. However, since the manual should be supplied to the audit in the language, within which it seems to have been worked out primarily, this remains a side note. More translations are also desirable within other languages and can by any user created through an entry in Wikibook by means of own contribution.

Der Vergleich mit dem englischen Handbuch sieht dagegen etwas unvollständiger aus: Es ist in einigen Abschnitten aus dem deutschen Originaldokument noch weitergehende Übersetzungs- bzw. Lektoratsarbeit vorzusehen. Da jedoch das Handbuch in der Sprache dem Audit zugeführt werden soll, in dem es vorwiegend erarbeitet worden zu sein scheint, bleibt dieses eine Randbemerkung. Weitere Übersetzungen, auch in andere Sprachen, sind wünschenswert und können von jedem Nutzer durch die Anlage z.B. als Wikibook mittels eines eigenen Beitrags eingepflegt werden.

3.8.4 Evaluation of the results with regard to weaknesses, risks, potentials for improvements and strengths

For the German user manual therefore remain after our review of quantitative and qualitative review no improvements. Basically every reader wishes depending on prior knowledge here and there a some deeper description, in our estimation, however, is any significant main function of the client described comprehensively and within sufficient depth and also very understandable.

Für das deutsche Benutzermanual verbleiben daher nach unserer Durchsicht keine quantitativen und qualitativen Verbesserungsvorschläge. Grundsätzlich wünscht sich jeder Leser je nach Vorkenntnissen hier oder da eine noch tiefer gehendere Beschreibung, nach unserer Einschätzung ist jedoch jede wesentliche Haupt-Funktion des Klienten umfassend sowie in ausreichender Tiefe und sehr verständlich beschrieben.

In a recommendation - and this is true in principle and separated from the rated application - it is always desirable to be able to find the changes also regularly in the current user manual for each new release. Furthermore, the changes in new versions of the application are also shown in full detail within the release notes of the source documents.

In einer Empfehlung - und das gilt grundsätzlich und losgelöst von der bewerteten Applikation - ist es immer wünschenswert, bei neuen Releases die Veränderungen ebenso regelmäßig im aktuellen Handbuch wiederfinden zu können. Darüber hinaus sind bislang die Veränderungen innerhalb der Applikation von neuen Versionen ja ausführlichst in den Release-Notes des Quellcodes dokumentiert.

Table 28: Description of findings 3.08

#	Area	Description of the finding	Valuation Severity Category / Difficulty Level / Innovation & Improvement Class / Strength Dimension
	Weakness / Schwäche	./.	./.
	Risk / Risiko	./.	./.
	Potential for Improvement / Verbesserungspotential	./.	./.
	Strength / Stärke	./.	./.

3.8.5 Appraisal of good practices in comparison with other similar applications

The installation files of the to be compared programs have basically integrated no documentation or even source code. Some programs documented within a short FAQ or Wiki the essential questions, however, a detailed documentation of the encryption and the process functions in a format understandable for end users is not, hardly, or only rarely given.

Die Installationsdateien der zu vergleichenden Programme haben grundsätzlich keine Dokumentation oder gar den Quellcode integriert. Einige Programme dokumentieren in einem kurzen FAQ oder Wiki die wesentlichen Fragen, jedoch ist eine ausführliche Dokumentation der Verschlüsselung und der Prozessfunktionen in einem für End-Nutzer verständlichen Format nicht, kaum, oder nur selten gegeben.

GoldBug Messenger has a very detailed user manual in comparison to further open source messengers.

GoldBug Messenger hat ein sehr ausführliches Benutzermanual im Vergleich zu den weiteren quelloffenen Messengern.

The explanation of crypto functions therein is also documented extensively. The further applications have their cryptologic functions based - as part of the full documentation - only less in an integrated approach of documentation and remain therefore only fair to poor within our review.

Die Erläuterung von Crypto-Funktionen ist darin ebenso ausführlich dokumentiert, die weiteren Applikationen haben ihre kryptologischen Funktionen als Teilbereich der Gesamtdokumentation wenig auf ein integriertes Dokumentationskonzept bezogen und bleiben daher in unserer Bewertung nur ausreichend bis mangelhaft.

Table 29: Indicative BIG SEVEN context references 3.08

Logo	Application	Comments
	Cryptocat	https://github.com/cryptocat/cryptocat/wiki - 14 short article pages in a wiki.
	GoldBug	https://de.wikibooks.org/wiki/Goldbug - over 50 pages as documentation of a tutorial.
	OTR+XMPP	https://developer.pidgin.im/wiki/Using%20Pidgin - 8 categroies as FAQ one e.g. with up to 75 questions andshort answers, resulting in several pages. Less description text in terms of a tutorial or for crypto content.
	RetroShare	http://retroshare.sourceforge.net/wiki/index.php/Documentation - 36 Wiki Articles including tutorials.
	Signal	http://support.whispersystems.org/hc/en-us - hundred questions and short sentences as answer resulting in a few, circa 10 FAQ pages. Articles or tutorials or technical documentations are mostly rare.
	SureSpot	https://www.surespot.me/documents/how_surespot_works.html - circa 3 pages with 3 chapters and one FAQ with 23 questions.
	Tox	https://wiki.tox.chat/doku.php - circa 11 pages documentation including a few questions in the FAQ.

For the other applications it has to be pointed out, that many ad-hoc required information or questions from users are stored within other forms of communication e.g. in a wiki (Tox) or a forum (Retroshare) - or is stored in the archives of a mailing list, but does not systematically open up this as an information resource and often remains high under the standard of a manual documentation, as created by users of the community of the project GoldBug.

Hervorzuheben ist für die weiteren Applikationen, dass viele Ad-Hoc benötigten Informationen oder Fragen von Nutzern in anderen Kommunikationsformen wie einem Wiki (Tox) oder Forum (RetroShare) oder über das Archiv einer Mailingliste abgelegt sind, sich diese jedoch nicht systematisch als Informationsressource erschließen und auch oft qualitativ unter dem Standard einer Handbuchdokumentation bleiben, wie sie von Nutzern der Community des Projektes GoldBug unterstützt wurden.

The strongest Messengers in terms of documentation are Retroshare and GoldBug and some OTR-XMPP clients, in particular the most well-known client Pidgin presents an equally detailed documentation, but consisting

Die stärksten Messenger hinsichtlich einer Dokumentation sind RetroShare und GoldBug sowie einige OTR-XMPP Klienten, wobei insbesondere der wohl bekannteste Klient Pidgin eine ebenso ausführliche

only of FAQs and containing no dedicated crypto chapter or tutorials.

Dokumentation vorlegt, die jedoch nur aus FAQ´s bestehen und keine dedizierte Crypto-Kapitel oder Tutorials enthält.

Table 30: Good Practice Insights #08

Good Practice Insight # 08	
with GoldBug Multi-Encrypting Communication Suite	
Case	I have heard in this study for the first time of GoldBug, and would like to gladly read in depth about Crypto-Messaging. Where can I do that?
	Ich habe in dieser Studie das erste Mal von GoldBug gehört, und möchte mich gerne vertiefend zum Thema Crypto-Messaging einlesen. Wo kann ich das tun?
Solution	GoldBug has deposited an extensive manual at Wikibooks and the project site. The texts are also like the program all open source, so that users can also translate into their referring languages.
	GoldBug hat ein umfangreiches Handbuch bei Wikibooks und der Projektseite hinterlegt. Die Texte sind wie das Programm alle quelloffen, so dass Nutzer es auch in ihre Landessprache übersetzten können.

Source: Own Case.

3.9 Inclusion of other Audit-Reports & Comparison with other Open-Source Messaging Software

An audit should never be done isolated only for a particular application, but an auditor - as well as a developer and a community member, who feels close to an application - should include ideally the "neighborhood", the context to the further, comparable developments, and a state-of-the-art at least for two comparable applications into the research, field testing respectively development proposals.

Below should therefore on the basis of already written audit reports to the similar, possibly comparable open source messenger applications first

- initially put together an overview of available audit reports. Here is certainly to be considered, that for applications, that already exist for several years, relevant audit reports may already be given (including inventory taking of given audit metrics).

- Second, is to be investigated, whether the relevant audit reports, the texts of other assessments are included by the auditors (view of the auditors). It should be noted, that many auditors get only active, when there is a financed contract. Often with just a few pages of text, the application-brand is then revalued for marketing purposes with the brand of the audit-company. Thus, free and gratuitous auditors are therefore to promote and requested, that they include comparisons to other audits and applications in a dedicated audit particularly. A funded audit will though rarely embed comparisons.

- Third, also should an impression be examined and combined, whether this claim is also lived by the developers and teams of the comparable Crypto-

Ein Audit sollte nie isoliert nur für eine jeweilige Applikation durchgeführt werden, sondern ein Auditor – wie auch ein Entwickler und auch ein Community Mitglied, das sich einer Applikation verbunden fühlt – bezieht idealerweise die „Nachbarschaft", den Kontext zu den weiteren, vergleichbaren Entwicklungen, sowie ein State-of-the-Art mindestens zweier vergleichbarer Applikationen mit in die Untersuchungen, Praxistests bzw. Entwicklungsvorschläge mit ein.

Im Folgenden soll daher anhand der bereits geschriebenen Audit-Berichte zu den ähnlichen, ggf. vergleichbaren quelloffenen Messenger-Applikationen zunächst

- erstens eine Übersicht an verfügbaren Audit-Reporten zusammen gestellt werden. Hier ist sicherlich zu berücksichtigen, dass zu Applikationen, die schon einige Jahre bestehen, auch entsprechende Audit-Berichte vorliegen können (inkl. Bestandsaufnahme der vorliegenden Audit-Metrics).

- Zweitens soll untersucht werden, ob die entsprechenden Audit-Reporte die Texte anderer Assessments seitens der Auditoren einbeziehen (Sichtweise der Auditoren). Hierbei ist anzumerken, dass viele Auditoren nur aktiv werden, wenn es sich um einen finanzierten Auftrag handelt. Oft mit nur wenigen Seiten Text wird sodann mit der Marke der Auditierenden die Applikationsmarke zu Marketingzwecken aufgewertet. Somit sind auch freie, unentgeltliche Auditoren daher besonders zu fördern und anzusprechen, dass sie auch in ein dezidiertes Audit Vergleiche zu anderen Audits und Applikationen einbeziehen. Ein finanziertes Audit wird selten Vergleiche einbetten.

- Drittens soll auch untersucht und ein Eindruck zusammengefasst werden, ob dieser Anspruch auch von den Entwicklern und Teams der

Messengers: contributing to a good-pratices sharing community, respectively being committed to reflect and document options for innovation: How is the community networking within this (even special) field of Crypto-Messengers? And will the in the communities praised and supported products being able to replace the unencrypted applications soon?

Innovations, successful integrations, good-practices models should be shared jointly and valued - and not sacrificed quietly as plagiarism. The shared learning takes place by mutual reviews, community contacts and evaluations and verifications in regard to the common approach - this is technically e.g. created by bridges, conversion-options or standardization of certain functions; and also this spirit is created by auditors bringing good practice models respectively blogger mentioning various alternatives within their references. References and mutual credits are the principle of a woven web as well as mutual learning. It is therefore critical to understand, why, for example, the word "Torrent" should not be mentioned on various edonkey-boards or even not linked with an URL - while nobody complains about censorship!

vergleichbaren Crypto-Messenger gelebt wird, zu einer good-pratice Sharing-Community beizutragen bzw. Innovationsoptionen engagiert zu reflektieren und zu dokumentieren. Wie stellt sich die Community in diesem (noch Spezial-) Gebiet der Crypto-Messenger auf? Und werden diese gepriesenen und unterstützten Produkte der Communities die unverschlüsselten Applikationen bald ersetzen können?

Innovationen, gelungene Integrationen, good-practice-Modelle sollten gemeinsam geteilt und wertgeschätzt - und nicht still und heimlich einem Plagiarismus geopfert werden. Das gemeinsame Lernen erfolgt auch durch gegenseitige Reviews, Community Kontakte und Evaluationen sowie Überprüfungen der gemeinsamen Ausrichtung – sei es technisch z.B. durch Bridges, Konvertierungsoptionen oder Standardisierungen von bestimmten Funktionen und, indem Auditoren auch good practice Modelle bzw. Blogger verschiedene Alternativen in ihren Referenzierungen einbringen. Verweise und gegenseitige Credits sind das Prinzip eines verwobenen Webs wie auch des gemeinsamen Lernens. Es ist daher unverständlich, warum z.B. das Wort "Torrent" auf verschiedenen Edonkey-Boards nicht erwähnt oder gar mit einer URL verlinkt werden darf - und sich niemand über Zensur beschwert.

3.9.1 Inventory taking, structural analysis and descriptions of the functions

For the GoldBug Communications Suite consists far besides the manual by Scott Edwards (Editor and other authors, 2014) numerous reviews and analysis assessments of the functions by editors, experts and bloggers (compare e.g. Cakra 2014 / Constantinos 2014 / Demir 2014 / Joos PCWelt 2014 / Lindner 2014 / Security Blog 2014 / Weller 2014, Dragomir 2016, et al.). These contexts we have considered for the planning of this audit.

The written source code, the programming of the functions as well as the detailed release changes ("release notes") provide valuable additional information on the dimensions, that an audit can address. In addition, applied

Zur GoldBug Communications Suite besteht bislang neben dem Handbuch von Scott Edwards (Editor und weitere Autoren, 2014) zahlreiche Review- und Analyse-Einschätzungen hinsichtlich der Funktionen von Editoren, Fachexperten und Bloggern (vgl. z.B. Cakra 2014 / Constantinos 2014 / Demir 2014 / Joos PCWelt 2014 / Lindner 2014 / Security Blog 2014 / Weller 2014, Dragomir 2016, et al.). Diese Kontexte haben wir für die Planung dieses Audits berücksichtigt.

Der geschriebene Quellcode, die Programmierung der Funktionen sowie auch die detaillierten Veröffentlichungs-Veränderungen („Release Notes") geben zusätzlich wertvolle Informationen über die

should be also standard methods and implications issued by the guidelines of the audit manuals.

The audit - as carried out here and derived within the first two chapters - should cover not only a code review and the essential functions of the application, but also include the essential audit areas, instruments and methods of the international prevailing IT-audit-manuals with the aim of to achieve maximum inspection width.

As seen, it is then not just

- about mathematical, cryptologic or programmed functions particularly in a code review, but e.g. also
- about an opinion regarding the awareness of the user, to be able to use functions with awareness of the corresponding set-up or
- about the contextual relationship of the individual functions in relation to transparency, confidentiality, proper implementation of an interaction, where necessary, and not least
- about an assessment also of process and operator safety
- as well as about an indicative assessment of the environment of the other, comparable applications, in which the to be investigated application is being audited,
- and many more ..

In our self-reflection, we note, that this audit has spent a lot of time on a broad-based research, and that the documentations, that are available about the client GoldBug, include numerous references and links.

Dimensionen, die ein Audit adressieren kann. Ebenso sind die Standard-Methoden und seitens der Audit-Manuale vorgegebenen Implikationen anzuwenden.

Das Audit, wie hier durchgeführt und in den ersten beiden Kapiteln hergeleitet, soll nicht nur ein Code Review und die wesentlichen Funktionen der Applikation abdecken, sondern auch die wesentlichen Audit-Felder, Instrumente und Methoden der internationalen vorherrschenden IT-Audit-Manuale einbeziehen mit dem Ziel, eine größtmögliche Untersuchungsbreite zu erzielen.

Wie gesehen geht es dann dabei nicht nur

- um mathematische, kryptologische oder programmierte Funktionen insbesondere in einem Code-Review, sondern z.B. auch
- um eine Einschätzung hinsichtlich des Bewusstseins des Nutzers, Funktionen in der entsprechenden Ausgestaltung auch bewusst nutzen zu können, oder
- um den kontextuellen Zusammenhang der einzelnen Funktionen in Bezug zu Transparenz, Vertraulichkeit, korrekter Implementierung eines Zusammenspiels, wo notwendig, sowie nicht zuletzt
- um eine Beurteilung auch von Prozess- und Bedienersicherheit
- sowie um eine indikative Einschätzung des Umfeldes anderer, vergleichbarer Applikationen, in dem die zu auditierende Applikation untersucht wird,
- u.v.m..

In unserer Selbst-Reflexion stellen wir fest, dass dieses Audit viel Zeit mit einer breit angelegten Recherche verbracht hat; und die Dokumentationen, die über den Klienten GoldBug verfügbar sind, auch zahlreiche Verweise und Verlinkungen einbinden.

3.9.2   Selected method for studying and function reference

To examine the developmental activity of the application GoldBug, the project should be examined therefore in terms of the source code, the release notes and existing documents, which passages are to be considered for the now present audit.

Um die Entwicklungs-Aktivität der Applikation GoldBug zu untersuchen, soll das Projekt daher hinsichtlich des Qellcodes, der Veröffentlichungsnotizen („Release Notes") sowie der vorhandenen Dokumente untersucht werden, welche Passagen dazu für das

The chosen method is therefore a document analysis, which should relate to three areas:

nunmehr vorliegende Audit insbesondere berücksichtigt werden können. Die gewählte Methode ist also eine Dokumentenanalyse, die drei Bereiche betreffen soll:

This relates to the reflection of our own work as auditors: Have we included enough broad references?

Dieses betrifft die Reflexion unserer eigenen Arbeit als Auditoren: Haben wir genügend breit angelegte Referenzen eingebunden?

Likewise, should on this basis, the reflection of the developers of the application and the kernel examined, whether they indicate, that learning, reviews and audit reports of other applications or theoretical concepts from the literature have been included in the development.

Ebenso soll auf dieser Basis die Reflexion der Entwickler der Applikation und des Kernels untersucht werden, ob sie Hinweise geben, dass bei der Entwicklung Lernprozesse, Reviews und Audit-Reporte anderer Applikationen oder theoretischer Konzepte aus der Literatur einbezogen worden sind.

Finally, the existing audit reports and texts are used of the further comparable open source applications to evaluate their processes in terms of reviews, learning and creating a contextual environment.

Schließlich werden auch die bestehenden Audit-Reporte und Berichte zu den weiteren vergleichbaren quelloffenen Applikationen genutzt, um deren Prozesse hinsichtlich Reviews, Lernen und Herstellung eines Kontextbezuges einzuschätzen.

3.9.3 Conduction and findings of the examinations

As shown above, there are numerous reviews of GoldBug on the web (see above), which provide a first basis for further parts of an audit report. Moreover, in addition to an external review as well the processes of internal self-assessment by the developers shall be included:

Wie oben dargestellt, bestehen zahlreiche Reviews von GoldBug im Web (s.o.), die eine erste Grundlage für weitere Bereiche eines Audit-Berichtes bieten. Darüber hinaus ist neben externer Bewertung auch der Prozess der internen Selbstbewertung durch die Entwickler einzubeziehen:

The development of the GoldBug client shows a significant commitment in the sense of a research project. Both, the architecture of the kernel spot-on and each interface, Spot-On GUI as well as the here corresponding GoldBug GUI, are developed by the developers as a hobby in their free time. There are according to their statements on the websites no third financial resources available and the development is made possible by the investment of private time. The project test server should have been funded also by private funds.

Die Entwicklung des GoldBug-Klienten zeigt eine starke Ausrichtung im Sinne eines Forschungsprojektes. Sowohl die Architektur des Kernel Spot-On als auch beide Benutzeroberflächen Spot-On-GUI wie auch die hier betreffende GoldBug-GUI werden von den Entwicklern als Hobby in der Freizeit entwickelt. Es stehen nach deren Aussagen auf den Webseiten keine dritten finanziellen Mittel zur Verfügung und die Entwicklungen werden durch die Investition von privater Zeit ermöglicht. Der Projekt-Test-Server sei ebenso aus privaten Mitteln finanziert.

The source code has many existing standards implemented and also with newer ideas (and partly for the first time worldwide) taken much forward, to mention e.g.

Der Quellcode hat viele bestehende Standards implementiert und auch mit neueren Ideen wesentlich (und z.T. weltweit erstmalig) vorangebracht, zu nennen sind z.B.

- the magnet URI standard was based on cryptologic functions and values,
- Introduction of the concept of Callings for end-to-end secured (a)symmetrical communication,
- use of numerous solutions in terms of the key transport problem (Geminis, Instant Perfect Forward Secrecy, Repleo etc.)
- Implementation of Socialist Millionaire Process (SMP),
- encryption using the NTRU algorithm & ElGamal algorithm next to RSA,
- possibility of communication between users of different encryption algorithms (for example, RSA to ElGamal)
- Supply of ephemeral Forward Secrecy keys in the existing email-client of GoldBug,
- Chat via e-mail server (POPTASTIC)
- P2P-URL-network for a web search, the data will be encrypted and stored as it is not yet comparable,
- Groupchat based on symmetric encryption,
- Possibility of manual definition of end-to-end passphrases for encryption (and not only for an authentication function as within the SMP function)
- network-oriented examination method for decoding within the echo protocol to minimize metadata recordings,
- encrypted chat and file transfer via Bluetooth,
- and further, to name just a few innovations.

- der Magnet URI-Standard wurde bezogen auf kryptologische Funktionen und Werte,
- Einführung des Begriffs des Callings für Ende-zu-Ende abgesicherter (a)symmetrischer Kommunikation,
- Anwendung von zahlreichen Lösungen hinsichtlich des Schlüssel-Transport-Problems (Geminis, Instant Perfect Forward Secrecy, Repleo etc.),
- Implementierung des Socialist Millionaire Prozesses (SMP),
- Verschlüsselung mit dem NTRU Algorithmus & ElGamal Algorithmus neben RSA,
- Möglichkeit der Kommunikation zwischen Nutzern verschiedener Verschlüsselungsalgorithmen (z.B. RSA zu ElGamal),
- Bezug von ephemeralen Forward Secrecy Schlüsseln im vorhandenen E-Mail-Kienten von GoldBug,
- Chat über E-Mail-Server (POPTASTIC),
- P2P-URL-Netzwerk für eine Websuche, deren Daten verschlüsselt übertragen und gespeichert werden, wie es bislang nicht vergleichbar ist,
- Gruppenchat auf Basis symmetrischer Verschlüsselung,
- Möglichkeit der manuellen Definition von Ende-zu-Ende Passphrasen für eine Verschlüsselung (und nicht nur für eine Authentifizierungsfunktion wie bei der SMP Funktion),
- Netzwerk-orientierte Prüfungsverfahren zur Decodierung im Echo-Protokoll, um Metadaten-Aufzeichnungen zu minimieren,
- Verschlüsselter Chat und Dateitransfer über Bluetooth,
- und weiteres, um nur einige Innovationen zu nennen.

In addition to the innovations, the references to existing libraries, concepts and comparable models are sufficiently well referenced and documented, so it can be concluded, that the developers are trying to consider the state of the art relatively good and to implement the developments, that are not yet included in other clients, in an innovative way.

It can thus be concluded that the project development from GoldBug respectively the

Neben den Innovationen sind auch die Referenzen zu bestehenden Bibliotheken, Konzepten und Vergleichsmodellen ausreichend gut referenziert und dokumentiert, so dass geschlossen werden kann, dass die Entwickler versuchen, den State of the Art vergleichsweise gut zu berücksichtigen und die Entwicklungen, die in anderen Klienten nicht enthalten sind, innovativ zu implementieren.

Es kann somit geschlossen werden, dass die Projektentwicklung von GoldBug bzw. des

Spot-On kernel includes numerous references for market standards and innovation options. Thus, due to the range of functions within GoldBug, certainly further research is needed to expand the fields mentioned above and also to compare our review dimensions within special (respectively even dedicated) reports.

Spot-On-Kernels zahlreiche Referenzen zu Marktstandards und Innovations-Optionen einbezieht. So besteht aufgrund des Funktionsumfangs in GoldBug durchaus weiterer Forschungsbedarf, die oben genannten Felder und auch unsere Review-Dimensionen in Spezialreporten noch zu erweitern bzw. dediziert zu vergleichen.

We as auditors have us accordingly familiarized also with other similar open source applications - such as already presented above - and carried out a search for their audit reports: With the question of whether these have put out their feelers for some context variables.

Auch wir als Auditoren haben uns dementsprechend ebenso mit weiteren vergleichbaren quelloffenen Applikationen wie schon oben vorgestellt vertraut gemacht und auch eine Recherche zu deren Auditberichten durchgeführt: Mit der Fragestellung, ob auch diese ihre Fühler zu den Kontextvariablen ausstrecken.

Therefore should for the each said seven applications - our BIG SEVEN - also the following chart of audit metrics be created about conducted audit reports respectively therein referenced findings:

Daher soll für die jeweils genannten sieben Applikationen - unsere BIG SEVEN -, auch folgende Übersicht an erfolgten Audit-Reporten bzw. darin verwiesenen Findings als Audit-Metrics erstellt werden:

Table 31: Open Source Crypto Messenger Applications and their Review Reports

Logo	Application	Authors of Security Review Audits etc.	# of Findings	# of ext. refs/lit	Extent / # Pages
	Cryptocat	Thomas (2013).	1	5	1
		Wilcox (2013).	7	10	27
		Diquet et al. (2014).	17	13	35
		Green (2014) [Blog-Entry].	several.	12	1
	GoldBug	Edwards, Scott (Ed.) et al. (2014).	./.	50	50
		2014/2015: Reviews as given (aaO).	as given.	12	as given.
		2016: This Review & Audit.	as found.	see Lit.	as found.
	OTR+ XMPP	Usage-Study by Developer GoldBerg et al. (2008)	./.	./.	./.
		Green (2014) [Blog-Posting]	0	20	10
		Quarkslab SAS (2015)	14	5	40
	Retro Share	./.	./.	./.	0
	Signal	Bader et al. (2014)	several.	49	17
	SureSpot	./.	./.	./.	0
	Tox	Developer-Comment from „Ex-Contributor" (2014)	1	0	1

Source: Own collection and research, to be further extended.

Very few of the audit reports reflect references respectively comparisons, benchmarks or good-practice models specified in detail for other similarly open source, and thus comparable, messengers for the reader. Also not all audit reports refer to referencing literature; that are mostly not over a dozen citations.

Also for the variety of proprietary, non-open source Messengers such as Threema (Cnlab 2015) and further are security audits of so-called "peers" available, that supposedly may have looked through the closed source code. However, these are often only brief and consist of up to 10-15 pages (in the case of Threema even only one (!) text page) and thus remain just a formal confirmation, that a peer has seen parts of the application. An audit of a closed source crypto-application is not replicable and scientifically therefore not acceptable! It remains a Black-Box.

These - not open source applications and audits - should from our view be excluded for a professional involvement and a practical application, because "Cryptology" with "non-open source" is incompatible. Their auditor reports rather have a formal seal function for the marketing of non-open-source applications. Also the IT-media brings up from time to time and depending on the application also reports of non-open-source crypto messengers without naming corresponding open-source alternatives, or to point at the issue of non-accessible source code of such crypto applications.

Considering OTR merely as key exchange protocol or tube, and cryptocat as a created symmetric key chat room, seem RetroShare and Tox to have the greatest proximity to GoldBug with all its advanced security features. Although both have no audit report respectively OTR and CryptoCat as clients with a particularly long history have correspondingly different investigation reports, they should be renewed in order to include the recent developments in the market and to the standard. These reviews for OTR and CrypoCat are therefore more likely to be called bug fix reports or feasibility studies and should actually be repeated in the post-Snowden-time

Nur sehr wenige der Audit-Reporte beziehen Referenzen bzw. Vergleiche, Benchmarks oder good-practice-Modelle zu anderen ebenso quelloffenen und damit vergleichbaren Messengern für den Leser in entsprechender Ausführlichkeit mit ein. Nicht alle Audit-Berichte verweisen auch auf referenzierende Literaturangaben, die selten über ein Dutzend an Literaturangaben liegen.

Auch für die Vielzahl proprietärer, nicht-quelloffene Messenger wie z.B. Threema (Cnlab 2015) und weitere liegen Security-Audits von sogenannten „Peers" vor, die den geschlossenen Quellcode angeblich haben durchblicken dürfen. Diese sind jedoch oft nur kurz sind und umfassen bis maximal 10-15 Seiten (im Falle von Threema sogar nur eine (!) Text-Seite) und bleiben somit nur eine formale Bestätigung, dass ein Peer Teile der Applikation durchgesehen habe. Ein Audit einer nicht quelloffenen Crypto-Applikation ist nicht replizierbar und wissenschaftlich somit nicht haltbar! Es bleibt eine Black-Box.

Diese - nicht quelloffenen Applikationen und Audits - scheiden somit aus unserer Sicht für einen fachlichen Einbezug sowie eine praktische Anwendung aus, weil "Kryptologie" sich mit "nicht-quelloffen" nicht verträgt. Deren Auditorenberichte haben eher eine formale Siegelfunktion für das Marketing der nicht-quelloffenen Applikationen. Auch die IT-Medien lanchieren zeitweise und je nach Applikation ebenso Berichte von nicht-quelloffenen Crypto-Messengern ohne entsprechende quelloffene Alternativen zu benennen oder auch auf die Problematik nicht einsehbarer Quelltexte von diesen Crypto-Applikationen hinzuweisen.

Betrachtet man OTR lediglich als Schlüssel-Austausch-Röhre oder –Protokoll, und CryptoCat als einen mit symmetrischen Schlüsseln erstellten Chat-Raum, so scheinen RetroShare und Tox die größte Nähe zu GoldBug mit all ihren erweiterten Sicherheitsfunktionen zu haben. Auch wenn beide über keinen Audit-Bericht verfügen bzw. OTR und CryptoCat als Klienten mit besonders langer Historie entsprechend verschiedene Untersuchungsberichte aufweisen, sollten sie erneuert werden, um auch die neueren Entwicklungen am Markt und zum Standard einzubeziehen. Diese Reviews für OTR und CrypoCat sind daher eher als Bug-Fix-Reporte

- with the following angles:

oder Machbarkeitsstudien zu bezeichnen und müssten eigentlich in der Nach-Snowden-Zeit wiederholt werden - mit folgenden Blickwinkeln:

Regarding CryptoCat particular on the feasibility of the use of decentralized chat server and symmetric encryption (including the problem of transporting the key online); as well regarding OTR in particular the inclusion of asynchronous methods, the use also of other algorithms besides RSA and safety of plug-in solutions and the introduction of a standard to encrypt the host of plugins (e.g. regarding login key length or encryption of data to be stored on the hard disk);

Hinsichtlich CryptoCat insbesondere zur Praktikabilität der Nutzung dezentraler Chat-Server und symmetrischer Verschlüsselung (inkl. des Schlüsseltransportproblems); sowie hinsichtlich OTR insbesondere auf den Einbezug von asynchronen Methoden, der Anwendung auch von anderen Algorithmen neben RSA und der Sicherheit von Plugin-Lösungen und der Einführung eines Standards an Verschlüsselung beim Host des Plugins (z.B. Hinsichtlich Login-Schlüssellänge oder Verschlüsselung der Daten, die auf die Festplatte gespeichert werden sollen);

regarding RetroShare it is also desirable due to the long development time to include a comprehensive and current audit with context references (for example, to GoldBug).

hinsichtlich RetroShare ist es aufgrund der langen Entwicklerzeit ebenso wünschenswert aktuell ein umfassendes Audit mit Kontextreferenzen (z.B. zu GoldBug) einbeziehen zu können.

3.9.4 Evaluation of the results with regard to weaknesses, risks, potentials for improvements and strengths

Regarding the development of GoldBug, we have no reason to note or to recommend that more external contexts and references should be included. For our own audit, we tried by the appropriate analysis, derivation and the inclusion of other open-source applications to consider this ambition: to focus not isolated on one application alone.

Hinsichtlich der Entwicklung von GoldBug haben wir keinen Anlass, festzustellen oder zu empfehlen, dass mehr externe Kontexte und Referenzen einbezogen werden sollten. Für unser eigenes Audit haben wir durch die entsprechende Analye, Herleitung und den Einbezug der weiteren quelloffenen Applikationen versucht, diesen Anspruch umzusetzen: nicht isoliert auf eine Applikation allein zu fokussieren.

Table 32: Description of findings 3.09

#	Area	Description of the finding	Valuation Severity Category / Difficulty Level / Innovation & Improvement Class / Strength Dimension
	Weakness / Schwäche	./.	./.
	Risk / Risiko	./.	./.
	Potential for Improvement / Verbesserungspotential	./.	./.
3.09.4.A	Strength / Stärke	This Audit shows indicative references to other comparables Messengers	Medium.

3.9.5   Appraisal of good practices in comparison with other similar applications

In this partial section we now want to continue to make an assessment based on our research, how far the comparable BIG SEVEN Messengers include references and context variables and innovative developments.

In diesem Teil-Abschnitt wollen wir nun aufgrund unserer Recherchen weiterhin eine Einschätzung abgeben, in wie weit die vergleichbaren BIG SEVEN Messenger Referenzen und Kontextvariablen und innovative Entwicklungen einbeziehen.

Table 33: Indicative BIG SEVEN context references 3.09

Logo	Application	Comments
	Cryptocat	New development goal to offer also a desktop client next to the browser plugin. Addresses the goal to lead the market in comparision to XMPP.
	GoldBug	Good references to other libraries, integrated approach of new innovations. Development includes code review tickets in other projects.
	OTR+XMPP	OTR has a long history, development seems to be established or slowing down or even being stalled. Newer developments in encryption present a better approach (e.g. Perrin 2014).
	RetroShare	Includes a common learning within the development community.
	Signal	Tries to be innovative and establishes with many marketing references on the market.
	SureSpot	Shows a good practice and established model, though with less references to other developments.
	Tox	Does not solve needs of others and ignores external context variables due to internal co-developers references.

Consolidation of Inclusion of References

Konsolidierung der Einbezüge von Referenzen

The Messenger market appears in the community between the various development projects in our assessment of the development communities and their willingness to involve contexts and external references in their development, to be quite widely, partly fragmented and competitive:

Der Messenger Markt scheint in der Community zwischen den einzelnen Entwicklungsprojekten in unserer Einschätzung der Entwicklungsgemeinschaften und deren Bereitschaft, Kontexte und externe Referenzen in ihre Entwicklung einzubeziehen, durchaus sehr unterschiedlich, zum Teil auch fragmentiert und umkämpft zu sein:

Cryptography and app development has been very dominated by a few individual experts.

Kryptographie und die App-Entwicklung war bislang sehr von einzelnen wenigen Experten

The further community as multipliers wants to celebrate their developers and projects partly as their "Messiah". This means that the further end users are steered. Second, it must be noted, that a further established reputation propaganda is also dependent on the financial facilities of the respective projects.

Currently, in the era after the Snowden publications there are numerous crypto-messenger projects, that compete in particular for the non-open source field among each other and have appeared on the market.

Thus, also for the remaining open-source crypto messengers and their users, it is particularly important to consider critical messages also from non-specialists references, and also to make themselves on the way to learn in the different areas, to judge the relationships to the individual development projects themselves and to not have only the functioning or non-functioning of the application respectively the source code in the view.

So we also hope with the conduction of our audit to interest a broad audience, because in a few years, the brand name of the Crypto Messengers will be more present at the end-users and be judged by how much the applications are elaborated.

Three levels of internal Crypto-Wars

The much-quoted crypto war thus appears initially to take place by incorporating appropriate elaboration of the functions in the applications at the level of the development of crypto projects themselves.

For example: a browser plug-in or a mobile messenger is to be published as a desktop version or the encryption should be supplemented by other types of symmetric respectively asymmetric encryption.

Then it comes at a second level to the community of multipliers and cryptologic experts, who advocate for specific applications - or not - or choose to ignore or even let

dominiert. Die weitere Community als Multiplikatoren will ihre Entwickler und Projekte z.T. als ihren „Messias" feiern. Damit werden auch die weiteren End-Nutzer gesteuert. Zweitens muss festgehalten werden, dass eine festgestellte weitere Leumund-Propaganda auch von den finanziellen Ausstattungen der jeweiligen Projekte abhängig ist.

Derzeit in der Ära nach den Snowden-Veröffentlichungen gibt es zahlreiche Crypto-Messenger-Projekte, die insbesondere für den nicht-quelloffenen Bereich miteinander konkurrieren und auf dem Markt erschienen sind.

Somit zeigt sich auch für die verbleibenden quelloffenen Crypto-Messenger und deren Nutzer, dass es insbesondere wichtig ist, kritische Meldungen auch von fachfremden Referenzen zu berücksichtigen, und sich auch selbst auf den Weg zu machen, in den einzelnen Gebieten zu lernen, um die Zusammenhänge der einzelnen Entwicklungsprojekte selbst beurteilen zu können und nicht nur das Funktionieren oder Nicht-Funktionieren der Anwendung bzw. den Quellcode im Blick zu haben.

So hoffen wir auch mit der Durchführung unseres Audits eine breite Leserschaft zu interessieren, denn in wenigen Jahren werden die Markennamen der Crypto-Messenger auch bei den Endnutzern präsenter sein und danach beurteilt werden, wie sehr die Applikationen elaboriert sind.

Drei Ebenen des fachinternen Crypto-Wars

Der vielzitierte Crypto-War scheint also zunächst auch auf Ebene der Entwickler von Crypto-Projekten selbst stattzufinden, indem sie entsprechende Ausarbeitungen der Funktionen in die Applikationen einbauen.

Beispiel: Ein Browser-Plugin oder auch ein mobiler Messener soll auch als Desktop-Version veröffentlicht werden, oder die Verschlüsselung soll um weitere Arten von symmetrischer bzw. asymmetrischer Verschlüsselung ergänzt werden.

Sodann geht es auf einer zweiten Ebene um die Community der Multiplikatoren und kryptologischen Experten, die sich für bestimmte Applikationen aussprechen - oder

Wikipedia entries delete *). Here the expressions of opinion emerging in blog and mailing lists are to be distinguished from written documentaries, that have a scientific or popular-scientific descriptive, but also comparative claim.

nicht - oder diese ignorieren oder gar Wikipedia-Einträge wieder löschen lassen*). Hier sind die in Blog und Mailinglists auftauchenden Meinungsäußerungen zu unterscheiden von verschriftlichen Dokumentationen, die einem wissenschaftlichen oder populär-wissenschaftlich beschreibenden, aber auch vergleichenden Anspruch haben.

*) In the case of GoldBug is e.g. the German-language Wikipedia entry proposed to extinction its existence by the user "Hanno" (aka Hanno B.) in the third year (compare also Teets in regard of this at Twitter 01/2016: https://twitter.com/GoldBugIM/status/694263996044689408, https://twitter.com/GoldBugIM/ status/693440868271939584, https://twitter.com/GoldBugIM/ status/689540775416369153).
As arguments were raised the in the Wikipedia often used, but very vague categories of "relevance" and "writing style" (related to two quoted sentences). Behind the user is a free IT journalist with cryptologic school knowledge, which would have been perfectly able to improve the wikipedia entry or to evaluate the functions of GoldBug professionally even in a separate post. After one week the three years existing entry has been deleted, a day later, however, the text page was acquired in another wiki.

*) Im Falle von GoldBug ist z.B. der deutschsprachige Wikipedia-Eintrag im dritten Jahr seiner Existenz durch den Nutzer „Hanno" (aka Hanno B.) zur Löschung vorgeschlagen worden (vgl. auch Teets dazu bei Twitter 01/2016: https://twitter.com/GoldBugIM/status/694263996044689408, https://twitter.com/GoldBugIM/ status/693440868271939584, https://twitter.com/GoldBugIM/ status/689540775416369153).
Als Argumente wurden die in der Wikipedia oftmals genutzten, aber sehr schwammigen Kategorien der „Relevanz" und des „Schreibstils" (festgemacht an zwei zitierten Sätzen) vorgebracht. Hinter dem Nutzer steht ein freier IT-Journalist mit kryptologischer Ausbildung, der durchaus in der Lage gewesen wäre, den Eintrag anzupassen oder die Funktionen von GoldBug fachlich sogar in einem eigenen Beitrag zu beurteilen. Nach einer Woche wurde der drei Jahre bestehende Eintrag gelöscht, einen Tag später war die Textseite jedoch in einem anderen Wiki übernommen worden.

URL: http://marjorie-wiki.de/wiki/GoldBug_(Instant_Messenger)

URL: http://marjorie-wiki.de/wiki/GoldBug_(Instant_Messenger)

From a scientific perspective, we feel this is less constructive in regard of a contribution to the accumulation of knowledge, and when cryptologists propose cryptologic tools to extinction, we consider this not only scientifically obsolete, but also as writing experts we see this reserved to a so-called bias. Is GoldBug on the way to be a "Sacre du Printemps"? It therefore remains only to suggest, that new generations of learners conduct the comparative analysis with more commitment and from a neutral point of view, than to deliver themselves to a destruction, based on whatever strategic motives.

Aus wissenschaftlicher Sicht halten wir dieses für wenig konstruktiv, um zu der Wissensmehrung beizutragen, und, wenn Kryptologen kryptologische Werkzeuge zur Löschung vorschlagen, halten wir diese nicht nur wissenschaftlich für obsolet, sondern auch als schreibende Fachexperten einem sog. Bias vorbehalten. Ist GoldBug auf dem Weg ein "sacre du printemps" zu werden? Es bleibt daher nur zu vermuten, dass neue Generationen an Lernenden die vergleichende Analyse mit mehr Engagement und aus einem neutraleren Blickwinkel umsetzen, als sich einer aus welchen Motiven auch immer strategischen Destruktion ausliefern.

Thirdly, the education process in a few years will have transported knowledge also to the user level, so that anyone can evaluate the technology of encryption over the Internet (and possibly even learned to compile it under Linux). Many dedicated participants and speakers on Crypto-Parties contribute to the BIG SEVEN Messengers to be tried in practice; that one finds an interested counterpart for a test. First locally, then remotely.

Drittens schließlich wird der Bildungsprozess in wenigen Jahren auch das Wissen auf Nutzerebene transportiert haben, so dass auch jedermann diese Technologie der Verschlüsselung über das Internet beurteilen kann (und ggf. auch selbst unter Linux kompilieren erlernt). Viele engagierte Teilnehmer und Referenten auf Crypto-Parties tragen dazu bei, dass die BIG SEVEN Messenger in der Praxis ausprobiert werden, man ein interessiertes Gegenpart zum Testen findet. Zunächst vor Ort, sodann remote.

It is therefore an object, not to ignore the modern functional developments, and it remains nonsense, to insinuate other plaintext scandals or to delete accumulation of

Es ist daher Ziel, die modernen Funktions-Entwicklungen nicht zu ignorieren, und es bleibt Unsinn, anderen Plaintext-Skandale zu inzenieren oder Wissensmehrung zu löschen, -

knowledge - in the hope, that the popularization of cryptologic knowledge would develop slower or that the knowledge would lose quality or respectively, that other applications would have more time for qualitative developments, such as the following case studies illustrate. Only a broad public discussion helps, when supposed experts share their knowledge exclusively in alleged expert circles. We are on the way, that cryptologic expertise will be commonplace. Also, this shows still an indicator of the digital division of our society.

in der Hoffnung, dass sich die Popularisierung des kryptologischen Wissens dadurch langsamer entwickele oder das Wissen an Qualität verliere bzw. andere Applikationen mehr Zeit für qualitative Entwicklungen hätten, wie die folgenden Fallbeispiele verdeutlichen. Nur eine breite öffentliche Diskussion hilft, wenn vermeintliche Experten ihr Wissen ausschließlich in vermeintlichen Experten-Zirkeln teilen wollen. Wir sind auf dem Weg, dass kryptologisches Know-How alltäglich wird. Auch dieses bezeichnet noch einen Indikator der digitalen Spaltung unserer Gesellschaft.

Influence of the public Crypto-Wars on the internal Crypto-War

Einfluss des öffentlichen Crypto-Wars auf den fach-internen Crypto-War

With these three stages of the crypto-war the crypto-war is therefore initially considered as an internal self-destruction of the individual projects, which would not be necessary. The external crypto-war, which is defined by privacy advocates and in political discussions, may perhaps also influence the internal development of the crypto-projects, if (induced) funds and marketing options are made available for the projects.

Mit diesen drei Stufen des Crypto-Wars wird der Crypto-War also zunächst einmal als interne Selbstzerfleischung der Einzelprojekte betrachtet, die gar nicht notwendig wäre. Der externe Crypto-War, der sich durch Datenschützer und in politischen Diskussionen definiert, mag vielleicht auch Einfluss auf die internen Entwicklungen der Crypto-Projekte nehmen, indem den Projekten Gelder und Marketing-Optionen zur Verfügung gestellt werden.

It is therefore necessary to look closely each, why a corresponding crypto solution, reporting or community steering in the public perception exists or is advertised.

Es ist daher jeweils genau zu schauen, warum eine entsprechende Crypto-Lösung, Berichterstattung oder auch Community-Steuerung in der öffentlichen Wahrnehmung besteht oder beworben wird.

BIG SEVEN Crypto-Parties as a decentralized solution out of the Crypto-War

BIG-SEVEN Crypto-Parties als dezentraler Lösungsansatz aus dem Crypto-War

From our recommendation decentralized crypto-parties, organized by many individual people, are one ideal way to bring up contextual references: if these, for example, introduce at the beginning here said BIG SEVEN Messengers and then present the participants not only the individual applications and encryption methods, but also explain the available functions and methods, and how it can be learned, how these can be assessed in comparison to other encryption tools by themselves.

Aus unserer Empfehlung heraus sind dezentrale, durch viele individuelle Personen organisierte Crypto-Parties eine ideale Methode, um kontextuelle Referenzen zu thematisieren: wenn diese zu Beginn z.B. die hier genannten BIG SEVEN Messenger vorstellen und sodann den Teilnehmer nicht nur die einzelnen Applikationen und Verschlüsselungsverfahren vorstellen, sondern auch die vorhandenen Funktionen erläutern und Methoden mitgeben, wie man diese im Vergleich zu anderen Verschlüsselungs-Werkzeugen selbst beurteilen lernt.

Crypto-parties should not have the aim to serve one application, or to understand encryption methods, but the learning goal is to

Crypto-Parties sollten daher nicht das Ziel haben, eine Applikation bedienen zu können, oder Verschlüsselungsverfahren zu verstehen,

learn methods for comparative evaluation in the crypto functions!

sondern das Lernziel ist, in den Crypto-Funktionen Methoden zur vergleichenden Beurteilung zu erlernen!

In further course of time, while there may be a consolidation that e.g. all crypto applications have installed a SMP process, and all applications hold in addition to chat an e-mail client, or enable chat via e-mail-server, and hold native encryption without plug-ins - because this denotes precisely the current exchange and learning processes in the community, that this audit section wants to take also in the viewing angle.

Im weiteren Zeitverlauf mag es zwar eine Konsolidierung geben, dass z.B. alle Crypto-Applikationen einen SMP-Prozess eingebaut haben, alle Applikationen neben Chat auch einen E-Mail-Klienten vorhalten oder Chat über E-Mail-Server ermöglichen sowie native Verschlüsselung ohne Plug-Ins vorhalten - denn dieses bezeichnet ja gerade die aktuellen Austausch- und Lernprozesse in der Community, die dieser Audit-Abschnitt ebenso in den Blickwinkel nehmen will.

Examples regarding of attempts of confidence shocks and marketing strategies for some crypto messenger projects

Beispiele an Versuchen hinsichtlich Vertrauenserschütterungen und Marketingstrategien bei einigen Crypto-Messenger-Projekten

Therefore the following examples may be documented as examples for the current behavior in the community:

Für das derzeitige Gebaren in der Community seien daher folgende Beispiele exemplarisch dokumentiert:

Case: Signal & Co.

An example is given with the Twitter exchange between the on the server non-open source (and therefore here not considered) Messenger Telegram and the (also only with a central server available) Messenger Signal.

Ein Exempel statuiert der Twitter-Austausch zwischen dem im Server nicht quelloffenen (und daher hier nicht berücksichtigten Messenger) Telegram und dem (ebenso nur mit einem zentralen Server verfügbaren) Messenger Signal.

A first message came from Signal Messenger over their account OpenWhisperSystems, in which it was informed, that all messages from Telegram would be stored in plaintext on the Telegram server (which is not really open source) and thus the supplier can eavesdrop on it!

Eine erste Meldung kam vom Signal-Messenger im Account Openwhisperystems, in der mitgeteilt wurde, dass alle Nachrichten von Telegram im Plaintext auf dem Telegramserver (der ja nicht quelloffen ist) gespeichert würden und somit dem Anbieter zur Verfügung stünden!

This message has been resent from the user "Ptacek" as a retweet and repeated again as an own statement. Also this message was again forwarded to hundreds of times by his readers to others.

Diese Meldung wurde dann vom Nutzer „Ptacek" als Re-tweet erneut gesendet und nochmals wiederholt als seine eigene Aussage. Auch diese Nachricht wurde hundertfach von seinen Leser wiederum an andere weitergeleitet.

Then commented Edward Snowden, who is also praising the Signal Messenger as the only true Messenger on their website (see also remarks in a previous section), not the original message of OpenWhisperSystems, but the message from the user "Ptacek".

Sodann kommentierte Edward Snowden, der auf der Webseite auch den Signal Messenger als den einzig wahren Messenger preist (s.a Ausführungen in einem vorherigen Abschnitt), nicht etwa die Originalmeldung von Openwhispersystems, sondern die Nachricht vom Nutzer „Ptacek".

Snowden was then forwarded more than thousand times by his readers, among others, also by the other alleged followers and heroes of the crypto-scene, possibly without questioning the origin and the strategic implication of the message. Because: It makes a difference, whether it is a descriptive statement, that a server save messages, or whether it is a statement, that has been launched as an attributed weakness by competitors.

Snowden wurde sodann über tausendmal von seinen Leser weitergeleitet, u.a. auch von den weiteren vermeintlichen Jüngern und Helden der Cryptoszene, ggf. ohne den Ursprung und die strategische Implikation der Message zu hinterfragen. Denn: Es macht ein Unterschied, ob es eine deskriptive Aussage ist, ein Server speichere Nachrichten, oder ob es eine Aussage ist, die als attribuierte Schwäche von der Konkurrenz lanchiert wird.

https://twitter.com/whispersystems/status/678036048815906818
Open Whisper Systems @whispersystems Dec 19
@CTZN5 @timcameronryan By default Telegram stores the plaintext of every message every user has ever sent or received on their server.

Thomas H. Ptacek Retweeted
https://twitter.com/tqbf/status/678065993587945472
Thomas H. Ptacek @tqbf Dec 19 Austin, Chicago
By default Telegram stores the PLAINTEXT of EVERY MESSAGE every user has ever sent or received on THEIR SERVER.

https://twitter.com/Snowden/status/678271881242374144
Jacob Appelbaum and 1 other Retweeted
Edward SnowdenVerified account @Snowden 16h16 hours ago
Edward Snowden Retweeted Thomas H. Ptacek
I respect @durov, but Ptacek is right: @telegram's defaults are dangerous. Without a major update, it's unsafe.

Edward Snowden added,
Thomas H. Ptacek @tqbf
By default Telegram stores the PLAINTEXT of EVERY MESSAGE every user has ever sent or received on THEIR SERVER.
1,092 retweets 836 likes
Reply Retweet 1.1K
Like 836

The background is that the messenger Telegram was represented at that time very much in the media, and supposed to have been used by terrorists. In addition it is developed in Germany by a Russian, and thus the users are not in the U.S. access.

Hintergrund ist, dass der Messenger Telegram zu dieser Zeit sehr stark in den Medien vertreten war, und angeblich von Terroristen genutzt worden sein soll. Zudem wird er in Deutschland von einem Russen entwickelt und somit sind die Nutzer nicht im US-amerikanischen Zugriff.

Through clever retweeting and forwarding of tweets as rumors and personal views, the initiator of the message and its underlying objective is obscured. The messenger Signal possibly wanted the messenger Telegram attributing a confidentiality gap, so it was not considered as a direct attack, but intermediate multipliers have been used. One must not have a common plot suspect behind, but it shows on the one hand quite unfriendly marketing effects, that will redound to alleged vulnerabilities in other applications for detriment, and secondly, on the other hand also shows the role of supposed experts, who can be more interpreted as community-strategists.

Would this mean, that chats, that do not run on American servers, are particularly safe? And that now an envy-debate among the messenger itselves is created, if they are "terrorist"-approved (Stahl 2016)? and then, that the stakeholders have sacrificed their neutral technical expertise of membership in strategic agreements?

Nevertheless: Telegram provides good reasons to believe, that something is wrong with the faith in a non-open source messenger. An open source Messenger requires no faith, because it is verifiable. Nevertheless, we want here only to briefly touch on this non-open source messenger:

The Telegram messenger explains in its FAQ section of the website, for example, that the client-to-server connection is regularly not encrypted, and also the end-to-end client-to-client encryption is explained, in which a symmetric key over the Diffie-Hellmann method (EDH) is sent.

The users should compare the symmetrical end-to-end encryption passphrase on the smartphone with the same on the phone of a friend. If it is the same, one could be sure, that the connection is secret – so the technical documentation according to the webstite. But this is not the case, because the criterion is that the passphrase is not known with third parties, such as Telegram.

Durch geschicktes Re-Tweeten und weiterleiten von Tweets, also Gerüchten und persönlichen Ansichten, wird der Initiator der Nachricht und seine dahinterstehende Absicht verschleiert. Der Messenger Signal wollte dem Messenger Telegram ggf. eine Vertraulichkeitslücke attribuieren, damit es nicht als direkter Angriff gewertet wurde, sind intermediäre Multiplikatoren genutzt worden. Man muss kein gemeinsames Komplott dahinter vermuten, aber es zeigt zum einen durchaus die unfreundliche Marketingeffekte, die mit vermeintlichen Sicherheitslücken anderer Applikationen zum Schaden gereichen sollen und zum anderen zeigt es auch die Rolle der vermeintlichen Fachexperten, die sich mehr als Community-Strategen deuten lassen.

Denn hiesse dieses, dass Chats, die nicht über amerikanische Server laufen, besonders sicher sind? Und, dass inzwischen eine Neid-Debatte der Messenger untereinander entstanden ist, wenn sie "Terrorist"-approved (Stahl 2016) sind? und sodann, dass die handelnden Akteure ihre neutrale Fachexpertise einer Mitgliedschaft in strategischen Absprachen geopfert haben?

Nichtsdesto trotz: Telegram liefert gute Gründe, anzunehmen, dass etwas nicht in Ordnung ist mit dem Vertrauen in einen nicht-quelloffenen Messenger. Ein quelloffener Messenger benötigt kein Vertrauen, weil es nachprüfbar ist. Dennoch wollen wir hier nur kurz auf den nicht-quelloffenen Messenger eingehen:

Der Telegram Messenger erläutert in seinen FAQ der Webseite beispielsweise die Client-zu-Server Verbindung, die regulär nicht verschlüsselt ist, und auch die Ende-zu-Ende Client-zu-Client Verschlüsselung, bei dem ein symmetrischer Schlüssel über das Diffie-Hellmann-Verfahren (EDH) gesandt wird.

Die Nutzer mögen ihre symmetrische Ende-zu-Ende Verschlüsselungs-Passphrase auf dem Smartphone vergleichen mit demselben auf dem Telefon des Freundes. Wenn sie dieselbe sei, könne man sicher sein, dass die Verbindung geheim sei – so die technische Erläuterung der Webseitendokumentation. Dieses ist aber mit Nichten der Fall, denn das Kriterium ist, dass die Passphrase nicht bei Dritten, wie Telegram, bekannt sei.

In addition, the user has no way to manually edit the end-to-end encrypting passphrase or to determine it.
The transmission protocols in Telegram and the implementation of the Diffie-Hellman method is not revisable and justified by open-source code.
In addition, the connection is created via a chat server, which is also not open-source.

The public key of the asymmetric encryption for the transfer of the symmetric key is at this messenger also not reviewable. Also is not explained, where the private key is stored (at the company or on the telephone of the user). Likewise, nothing is stated about the encryption respectively the protection of the private key for EDH.

It is therefore to be regarded as highly critical, that Telegram should have according to own words no copy of the symmetric key available.

Also, the end-to-end encryption is a permanent one, which the user therefore cannot like in GoldBug renew instantly – by means of "Instant Perfect Forward Secrecy" (IPFS) at any time.
A manual definition and immediate renewability of symmetric keys in GoldBug are a unique proposition!

Telegram reminds one of the sleight of shell game gamblers on holiday: compare both keys and assume that you're safe. But whether Telegram has a copy of the between two friends in secret shared key, remains the secret of the not open-source protocol and not open-source chat server. On the contrary, the above indications suggest, that Telegram could receive a copy of the key and the user is not really free, to manually create a secret, symmetric passphrase and to share it with a friend in secret.

Willfully foist an encrypting messenger a plaintext affair as matter-of-fact-presumption, as addressed by Signal to Telegram, can in itself be deemed a strategic communication, such as to communicate a farmer's milk would be pure hydrogen cyanide.

Zudem hat der Nutzer keine Möglichkeit, die Ende-zu-Ende-verschlüsselnde Passphrase manuell selbst zu edieren oder zu bestimmen.
Die Übertragungsprotokolle bei Telegram und die Implementierung des Diffie-Hellman Verfahrens ist nicht bekannt und durch quelloffenen Code belegt.
Zudem geht die Verbindung über einen Chat-Server, der ebenso nicht quelloffen ist.

Der öffentliche Schlüssel aus der asymmetrischen Verschlüsselung für den Transfer des symmetrischen Schlüssels ist bei diesem Messenger ebenso nicht einsehbar. Ebenso wird nicht erläutert, wo der private Schlüssel abgelegt ist (beim Anbieter oder auf dem Telefon des Nutzers). Ebenso wird keine Aussage getroffen über die Verschlüsselung bzw. den Schutz des privaten Schlüssels für EDH.

Es ist daher als höchst kritisch zu beurteilen, dass Telegram nach eigenen Angaben angeblich keine Kopie des symmetrischen Schlüssels zur Verfügung habe.

Auch ist die Ende-zu-Ende Verschlüsselung eine permanente, die der Nutzer also nicht „instant" wie bei GoldBug mittels „Instant Perfect Forward Secrecy" (IPFS) jederzeit erneuern kann.
Eine manuelle Definition und die sofortige Erneuerbarkeit der symmetrischen Schlüssel in GoldBug sind ein Alleinstellungsmerkmal!

Telegram erinnert einen an die Taschenspielertricks der Hütchenspieler im Urlaub: Vergleiche beide Schlüssel und nehme an, dass Du sicher bist. Aber ob Telegram eine Kopie des zwischen zwei Freunden im Geheimen geteilten Schlüssels hat, bleibt das Geheimnis des nicht quelloffenen Protokolls und nicht quelloffenen Chat-Servers. Im Gegenteil sprechen die oben genannten Indizien dafür, dass Telegram eine Kopie des Schlüssels erhalten könnte und der Nutzer nicht wirklich frei ist, eine geheime, symmetrische Passphrase manuell zu erstellen und mit einem Freund im Geheimen zu teilen.

Einem verschlüsselnden Messenger jedoch mutwillig eine Plaintext-Affäre als Tatsachen-Vermutung unterzujubeln, wie von Signal an Telegram adressiert, kann schon als eine strategische Kommunikation gewertet werden, wie einem Landwirt mitzuteilen, seine Milch sei pure Blausäure.

Case: CryptoCat & Enigmail

Even if such plaintext-gaps may occur, as with Enigmail - where it was over 10 years not discovered that the BCC mails are not encrypted (Scherschel 2014), or as in CryptoCat where certain cryptographic functions have not been properly implemented (the Group Chat was decipherable (Thomas 2013)! and also the authentication model was inadequate (Diquet 2014)) - but it is rather the aggressiveness with that here strategy and policy is translated and must be accordingly assessed and considered.

Dealing with code improvements in neighboring projects is here in Signal used for pure strategic marketing purposes and apparently not claimed to conduct in the developer community something like "common assistance". Many developers are highly individualized people, who think with the point input by the return-key at the end of their source-code sentence to define the world very powerful.

Auch wenn solche Plaintextlücken vorkommen können - wie bei Enigmail, wo über 10 Jahre nicht festgestellt wurde, dass die BCC-Mails gar nicht verschlüsselt sind (Scherschel 2014), oder wie bei CryptoCat, wo bestimmte kryptographische Funktionen nicht richtig implementiert wurden (der GroupChat war entschlüsselbar (Thomas 2013)! und auch das Authentifizierungsmodell war unzureichend (Diquet 2014)) - ist es doch vielmehr die Aggressivität mit der hier Strategie und Politik umgesetzt werden und dementsprechend auch bewertet und berücksichtigt werden müssen.

Der Umgang mit Codeverbesserungen bei Nachbarprojekten wird hier bei Signal zu reinen strategischen Marketingzwecken benutzt und augenscheinlich nicht vorgetragen, um in der Entwicklergemeinde gemeinsam "Amtshilfe" zu betreiben. Viele Entwickler sind hochgradig individualisierte Personen, die mit der Punkt-Eingabe durch die Returntaste am Ende ihres Quellcode-Satzes meinen, die Welt sehr mächtig zu definieren.

Example: RetroShare

Many users rise the question, whether the data transfer of the messenger RetroShare, which is predominantly oriented to FileSharing, is secure: No, it should be not, because each file, respectively chunk of a file, that is passed through a friend, shows each node the hash of the file, so state even the developers in its internal community.
Since the file search is working over this hash, each file, that is passed over my own node, has to be regarded as critical (in the sense of questionable) and identifiable.

Viele Nutzer fragen, ob der Datei-Transfer des vorwiegend auf FileSharing ausgerichteten Messengers RetroShare sicher sei: Nein, sei es nicht, denn jede Datei bzw. Chunk einer Datei, die durch einen Freund geleitet wird, zeige jedem Knotenpunkt den Hash der Datei an, so die Entwickler selbst in ihren internen Forenbeiträgen.
Da die Dateisuche über diesen Hash funktioniert, ist jede Datei kritisch (im Sinne von: zu hinterfragen) und identifizierbar, die über meinen eigenen Kontenpunkt geleitet wird.

Likewise, the chat applications, that use only a central server, could be assessed in this regard as potentially unsafe. Remain in this consideration therefore only OTR-XMPP-server, GoldBug, CryptoCat and Tox, while OTR is not designed for file-transfer respectively file-sharing and XMPP-servers were not originally designed for continuous end-to-end encryption.

Ebenso sind die Chat-Applikationen in dieser Hinsicht als potentiell unsicher einzuschätzen, die nur einen zentralen Server nutzen. Bleiben in dieser Betrachtung also nur OTR-XMPP Server, GoldBug, Cryptocat und Tox übrig, wobei OTR nicht für Dateiübertragung bzw. Filesharing ausgelegt ist und XMPP Server nicht für durchgehende Ende-zu-Ende Verschlüsselung ursprünglich designed wurden.

Case: Tox Messenger

Socially responsible cooperation amongst projects should be fostered by a successful crypto project and not be mistaken for strategic alliance agreements in the multipliers community, that can often also have financial backgrounds.

So was also the criticism of the Co-Developer meant (Contributor 2014), who left the main developer of the project of Tox, because he refused to implement certain innovations and security enhancements.

If it were even deeper scientific analyses in addition to our indicative documented examples, one would possibly come to the conclusion, that only three out of our BIG SEVEN Messengers are friendly to each other involved in an extended community: RetroShare-, Tox and GoldBug developers are also on the road in other context-projects, to fix bugs, to provide each other mutual assistance, and jointly bring the projects and their own forward.

Although many developers are active in numerous sub-projects in the OTR-XMPP community, is the willingness to deal with anything other than OTR and XMPP is yet to be assessed for many especially in this community rather than low. OTR can not be regarded as savior for the security questions, that the hosts of this plugin can not standardize in a common response despite various manifest attempts (Saint-Andre 2014, Schmaus 2016). Possibly one must then also take away no longer compliant clients the XMPP status, or establish a new brand like "NTRU-XMPP", to guarantee native encryption, or find an account solution in the server programming, that throws off unencrypted transfers and does not allow a connection of unencrypted transfers (and also requires password lengths and key sizes as the minimum standard for a NTRU-XMPP).

Case: CryptoCat & OTR-XMPP

Then also posted the CryptoCat developers regarding XMPP a message, that is likely to be understood as an attack: that he was preparing a development to see "Pidgin dead soon":

sehen:

---

https://twitter.com/kaepora/status/670725803404075008
Nadim Kobeïssi @kaepora
Cryptocat rewrite is native desktop client, no web, no mobile. Uses Axolotl, has buddy lists.
Goal: kill Pidgin.

The succinctness of this message may not just the 140-character limit to be owed by Twitter, but each message is indeed a matter of information about one's own self-image - and also on the possibly rightly so expressed and in part above described serious problems of OTR-XMPP-encryption.

Die Prägnanz dieser Nachricht mag nicht nur dem 140-Zeichen Limit von Twitter geschuldet sein, sondern jede Nachricht gibt ja auch eine Selbstauskunft über das eigene Selbstverständnis – wie auch über die ggf. zu Recht damit ausgedrückten und z.T. oben beschriebenen ernsthaften Probleme von OTR-XMPP Verschlüsselung.

Our statement:

All may have given their valid contribution and in the professional world and in community meeting also all want to receive honor - and finally all somehow have to finance. But our recommendation is to readers and end-users, to recognize the critics of the glorified, and the strategic relationships within the scene and funded marketing better - and possibly to make even better a bow around the all-too-familiar faces of the scene:

Es mögen alle ihren validen Beitrag geleistet haben und in der Fachwelt und auf Community-Treffen auch Ehre erhalten wollen und sich schließlich auch irgendwie finanzieren müssen, dennoch ist unsere Empfehlung an die Leser und Endnutzer, die Kritiker der Glorifizierten und auch die strategischen Zusammenhänge der Szene und des finanzierten Marketings besser zu erkennen - und um die allzu-bekannten Gesichter der Szene ggf. sogar besser einen Bogen zu machen:

It must not at every IT-community-meeting speak a supposed "Star", but unknown experts, that make a technical contribution, or persons, which are critical to existing systems, procedures, or strategic and financial contexts, should be payed much more attention.

Es muss nicht auf jedem Treffen von IT-Interessierten ein vermeintlicher "Star" referieren, sondern unbekannte Fachexperten, die einen fachlichen Beitrag leisten, oder Personen, die Kritik an bestehenden Systemen, Prozeduren oder strategischen und finanziellen Zusammenhängen üben, wäre viel mehr Beachtung zu schenken.

Activists, who need a stage, and have not been known from their technical comparative writings and are only known from the stage, are to be regarded as critical, when they promote their messages.

Aktivisten, die eine Bühne brauchen und die auch nur von der Bühne her und nicht ihren fachlich vergleichenden Schriftstücken her bekannt sind, sind kritisch zu sehen, wenn sie ihre Botschaft preisen.

It appears currently that with mutual accusations of vulnerabilities the community should be frightened in order to damage the image of individual applications.

Es zeigt sich derzeit, dass mit gegenseitigen Vorwürfen von Sicherheitslücken die Community aufgeschreckt werden soll, um das Image einzelner Applikationen zu beschädigen.

One conclusion is, that there should be a *process of education and learning* for each participant in order not to be dependent on so-called experts and multipliers.

Eine Schlussfolgerung ist, dass es einen *Prozess der Bildung/des Lernens* bei einem jeden Teilnehmer geben sollte, um nicht von sogenannten Experten und Multiplikatoren abhängig zu sein.

It therefore seems to be more than necessary, that every user can make professional decisions for or against an encryption solution independently and with appropriate knowledge and can recognize strategic marketing initiatives - to become more independent of multipliers and so-called experts within crypto.

Ideally, everyone should test several alternative applications and make their own image by investing the own time in reading the manuals and audit-reports of the applications, as we have undergone this process for documenting our findings also time-consuming during the analysis.

It depends on the in part easily recognizable attitude, that an expert member show in thier paper about crypto solutions for a community, whether it is a benevolent and balanced teaching or in the malicious sense represents a burning criticism without comparisons and constructive solution perspectives. Just to offer own assistance in what is criticized, should still be commendable.

Also speakers on a crypto-party are therefore to provide logically always the question of what further functions, encryption types and alternative messenger they have now not presented, are even not sufficiently familiar with or why they rated a tool as insufficient - respectively why not a focus on open-source processes is placed.

A crypto-party should be in our view "BIG SEVEN APPROVED", that is, therefore to consider all the above-identified open-source applications at an initial course to exploratory involve the participants in learnings about the different configurations and functions.

Other auditors, we would like to encourage, to also create references to other applications, if they are allowed to write independently and without financial loss for an audit.

Es scheint somit mehr als erforderlich zu sein, dass jeder Nutzer fachliche Entscheidungen für oder gegen eine Verschlüsselungslösung selbständig und mit entsprechendem Wissen treffen kann sowie auch strategische Marketinginitiativen erkennen lernt – um von Multiplikatoren und sogenannten Fachexperten auf dem Crypto-Gebiet unabhängiger zu werden.

Idealerweise sollte jeder mehrere alternative Applikation austesten und sich sein eigenes Bild machen, indem die eigene Zeit auch darin investiert wird, die Manuale und Audit-Berichte zu den Applikationen zu lesen, so wie wir den Prozess für die Dokumentation unserer Findings ebenso zeitintensiv während der Analysen durchlaufen haben.

Es kommt auf die z.T. leicht erkennbare Haltung an, die ein Experten-Mitglied bei seinem Referat über Krypto-Lösungen für eine Community an den Tag legt, ob es eine wohlwollende und ausgewogene Didaktik oder eine im böswilligen Sinn zündelnde Kritik ohne Vergleiche und konstruktive Lösungsperspektiven darstellt. Einfach mal die eigene Mithilfe anzubieten bei dem, was man kritisiert, sollte anerkennenswert bleiben.

Auch einem Referenten auf einer Crypto-Party ist daher folgerichtig immer die Frage zu stellen, welche weiteren Funktionen, Verschlüsselungsarten und alternativen Messenger er jetzt nicht genannt hat, selbst nicht ausreichend kennt oder warum er sie als nicht ausreichend bewertet bzw. warum ggf. ein Schwerpunkt auf nicht quelloffene Prozesse gelegt wird.

Eine Crypto-Party sollte daher aus unserer Sicht „BIG SEVEN APPROVED" sein, d.h. also alle die oben identifizierten quelloffenen Applikationen bei einer Einführungs- veranstaltung berücksichtigen, um die Teilnehmer an den unterschiedlichen Ausgestaltungen und Funktionen explorativ in das Lernen einzubeziehen.

Andere Auditoren möchten wir ermuntern, ebenso auch Referenzen zu anderen Applikationen zu erstellen, wenn sie denn unabhängig und ohne finanzielle Einbußen für ein Audit schreiben dürfen.

Table 34: Good Practice Insights # 09

Good Practice Insight # 09	
with GoldBug Multi-Encrypting Communication Suite	
Case	I have now tried different applications. Although the user interface is habituation needy in any program, I want to use the product for my safety, which is regarding the safety orientation modern and technically excellent. Where can I get more information about other applications and their technical quality approach? *Ich habe inzwischen verschiedene Applikationen ausprobiert. Auch wenn die Benutzeroberfläche in jedem Programm gewöhnungsbedürftig ist, möchte ich für meine Sicherheit das Produkt nutzen, das hinsichtlich Sicherheitsorientierung modern und technisch excellent ist. Wo kann ich von anderen Programmen mehr Informationen über technische Qualität erhalten?*
Solution	Each program offers on the website numerous information. Some applications also have more in-depth instructions for encryption and security aspects. Some also link an audit study. GoldBug is aligned with its processes extensively to encryption and has these documented accordingly in the open source-code, in the project documentation, as well as in user manuals. *Jedes Programm bietet auf der Webseite zahlreiche Informationen an. Einige Applikationen haben auch tiefergehende Hinweise auf Verschlüsselung und Sicherheitsaspekte. Manche verlinken auch eine Audit-Studie. GoldBug ist mit seinen Prozessen umfänglich auf Verschlüsselung ausgerichtet und hat diese auch entsprechend im quelloffenen Source Code, in der Projektdokumentation wie auch Benutzer-Manualen dokumentiert.*

Source: Own Case.

3.10 Description of Process and Function: POPTASTIC E-Mail-Client

POPTASTIC is a function, which creates within the application on the one hand a regular and also encrypted e-mail client and beyond that also introduces a so far innovative function: the presence chat over a regular (POP3 or IMAP) email account.

POPTASTIC ist eine Funktion, die das Programm einerseits zum vollwertigen – verschlüsselnden – E-Mail-Klienten macht und darüber hinaus – auch eine bislang innovative Funktion einführt: den Präsenz-Chat über einen regulären (POP3 oder IMAP) E-Mail-Account.

3.10.1 Inventory taking, structural analysis and descriptions of the functions

POPTASTIC enables direct encryption of e-mails and uses POP3 e-mail server for both, e-mail, as well as for chat.

POPTASTIC ermöglicht die direkte Verschlüsselung von E-Mails und nutzt POP3-E-Mail-Server sowohl für E-Mail, als auch für Chat.

This not only means, that messaging is now bundling offline and offline friends, but also, that the encryption is provided continuously by default and requires only a one-time key exchange with own communication partners. Second, it must not no longer any individual communication be manually encrypted with a key and possibly signed, instead the effort for the user is reduced to a minimum without loss of security! After the one-time key-exchange any communication through GoldBug will be encrypted continuously.

Das bedeutet nicht nur, dass Messaging zu Offline- und Offline-Freunden gebündelt wird, sondern, dass die Verschlüsselung kontinuierlich standardmäßig vorgesehen ist und nur einen einmaligen Schlüsseltausch mit seinem Kommunikationspartner erfordert. Sodann muss nicht mehr jede einzelne Kommunikation manuell mit einem Schüssel verschlüsselt und ggf. signiert werden, sondern der Aufwand für den Nutzer wird auf ein Minimum reduziert ohne Sicherheitsverluste! Nach dem einmaligen Schlüsseltausch wird jede Kommunikation durch GoldBug kontinuierlich verschlüsselt sein.

With regard to the chats with POPTASTIC this means, that the regular e-mail server based on POP3 and IMAP also can be used as a chat server (see also Lindner 2014).

Hinsichtlich des Chats mit POPTASTIC bedeutet dieses, dass die regulären E-Mail-Server auf Basis von POP3 und IMAP auch eingesetzt werden können als Chat-Server (siehe auch Lindner 2014).

Principally, there are then no special chat servers, no XMPP- or any proprietary IM servers no longer necessary! Even with those encrypting Messengers, that make the chat client open source, but not offering the chat-server open source, it is getting clear, that the existing infrastructure easily and efficiently can be used for e-mail and chat for encrypted communications.

Es sind daher prinzipiell keine gesonderten Chat-Server, keine XMPP oder proprietären Chat-Server mehr notwendig! Auch bei manchen verschlüsselnden Messengern, die den Chat-Clienten zwar quelloffen machen, aber den Chat-Server nicht-quelloffen anbieten, wird deutlich, dass die bestehenden Infrastrukturen einfach und effizient zur verschlüsselnden Kommunikation bei E-Mail und Chat genutzt werden können.

By a flag or through the appropriate key (see below) for the encrypted chipertext the receiving client is informed, whether to decipher the text in an e-mail-message or a chat-message and then displays the message

Durch einen Flag im bzw. durch den entsprechenden Schlüssel (s.u.) für den verschlüsselten Chipertext weiss der empfangende Klient, ob er diesen in eine E-Mail oder eine Chat-Nachricht dechiffrieren

to the user, either in the chat-tab or in the e-mail-tab.

Another advantage is, that the port for email is enabled almost in every firewall and you can therefore chat and mail-out encrypted from almost any environment - and even attachments can be sent encrypted.

To activate the POPTASTIC function it is only necessary - like in any other e-mail client as well - to deposit the POP3- or alternatively IMAP-Server-details in the settings to send and receive e-mails.

Then, with the exchange of the POPTASTIC key between two friends, the encryption is installed within one step, and, from this time on, it is possible - without further processes - to communicate easily and securely with each other.

muss und zeigt sodann die Nachricht entweder im Chat-Tab oder im E-Mail-Tab dem Nutzer an.

Ein weiterer Vorteil ist, dass der Port für E-Mail in fast jeder Firewall freigegeben ist und man daher aus fast jeder Umgebung heraus verschlüsselt chatten und mailen kann – und auch Anhänge verschlüsselt senden kann.

Um die POPTASTIC Funktion zu aktivieren, ist es lediglich erforderlich – wie bei jedem anderen E-Mail-Klienten auch –, die POP3 oder wahlweise IMAP Serverdetails zum Senden und Empfangen von E-Mails in den Einstellungen zu hinterlegen.

Sodann wird mit dem Austausch der POPTASTIC-Schlüssel zwischen zwei Freunden die Verschlüsselung mit nur einem Schritt installiert und fortan ist es möglich, ohne weitere Prozesse einfach und sicher miteinander zu kommunizieren.

Figure 11: POPTASTIC Settings

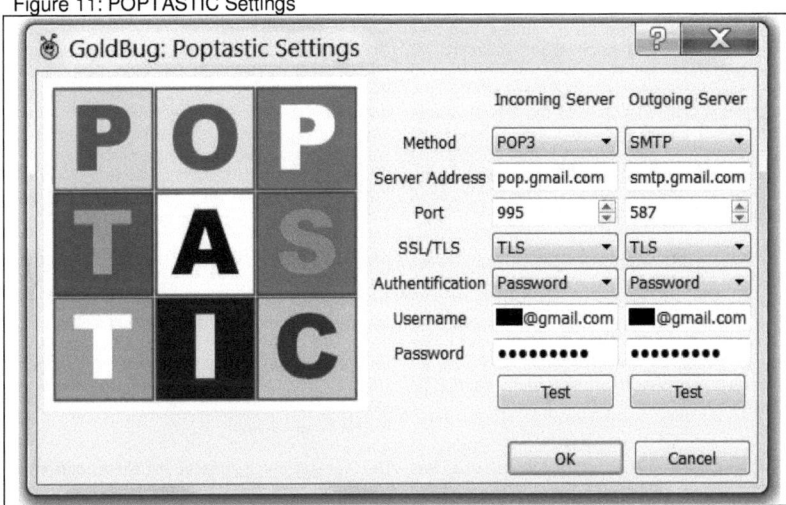

Source: https://de.wikibooks.org/wiki/Goldbug#POP3

In addition to encryption via adjacent nodes over the echo protocol of the messenger, POPTASTIC is added as a second protocol, that enables encryption using the existing infrastructure: POP3- and IMAP-servers.

Neben der Verschlüsselung über benachbarte Knotenpunkte des dem Messenger originären Echo-Protokolls wird mit POPTASTIC ein zweites Protokoll hinzugefügt, dass die Verschlüsselung über die bestehende Infrastruktur – von POP3- und IMAP-Servern – ermöglicht.

The function and operation of POPTASTIC is documented in detail in the user manual.

Die Funktionsweise von POPTASTIC ist ausführlich im Benutzer-Manual dokumentiert.

As it always comes to the inclusion of manual documentation during an audit, this aspect should be included with the example of the POPTASTIC function in this assessment.

Da es bei einem Audit auch immer um den Einbezug der Handbuch-Dokumentationen geht, soll dieser Aspekt am Beispiel der Funktion POPTASTIC in diesem Assessment einbezogen sein.

3.10.2 Selected method for studying and function reference

To test the POPTASTIC function, the user manual as process description should be used and assessed, whether a user being aware of this manual description can enter the e-mail server account details within the POPTASTIC function.

Um die POPTASTIC Funktion zu testen, soll das Handbuch als Prozessbeschreibung zugrunde gelegt werden und beurteilt werden, ob ein Nutzer in Kenntnis dieser Beschreibung die Server-Details seines E-Mail-Accounts in der POPTASTIC Funktion eingeben kann.

3.10.3 Conduction and findings of the examinations

The POPTASTIC function was tested qualitatively with three users, without that they knew the GoldBug application previously. At the beginning everyone was allowed for 15 minutes to read the user manual for the corresponding function, and the e-mail usage. The setup of the application was carried out jointly, as it is here focused only on entering the server details in the POPTASTIC function and as well the understanding and application of the process.

Die POPTASTIC-Funktion wurde mit drei Nutzern qualitativ getestet, ohne dass sie das GoldBug Programm zuvor kannten. Zu Beginn durfte sich jeder 15 Minuten mit dem Benutzermanual zur entsprechenden Funktion und der E-Mail-Nutzung einlesen. Der Setup des Programmes wurde gemeinsam vorgenommen, da es hier lediglich um die Eingabe der Server-Details in die POPTASTIC Funktion sowie um das Verständnis und die Anwendung des Prozesses geht.

All three users could enter the server details within a few minutes after reading the manual. Helpful was the button of the test function in the settings, with which the correctness of the entered server settings is confirmed. The server-details regarding domain and port for the own e-mail-account should of course be known by the user.

Alle drei Nutzer konnten nach Lesen des Handbuches innerhalb weniger Minuten die Serverdetails eingeben. Hilfreich war der Knopf der Test-Funktion in den Einstellungen, mit dem die Richtigkeit der eingegebenen Servereinstellungen bestätigt wird. Die Server-Details hinsichtlich Domain und Port für den eigenen E-Mail Account sollten natürlich beim Nutzer bekannt sein.

The exchange of keys with a different user was then just a simple process and the three subjects could each start an encrypted chat.

Der Tausch der Schlüssel mit einem anderen Anwender war sodann ebenso ein einfacher Prozess und die drei Probanden konnten jeweils einen verschlüsselten Chat starten.

POPTASTIC uses - also verified in a further analysis of the source code - therefore its own POPTASTIC key pair for the chat, and also the permanent e-mail key. Both keys are included in the key transfer, so that both, chat and e-mail, will get functional.

POPTASTIC nutzt - auch verifiziert in einer weiteren Analyse des Quellcodes - dazu ein eigenes POPTASTIC-Schlüsselpaar für den Chat, sowie aber auch den permanenten E-Mail-Schlüssel. Beide Schlüssel werden bei der Schlüsselübertragung berücksichtigt, damit

For the emerging friend in the chat tab the e-mail address will be displayed with the @ symbol, and therefore differs also chat-friends with a chat-key of chat-friends with a POPTASTIC-key.

sowohl Chat als auch E-Mail funktionsfähig werden.
Für den im Chat-Tabulator auftauchenden Freund wird die E-Mail-Adresse mit dem @-Symbol angezeigt und unterscheidet daher auch Chat-Freunde mit dem Chat-Schlüssel von Chat-Freunden mit dem POPTASTIC-Schlüssel.

3.10.4 Evaluation of the results with regard to weaknesses, risks, potentials for improvements and strengths

In an evaluation it can be said, that all three subjects were able to implement the process description of the manual for the application of the POPTASTIC function very well and succeeded completely, to apply the function. The technical-procedural analysis and the source code show transparently the use of another key pair for the POPTASTIC function.

In einer Bewertung lässt sich festhalten, dass alle drei Probanden den Beschreibungs-prozess des Handbuches zur Anwendung der POPTASTIC Funktion sehr gut umsetzen konnten und es vollständig gelang, die Funktion anzuwenden. Die technisch-prozessurale Analyse sowie Analyse des Quellcodes zeigt transparent die Nutzung eines weiteren Schlüsselpaares für die POPTASTIC-Funktion auf.

By chat friends, who are displayed with an email address within POPTASTIC, this function is also indicating transparently in the user interface. Further, the e-mail function is also explained in greater depth in the manual.

Indem die Chatfreunde bei POPTASTIC mit einer E-Mail-Adresse abgebildet sind, wird diese Funktion auch ebenso transparent in der Benutzeroberfläche angezeigt. Die E-Mail-Funktion wird weitergehend im Handbuch ebenso vertiefend erläutert.

Table 35: Description of findings 3.10

#	Area	Description of the finding	Valuation Severity Category / Difficulty Level / Innovation & Improvement Class / Strength Dimension
	Weakness / Schwäche	./.	./.
	Risk / Risiko	./.	./.
3.10.4.A	Potential for Improvement / Verbesserungspotential	Update of Screenshots in the manual to the current version of the application.	Informational
3.10.4.B	Strength / Stärke	E-Mail and chat in one application, incorporating the existing infrastructure of IMAP and POP3 e-mail server, Own key for this feature.	High

As a suggestion for improvement has been identified by the subjects, that the screenshot used in the manual of the POPTASTIC function is not quite up to date in the layout, so the recommendation to give is to continuously update the user manual also in this screenshot to the referring software version.

Als Verbesserungsvorschlag wurde von den Probanden identifiziert, dass der im Handbuch verwendete Screenshot von der POPTASTIC-Funktion im Layout nicht ganz aktuell ist, so dass die Empfehlung zu geben ist, das Nutzermanual auf die jeweilige Softwareversion kontinuierlich auch in den Screenshots zu aktualisieren.

All in all, with POPTASTIC next to the echo protocol a second innovative protocol is given in GoldBug Messenger, that is - taking into account the user manual - easily to understand and allows encryption for both, for e-mail and for chat, over POP3 and IMAP servers.

Alles in allem ist mit POPTASTIC neben dem Echo-Protokoll ein zweites, innovatives Protokoll im GoldBug Messenger vorhanden, das unter Berücksichtigung des Nutzerhandbuches einfach zu verstehen ist und Verschlüsselung sowohl für E-Mail, als auch für einen Chat, über POP3- und IMAP-Server ermöglicht.

3.10.5 Appraisal of good practices in comparison with other similar applications

Compared with the other selected open source encryption applications, there is no application that allows a chat over an e-mail server and no application that can send an email - whether encrypted or unencrypted - over an IMAP- or POP3-server.

Im Vergleich mit den ausgewählten weiteren quelloffenen Verschlüsselungsanwendungen gibt es keine Applikation, die einen Chat über E-Mail-Server ermöglicht und auch keine Anwendung, die ein E-Mail – ob nun verschlüsselt oder unverschlüsselt – über einen IMAP oder POP3-Server senden kann.

Here is particularly the GoldBug Messenger to attest a strength that it is incorporating over an intelligent and innovative way existing infrastructure in the processes of encryption.

Hier ist insbesondere dem GoldBug Messenger eine Stärke zu attestieren, die darin besteht, vorhandene Infrastrukturen in die Prozesse der Verschlüsselung intelligent und innovativ einzubeziehen.

Compared to the regular given email encryption exists the advantage that each e-mail is provided by default for encryption, the user does not have to start an encryption process for each e-mail manually.

Gegenüber der sonst vorhandenen E-Mail-Verschlüsselung besteht der Vorteil, dass jedes E-Mail per Voreinstellung zur Verschlüsselung vorgesehen ist - der Nutzer also nicht bei jeder E-Mail manuell einen eigenen Verschlüsselungsprozess starten muss.

An e-mail-related function contains only the application RetroShare, but it does not allow sending e-mails to friends, which are offline.

Eine e-mail-ähnliche Funktion enthält lediglich die Applikation RetroShare, jedoch erlaubt sie keine Versendung zu Freunden, die offline sind.

The e-mail of RetroShare does not work, when either friends are offline, or in other words, it only works, if both parties are successful in proceeding a handshake, so if both are online. But then you could also chat and transmit the message via presence chat.

Das E-Mail von RetroShare funktioniert nicht, wenn beide Freunde offline sind, oder anders ausgedrückt, es funktioniert nur, wenn beiden Teilnehmern ein sog. „Handshake" gelingt, also wenn beide online sind. Aber dann könnte man auch chatten bzw. die Nachricht auch über einen Präsenz-Chat übertragen.

The RetroShare email function is therefore in development, as it actually shows an online chat in an inbox instead of in a chat window (based on the latest revision).

Die RetroShare E-Mail-Funktion ist daher in Entwicklung, da sie eigentlich einen Online-Chat in einer E-Mail-Inbox statt in einem Chat-Fenster anzeigt (bezogen auf den letzten Revisionsstand).

Also RetroShare does not utilize an own e-mail-key, but instead sends the e-mail-message ongoing through the only available chat-, respective application-key.

Auch nutzt RetroShare keinen eigenen E-Mail-Schlüssel, sondern sendet die E-Mail-Nachricht weiterhin über den einzig vorhandenen Chat- bzw. Applikations-Schlüssel.

Table 36: Indicative BIG SEVEN context references 3.10

Logo	Application	Comments
	Cryptocat	No support for POP3 or IMAP for message transfers.
	GoldBug	Implementation of POP3 and IMAP in the Poptastic function with its own key. Innovative chat function via e-mail servers.
	OTR+XMPP	No support for POP3 or IMAP for message transfers.
	RetroShare	No support for POP3 or IMAP for message transfers. UI for e-mail, but transfer only, if both participants are online. No specific e-mail-key.
	Signal	No support for POP3 or IMAP for message transfers.
	SureSpot	No support for POP3 or IMAP for message transfers.
	Tox	No support for POP3 or IMAP for message transfers.

To understand messaging holistically - that is, the transmission of messages to chat-friends and e-mail-partners - it makes sense, that the here encountered standard of IMAP and POP3 is possibly considered to be included also in the other open-source encrypting applications.

GoldBug as a client emphasizes with this the core competency to integrate within one application both, e-mail and chat, as it can not be found in almost any other comparable application.

Rogers illustrates in his book "Diffusion of Innovations" (1962, 2003) the processes how innovation first by a group of the so called "innovators" and then by a group of "early adopters" is tested.

The POPTASTIC function is a worldwide first implementation, in which you can send chat (and e-mail) via e-mail-server - and also still encrypts everything.

Therefore, it makes sense to relate this theoretical construct of phased interpenetration of ideas through communication in the social system as a perspectivistic issue as well for one of the main innovations in this client.

Um Messaging – also die Übertagung der Nachrichten an Chat-Freunde und E-Mail-Partner – ganzheitlich zu verstehen, macht es Sinn, diesen hier vorgefundenen Standard von IMAP und POP3 ggf. auch in die weiteren quelloffen verschlüsselnden Applikationen einzubeziehen.

GoldBug stellt darüber hinaus als Klient auch seine Kernkompetenz heraus, in einer Applikation beides zu integrieren, E-Mail und Chat, wie es bei fast keiner vergleichbaren anderen Applikation zu finden ist.

Rogers stellt in seinem Buch "Diffusion of Innovations" (1962, 2003) die Prozesse dar, wie Innovationen zunächst durch eine Gruppe der sogenannten "Innovatoren" und sodann durch "Early Adopters" ausgetestet werden.

Die POPTASTIC Funktion ist eine weltweit erstmalige Implementation, bei der Chat (und E-Mail) über E-Mail-Server gesendet wird - und zudem auch noch alles verschlüsselt.

Daher macht es Sinn, dieses theoretische Konstrukt der phasenweisen Durchdringung von Ideen durch Kommunikation im Sozialen System als perspektivistische Fragestellung ebenso auf eine der wesentlichen Innovationen in diesem Klienten zu beziehen.

Figure 12: Diffusion of POPTASTIC Innovation as theoretical construct

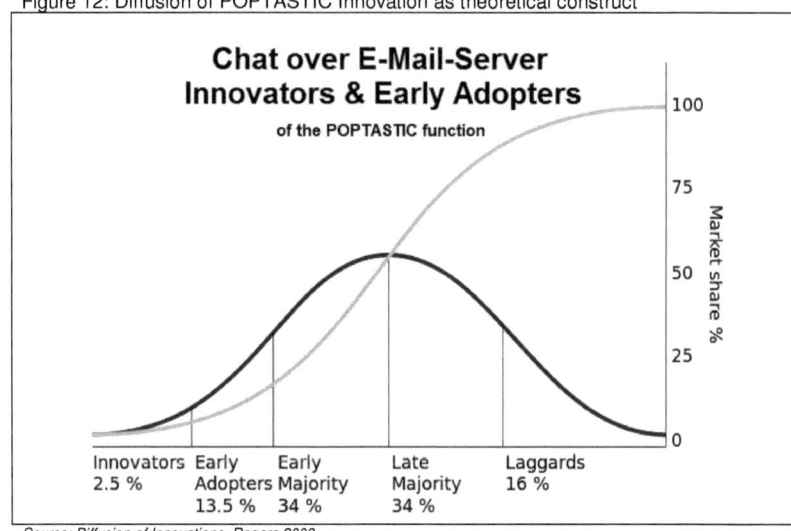

Chat over E-Mail-Server
Innovators & Early Adopters
of the POPTASTIC function

| Innovators
2.5 % | Early
Adopters
13.5 % | Early
Majority
34 % | Late
Majority
34 % | Laggards
16 % |

Source: Diffusion of Innovations, Rogers 2003.

The graph shows that a group of innovators is needed during the beginning of innovation, which provide and test a new techology via different communication channels, before it is tested by other people from the group of early adopters: the scientists, the curious thinker, the questioners, the communicators, the ones who ask, the librarians, the archivists etc. ... .

POPTASTIC is not just chat via e-mail, but rather at the same time encrypts regular e-mail accounts too.
Actually, the solution after which each one is currently looking for regarding e-mail?
One will over time also be able to analyze with this example, if communication about how we communicate (e.g. via POPTASTIC), also a first social penetration in the other group of "adapters" constitutes - or due to the existing multifarious options of communication channels this innovation will be considered as a niche – and/or only, if it comes to default encrypted communication, one recognizes, that chat and email can ideally run through e-mail servers also in this bundle.

Die Grafik verdeutlicht, dass es beim Beginn von Innovationen eine Gruppe an Innovatoren benötigt wird, die über verschiedene Kommunikationskanäle eine neue Techologie vermitteln und erproben, bevor sie durch weitere Personen aus der Gruppe der Early Adopters ausgetestet wird: der Wissenschaftler, der neugierigen Denker, der Fragenden, der Kommunikatoren, des Bibliothekenpersonals und der Aktivisten, um nur einige zu nennen... .

POPTASTIC ist nicht nur Chat über E-Mail, sondern verschlüsselt zugleich auch reguläre E-Mail-Konten?
Eigentlich die Lösung, nach der jeder derzeit für E-Mail sucht?
Man wird im Zeitverlauf auch an diesem Beispiel analysieren können, ob Kommunikation darüber, wie wir kommunizieren (z.B. über POPTASTIC), auch eine erste soziale Durchdringung in die weitere Gruppe von "Adaptoren" beinhaltet - oder ob aufgrund der bestehenden Möglichkeitsvielfalt an Kommunikationswegen diese Innovation als Nische betrachtet wird – und/oder man erst wenn es zu ausschließlich verschlüsselter Kommunikation kommt, erkennt, dass Chat und E-Mail idealerweise über E-Mail-Server in dieser Bündelung auch laufen kann.

Table 37: Good Practice Insights #10

Good Practice Insight # 10	
with GoldBug Multi-Encrypting Communication Suite	
Case	I want to transfer a file encrypted to a friend, how to proceed? Ich möchte eine Datei zu einem Freund verschlüsselt übertragen, wie gehe ich da am besten vor?
Solution	GoldBug provides once with the File Encryption tool the option to securely encrypt a file with high encryption values. Then the file can be sent through any channel or be stored in a cloud. Another option is the file transfer of the file within the Messenger. Each file will be always transmitted in encoded form. It is also possible to place an additional symmetric encryption with an AES-256, on the file - so to speak: a password. Furthermore an encrypted file can be send as an attachment of an e-mail via a regular e-mail account, which is set up with the POPTASTIC function within GoldBug. GoldBug bietet einmal mit dem Werkzeug des Fileencryptors die Möglichkeit, eine Datei mit hohen Verschlüsselungswerten sicher zu verschlüsseln. Dann kann die Datei über jeglichen Kanal gesandt werden oder auch in einer Cloud abgelegt werden. Eine weitere Möglichkeit besteht in dem Dateiversand der Datei innerhalb des Messengers. Dabei wird jede Datei grundsätzlich nur verschlüsselt übertragen. Zudem besteht die Möglichkeit eine zusätzliche, symmetrische Verschlüsselung mit einem AES-256 auf die Datei zu legen - sozusagen: ein Passwort. Schließlich kann die verschlüsselte Datei auch als Anhang einer E-Mail versand werden, auch über reguläre E-Mail-Konten, die mit der POPTASTIC-Funktion in GoldBug erstellt werden.

Source: Own Case.

3.11 Description of Process and Function: Example of a File-Transfer with StarBeam

The StarBeam function within GoldBug messenger describes the file-sharing respectively file-transfer function. By means of a link in the magnet-URI standard - that means similar to an Edonkey-ED2K-link or a torrent or Gnutella-link, now encrypted files can be transmitted securely and safely.

Die StarBeam-Funktion bezeichnet im GoldBug Messenger die FileSharing- bzw. Datei-Transfer-Funktion. Mittels eines Links im Magnet-URI Standard – also ähnlich einem Edonkey-ED2K-Link bzw. eines Torrent- oder Gnutella-Links, können damit Dateien verschlüsselt und sicher übertragen werden.

3.11.1 Inventory taking, structural analysis and descriptions of the functions

The data transfer can be easily understood: Either the file is transferred in the tab StarBeam (SB) - there you will find the sub-tabs: "downloads", "uploads" and "define magnet" - or the file is even easier transmitted in a Chat-Pop-up window with a simple mouse click.

Die Datei-Übertragung lässt sich ganz einfach verstehen: Entweder wird die Datei im Tabulator StarBeam (SB) übertragen – dort finden sich die Sub-Tabs: „Downloads", „Uploads" und „Magneten definieren" – oder aber die Datei wird noch einfacher im Chat-Pop-up-Fenster mittels eines einfachen Mausklicks übertragen.

The StarBeam function can be explained as follows:

Die StarBeam-Funktion lässt sich wie folgt erläutern:

A magnet-URI is a standard, which is known from many file-sharing programs (it has been widely used in the Gnutella network) and in the operatings also corresponds to an eDonkey / eMule ed2k link or a torrent link.

Ein Magnet-URI ist ein Standard, der aus vielen File-Sharing Programmen bekannt ist (er wurde vielfach im Gnutella Netzwerk eingesetzt) und in der Funktionsweise ebenso den eDonkey/Emule ed2k-Links oder auch Torrent-Links entspricht.

The development of the magnet-URI standard through the GoldBug messenger underlying Spot-On library is the embodiment of the magnetic-URI with encryption values. Magnets are thus used to create a package of cryptologic information and bundling it together.

Die Weiterentwicklung des Magnet-URI Standards durch die dem GoldBug Messenger zugrunde liegende Spot-On Bibliothek liegt in der Ausgestaltung des Magnet-URI mit Verschlüsselungswerten. Magneten werden also genutzt, um ein Bündel an kryptologischen Informationen zu erstellen und zusammen zu halten.

Thus between the nodes in the echo network an end-to-end encrypted, symmetric channel is created, through which a file can then be sent.

Zwischen den Knotenpunkten im Echo-Netzwerk wird somit ein Ende-zu-Ende verschlüsselter, symmetrischer Kanal geschaffen, durch den eine Datei dann gesendet werden kann.

It can then also be sent any other file. The magnet is thus not allocated to a specific file, but only opens a secure channel. The SB-magnet can therefore be seen as a channel, through which an instance can constantly and permanently send files. - Or it is created a one-time magnet, which is deleted immediately

Es kann sodann auch jede andere Datei gesandt werden. Der Magnet ist somit keiner bestimmten Datei zugeordnet, sondern eröffnet nur einen sicheren Kanal. Der SB-Magnet ist also wie ein Channel zu verstehen, durch den eine Instanz laufend und dauerhaft Dateien senden kann. - Oder aber es wird ein One-

after a single use. Then each magnet corresponds to only one file.

Through this dual-use effect a magnet can not be assigned to a single file or a specific IP address. Also a specific file-name does not appear in the SB-magnet (- as even it is yet the case for the more advanced links - for example, by OffSystem or RetroShare - compard to Gnutella, eMule and Torrent links). Thus it is clear, that in StarBeam no specific file is swapped, instead there are basically swapped only encrypted channels.

The use of magnets is very simple and the user interface automates the magnet transfer in the chat window: a single click sends a file via the "Share" button to the chat friend.

Time-Magnet erstellt, der nach der einmaligen Nutzung gleich wieder gelöscht wird. Dann entspricht jeder Magnet auch nur einer Datei.

Durch diesen Dual-Use-Effekt kann ein Magnet nicht einer einzelnen Datei oder einer bestimmten IP-Adresse zugeordnet werden. Auch ein Dateiname taucht in dem SB-Magneten nicht auf (- wie es selbst bei den - gegenüber Gnutella, Emule und Torrent-Links - fortschrittlicheren Verlinkungen beispielsweise von OFFSystem oder RetroShare noch der Fall ist). Somit wird deutlich, dass in StarBeam keine bestimmte Datei getauscht wird, sondern es werden grundsätzlich nur verschlüsselte Kanäle getauscht.

Die Anwendung der Magneten ist sehr einfach und die Benutzeroberfläche automatisiert den Magneten-Transfer im Chat-Fenster: mit einem Klick wird eine Datei zum Chat-Freund über den „Share"-Knopf gesandt.

Figure 13: GoldBug – File Transfer in the Chat Pop-up Window

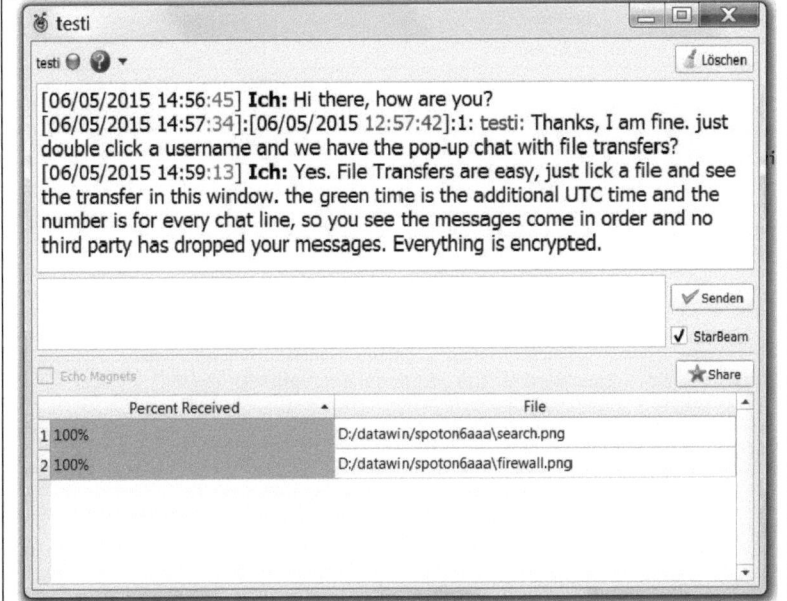

Source: https://de.wikibooks.org/wiki/Goldbug#FileSharing:_mit_StarBeam

Technically, the magnet URI standard, which has been extended by cryptographic values in GoldBug clients, can be explained in detail as follows:

Technisch detailliert lässt sich der Magnet-URI-Standard, der um kryptographische Werte im GoldBug Klienten erweitert worden ist, wie folgt erläutern:

Figure 14: Example of Magnet URI-Link for StarBeam-File-Transfer

```
magnet:?ct=aes256&ek=Iky44OlnaiJJLzR39n+KeRbjv90RL2iSPWK57gtBX+I=
&ht=sha512&mk=B1A0RrgmEToK4vttcPMZ8mRxlpOPjtVhA6S8yDsQv7
wzYLGS7bynKcSZNALp Z0fcaHhdKkr+MB/CUb0OtHW08Q==
&xt=urn:starbeam
```

Table 38: Overview of the Magnet-URI-Standards for cryptographic values

Short	Example	Description
rn	&rn=Spot-On_Developer_Channel_Key	Roomname
xf	&xf=10000	Exact Frequency
xs	&xs=Spot-On_Developer_Channel_Salt	Exact Salt
ct	&ct=aes256	Cipher Type
hk	&hk=Spot-On_Developer_Channel_Hash_Key	Hash Key
ht	&ht=sha512	Hash Type
xt=urn:buzz	&xt=urn:buzz	Magnet for IRC Chat
xt=urn:starbeam	&xt=urn:starbeam	Magnet for File-Transfer
xt=urn:institution	&xt=urn:institution	Magnet for E-Mail-Postbox

Source: own collection from the GoldBug Manual (2014).

As a SB-magnet transfers the file on the network to each node, which knows and has deposited the magnet, a passphrase for symmetric encryption can additionally protect the file. This function for, respectively Password on, SB-magnets is called: Nova.

Da ein SB-Magnet die Datei im Netzwerk zu jedem Knotenpunkt transferiert, der den Magneten kennt und hinterlegt hat, kann eine Passphrase einer symmetrischen Verschlüsselung die Datei zusätzlich schützen. Diese Funktion für bzw. Passwort auf SB-Magneten wird Nova genannt.

Optional: A Nova-Password for the additional encryption of the file

Before sending a specific file via the SB function, the option is offered, to protect it with a password via the Nova function. So what is called "GoldBug" within email: the password that encrypts the e-mail - is during the StarBeam-Upload called: "Nova".
The receiving friend thus only can open the file when the Nova password is entered. It is an additional symmetric encryption to secure a file-transfer.

Vor dem Versand einer Datei über die SB-Funktion besteht die Möglichkeit, sie mit einem Passwort über die Nova-Funktion zu schützen. Was also "GoldBug" im E-Mail heisst: das Passwort, das die E-Mail verschlüsselt - heisst beim StarBeam-Upload: "Nova".
Die Datei kann der empfangende Freund also nur dann öffnen, wenn er das Nova-Passwort eingibt. Es ist eine zusätzliche symmetrische Verschlüsselung, um einen Datei-Transfer abzusichern.

Thus it can be prevented, that a friend is forwarding the magnet for the requested file to any other person - they would have also to pass on the Nova.

The release of the password for the file therefore takes in this case place at a time, when the transfer of the file has already been completed. This nuanced consideration of setting a Nova password to a file should be left aside in this assessment for a first transfer and the function investigation.

So kann verhindert werden, dass ein Freund den Magneten für die angeforderte Datei anderen Personen zur Verfügung stellt - er müsste auch das Nova weitergeben.

Die Passwort-Freigabe der Datei erfolgt in diesem Fall also zu einem Zeitpunkt, wenn der Transfer der Datei längst abgeschlossen ist. Für einen ersten Transfer bzw. die Funktionsuntersuchung in diesem Assessment sollen diese differenzierteren Überlegungen der Setzung eines Nova-Passwortes auf eine Datei außer Acht gelassen werden.

3.11.2 Selected method for studying and function reference

To an audit belongs checking, whether the processes described in the manual may be conducted in practice. As stated above, this is to be analyzed by the POPTASTIC process and now the StarBeam file transfer.

While at the POPTASTIC function in the chapter above three subjects were employed to comprehend the description process in its qualitative grade, should here the description of the StarBeam function be based on the analysis of the team of authors and be tested in practice.

Zu einem Audit gehört die Überprüfung, ob die im Handbuch beschriebenen Prozesse in der Praxis abgebildet werden können. Wie zuvor dargestellt, soll dieses anhand des POPTASTIC-Prozesses und nun auch des StarBeam-Dateitransfers analysiert werden.

Während bei der POPTASTIC-Funktion im Kapitel zuvor drei Probanden eingesetzt wurden, um den Beschreibungsprozess in seiner qualitativen Güte nachzuvollziehen, soll hier bei der Beschreibung der StarBeam-Funktion die Analyse des Autorenteams in einer praktischen Durchführung zugrunde gelegt und getestet werden.

3.11.3 Conduction and findings of the examinations

In the experimental setup a chain of four nodes was formed:
- Alice connects to Mary and
- Mary to Ed and
- Ed to Bob. Bob now tried to send a file to Alice.

In the practice first a file from the chat pop-up window has been successfully transferred and then the same file again from the tab for the StarBeam file transfer function.

As a result, it can be said: The file has been transferred to 100% in both cases from one user to another successfully. The transfer was carried out according to the user manual and this describes the process adequately.

Im Versuchsaufbau wurde eine Kette von vier Knotenpunkten gebildet:
- Alice verbindet zu Maria und
- Maria zu Ed und
- Ed zu Bob. Bob versuchte nun eine Datei an Alice zu senden.

In der praktischen Durchführung wurde jeweils einmal eine Datei aus dem Chat-Pop-up Fenster erfolgreich übertragen sowie sodann dieselbe Datei nochmals aus dem Tabulator für die StarBeam-Dateitransfer-Funktion.

Als Ergebnis lässt sich festhalten: Die Datei wurde zu 100% in beiden Fällen von einem Nutzer zum anderen erfolgreich übertragen. Die Übertragung wurde entsprechend dem Benutzerhandbuch durchgeführt und dieses bildet den Prozess adäquat ab.

As there is additionally the analysis tool "StarBeam Analyzer" given, an attempt was made to repeat this experiment with it as follows: For this purpose the node of Ed was connected to three other users, which connected to his listener. These users now tried to transmit via the node of Ed also larger files. The goal was to increase the packet loading so that packets get lost in a simultaneous transfer from Bob to Alice.

Then Alice would have been able to check her resultant file with the StarBeam-Analyzer tool, which was possibly transferred to only 98%, and to define the missing blocks in a magnet, she sends to Bob. If Bob enters this magnet in his node and repeats the file transfer, only the missing blocks will be supplied - and not again the whole file.

However, in this repetition of the data transmission from Bob to Alice, the transmission was 100% accurate, so that the StarBeam-Analyzer-tool did not have to be used.
The data transmission via an e-mail attachment is in GoldBug Messenger as well possible, but at this point not element of an assessment. Larger files should be better transmitted in chat or using the StarBeam function.

As an improvement proposal it can be stated, possibly to complete the process of the usage of the StarBeam-Analyzer-tool a little more in detail with a pictorial representation, so that the initial user is more aware of how the analysis of the transmitted blocks can be visualized (figure of a screenshot in the manual).

If a file once has not been successfully transferred, this can be checked with the StarBeam-Analyser tool.

The file would itself also complete, if the transmitter sends it e.g. three times a day over the echo with the "Rewind"-function (= "Send again").

Note, that existing files in the download path

Da es zusätzlich das Analyse-Werkzeug „StarBeam-Analyzer" gibt, wurde versucht, dieses Experiment wie folgt damit zu wiederholen: Dazu wurde der Knotenpunkt von Ed mit drei weiteren Nutzern verbunden, die sich an seinen Listener verbanden. Diese Nutzer versuchten nun, über den Knotenpunkt von Ed ebenso größere Dateien zu übertragen. Ziel war, die Last so zu erhöhen, dass bei einer zeitgleich stattfindenden Übertragung von Bob an Alice Datenpakete verloren gehen.

Sodann wäre Alice mit dem StarBeam-Analyzer Werkzeug in der Lage gewesen, ihre erhaltene Datei, die ggf. nur zu 98 % übertragen wurde, zu überprüfen und die fehlenden Blöcke in einem Magneten zu definieren, den sie dann an Bob sendet. Wenn Bob diesen Magneten in seinem Knotenpunkt eingibt und die Dateiübertragung wiederholt, werden nur die fehlenden Blöcke nachgeliefert – und nicht nochmals die ganze Datei.

Jedoch war auch in dieser Wiederholung der Dateiübertragung von Bob an Alice die Übertragung zu 100 % korrekt, so dass das StarBeam-Analyzer Werkzeug nicht zum Einsatz kommen musste.
Die Datei-Übertragung mittels E-Mail-Anhang ist im GoldBug Messenger ebenso möglich, jedoch an dieser Stelle nicht Element eines Assessments. Größere Dateien sollten daher besser im Chat bzw. mit der StarBeam-Funktion übertragen werden.

Als Verbesserungsvorschlag lässt sich ggf. festhalten, den Prozess der Nutzung des StarBeam-Analyzer Werkzeuges noch etwas ausführlicher mit einer bildlichen Darstellung zu ergänzen, so dass dem Erst-Nutzer stärker verdeutlicht wird, wie man sich die Analyse der übertragenen Blöcke vorstellen kann (Abbildung eines Screenshots im Benutzerhandbuch).

Sollte eine Datei also mal nicht erfolgreich übertragen worden sein, kann dieses mit dem StarBeam-Analyser Werkzeug überprüft werden.

Die Datei würde sich auch vervollständigen, wenn der Sender sie z.B. dreimal am Tag über das Echo mit der „Rewind" (= „Erneut senden")-Funktion sendet.

Zu beachten ist, dass vorhandene Dateien im

(mosaic path under the installation path) will then be renewed, if no one-time magnet was used and the file is sent again to the same channel - as a magnet is a channel. A new shipment of the file by the uploader will overwrite the file obtained thus again, if the receiver does not set the lock option in the transmission table. With the check box "lock" in the transfer table, the file, that is being transferred, is then not deleted.

Download-Pfad (Mosaik-Pfad auf der Installationsebene) sodann erneuert werden, wenn kein One-Time-Magnet genutzt wurde und sie nochmals im gleichen Kanal gesendet werden, da ein Magnet ein Kanal ist. Ein erneuter Versand der Datei durch den Uploader wird die erhaltene Datei somit wieder überschreiben, wenn der Empfänger in der Übertragungstabelle keine Lock-Option fest legt. Mit der Check-Box „Lock" in der Transfer-Tabelle wird die Datei, die gerade transferiert wird, sodann nicht gelöscht.

With respect to a source-code assessment the process is found starting in the code-lines of "StarBeam-Analyzer.cc" file at the VOID "Analyze":

Hinsichtlich einer Quellcode-Beurteilung findet sich der Prozess startend in den Codezeilen der Datei „StarBeam-Analyzer.cc" ab dem VOID „Analyze":

Figure 15: Assessment of Codelines of spot-on-starbeamanalyzer.cc

```
void spoton_starbeamanalyzer::analyze(const QString &fileName,
                                      const QString &pulseSize,
                                      const QString &totalSize,
                            QAtomicInt *interrupt)
[...]
    /*
    ** Now that we've reviewed the file, let's review shadow portions.
    */

    if(!excessive && !interrupted)
      while(percent < 100)
        {
          problems += 1;

          double p = 100 * (static_cast<double> (problems) /
                            static_cast<double> (nPulses));

          if(p >= 75.00)
            {
              excessive = true;
              break;
            }

          if(first)
            {
              if(pos - ps >= 0)
                emit potentialProblem(fileName, pos - ps);

              first = false;
            }

          emit potentialProblem(fileName, pos);
          pos += ps;
          percent = static_cast<int>
            (qMin(static_cast<double> (100),
                  100 * static_cast<double> (pos) /
                  static_cast<double> (ts)));
```

```
if(percent > 0 && percent % 5 == 0)
    emit updatePercent(fileName, percent);

if(interrupt && interrupt->fetchAndAddRelaxed(0))
{
    interrupted = true;
    break;
}
}

if(excessive)
    emit excessiveProblems(fileName);
else if(!interrupted)
{
    if(rc == -1)
        emit updatePercent(fileName, 0);
    else
        emit updatePercent(fileName, 100);
}
}
else
    emit updatePercent(fileName, 0);
}
```

The source code shows no irregularities.   Der Quellcode zeigt keine Auffälligkeiten.

3.11.4 Evaluation of the results with regard to weaknesses, risks, potentials for improvements and strengths

In our overall assessment the process for sending data via the StarBeam function according to the manual documentation is fully understandable.

In unserer Gesamt-Bewertung ist der Prozess für den Dateiversand mittels der StarBeam-Funktion entsprechend der Handbuch-Dokumentation vollständig nachvollziehbar.

Table 39: Description of findings 3.11

#	Area	Description of the finding	Bewertung Severity Category / Difficulty Level / Innovation & Improvement Class / Strength Dimension
	Weakness / Schwäche	./.	./.
	Risk / Risiko	./.	./.
3.11.4.A	Potential for Improvement / Verbesserungspotential	StarBeam-Analyzer could be shown with screenshots in the manual.	Informational
3.11.4.B	Strength / Stärke	Development of the Magnet-URI-Standard with crpyto-values by the applied architecture of the GoldBug messenger is regarded as one strength.	High

3.11.5 Appraisal of good practices in comparison with other similar applications

Compared to other open source messengers files can be transferred with XMPP+OTR depending on the client's choice as well as the program Tox and RetroShare.

Im Vergleich zu den anderen quelloffenen Messengern lassen sich bei XMPP+OTR je nach Wahl des Klienten Dateien übertragen wie auch im Programm Tox und RetroShare.

Specifically RetroShare plays here fully with its core competencies: not only the file-transfer, but also the file-sharing is there an inherent function.

Insbesondere RetroShare spielt hier seine Kernkompetenz voll aus: nicht nur der Datei-Transfer, sondern auch das FileSharing ist dort eine inherente Funktion.

In addition, the applications that are available only for mobile devices, are often limited in the transfer of files, that are outside the normal file types, such as image or video.

Hinzu kommt, dass die Anwendungen, die lediglich mobil verfügbar sind, oftmals eingeschränkt sind in der Übertragung von Dateien, die außerhalb der üblichen Dateitypen, wie Bild oder Video, sind.

Table 40: Indicative BIG SEVEN context references 3.11

Logo	Application	Comments
	Cryptocat	Files and images can be transferred fast and simple to friends.
	GoldBug	Elaborated File-Transfer and File-Sharing with the enhanced Magnet-URI-Standard. E-Mail-Attachments und convenient 1-Click-Transfers out of the Chat-Windows.
	OTR+XMPP	Plugin-Encryption. File-Transfer depends on the XMPP-Client. Encryption has to be evaluated in reference to the plugin-architecture.
	RetroShare	Elaborated core competencies in regard of File Sharing and File-Transfer. The transferred file is - due to its indicated hash - known in all nodes of the path in the p2p network.
	Signal	File-transfer is offered since Version 2.0.
	SureSpot	File-Transfer for restrictive file types (images) possible.
	Tox	File-Transfer is possible.

As perspective it can be noted, that the encrypted data transmission possibly represents a decisive criterion in the usability of a communication application.

Als Perspektive lässt sich festhalten, dass die verschlüsselte Dateiübertragung ggf. ein entscheidendes Kriterium in der Nutzerfreundlichkeit einer Kommunikationsapplikation darstellt.

Applications available exclusively for mobile platforms should be tested for the usability of all file types. As well: Particularly in encrypting applications, that enable file transfer only via plugin solutions, it should be further examined sustainable, if the file encryption is performed in a continuous process with no gaps in the encryption and not refers only to the transmission of text messages.

Applikationen, die ausschließlich für mobile Plattformen angeboten werden, sollten auf die Nutzungsfreundlichkeit für alle Dateitypen hin geprüft werden. Sowie: Insbesondere bei Verschlüsselungs-Applikationen, die Dateiversand nur über Plugin-Lösungen ermöglichen, sollte weiterhin nachhaltig geprüft werden, ob die Dateiverschlüsselung in einem durchgängigen Prozess ohne Lücken in der Verschlüsselung erfolgt und sich nicht nur auf die Übermittlung von Textnachrichten bezieht.

Table 41: Good Practice Insights # 11

Good Practice Insight # 11	
with GoldBug Multi-Encrypting Communication Suite	
Case	At my workplace I have no opportunity to use a messenger. My current Messenger has also no e-mail function. How can I send people an encrypted message or file out of my Chat-Application, even if they are offline? An meinem Arbeitsplatz habe ich gar keine Möglichkeit, einen Messenger zu nutzen. Mein jetziger Messenger hat auch keine E-Mail-Funktion. Wie kann ich Personen eine verschlüsselte Nachricht oder Datei aus meinem Chat-Programm heraus senden senden, auch wenn sie offline sind?
Solution	Nevertheless, in restrictive IT-environments the email function or the corresponding port is mostly enabled for POP3 and IMAP. With GoldBug one can send either chat and e-mails to online and offline friends through e-mail server like POP3. E-mail-servers turn to a chat-server with the innovative POPTASTIC function. With POPTASTIC one can send out of the chat-application GoldBug both, encrypted text messages and encrypted files, to friends, which are currently offline. In restiktiven IT-Umgebungen ist dennoch meistens die E-Mail-Funktion bzw. der entsprechende Port für POP3 und IMAP freigegeben. Mit GoldBug kann man sowohl Chat als auch E-Mails an Online- und Offline-Freunde über E-Mail-Server wie POP3 senden. E-Mail-Server werden zu Chat-Servern mit der innovativen POPTASTIC-Funktion. Mit POPTASTIC kann man aus der Chat-Applikation GoldBug heraus Freunden, die offline sind, sowohl Textnachrichten als auch Dateien verschlüsselt zusenden.

Source: Own Case.

3.12   Data Analysis: Statistic Function in GoldBug

To analyze available data is also a relevant element of a review. In GoldBug various data are processed and stored in appropriate databases. They are found on the hard disk in the installation or user-specific sub-path under "/.spoton". As seen before e.g. in section 3.6 on the example of e-mail storage, data contained therein are stored in encrypted form.

Verfügbare Daten zu analysieren ist ebenso ein relevantes Element eines Reviews. In GoldBug werden verschiedene Daten verarbeitet und auch in entsprechenden Datenbanken gespeichert. Sie finden sich auf der Festplatte im Installations- bzw. nutzerspezifischen Unterpfad unter „/.spoton". Wie zuvor z.B. im Abschnitt 3.6 am Beispiel für die E-Mail-Speicherung gesehen, sind darin enthaltene Daten verschlüsselt abgelegt.

As a further basis for a possible analysis of data, the status and the process data of the application come into question, especially the one of the kernel.
These data are listed in the application GoldBug in a specially defined statistics area.

Als weitere Basis für eine mögliche Analyse von Daten kommen die Status- und Prozessdaten der Applikation in Frage, insbesondere auch die des Kernels.
Diese Daten sind in der Applikation GoldBug in einem eigens definierten Statistik-Bereich aufgeführt.

3.12.1   Inventory taking, structural analysis and descriptions of the functions

GoldBug has not only for the URL-Import-function of the RSS/Atom-reader a dedicated statistic captured and indexed, and then also for the p2p-web-search imported URLs. Also for the other functions and in particular data of the kernel are the user extensive information visible. They are shown in its own window for statistics.

GoldBug verfügt nicht nur für die URL-Import-Funktion des RSS-/Atom-Readers eine dezidierte Statistik über erfasste und indexierte sowie sodann auch für die p2p Websuche importierten URLs. Auch für die weiteren Funktionen und insbesondere Daten des Kernels sind dem Nutzer umfangreiche Angaben ersichtlich. Sie werden im eigenen Fenster für die Statistik gezeigt.

Figure 16: Statistics Window of GoldBug

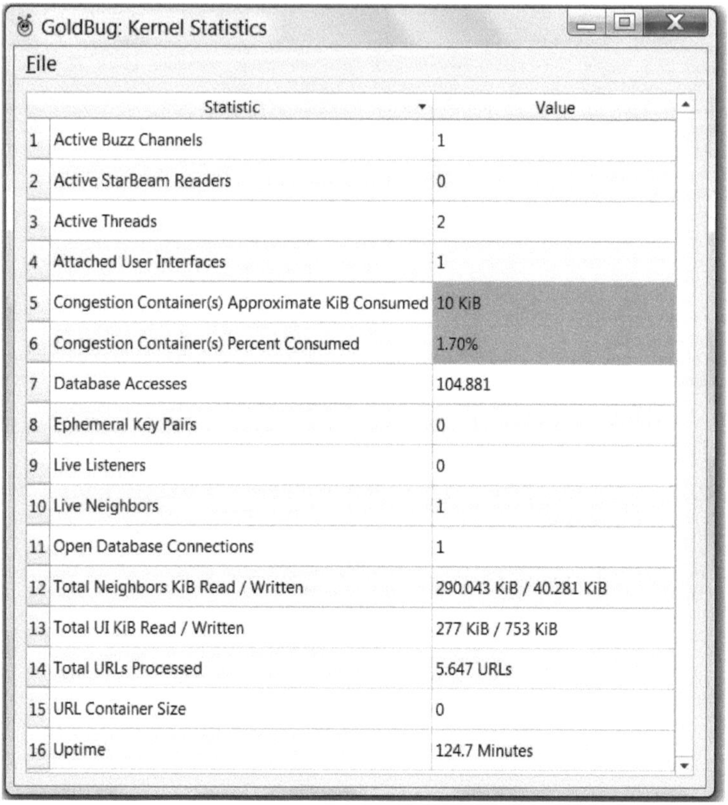

	Statistic ▾	Value ▲
1	Active Buzz Channels	1
2	Active StarBeam Readers	0
3	Active Threads	2
4	Attached User Interfaces	1
5	Congestion Container(s) Approximate KiB Consumed	10 KiB
6	Congestion Container(s) Percent Consumed	1.70%
7	Database Accesses	104.881
8	Ephemeral Key Pairs	0
9	Live Listeners	0
10	Live Neighbors	1
11	Open Database Connections	1
12	Total Neighbors KiB Read / Written	290.043 KiB / 40.281 KiB
13	Total UI KiB Read / Written	277 KiB / 753 KiB
14	Total URLs Processed	5.647 URLs
15	URL Container Size	0
16	Uptime	124.7 Minutes

GoldBug: Kernel Statistics — File

Source: Own Screenshot.

In addition to specifying "Uptime", that means how long the user is with the kernel already online, as well as the indication to the written and read data, one finds further information e.g. about the number of exchanged URLs at this time. Thus, for example, the performance of a kernel for this function in each client can be explored, such as the per minute with friends exchanged URLs.

Neben der Angabe „Uptime", also wie lange der Nutzer mit dem Kernel schon online ist, wie auch die Angabe zu geschriebenen und gelesenen Daten, finden sich ferner auch Angaben z.B. über die Anzahl der in dieser Zeit getauschten URLs. Somit kann z.B. auch die Performance eines Kernels für diese Funktion in jedem individuellen Klienten erkundet werden, wie z.B. die pro Minute mit Freunden getauschten URLs.

3.12.2 Selected method for studying and function reference

Based on two machines the research should explore now, how the statistics vary in performance, and also if possibly aspects for the assessment of the application in regard of trustfulness could be derived. Thus methodologically is to implement a practical examination in different environments, in order to be able to assess the transferred data and data flows from the values obtained.

Untersucht werden soll nun anhand von zwei Maschinen, wie die Statistiken variieren hinsichtlich der Performance, aber auch, ob daraus ggf. Aspekte für die Bewertung der Vertaulichkeit der Applikation abzuleiten sind. Methodisch ist also eine praktische Untersuchung in verschiedenen Umgebungen umzusetzen, um so aus den erhaltenen Werten die transferierten Daten und Datenflüsse einschätzen zu können.

3.12.3 Conduction and findings of the examinations

To carry out the analysis and the comparison, GoldBug has been installed on two machines each running Windows, one with a I5-CPU and one with a stronger I7-CPU.

Zur Durchführung der Analyse und eines Vergleiches wurde GoldBug auf zwei Maschinen jeweils unter Windows installiert, einmal mit einer I5-CPU und einmal mit einer stärkeren I7-CPU.

The kernel was in each case successively connected to a third node and the statistical values were read off after ten minutes.

Der Kernel wurde jeweils nacheinander mit einem dritten Knotenpunkt verbunden und die statistischen Werte wurden jeweils nach zehn Minuten abgelesen.

During the ten minutes the statistical curves were kept as well an eye on.

Während der zehn Minuten wurden die statistischen Verläufe ebenso im Auge behalten.

Table 42: Analyzing and comparing the statistcs after a practical monitoring test

DESCRIPTION	VALUE MACHINE i7 - 3612 QM Intel CPU @ 2,10 GH	VALUE MACHINE AMD - A10 5750M AMD CPU @ 2,5 GH
Active Buzz Channels	1	1
Active StarBeam Readers	0	0
Active Threads	1	1
Attached User Interfaces	1	1
Congestion Container(s) Appr. KiB Consumed	2 KiB	3 KiB
Congestion Container(s) Percent Consumed	0.53 %	0.52 %
Database Accesses	8.541	9.881
Display Open Database Connections	1	1
Ephemeral Key Pairs	1	1
Live Listeners	0	0
Live Neighbors	1	1
Open Database Connections	1	1
Total Neighbors KiB Read / Written	8545 KiB / 8.818 KiB	10.290 KiB / 9.145 KiB
Total UI KiB Read / Written	22 KiB / 32 KiB	27 KiB / 38 KiB
Total URLs Processed	264 URLs	339 URLs
URL Container Size	0	0
Uptime	10 min	10 min

The results show a good overview of the most relevant data, functions and processes that arise in the operation of the client GoldBug with its kernel. Disorders during the test and monitoring of data in the ten-minute frame were not found.

In particular, the data for Uptime, written data, as well as transferred URLs clearly show the greatest activity. Other information, such as the value for "Congestion container(s) Percent Consumed" remain relatively stable.

The data provide important information to the user about how intensively something is processed inside the application. The shown statistics increase the familiarity with the application like an information board allows a car drivers as well not only the possibility of the information and, if necessary, steering of the processes, but also makes the users with the processes familiar. Therefore, the data analysis is also used to support, to increase confidentiality and the consciousness of the user for the performed functions and processes.

The comparison of the data shows a different expression for some values, that are subject to continuous processings. Other findings don´t result from different values, which depend in particular on the performance of the CPU.

The statistics function can also be accessed via the console, as shown in following table for an operation of GoldBug on a Raspberry PI computer:

Die Ergebnisse zeigen eine gute Übersicht über die relevantesten Daten, Funktionen und Prozesse, die bei dem Betrieb des Klienten GoldBug mit seinem Kernel entstehen. Auffälligkeiten während des Versuches und des Monitorings der Daten im zehn Minuten Fenster wurden nicht festgestellt.

Insbesondere die Daten für Uptime, geschriebene Daten, als auch transferierte URLs zeigen deutlich die größten Aktivitäten an. Andere Daten wie der Wert für "Congestion Container(s) Percent Consumed" bleiben vergleichsweise stabil.

Die Daten geben wichtige Informationen an den Nutzer darüber, mit welcher Intensität wird. Die gezeigten Statistiken erhöhen die Vertrautheit der Applikation wie eine Board-Informationstafel dem Auto-Fahrer ebenso nicht nur die Möglichkeit der Information und ggf. Steuerung der Prozesse ermöglicht, sondern auch den Nutzer mit den Prozessen vertrauter macht. Die Datenanalyse dient daher auch der Unterstützung, die Vertraulichkeit und das Bewußtsein des Nutzers für die durchgeführten Funktionen und Prozesse zu erhöhen.

Der Vergleich der Daten zeigt eine unterschiedliche Ausprägung für manche Werte, die kontinuierlichen Prozessierungen unterliegen. Weitere Findings haben sich aus unterschiedlichen Werten, die insbesondere von Performance der CPU abhängen, nicht ergeben.

Die Statistik-Funktion kann auch über die Konsole abgerufen werden, wie es folgende Übersicht für einen Betrieb von GoldBug auf einem Raspberry-PI-Computer zeigt:

Figure 17: Console Statistic Function

```
GoldBug Messenger on the Raspberry PI - Statistics over Console
pi@snoopy:~ $ uname -a
Linux snoopy 4.1.13-v7+ #826 SMP PREEMPT Fri Nov 13 20:19:03 GMT 2015 armv7l GNU/Linux
pi@snoopy:~ $ sqlite3 .spot-on/kernel.db
SQLite version 3.8.7.1 2014-10-29 13:59:56
Enter ".help" for usage hints.
sqlite> .d
PRAGMA foreign_keys=OFF;
BEGIN TRANSACTION;
CREATE TABLE kernel_gui_server (port INTEGER PRIMARY KEY NOT NULL CHECK (port >= 0 AND port <= 65535));
INSERT INTO "kernel_gui_server" VALUES(38328);
CREATE TABLE kernel_statistics (statistic TEXT PRIMARY KEY NOT NULL, value TEXT);
INSERT INTO "kernel_statistics" VALUES('Active Buzz Channels','0');
INSERT INTO "kernel_statistics" VALUES('Active StarBeam Readers','0');
INSERT INTO "kernel_statistics" VALUES('Active Threads','1');
INSERT INTO "kernel_statistics" VALUES('Attached User Interfaces','0');
INSERT INTO "kernel_statistics" VALUES('Congestion Container(s) Approximate MiB Consumed','2 MiB');
INSERT INTO "kernel_statistics" VALUES('Congestion Container(s) Percent Consumed','0.46%');
INSERT INTO "kernel_statistics" VALUES('Database Accesses','465,717');
INSERT INTO "kernel_statistics" VALUES('Ephemeral Key Pairs','0');
INSERT INTO "kernel_statistics" VALUES('Live Listeners','1');
INSERT INTO "kernel_statistics" VALUES('Live Neighbors','3');
INSERT INTO "kernel_statistics" VALUES('Open Database Connections','1');
INSERT INTO "kernel_statistics" VALUES('Total URLs Processed','0 URLs');
INSERT INTO "kernel_statistics" VALUES('URL Container Size','0');
INSERT INTO "kernel_statistics" VALUES('Uptime','875.2 Minutes');
CREATE TRIGGER kernel_gui_server_trigger BEFORE INSERT ON kernel_gui_server BEGIN DELETE FROM kernel_gui_server; END;
COMMIT;
```

Source: https://twitter.com/GoldBugIM/status/672466304872378368

3.12.4 Evaluation of the results with regard to weaknesses, risks, potentials for improvements and strengths

The overview of the statistics is a valuable complementary function. Weaknesses or risks were not found. On the contrary, the user receives an information that fosters transparency and the usage the application with awareness.
As improvement is seen, that the statistical data from the RSS / Atom newsreader could be displayed as well in the overall statistical summary. One strength is that the kernel performance for the user is revealed.

Die Übersicht der Statistiken ist eine wertvolle ergänzende Funktion. Schwächen oder Risiken wurden nicht gefunden. Im Gegenteil, der Nutzer erhält eine Auskunft, die die Transparenz und den bewußten Umgang mit der Applikation fördert.
Als Verbesserungspotential wird gesehen, dass die statistischen Angaben aus dem RSS-/Atom-Newsreader ebenso in der statistischen Gesamtübersicht abgebildet werden könnten. Eine Stärke besteht darin, dass die Kernel-Performance für den Nutzer offengelegt wird.

Table 43: Description of findings 3.12

#	Area	Description of the finding	Valuation Severity Category / Difficulty Level / Innovation & Improvement Class / Strength Dimension
	Weakness / Schwäche	./.	./.
	Risk / Risiko	./.	./.
	Potential for Improvement / Verbesserungspotential	RSS-/Atom-Statistics could also be shown in the main stats panel.	Informational
	Strength / Stärke	Strength due to focus also on kernel statistics.	Medium

3.12.5 Appraisal of good practices in comparison with other similar applications

Compared to other open-source applications such detailed statistics as in GoldBug were there not found. The graphical user interfaces of the other, in particular of mobile applications, provide only little information about functions, data and processes of these messengers to the user. Also in this section remains GoldBug to be judge as the messenger, which presents the most statistical variables transparently to the user. This contributes to improve the use, the trustfulness and last not least the security of this application.

Im Vergeich zu den anderen quelloffenen Applikationen finden sich derart detaillierte Statistiken wie bei GoldBug dort nicht. Die Benutzeroberflächen der weiteren, insbesondere der mobilen Applikationen geben kaum Daten über Funktionen, Daten und Prozessabläufe dieser Messenger an den Nutzer bekannt. Auch in diesem Abschnitt bleibt GoldBug als der Messenger zu beurteilen, der die meisten statistischen Variablen dem Nutzer transparent präsentiert und so zur Verbesserung der Nutzung, der Vertrautheit und letztlich auch der Sicherheit mit dieser Applikation beiträgt.

Table 44: Indicative BIG SEVEN context references 3.12

Logo	Application	Comments
	Cryptocat	No statistics window.
	GoldBug	Comprehensive statistics window. User has an overview of main processes and the activity of the tool.
	OTR+XMPP	No statistics window (in regard of encryption, resp. per client).
	RetroShare	Some statistics are given in the GUI.
	Signal	No statistics available.
	SureSpot	No statistics available.
	Tox	No elaborated statistics available.

Table 45: Good Practice Insights #12

Good Practice Insight # 12

with GoldBug Multi-Encrypting Communication Suite

Case	From my file sharing clients I know the statistics function. Can you read relevant statistics values in a program for encryption? *Aus meinem File-Sharing Klienten kenne ich die Statistik-Funktion. Kann man auch in einem Programm zur Verschlüsselung entsprechende Statistik-Werte ablesen?*
Solution	Yes. GoldBug has its own statistics page, in which the various core processes with values are stored, in which users can read about the performance of their program. *Ja. GoldBug hat eine eigene Statistik-Seite, in der zahlreiche Kernprozesse mit Werten hinterlegt sind, in der der Anwender die Performance seines Programms ablesen kann.*

Source: Own Case.

3.13 Search-Engine-Requests & Security Nuggets: Key Handling & P2P-Websearch-Engine Code Review

The audit topic of the method of search engine queries respectively to get general information about encrypted applications over search engines (discovery of so-called "security nuggets") refers to the fact, that in the web deposited, smaller content is often detected by search engines and therefore - with a corresponding research - websites or information may be disclosed from protected areas, which would be otherwise available only with an authorization concept. Smaller snippets of information give then insight into potential vulnerabilities or may reveal the (public (asymmetric) or symmetric) key in regard to of encryption.

Der Audit Bereich der Methode der Suchmaschinenabfragen bzw. generelle Informationen verschlüsselter Applikationen über Suchmaschinen zu erhalten (Auffinden von sog. "Security Nuggets"), bezieht sich darauf, dass im Web hinterlegte, auch kleinere Inhalte von Suchmaschinen oftmals erfasst werden und somit - bei entsprechender Recherche - Webseiten bzw. Informationen aus geschützten Bereichen offenlegen könnten, die sonst nur mit einem Berechtigungskonzept verfügbar wären. Kleinere Informationsschnipsel geben sodann Einblick in potentielle Sicherheitslücken oder legen auch die (öffentlichen (asymmetrischen) oder symmetrischen) Schlüssel hinsichtlich von Verschlüsselungen unter Umständen offen.

This topic of the assessment in this section is to be transmitted from two perspectives on the GoldBug Messenger, with respect to an external search engine such as Startpage.com, DuckDuckGo.com, YaCy.net as well as Google.com (external view), and: also in regard to the internal p2p search engine GoldBug itself (internal view).

Dieser Bereich des Assessment in diesem Abschnitt soll aus zwei Perspektiven auf den GoldBug Messenger übertragen werden, einmal: hinsichtlich einer externen Suchmaschine wie Startpage.com, DuckDuckGo.com, YaCy.net sowie auch Google.com (externe Sichtweise), sowie: auch hinsichtlich der internen p2p Suchmaschine von GoldBug selbst (interne Sichtweise).

The external search engines should be investigated with the focus, if they could theoretically record the public key of the application GoldBug, because the Key-handling process would be a part, in which the user publicize their public key - even if it is called per sé as public: Thus, the public key of the asymmetric encryption is public, yet there are many users who want to see this not be published in public.
As seen earlier, GoldBug provides therefore the protective function of the Repleo, with which the own public key can be encrypted.

Die externen Suchmaschinen sollen fokussiert untersucht werden, ob sie die öffentlichen Schlüssel der Applikation GoldBug theoretisch aufzeichnen könnten, da der Key-Handling Prozess ein Teil wäre, in dem Nutzer ihren öffentlichen Schlüssel öffentlich machen - auch wenn dieser per sé als öffentlich bezeichnet wird: So ist der öffentliche Schlüssel der asymmetrischen Verschlüsselung zwar öffentlich, dennoch gibt es viele Nutzer, die diesen in der Öffentlichkeit nicht veröffentlicht sehen möchten. Wie schon weiter oben gesehen, bietet GoldBug dazu auch die Schutzfunktion des Repleo an, mit dem der eigene öffentliche Schlüssel verschlüsselt werden kann.

Furthermore, there is also criticism of PGP key servers that they are actually insecure if someone wants to find the key for encryption of a friend by name or email address: Often the key is incorrect, outdated and everyone can create an key-entry with any e-mail address, that needs not to belong to the owner.

Weiterhin besteht auch die Kritik an PGP-Schlüssel-Servern, dass diese eigentlich unsicher sind, wenn jemand per Namen oder E-Mail-Adresse den Schlüssel für die Verschlüsselung eines Freundes heraussuchen will: Oftmals ist der Schlüssel falsch, veraltet und jeder kann sich mit einer

How is an investigation processes in this context to design and how to evaluate the innovations provided by GoldBug for this?

Then the following statements should relate in a second step also to the built-in websearch-engine of GoldBug, whether it could reveal security information available from the client to others in the network, which is relating to the safety of its own instance.

ihm nicht gehörenden E-Mail-Adresse mit beliebigem Schlüssel eintragen. Wie ist ein Untersuchungsprozess in diesem Zusammenhang zu gestalten und wie können die Innovationen beurteilt werden, die GoldBug dazu bietet?

Sodann sollen sich die folgenden Ausführungen weiterhin in einem zweiten Schritt auch auf die eingebaute Web-Suchmaschine von GoldBug beziehen, ob sie sicherheitsrelevante Informationen aus dem eigenen Klienten an andere im Netzwerk preisgeben könnte, die die Sicherheit der eigenen Instanz betreffen.

3.13.1 Inventory taking, structural analysis and descriptions of the functions

External websearch-engines: like Startpage.com, DuckDuckGo.com, YaCy.net or Google.com

Externe Web-Suchmaschinen: wie Startpage.com, DuckDuckGo.com, YaCy.net oder auch Google.com

Goldbug as communication network with flow of information from one node to another is designed from scratch to encrypted transactions and sends the information always multi-encrypted. Therefore, no external, conventional search engine such as Startpage.com, DuckDuckGo.com, YaCy.net or Google.com can index portions or information of GoldBug, which could reveal unencrypted internal and security-related data.

GoldBug als Kommunikationsnetzwerk mit Informationsfluss von einem Knotenpunkt zum anderen ist von Grund auf auf verschlüsselte Vorgänge ausgelegt und sendet die Informationen immer mehrfach verschlüsselt. Daher kann keine externe, übliche Suchmaschine wie Startpage.com, DuckDuckGo.com, YaCy.net oder auch Google.com Bereiche oder Informationen von GoldBug indexieren, die unverschlüsselte interne und sicherheitsrelevante Daten preisgeben könnten.

Even if two nodes refrain of the connection using SSL/TLS in HTTPS and would build only an HTTP connection, the transmitted information remains ciphertext - this is the encrypted messages capsule.

Selbst wenn zwei Knotenpunkte auf die Verbindung mittels SSL/TLS im HTTPS verzichten und nur eine HTTP-Verbindung aufbauen, bleibt die übermittelte Information Ciphertext – nämlich die verschlüsselte Nachrichten-Kapsel.

It is thus excluded, that in GoldBug internal information of the user would be found in an external web search engine. The part, which the user possibly shows themself publicly, is mainly the public key. With regard to the above-mentioned problems of the public key must be noted that public keys are indeed basically public.

Es ist also ausgeschlossen, dass in GoldBug interne Informationen des Nutzers in einer externen Websuchmaschine aufzufinden wären. Der Teil, den der Nutzer ggf. selbst öffentlich zeigt, ist vor allem der öffentliche Schlüssel. Hinsichtlich dieser oben genannten Problematik des öffentlichen Schlüssels bleibt festzuhalten, dass öffentliche Schlüssel ja grundsätzlich öffentlich sind.

If anyone prefers though to transfer the public keys protected, exist in Goldbug at least three methods to be able to transfer the keys secured:

Wenn jemand also seine öffentliche Schlüssel lieber geschützt übertragen will, bestehen in GoldBug mindestens drei Methoden, diese gesichert übertragen zu können:

1. A user can thereto use the Repleo-function in GoldBug, as described at another section: If I get a key from a friend, my own public key with this can already be encrypted, so that it is protected during transmission.

1. Ein Nutzer kann dazu die Repleo-Funktion in GoldBug benutzen, wie auch an anderer Stelle beschrieben: Wenn ich einen Schlüssel eines Freundes erhalten habe, kann mein eigener öffentlicher Schlüssel mit diesem bereits verschlüsselt werden, so dass dieser bei der Übertragung geschützt ist.

2. Furthermore, there is also the possibility to transmit the key (or new keys) over an existing buzz respectively private IRC-like channel of the group chat feature in GoldBug.

2. Weiterhin besteht auch die Möglichkeit, die Schlüssel (oder neue Schlüssel) über einen bestehenden Buzz- bzw. privaten IRC-ähnlichen-Channel der Gruppenchatfunktion in GoldBug zu übermitteln.

3. After all thirdly, also offers the EPKS function - Encryption Public Key Sharing, found in the main menu under Tools - the possibility of transferring the key in the EPKS feature via a so-called community in GoldBug. The community name is a symmetrical end-to-end encryption password. Then, the own public (asymmetric) key is transmitted via a symmetrical end-to-end encrypted communication channel, while the password is known only to both participants and (possibly even prior verbally) agreed upon.

3. Schließlich bietet drittens auch die Funktion EPKS – Encrypted Public Key Sharing, im Hauptmenü unter Werkzeuge zu finden – die Möglichkeit, den Schlüssel in der EPKS-Funktion über eine sogenannte Community in GoldBug zu übertragen. Der Community-Name stellt ein symmetrisches Ende-zu-Ende Passwort für die Verschlüsselung dar. Dann wird der eigene öffentliche (asymmetrische) Schlüssel über einen symmetrisch ende-zu-ende verschlüsselten Kommunikationskanal übertragen, dessen Passwort nur die beiden Teilnehmer kennen und (ggf. auch vorab mündlich) vereinbaren.

The asymmetric and public keys are therefore kept in the application Goldbug with different methods for a transfer very well confidential.

Die asymmetrischen und öffentlichen Schlüssel werden daher in der Applikation GoldBug mit verschiedenen Methoden sehr gut für einen Transfer vertraulich gehalten.

In particular, the EPKS function has great potentials to complement the conventional key servers - if not even replace their disadvantages.

Insbesondere die EPKS-Funktion hat große Potentiale die üblichen Schlüssel-Server zu ergänzen - wenn nicht sogar deren Nachteile zu ersetzen.

Figure 18: EPKS – Echo Public Key Sharing

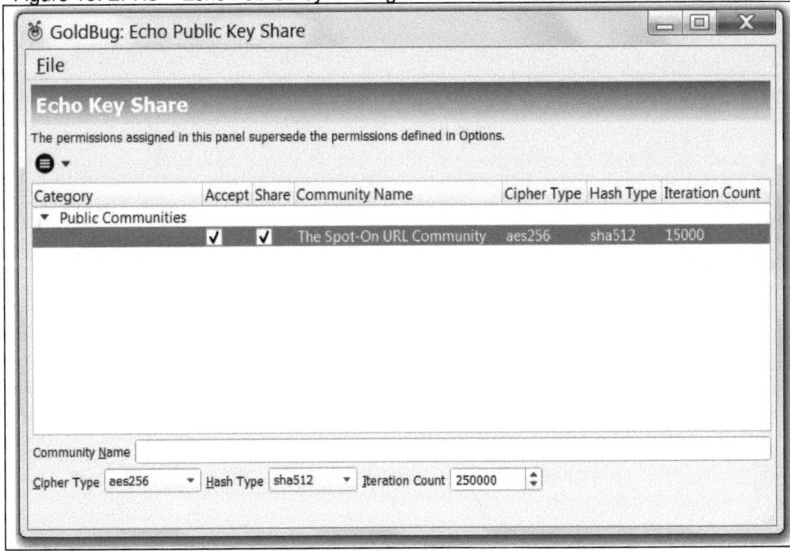

Quelle: Screenshot of GoldBug

Internal P2P search engine: GoldBug Web Search

Since the contents of the communication between two users as well as the contents of a public key as security nuggets in ordinary external Web search engines are not given within the GoldBug client - or only in theory extremely unlikely could occur (unless users release the keys, consciously and voluntarily, e.g. in a web forum, which can be detected by search engines) - the area of spying on smaller information through search engines hereafter should no longer be based on the external Web search engines.

Instead, in addition should the examination question also be transformed from the external Web search to the in GoldBug as well implemented p2p web search: Are there security risks, when someone uses the function of URL indexing for own web search, which could reveal the communication-content of the other GoldBug communication-functions?

Interne P2P-Suchmaschine: GoldBug Websearch

Da die Inhalte der Kommunikation von zwei Nutzern wie auch die Inhalte eines öffentlichen Schlüssels als Security Nuggets in üblichen externen Web-Suchmaschinen beim GoldBug Klienten nicht preisgegeben werden - oder nur theoretisch und äußerst unwahrscheinlich vorkommen könnten (es sei denn der Nutzer veröffentlicht selbst, bewusst und freiwillig seinen öffentlichen Schlüssel in z.B. einem Web-Forum, das von Suchmaschinen erfasst werden kann), - soll der Bereich des Ausspionierens von kleineren Informationen durch Suchmaschinen im folgenden nicht weiter auf die externe Web-Suchmaschinen bezogen werden.
Stattdessen soll ergänzend die Untersuchungsfragestellung auch transformiert werden von der externen Web-Suche auf die in GoldBug ebenso implementierte p2p Web-Suche: Gibt es Sicherheitsrisiken, wenn jemand die Funktion der URL-Indexierung für die eigene Websuche nutzt, die den Kommunikationsinhalt der anderen GoldBug-Kommunikationsfunktionen preisgeben könnte?

The Web search in GoldBug is an extension of the functions in regard to encrypted communication. With the web search exists the option to conduct a search for a keyword in an encrypted URL database on the own machine of the user.

It is thus requested no remote database as a web service and other nodes in the peer-to-peer network are not queried with the search word. Thus no so-called "QueryHit" in other nodes, as it would be the case e.g. in the p2p web search YaCy. The architecture of these two p2p web searches differentiate by the fact.

The search results the Web search of GoldBug are displayed to the user locally from the database - currently the most recent links are displayed on the first place, so with a simple sorting. Even AND and OR associations with several different key words are possible.

The URL database (SQLite, or optionally PostgreSQL) on the user's hard drive is fully encrypted - like all other databases of the application Goldbug as well!
The URLs get into the local database of the own node by friends and neighboring nodes of the peer-to-peer network. To that extent shared and new URLs are to be distinguished.

The import of new URLs in the own Goldbug client is carried out by manual page imports from the Web browser Dooble (another application), via the Web crawler Pandamonium (other application) or through the RSS function in the Goldbug client (accessable via the main menu of Goldbug as a separate Window).

The RSS function allows to add URLs in a large amount to the own client (new URLs).

More links then are added through the online connection of friends with whom one has swapped the URL key (shared URLs).

Die Websuche in GoldBug ist eine Erweiterung der Funktionen hinsichtlich von verschlüsselter Kommunikation. Bei der Web-Suche besteht die Möglichkeit, in einer verschlüsselten URL Datenbank auf der eigenen Maschine des Nutzers eine Abfrage nach einem Suchwort durchzuführen.

Es wird also keine Remote-Datenbank wie bei einem Webservice abgefragt und auch andere Knotenpunkte in dem Peer-to-Peer-Netz werden nicht mit dem Suchwort abgefragt. Es entsteht somit kein sogenannter „Queryhit" in anderen Knotenpunkten, wie es z.B. bei der p2p-Websuche von YaCy der Fall wäre. Die Architektur dieser beiden p2p Websuchen differenziert sich dadurch.

Die Such-Ergebnisse werden bei der Goldbug Websuche dem Nutzer aus dem Datenbestand lokal angezeigt - derzeit mit einer einfachen Sortierung, so dass die aktuellsten Weblinks jeweils an erster Stelle angezeigt werden. Auch UND sowie ODER Verknüpfungen mit mehreren, verschiedenen Stichworten sind möglich.

Die URL-Datenbank (SQLite, oder auch wahlweise PostgreSQL) auf der Festplatte des Nutzers ist vollständig verschlüsselt - wie alle anderen Datenbanken der Applikation GoldBug auch!
Die URLs kommen in die lokale Datenbank des eigenen Knotenpunktes durch Freunde und benachbarte Knotenpunkte des Peer-to-Peer-Netzwerkes. Insofern sind geteilte und neue URLs zu unterscheiden.

Der Import von neuen URLs in den eigenen GoldBug Klienten erfolgt durch manuelle Seitenimporte aus dem Web Browser Dooble (weitere Applikation), über den Webcrawler Pandamonium (weitere Applikation) oder über die RSS-Funktion im GoldBug Klienten (aufzurufen über das Hauptmenü von GoldBug als eigenständiges Fenster).

Die RSS-Funktion erlaubt es, URLs in großer Menge dem eigenen Klienten hinzuzufügen (neue URLs).

Weitere Weblinks kommen dann über die Online-Verbindung von Freunden hinzu, mit denen man den URL-Schlüssel getauscht hat (geteilte URLs).

Figure 19: RSS-Function in the GoldBug client

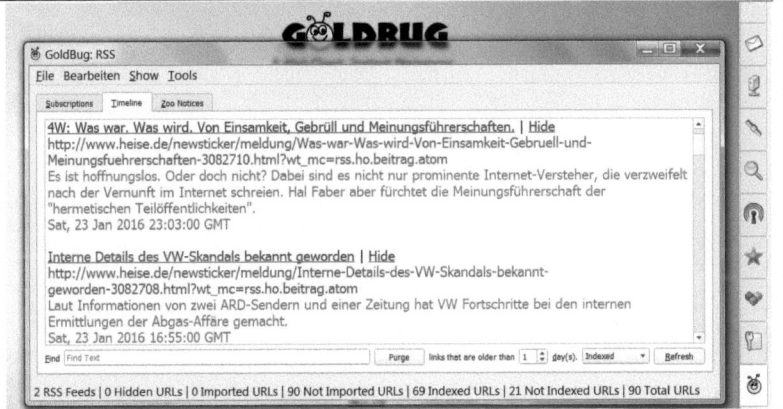

Source: Screenshot of RSS-/Atom-Reader in GoldBug.

3.13.2 Selected method for studying and function reference

To investigate the separation of the URL Web search from the other communication functions, a code review should be provided as well as a process-review.

With the code review of the URL and RSS function is to ensure that content from the areas of communication such as chat, group chat, and email not enter the field of web URLs.

With the processes review is to ensure that both, the structure (e.g. of the functions or especially of the databases, in which the information is stored), as also by the user clicking routines no confidential information in the URL indexing is added and is possibly spread inadvertently to other friends or subscribers.

The method of investigation of safety information, which could end up as so-called "security nuggets" in external search engines, has been excluded above by theoretical assumptions and as well by a code review.

Um die Trennung der URL-Websuche von den übrigen Kommunikationsfunktionen zu untersuchen, ist ein Code-Review vorzusehen sowie auch ein Prozess-Review.

Mit dem Code-Review der URL- und RSS-Funktion soll sichergestellt werden, dass Inhalte aus den Kommunikationsbereichen wie Chat, Gruppenchat und E-Mail nicht in den Bereich der Web-URLs gelangen.

Mit dem Prozess-Review soll sichergestellt werden, dass sowohl von der Struktur (z.B. der Funktionen oder besonders der Datenbanken, in denen die Informationen gespeichert werden), als auch von den Nutzer-Klick-Routinen keine vertraulichen Informationen in die URL-Indexierung aufgenommen und ggf. an andere Freunde oder Teilnehmer versehentlich verteilt werden.

Die Methode der Untersuchung von sicherheitsrelevanten Informationen, die als sogenannte "Security Nuggets" in externe Suchmaschinen gelangen könnten, wurde oben durch theoretische Annahmen und ebenso durch eine Code-Review ausgeschlossen.

Both approaches of a judgment as to whether an external search engine or the internal search engine of Goldbug might tap security-related information from the client, therefore come to the following conclusion:

Beide Ansätze einer Beurteilung, ob eine externe Suchmaschine oder die interne Suchmaschine von GoldBug sicherheitsrelevante Informationen aus dem Klienten abgreifen könnte, kommen daher zu folgendem Ergebnis:

3.13.3 Conduction and findings of the examinations

The case, whether external Web search engines could record the communication of two users of the client GoldBug, is almost impossible. The investigation of these "security nuggets" of unprotected portions has therefore then been based in a second perspective on the Websearch feature, which is implemented in GoldBug itself internally.

Die Fragestellung, ob externe Web-Suchmaschinen die Kommunikation zweier Nutzer des Klienten GoldBug aufzeichnen könnten, ist nahezu ausgeschlossen. Die Untersuchung von diesen "Security Nuggets" ungeschützter Bereiche ist daher sodann in einer zweiten Sichtweise auch auf die in GoldBug selbst implementierte interne Websuch-Funktion bezogen worden.

For this purpose a code review and a process analysis of the user interface has been conducted.

Dazu wurde ein Code-Review und eine Prozess-Analyse der Bedienoberfläche durchgeführt.

Figure 20: Code for the URL-Database Distribution to other participants

```
void spoton_urldistribution::slotTimeout(void)
{
  QTimer *timer = qobject_cast<QTimer *> (sender());

  if(timer)
    if(1000 * spoton_common::KERNEL_URL_DISPATCHER_INTERVAL !=
      timer->interval())
      timer->setInterval
        (1000 * spoton_common::KERNEL_URL_DISPATCHER_INTERVAL);

  spoton_crypt *s_crypt1 = spoton_kernel::s_crypts.value("url", 0);

  if(!s_crypt1)
    {
      spoton_misc::logError("spoton_urldistribution::slotTimeout(): "
                            "s_crypt1 is zero.");
      return;
    }

  spoton_crypt *s_crypt2 = spoton_kernel::s_crypts.value("url-
signature", 0);

  if(!s_crypt2)
    {
      spoton_misc::logError("spoton_urldistribution::slotTimeout(): "
                            "s_crypt2 is zero.");
      return;
    }

  QString connectionName("");

  /*
  ** Now, retrieve polarizers.
```

```
*/

QList<QPair<QUrl, QString> > polarizers;

{
  QSqlDatabase db = spoton_misc::database(connectionName);

  db.setDatabaseName(spoton_misc::homePath() + QDir::separator() +
                     "urls_distillers_information.db");

  if(db.open())
    {
      QSqlQuery query(db);
      bool ok = true;

      query.setForwardOnly(true);
      query.prepare("SELECT domain, permission FROM distillers WHERE "
                    "direction_hash = ?");
      query.bindValue(0, s_crypt1->keyedHash(QByteArray("upload"),
                                             &ok).toBase64());

      if(ok && query.exec())
        while(query.next())
          {
            QByteArray domain;
            QByteArray permission;
            bool ok = true;

            domain = s_crypt1->
              decryptedAfterAuthenticated(QByteArray::
                                          fromBase64(query.
                                                     value(0).
                                                     toByteArray()),
                                          &ok);

            if(ok)
              permission = s_crypt1->
                decryptedAfterAuthenticated(QByteArray::
                                            fromBase64(query.
                                                       value(1).
                                                       toByteArray()),
                                            &ok);

            if(ok)
              {
                QUrl url(QUrl::fromUserInput(domain));

                if(!url.isEmpty())
                  if(url.isValid())
                    {
                      QPair<QUrl, QString> pair;

                      pair.first = url;
                      pair.second = permission.constData();
                      polarizers.append(pair);
                    }
              }

            if(m_quit.fetchAndAddRelaxed(0))
              break;
          }
    }
```

```
   db.close();
}

QSqlDatabase::removeDatabase(connectionName);

if(m_quit.fetchAndAddRelaxed(0))
  return;

/*
** Let's retrieve the public keys.
*/

QList<QByteArray> publicKeys;

{
   QSqlDatabase db = spoton_misc::database(connectionName);

   db.setDatabaseName(spoton_misc::homePath() + QDir::separator() +
                      "friends_public_keys.db");

   if(db.open())
     {
        QSqlQuery query(db);
        bool ok = true;

        query.setForwardOnly(true);
        query.prepare("SELECT public_key "
                      "FROM friends_public_keys WHERE "
                      "key_type_hash = ? AND neighbor_oid = -1");
        query.bindValue
          (0, s_crypt1->keyedHash(QByteArray("url"), &ok).toBase64());

        if(ok && query.exec())
          while(query.next())
            {
               QByteArray publicKey;
               bool ok = true;

               publicKey = s_crypt1->decryptedAfterAuthenticated
                 (QByteArray::fromBase64(query.value(0).toByteArray()),
                  &ok);

               if(ok)
                 publicKeys.append(publicKey);

                 if(m_quit.fetchAndAddRelaxed(0))
                   break;
            }
     }
   db.close();
}

QSqlDatabase::removeDatabase(connectionName);

if(m_quit.fetchAndAddRelaxed(0))
  return;

if(publicKeys.isEmpty())
  {
     spoton_misc::logError("spoton_urldistribution::slotTimeout(): "
```

```
                              "publicKeys is empty.");
      return;
   }

spoton_crypt *urlCommonCredentials =
  spoton_misc::retrieveUrlCommonCredentials(s_crypt1);

if(!urlCommonCredentials)
  {
    spoton_misc::logError("spoton_urldistribution::slotTimeout(): "
                          "urlCommonCredentials is zero.");
    return;
  }

/*
** Next, retrieve some URL(s).
*/

QByteArray data;

{
  connectionName = spoton_misc::databaseName();

  QSqlDatabase db;

  if(spoton_kernel::setting("gui/sqliteSearch", true).toBool())
    {
      db = QSqlDatabase::addDatabase("QSQLITE", connectionName);
      db.setDatabaseName
        (spoton_misc::homePath() + QDir::separator() + "urls.db");
      db.open();
    }
  else
    {
      QByteArray password;
      QString database
        (spoton_kernel::setting("gui/postgresql_database", "").
         toString().trimmed());
      QString host
        (spoton_kernel::setting("gui/postgresql_host", "localhost").
         toString().trimmed());
      QString name
        (spoton_kernel::setting("gui/postgresql_name", "").toString().
         trimmed());
      QString str("connect_timeout=10");
      bool ok = true;
      bool ssltls = spoton_kernel::setting
        ("gui/postgresql_ssltls", false).toBool();
      int port = spoton_kernel::setting
        ("gui/postgresql_port", 5432).toInt();

      password = s_crypt1->decryptedAfterAuthenticated
        (QByteArray::
         fromBase64(spoton_kernel::setting("gui/postgresql_password",
""));
                    toByteArray()), &ok);

      if(ssltls)
        str.append(";requiressl=1");

      db = QSqlDatabase::addDatabase("QPSQL", connectionName);
      db.setConnectOptions(str);
```

```
         db.setDatabaseName(database);
         db.setHostName(host);
         db.setPort(port);

         if(ok)
            db.open(name, password);
      }

   if(db.isOpen())
      {
         QDataStream stream(&data, QIODevice::WriteOnly);
         QSqlQuery query(db);
         QString querystr("");

         query.setForwardOnly(true);

         for(int i = 0; i < 10 + 6; i++)
            for(int j = 0; j < 10 + 6; j++)
               {
                  QChar c1;
                  QChar c2;

                  if(i <= 9)
                     c1 = QChar(i + 48);
                  else
                     c1 = QChar(i + 97 - 10);

                  if(j <= 9)
                     c2 = QChar(j + 48);
                  else
                     c2 = QChar(j + 97 - 10);

                  if(i == 15 && j == 15)
                     querystr.append
                        (QString("SELECT url, title, description, content, "
                                 "date_time_inserted, unique_id "
                                 "FROM spot_on_urls_%1%2 "
                                 "WHERE LENGTH(content) <= %3 AND unique_id > "
%4 ").
                        arg(c1).arg(c2).
                        arg(spoton_common::URL_CONTENT_SHARE_MAXIMUM_SIZE).
                        arg(m_lastUniqueId));
                  else
                     querystr.append
                        (QString("SELECT url, title, description, content, "
                                 "date_time_inserted, unique_id "
                                 "FROM spot_on_urls_%1%2 "
                                 "WHERE LENGTH(content) <= %3 AND unique_id > "
%4 "
                                 "UNION ").
                        arg(c1).arg(c2).
                        arg(spoton_common::URL_CONTENT_SHARE_MAXIMUM_SIZE).
                        arg(m_lastUniqueId));
               }

         querystr.append(" ORDER BY 5 "); // date_time_inserted
         querystr.append(QString(" LIMIT %1 ").arg(m_limit));

         quint64 count = 0;

         if(query.exec(querystr))
            do
```

```
{
   if(!query.next())
   {
      if(count != m_limit)
        m_lastUniqueId = -1;

      break;
   }

   bool ok = true;

   if(data.isEmpty())
   {
      QByteArray myPublicKey(s_crypt1->publicKey(&ok));
      QByteArray myPublicKeyHash;

      if(ok)
        myPublicKeyHash = spoton_crypt::sha512Hash
           (myPublicKey, &ok);

      if(ok)
      {
         stream << myPublicKeyHash;

         if(stream.status() != QDataStream::Ok)
         {
            data.clear();
            ok = false;
         }
      }
   }

   QList<QByteArray> bytes;

   if(ok)
     bytes.append
       (urlCommonCredentials->
        decryptedAfterAuthenticated(QByteArray::
                                 fromBase64(query.value(0).
                                        toByteArray()),
                                 &ok));

   if(ok)
   {
      /*
      ** Apply polarizers.
      */

      ok = false;

      for(int i = 0; i < polarizers.size(); i++)
      {
         QString type(polarizers.at(i).second);
         QUrl u1(polarizers.at(i).first);
         QUrl u2(QUrl::fromUserInput(bytes.value(0)));

         if(type == "accept")
         {
            if(u2.toEncoded().startsWith(u1.toEncoded()))
            {
               ok = true;
               break;
```

```
                            }
                        }
                    else
                        {
                            if(u2.toEncoded().startsWith(u1.toEncoded()))
                                {
                                    ok = false;
                                    break;
                                }
                        }
                    }
                }

            if(ok)
                bytes.append
                    (urlCommonCredentials->
                    decryptedAfterAuthenticated(QByteArray::
                                        fromBase64(query.value(1).
                                                toByteArray()),
                                        &ok));

            if(ok)
                bytes.append
                    (urlCommonCredentials->
                    decryptedAfterAuthenticated(QByteArray::
                                        fromBase64(query.value(2).
                                                toByteArray()),
                                        &ok));

            if(ok)
                bytes.append
                    (urlCommonCredentials->
                    decryptedAfterAuthenticated(QByteArray::
                                        fromBase64(query.value(3).
                                                toByteArray()),
                                        &ok));

            if(ok)
                m_lastUniqueId = qMax
                    (m_lastUniqueId, query.value(5).toLongLong());

            if(ok)
                {
                    stream << bytes.value(0)  // URL
                           << bytes.value(1)  // Title
                           << bytes.value(2)  // Description
                           << bytes.value(3); // Content

                    if(stream.status() != QDataStream::Ok)
                        {
                            data.clear();
                            ok = false;
                        }
                }

            count += 1;

            if(m_quit.fetchAndAddRelaxed(0))
                break;
        }
    while(true);
}
```

```
  db.close();
}

QSqlDatabase::removeDatabase(connectionName);
delete urlCommonCredentials;

if(data.isEmpty())
  {
    spoton_misc::logError("spoton_urldistribution::slotTimeout(): "
                          "data is empty.");
    return;
  }

if(m_quit.fetchAndAddRelaxed(0))
  return;

QByteArray cipherType
  (spoton_kernel::setting("gui/kernelCipherType",
                          "aes256").toString().toLatin1());
QByteArray hashType
  (spoton_kernel::setting("gui/kernelHashType",
                          "sha512").toString().toLatin1());
size_t symmetricKeyLength = spoton_crypt::cipherKeyLength
  (cipherType);

if(symmetricKeyLength <= 0)
  {
    spoton_misc::logError
      ("spoton_urldistribution::slotTimeout(): "
       "cipherKeyLength() failure.");
    return;
  }

data = qCompress(data, 9);

for(int i = 0; i < publicKeys.size(); i++)
  {
    QByteArray hashKey;
    QByteArray symmetricKey;

    hashKey.resize(spoton_crypt::SHA512_OUTPUT_SIZE_IN_BYTES);
    hashKey = spoton_crypt::strongRandomBytes
      (static_cast<size_t> (hashKey.length()));
    symmetricKey.resize(static_cast<int> (symmetricKeyLength));
    symmetricKey = spoton_crypt::strongRandomBytes
      (static_cast<size_t> (symmetricKey.length()));

    QByteArray keyInformation;
    QByteArray message;
    QByteArray messageCode;
    QByteArray signature;
    QDataStream stream(&keyInformation, QIODevice::WriteOnly);
    bool ok = true;

    stream << QByteArray("0080")
           << symmetricKey
           << hashKey
           << cipherType
           << hashType;

    if(stream.status() != QDataStream::Ok)
```

```
      ok = false;

  if(ok)
    keyInformation = spoton_crypt::publicKeyEncrypt
      (keyInformation, publicKeys.at(i), &ok);

  if(ok)
    if(spoton_kernel::setting("gui/urlSignMessages", true).toBool())
      signature = s_crypt2->digitalSignature(keyInformation + data,
&ok);

  if(ok)
    {
      QByteArray bytes;
      QDataStream stream(&bytes, QIODevice::WriteOnly);
      spoton_crypt crypt(cipherType,
                          hashType,
                          QByteArray(),
                          symmetricKey,
                          hashKey,
                          0,
                          0,
                          "");

      stream << data
             << signature;

      if(stream.status() != QDataStream::Ok)
        ok = false;

      if(ok)
        message = crypt.encrypted(bytes, &ok);

      if(ok)
        messageCode = crypt.keyedHash(keyInformation + message,
&ok);
    }

  if(ok)
    message = keyInformation.toBase64() + "\n" +
      message.toBase64() + "\n" +
      messageCode.toBase64();

  if(ok)
    emit sendURLs(message);

  if(m_quit.fetchAndAddRelaxed(0))
    return;
  }
}
```

Source: Source Code of GoldBug.

The review of the code in this regard in the chat messenger respectively in the e-mail client area and in particular in the function of the Web search of GoldBug shows no irregularities, from which a risk is to assume, that the separate functions of the private communication transmission could interfere in the URL database respectively in the Web search, or even could be found in the URL data

Die Durchsicht des Codes diesbezüglich im Chat-Messenger bzw. im E-Mail Klient-Bereich als auch insbesondere im Funktionsteil der Websuche von GoldBug zeigt keine Auffälligkeiten, aus denen ein Risiko anzunehmen wäre, dass die getrennten Funktionen der privaten Kommunikationsübermittlung sich in der Websuche bzw. der URL-Datenbank

exchange to a peer. The URL web search shares with the neighbors just URLs. Furthermore the URL database can also be operated locally without a network connection.

Also the user interface with its click and process routines remained without any idea of an incorrect operation, that could cause that private information could fraudulently brought into the functional area of the p2p URL database.

The path that a chat message enters in the URL database respectively website function is therefore highly unlikely.

While researching we looked also at the global external web search engines, which Top 10 search results they produce for the keyword "GoldBug Messenger". Essentially, there are software review portals, which are reflected in the ten relevant URL results. The average rating of the URL location by web search engines of the respective portal, we have shown in the following table.

It should be noted, that this only the sorting of the search engine algorithm was analyzed, it says no statement about the continuous adaptation of the portal to the latest version of GoldBug, about corresponding download numbers or even editorial quality of the review and reporting contribution.

Downloadportals are able to significantly develop in the subject area of the Crypto Messenger, if they report in an editorial and qualitative style about software - and not mirror only a download option of a file.

niederschlagen könnten oder gar sich in dem URL-Datenaustausch zu einem Peer wiederfinden könnten. Die URL-Websuche teilt mit den Nachbarn nur URLs. Zudem kann die URL-Datenbank auch lokal ohne Netzwerk-Verbindung betrieben werden.

Auch die Benutzeroberfläche mit ihren Klick- und Prozess-Routinen blieb ohne jegliche Idee einer falschen Bedienung, die dazu führen könnte, dass private Informationen in den Funktionsbereich der p2p URL-Datenbank unbefugt gelangen könnten.

Der Weg, dass eine Chat-Nachricht in die URL-Datenbank bzw. Webseitenfunktion gelangt, ist daher absolut unwahrscheinlich.

Bei unseren Recherchen haben wir uns auch die globalen externen Websuchmaschinen angeschaut, welche Top 10 Suchergebnisse sie zur Stichwortsuche "GoldBug Messenger" hervorbringen. Im Wesentlichen sind es Software-Review-Portale, die sich in den jeweiligen zehn relevanten URL-Ergebnissen wiederfinden. Die durchschnittliche Bewertung der URL-Position durch die Websuchmaschinen von dem jeweiligen Portal haben wir in der folgenden Tabelle dargestellt.

Es sei angemerkt, dass damit nur die Sortierung des Suchmaschinenalgorithmus untersucht wurde, es jedoch keine Aussage über die kontinuierliche Anpassung des Portals auf die aktuelle Version von GoldBug, entsprechende Downloadzahlen oder gar redaktioneller Qualität des Reviews und Berichtsbeitrages aussagt.

Downloadportale können sich wesentlich auch im Themenfeld der Crypo-Messenger entwickeln, wenn Sie redaktionell und qualitativ über Software berichten - und nicht nur eine Downloadmöglichkeit einer Datei spiegeln.

Table 46: Within Top 10 search results of main search engines for query: GB Messenger

URL TO WEBSITE OF	AVERAGE POSITION	START PAGE	METAGER & YACY	DUCK DUCKGO	GOOGLE	BING	YANDEX	BAIDU
Sourceforge	2,1	☑	☑	☑	☑	☑	☑	☑
Softpedia	3,5	☑		☑	☑	☑	☑	☑
Download	3,8	☑		☑	☑	☑	☑	☑
Softonic	5,0	☑	☑	☑	☑	☑	☑	☑
Twitter	5,3	☑	☑	☑	☑	☑	☑	☑
Heise DL	5,3		☑		☑	☑		
Download 3K	6,3	☑	☑		☑	☑	☑	☑
Soft 82	7,3		☑	☑			☑	☑
Qt Showroom	7,3				☑	☑	☑	☑
Shareware	7,5		☑			☑		
FF Betanews	7,8	☑	☑	☑				
Afterdawn	8,0	☑		☑				
UptoDown	8,0		☑					☑
Freewarefiles	8,3	☑		☑	☑		☑	☑
Majorgeeks	9,2	☑	☑	☑	☑	☑	☑	

Source: Own research.

3.13.4 Evaluation of the results with regard to weaknesses, risks, potentials for improvements and strengths

The opposite way, that an URL found in the GoldBug web search can be sent to a friend via a simple click through the e-mail function of GoldBug, is possibly in contrast most desirable (and not yet implemented at the time of the audit in GoldBug).

The URL database in GoldBug could therefore provide a function for sharing the URLs via chat or e-mail in order to forward them e.g. with a comment.

Der umgekehrte Weg, dass eine in der GoldBug-Websuche gefundene URL über einen einfachen Klick über die E-Mail-Funktion von GoldBug an einen Freund gesandt werden kann, ist demgegenüber ggf. absolut wünschenswert (und zum Zeitpunkt des Audits in GoldBug noch nicht implementiert).

Die URL-Datenbank in GoldBug könnte daher eine Funktion zum Teilen der URLs per Chat oder E-Mail vorsehen, um sie mit einem Kommentar weiterzuleiten.

Table 47: Description of findings 3.13

#	Area	Description of the finding	Valuation Severity Category / Difficulty Level / Innovation & Improvement Class / Strength Dimension
	Weakness / Schwäche	./.	./.
	Risk / Risiko	./.	./.
	Potential for Improvement / Verbesserungspotential	./.	./.
	Strength / Stärke	./.	./.

Security risks or weaknesses from were not found for this assessment part.

Sicherheits-Risiken oder -Schwächen wurden für diesen Assessment-Teil nicht gefunden.

3.13.5   Appraisal of good practices in comparison with other similar applications

All said other communication solutions have integrated no URL database or Web search - except of RetroShare. Thus it is also not possible to send bookmarks or URLs from one friend to another for a search indexing.

Alle genannten anderen Kommunikations-lösungen haben - bis auf RetroShare - keine URL-Datenbank oder Websuche integriert. Damit ist es auch nicht möglich, Bookmarks oder URLs von einem Freund zum anderen für eine Indexierung zu senden.

The extent to which other communication solutions have separate areas of activity, that a function does not reveal another function sensitive information, respectively the programmings of the individual functions are clearly separated from each other, can not further and not deeper be compared in the context of this audit. For this purpose individual audits of each application should be performed.

Inwieweit die weiteren Kommunikationslösungen getrennte Funktionsbereiche haben, dass eine Funktion nicht einer anderen Funktion sensible Informationen offenbart, bzw. die Programmierungen der Einzelfunktionen voneinander sauber getrennt sind, kann im Rahmen dieses Audits nicht weiter und tiefergehend verglichen werden. Dazu sollten individuelle Audits der jeweiligen Applikation durchgeführt werden.

RetroShare as well provides the function of a link-, respectively URL-sharing to existing friends. This is offered for individual URL bookmarks with a comment and scoring function, is so far technically be regarded even as an advanced solution in these two features. However, the URL search does not include indexing with keywords, also including website content for indexing is not given and the function shares the URLs with friends only, if they click manually on each individual URL and confirm an sharing with friends. In the absence of the implementation of URL filtering (URL Distiller function) the URL function therefore at Retroshare can only be described as rudimentary respectively as equipped with a different focus than for a web search. It is more a shared link list with comments between only two friends.

RetroShare bietet ebenso die Funktion eines Link bzw. URL-Versandes an bestehende Freunde. Dieses wird für einzelne URL-Bookmarks mit einer Kommentar- und Bewertungsfunktion angeboten, ist insofern technisch in diesen beiden Ausgestaltungen sogar als fortschrittliche Lösung zu werten. Jedoch umfasst die URL-Suche keine Indexierung mit Stichworten, bezieht den Webseiten Content bei der Indexierung nicht mit ein und teilt die URLs nur mit Freunden, wenn sie manuell auf jede einzelne URL klicken und eine Teilung mit Freunden bestätigen. In Ermangelung der Implementierung von URL-Filtern (URL-Distiller-Funktion) kann bei RetroShare die URL-Funktion daher nur als rudimentär bzw. mit einem anderen Fokus als der für eine Websuche bezeichnet werden. Es ist eine nur zwischen zwei Freunden geteilte Link-Liste mit Kommentarfunktion.

Also at RetroShare is no browser-import available, and no web-crawler respectively the compound of the RSS function to the URL-sharing available.
The p2p web search in GoldBug is therefore conceptually possibly meaningful to compare with the established p2p web search YaCy - even if both p2p web search engines have experienced different elaborations based on previous history and practical usages.

Auch steht bei RetroShare kein Webbrowser-Import, kein Web-Crawler bzw. die Verbindung der RSS-Funktion mit dem URL-Sharing zur Verfügung.
Die p2p Websuche in GoldBug ist daher konzeptionell ggf. sinnvoller mit der etablierten p2p-Websuche von YaCy zu vergleichen – wenn gleich auch beide p2p Web-Suchen aufgrund der bisherigen Historie unterschiedliche Elaborationen und Praxisanwendungen erfahren haben.

Table 48: Indicative BIG SEVEN context references 3.13

Logo	Application	Comments
	Cryptocat	Has not been assessed in terms of lacks of so called security nuggets left to external web search engines. Has no own p2p websearch function.
	GoldBug	Secures the information to external search engines. Even one possibly public element, the public key, is secure-able. Has an internal p2p-Websearch engine, which is well separated – as a code review shows.
	OTR+XMPP	Has not been assessed in terms of lacks of so called security nuggets left to external web search engines. Has no own p2p websearch function.
	RetroShare	Has not been assessed in terms of lacks of so called security nuggets left to external web search engines. Local database to manually share bookmarks to one hop friend but not filter distiller implemented.
	Signal	Has not been assessed in terms of lacks of so called security nuggets left to external web search engines. Has no own p2p websearch function.
	SureSpot	Has not been assessed in terms of lacks of so called security nuggets left to external web search engines. Has no own p2p websearch function.
	Tox	Has not been assessed in terms of lacks of so called security nuggets left to external web search engines. Has no own p2p websearch function.

The following analysis in this context of the above-mentioned Download portals should be as well documented:

Focussing an essential DownloadPortal as key player - because it is manually created and maintained, provided with its own test screenshot and reviews - one finds in the category "Instant Messenger" 59 Programs, of which 24 Messenger have published a release since 2013, so can be considered as active projects.

Folgende Analyse in diesem Zusammenhang der o.g. Downloadportale soll ebenso dokumentiert werden:

Nimmt man ein wesentliches, weil manuell erstellt und gepflegtes, mit eigenen Test-Screenshots und Reviews versehenes, Downloadportal heraus - wir wollen uns auf das Expertenportal Majorgeek für technische Werkzeuge beziehen - so findet man dort in der Kategorie "Instant Messenger" insgesamt 59 Programme, von denen 24 Messenger seit 2013 ein Release veröffentlicht haben, also als aktive Projekte gelten können.

Table 49: Overview of other Messengers in the Portal Majorgeeks

APP NAME	VERSION	ENCRYPTION	RELEASE-DATE	LICENSE	DOWNLOADS	RATING
GoldBug Secure Email Client & Instant Messenger	2.9	yes	2016-01-31	Open Source	21.169	5
RetroShare	0.6.0 RC2.8551	yes	2015-06-24	Open Source	5.276	4
Mumble	1.2.13	No Encryption	2016-01-11	Open Source	3.034	5
Pidgin XMPP	2.10.12	Encryption only with OTR Plug	2016-01-02	Freeware	92.213	5
Viber	5.4.0.1664	No Encryption	2015-12-21	Freeware	45.329	4
Raidcall	7.3.6	No Encryption	2014-06-11	Freeware	32.775	4
ooVoo	3.6.9.10	No Encryption	2015-11-06	Freeware	32.273	4
MicroSIP	3.10.10	No Encryption	2015-12-13	Freeware	32.114	4
Speak-A-Message	10.2.1	No Encryption	2015-07-24	Freeware	29.162	3
TeamTalk	5.1.1.4434	No Encryption	2015-10-02	Freeware	26.288	3
Nokia Suite	3.8.54	No Encryption	2014-12-19	Freeware	17.460	5
Ventrillo	3.0.8	No Encryption	2013-10-15	Freeware	16.582	4
Nimbuzz	2.9.5	No Encryption	2015-05-18	Freeware	12.951	5
SSuite	e.g. NetVine	No Encryption	2016-01-13	Freeware	11.408	5
MP3 Skype Recorder	4.6	No Encryption	2014-08-14	Freeware	5.799	2
UltraCam Video Phone	2.01	No Encryption	2015-01-10	Freeware	2.539	5
Telegram	0.9.18	closed source Crypto	2016-01-08	Freeware	1.925	5
Cryptocat	2.2.1	yes	2014-05-16	Freeware	1.876	5
Skype	7.18.32.109	No Encryption	2016-01-20	Ad-Supported	661.947	5
Trillian	5.6.0.5	No Encryption	2015-05-27	Ad-Supported	124.905	5
Miranda IM	0.10.45	Encryption only with OTR Plug	2016-01-28	Ad-Supported	112.630	5
ICQ	10.0.10244	No Encryption	2016-01-20	Ad-Supported	76.659	4
ManyCam	5.1.0	No Encryption	2015-12-21	Ad-Supported	61.619	3
Camfrog	6.11.511	No Encryption	2015-12-22	Ad-Supported	46.903	3
TeamSpeak	3.0.18.2	No Encryption	2015-10-22	Ad-Supported	27.660	3

Source: Own overview per 02/2016 from http://www.majorgeeks.com/mg/sortdate/messaging.html

The survey clearly shows that GoldBug not only in the user review, but also in the number of downloads of the respective license category has high relevance.
Looking at this background of numerous articles, blogs, and reviews of the download portals, is the discussion for a Wikipedia entry or its deletion, as have happened in history, with the criterion "Relevance" incomprehensible.

GoldBug has has among the BIG SEVEN messengers an important high relevance in terms of popularity among users, in the number of downloads of this portal as well as compared to the BIG SEVEN Open Source messengers: Here are not the Messenger Tox, SureSpot, Signal in this exemplary Download-portal listed. Nevertheless, the relevance of an

Die Übersicht zeigt deutlich, dass GoldBug nicht nur in der Nutzerbewertung, sondern auch in den Downloadzahlen der jeweiligen Lizenz-Kategorie hohe Relevanz hat. Vor diesem Hintergrund zahlreicher Artikel, Blogs und Reviews der Downloadportale ist die Diskussion für einen Wikipedia-Eintrag oder dessen Löschung, wie wohl in der Historie geschehen, mit dem Kriterium "Relevanz" unverständlich.

GoldBug hat unter den BIG SEVEN Messengern eine sehr hohe Relevanz in der Beliebtheit bei den Nutzern, in den Downloadzahlen dieses Portals wie auch im Vergleich zu den BIG SEVEN Open Source Messengern: Hier sind die Messenger Tox, Surespot, Signal in diesem exemplarischen Downloadportal gar nicht aufgeführt.

innovative and cryptologic evaluation of processes and programming should be considered as well. It is about the judgement of the quality of the tool, e.g. its codings, and not about the popularity.

The Portal Major Geek has thus listed for approximately 50 Messenger 5 Messenger offering encryption. The XMPP-Messenger Pidgin and Miranda offer encryption only over a retrofit e.g. with an OTR-plugin, the three native encrypted open source applications are therefore again: GoldBug, RetroShare and CryptoCat.

Even if the download numbers speak only for this site and each application generates Downloads in other portals or release paths, is the qualitative assessment that GoldBug beside Retroshare and CryptoCat plays an essential role, and additionally the only messenger is, that offers both, encrypted chat and e-mail.

Pidgin as popular XMPP representative is also open source and possibly therefore not sorted quite right in the freeware Categorie, however, the download figures are there referred to a version without encryption plugin. The number of users of Pidgin with the OTR plugin is therefore unknown. Nor are there any efforts at XMPP, natively and necessarily predetermine the encryption in XMPP clients from default setting.

In the German-speaking area, we have made at this time an additional assessment based on the renowned and excellent maintained download section of the portal Heise.de: Thereafter GoldBug achieved a download ranking of 5513, OTR-XMPP e.g. with the OTR-integrated client ChatSecure a value of 6529, SureSpot is at 9162 and on the last places is Retroshare with 11340 and CryptoCat with 17130 brings up the rear. (For Signal and Tox exist there no download options). This also shows, taking into account that the clients offer also on their respective web page downloads, at least indicative, that users, who want to explore this download portal, again at the BIG SEVEN Crypto messengers put their interest also in GoldBug.

Gleichwohl sollte sich die Relevanz aus einer innovativen und kryptologischen Beurteilung der Prozesse und Programmierung ebenso ergeben. Es geht um die Beurteilung der Qualität eines technischen Tools und dessen Programmierung und nicht um dessen Popularität.

Das Portal Majorgeek hat also aus rund 50 Messenger nur 5 Messenger gelistet, die eine Verschlüsselung anbieten. Die XMPP-Messenger Pidgin und Miranda bieten Verschlüsselung nur über eine Nachrüstung mit einem OTR-Plugin an, die drei nativen verschlüsselnden quelloffenen Applikationen sind daher wieder: GoldBug, RetroShare und CryptoCat.

Auch wenn die Downloadzahlen nur für dieses Portal sprechen und jede Applikation auch in anderen Portalen oder Release-Pfaden Downloads generiert, ist die qualitative Bewertung, dass GoldBug neben RetroShare und CryptoCat eine wesentliche Rolle spielt, und dabei der einzige Messenger ist, der sowohl Chat, als auch E-Mail verschlüsselt anbietet.

Pidgin als populärer XMPP Vertreter ist ebenso quelloffen und ggf. daher in der Freeware-Categorie nicht ganz richtig einsortiert, jedoch beziehen sich die Downloadzahlen dort auf die Version ohne Verschlüsselungs-Plugin. Die Anzahl der Nutzer von Pidgin mit OTR-Plugin ist daher unbekannt. Ebenso bestehen keine Bestrebungen bei XMPP, die Verschlüsselung in XMPP-Klienten nativ und zwingend ab Werkseinstellung vorzugeben.

Auch im deutschsprachigen Raum haben wir zu dieser Zeit eine ergänzende Einschätzung auf Basis der renommierten und excellent gepflegten Download-Sektion des Portals Heise.de vorgenommen: Danach erreicht GoldBug ein Download-Ranking von 5513, OTR-XMPP z.B. mit dem OTR-integrierten Clienten Chatsecure einen Wert von 6529, Surespot liegt bei 9162 und auf den letzten Plätzen liegt RetroShare mit 11340 und CryptoCat mit 17130 bildet das Schlusslicht. (Für Signal und Tox bestehen dort keine Downloadmöglichkeiten). Auch hier zeigt sich unter Berücksichtigung, dass die Klienten jeweils auch auf ihrer Webseite Downloads anbieten, zumindest indikativ, dass die Nutzer, die dieses Downloadportal erkunden, bei den BIG SEVEN Crypto Messengern wiederum ihr Interesse auch in GoldBug setzen.

Assuming that the user wishes to continue to use in future elaborated programs, in Goldbug is noted in a strategic assessment in this regard a clear perspective of an "Unique Structure Proposition" (USP) - a base for the anticipated, maximized usage-characteristics due to the previously developed functional scope compared to other applications.

Unter der Annahme, dass der Nutzer in Zukunft weiterhin elaborierte Programme nutzen will, ist bei GoldBug in einer strategischen Beurteilung in dieser Hinsicht eine klare Perspektive für eine "Unique Structure Proposition" (USP) festzustellen - eine Ausgangsbasis für die anzunehmenden, größtmöglichen Nutzungseigenschaften aufgrund des bislang erarbeiteten Funktionsumfanges im Vergleich zu anderen Applikationen.

Table 50: Good Practice Insights #13

Good Practice Insight # 13	
with GoldBug Multi-Encrypting Communication Suite	
Case	I do not want, that my public key is known to other persons or search engines than to the friends I communicate with. How can I protect the key?
	Ich möchte nicht, dass mein öffentlicher Schlüssel anderen Personen oder Suchmaschinen bekannt wird als den Freunden, mit denen ich kommuniziere. Wie kann ich den Schlüssel schützen?
Solution	In GoldBug you need not to make your public key public. There are numerous protective measures and ways to be able to send the key securely to a friend. One possibility is e.g. the use of the Repleo function. With this, your own key will be already encrypted with the key obtained from the friend. As another option, it is recommended to exchange the own key within GoldBug, e.g. in a private chat room of the Buzz-IRC-function. This works with symmetric encryption and with the friend is simply a password to share, that opens then private room. Also the EPKS function is given with a similar proxess.
	In GoldBug muss man seinen Schlüssel nicht öffentlich machen. Es bestehen zahlreiche Schutzmaßnahmen und –wege, den Schlüssel sicher an einen Freund senden zu können. Eine Möglichkeit ist z.B. die Nutzung der Repleo-Funktion. Damit wird der eigene Schlüssel bereits mit dem vom Freund erhaltenen Schlüssel verschlüsselt. Als weitere Option ist es zu empfehlen, den eigenen Schlüssel innerhalb von GoldBug zu tauschen, z.B. in einem privaten Chat-Raum der Buzz-IRC Funktion. Dieser funktioniert mit symmetrischer Verschlüsselung und mit dem Freund ist lediglich ein Passwort zu teilen, das den dann privaten Raum eröffnet. Ebenso steht auch die EPKS-Funktion mit einem ähnlichen Prozess zur Verfügung.

Source: Own Case.

3.14 Physical Interaction of Components: e.g. GUI-Kernel-Interaction

A classical approach to app-programming is that a kernel and a user interface are used. So the stability-oriented kernel may perform its tasks and functions and the user interface is independent of it and can be created in different variations.

As an example of a physical interaction the GUI-kernel-interaction should be regarded, since two physical binaries exchange data on a machine via a secure connection.

Eine klassische Vorgehensweise bei der App-Programmierung ist, dass ein Kernel und eine Benutzeroberfläche genutzt werden. So kann der auf Stabilität ausgerichtete Kernel seine Aufgaben und Funktionen durchführen und die Benutzeroberfläche ist davon unabhängig und kann in verschiedenen Varianten erstellt werden.

Als Beispiel für eine physikalische Interaktion soll die GUI-Kernel-Interaktion betrachtet werden, da hier zwei physische Binärdateien Daten auf einer Maschine über eine gesicherte Verbindung austauschen.

3.14.1 Inventory taking, structural analysis and descriptions of the functions

There are thus correspondingly two binaries for GoldBug available, which keep the application functioning: On the one hand the kernel ("spoton-kernel.exe") and the user interface ("goldbug.exe"), also GUI (Graphical User Interface) called.

Es sind somit entsprechend zwei Binär-Dateien für GoldBug vorhanden, die die Applikation funktionstüchtig erhalten: Einmal der Kernel („spoton-kernel.exe") sowie . die Benutzeroberfläche („goldbug.exe"), auch GUI (Graphical User Interface) genannt.

In this architecture exists especially with deployed encryption of course the need to securely connect the interface with the kernel. This should be taken into account in the present review.

In dieser Architektur besteht insbesondere bei genutzter Verschlüsselung natürlich auch die Notwendigkeit, die Benutzeroberfläche sicher mit dem Kernel zu verbinden. Dieses soll beim vorliegenden Review entsprechend berücksichtigt werden.

GoldBug uses a local TLS/SSL connection between the GUI and the kernel. The kernel is therefore not influenced by attacks from the middle - a user can only log in with the appropriate login data in the kernel and sees there also the status information, if the kernel is tied with a secure connection.

GoldBug nuzt eine lokale TLS/SSL-Verbindung zwischen der Benutzeroberfläche und dem Kernel. Der Kernel ist daher nicht durch Angriffe aus der Mitte beeinflussbar - ein Nutzer kann sich nur mit den entsprechenden Logindaten in den Kernel einloggen und sieht dort auch die Statusinformationen, ob der Kernel mit einer sicheren Verbindung angebunden ist.

Figure 21: GoldBug - Tooltip for the encryption of GUI to kernel

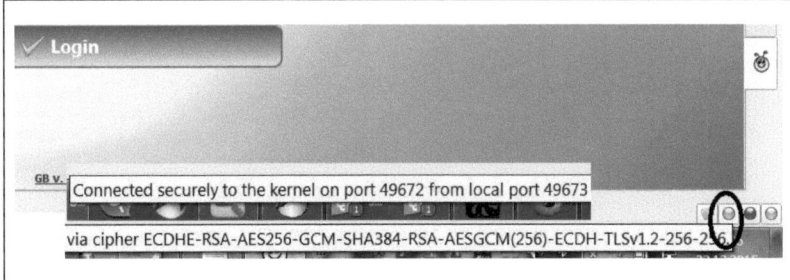

Source: Own screenshot of GoldBug.

The figure shows the prominent at first glance status information via a tooltip, if the kernel is connected safely or not. Additional safety information can as well be read from it.

Die Abbildung zeigt die gleich auf den ersten Blick präsente Statusinformation über einen ToolTip, ob der Kernel sicher angebunden ist oder nicht. Weitere Sicherheitsinformationen können ebenso daraus abgelesen werden.

3.14.2 Selected method for studying and function reference

As analysis the mentioned physical interaction of the GUI should be examined with the kernel. For this, the traffic is recorded with the tool Wireshark on the local machine. Furthermore, it was also looked in the source code, how the kernel-GUI-connection function is implemented.

Als Analyse soll die genannt physikalische Interaktion der Benutzeroberfläche mit dem Kernel untersucht werden. Dazu wird der Traffic mit dem Werkzeug Wireshark auf der lokalen Maschine aufgezeichnet. Weiterhin wurde auch im Quellcode geschaut, wie die Funktion der Kernel-GUI-Anbindung implementiert wurde.

3.14.3 Conduction and findings of the examinations

When analyzing the Wireshark records, it is shown, that the recorded traffic consists exclusively of ciphertext.

Bei der Analyse der Wirkeshark Aufzeichnungen zeigt sich, dass der aufgezeichnete Traffic ausschließlich aus Ciphertext besteht.

From the code review appears that the encryption of the connection is established from the GUI to the kernel via the established standard crypto libraries and its result in the slot "slotKernelSocketState" with these following lines of code in the tooltip summarized is represented.

Aus dem Code-Review zeigt sich, dass die Verschlüsselung der Verbindung von der GUI zum Kernel über die etablierten Standard-Crypto-Bibliotheken hergestellt wird und dessen Ergebnis im Slot "slotKernelSocketState" mit diesen folgenden Codezeilen im Tooltip zusammengefasst dargestellt werden.

The code review shows no irregularities.

Der Code Review zeigt keine Auffälligkeiten.

Figure 22: Code-Review for the encryption of the GUI Kernel connection

```
void spoton::slotKernelSocketState(void)
{
   QAbstractSocket::SocketState state = m_kernelSocket.state();
```

```
if(state == QAbstractSocket::ConnectedState)
    {
      m_kernelSocket.setSocketOption
        (QAbstractSocket::LowDelayOption,
        m_settings.value("gui/tcp_nodelay", 1).toInt()); /*
                                                   ** Disable
Nagle?
                                                   */
      if(m_kernelSocket.isEncrypted())
        {
          askKernelToReadStarBeamKeys();
          sendBuzzKeysToKernel();
          sendKeysToKernel();

          QSslCipher cipher(m_kernelSocket.sessionCipher());
          QString str(QString("%1-%2-%3-%4-%5-%6-%7").
                      arg(cipher.name()).
                      arg(cipher.authenticationMethod()).
                      arg(cipher.encryptionMethod()).
                      arg(cipher.keyExchangeMethod()).
                      arg(cipher.protocolString()).
                      arg(cipher.supportedBits()).
                      arg(cipher.usedBits()));

          m_sb.kernelstatus->setToolTip
            (tr("Connected to the kernel on port %1 "
                "from local port %2 via cipher %3.").
             arg(m_kernelSocket.peerPort()).
             arg(m_kernelSocket.localPort()).
             arg(str));
        }
      else
        m_sb.kernelstatus->setToolTip
          (tr("Connected to the kernel on port %1 "
              "from local port %2. Communications between the interface
and "
              "the kernel have been disabled.").
           arg(m_kernelSocket.peerPort()).
           arg(m_kernelSocket.localPort()));

#if SPOTON_GOLDBUG == 1
      m_sb.kernelstatus->setIcon
        (QIcon(QString(":/%1/status-online.png").
               arg(m_settings.value("gui/iconSet", "nouve").toString().
                   toLower())));
#else
      m_sb.kernelstatus->setIcon
        (QIcon(QString(":/%1/activate.png").
               arg(m_settings.value("gui/iconSet", "nouve").toString().
                   toLower())));
#endif
    }
  else if(state == QAbstractSocket::UnconnectedState)
    {
      m_keysShared["buzz_channels_sent_to_kernel"] = "false";
      m_keysShared["keys_sent_to_kernel"] = "false";
      m_sb.kernelstatus->setIcon
        (QIcon(QString(":/%1/deactivate.png").
               arg(m_settings.value("gui/iconSet", "nouve").toString().
                   toLower())));
      m_sb.kernelstatus->setToolTip
```

```
        (tr("Not connected to the kernel. Is the kernel "
        "active?"));
    }
}
```
Source: spot-on-a.cc: void spoton::slotKernelSocketState(void).

3.14.4 Evaluation of the results with regard to weaknesses, risks, potentials for improvements and strengths

The kernel is attached securely to the user interface. No risks or weaknesses were discovered. With regard to the implementation of the function this is felt to be adequate, that is, there is no need to obtain improvements. One strength of the GUI-kernel connection can be seen in the strong and modifiable encryption.

Der Kernel wird an die Benutzeroberfläche sicher angebunden. Es stellen sich keine Risiken oder Schwächen heraus. Hinsichtlich der Implementierung der Funktion wird diese als adäquat empfunden, d.h. es besteht keine Notwendigkeit, Verbesserungen zu erwirken. Eine Stärke der GUI-Kernel Anbindung kann in der starken und modifizierbaren Verschlüsselung gesehen werden.

Table 51: Description of findings 3.14

#	Area	Description of the finding	Valuation Severity Category / Difficulty Level / Innovation & Improvement Class / Strength Dimension
	Weakness / Schwäche	./.	./.
	Risk / Risiko	./.	./.
	Potential for Improvement / Verbesserungspotential	./.	./.
3.14.5.A	Strength / Stärke	Strong and adjustable connection of GUI and kernel as a strength of GoldBug.	High

3.14.5 Appraisal of good practices in comparison with other similar applications

Only Tox uses in comparable programs to GoldBug an explicit GUI-kernel architecture. Here, various interfaces are available for the kernel. A security audit of the there given user interface has not yet been carried out and the documentation of the Tox project considers this aspect also very limited.

Nur Tox nutzt bei den vergleichbaren Programmen zu GoldBug eine explizite GUI-Kernel Architektur. Hier sind für den Kernel auch verschiedene Benutzeroberflächen erhältlich. Eine Sicherheitsauditierung der dortigen Benutzeroberflächen ist bislang nicht erfolgt und die Dokumentationen des Tox-Projektes betrachten diesen Aspekt auch nur sehr eingeschränkt.

For OTR + XMPP applications a plugin is given with OTR, which needs to be questioned as well in all XMPP applications, respectively should be evaluated and audited in regard of the connection of the plug to the hosting application - as well, whether all the functions then will run then via this plugin.

Bei OTR+XMPP Applikationen ist mit OTR ein Plugin gegeben, das ebenso in allen XMPP Applikationen hinterfragt werden muss bzw. evaluiert und auditiert werden solle auf die Anbindung des Plugins an die hostende Applikation - sowie, ob auch alle Funktionen über dieses Plugin sodann tatsächlich laufen können.

So it occurred for example as known already in the application Enigmail as encrypting plugin for Thunderbird e-mail, that it was discovered only after years, that only the direct e-mail was encrypted, but not the BCC-copies of the e-mails (Scherschel 2014).

So ist es beispielsweise wie inzwischen bekannt bei der Applikation Enigmail als Verschlüsselungs-Plugin bei Thunderbird-E-Mail vorgekommen, dass man erst nach Jahren feststellte, dass nur das direkte E-Mail verschlüsselt wurde, aber nicht die BCC-Kopien des E-Mails (Scherschel 2014).

Table 52: Indicative BIG SEVEN context references 3.14

Logo	Application	Comments
	Cryptocat	Plugin in the browser to the underlaying processes.
	GoldBug	Authenticated and encrypted GUI-Kernel-Interaction. Transparent to the user.
	OTR+XMPP	OTR is a plugin referring to the XMPP client. Per client no or different approaches to secure the connection to the host.
	RetroShare	Local server and GUI implemented in one binary.
	Signal	Local client addressing to a central server.
	SureSpot	Local client addressing to a central server.
	Tox	GUI-Kernel-Interaction. Security depends on the referring and chosen GUI.

Table 53: Good Practice Insights #14

Good Practice Insight # 14
with GoldBug Multi-Encrypting Communication Suite

Case	I have a GoldBug respectively Spot-On kernel running on a server, and thus set up a chat server respectively e-mail mailbox. How can I make sure that this kernel nobody can change through the user interface?
	Ich habe einen GoldBug bzw. Spot-On-Kernel auf meinem Server laufen und damit einen Chat-Server bzw. E-Mail-Postfach eingerichtet. Wie kann ich sicherstellen, dass diesen Kernel niemand über die Benutzeroberfläche verändern kann?
Solution	The connection of the GUI to the kernel is encrypted in GoldBug as well. This is displayed as a tool tip in the status bar. The GUI can be set as well in a "LOCK" status, or can be closed. Then no one can operate the kernel respectively listener.
	Die Verbindung der GUI zum Kernel ist in GoldBug ebenso verschlüsselt. Dieses wird als Tooltip in der Statusbar angezeigt. Die GUI kann ebenso in einen „LOCK" Zustand versetzt werden, oder geschlossen werden. Dann kann niemand den Kernel bzw. Listener bedienen.

Source: Own Case.

3.15 Analog Communication: Gemini, GoldBug, Nova and Instant Perfect Forward Secrecy (IPFS)

GoldBug uses so far no options to transmit data packets in an analog communication, such as e.g. over beeps as we know it from a modem and this constituted still the regular way to the Internet a few years ago.

The use of the analog communication can then exist among users of GoldBug, when they e.g. want to commuicate a password orally to their friends. In the following therefore should the relevant part of the audit be layed on the inclusion of possible options of the analysis of analog communication, e.g. of the verbal communication of the end-to-end encrypted passwords.

GoldBug nutzt bislang keine Optionen, Datenpakete in einer analogen Kommunikation zu übertragen, wie z.B. über Signaltöne wie wir es von einem Modem her kennen und dieses vor einigen Jahren noch der reguläre Weg ins Internet darstellte.

Die Anwendung der analogen Kommunikation kann bei den Nutzern von GoldBug dann bestehen, wenn sie z.B. ein Passwort mündlich an ihre Freunde kommunizieren wollen. Im Folgenden soll daher der relevante Audit-Bestandteil des Einbezugs möglicher Optionen der Analyse von analoger Kommunikation auf die ggf. mündliche Kommunikation der Ende-zu-Ende verschlüsselnden Passworte gelegt werden.

3.15.1 Inventory taking, structural analysis and descriptions of the functions

GoldBug has its strength especially in the option of a manual creation of a symmetrical end-to-end encryption passphrase and in the numerous methodological ways that exist for the transmission of the end-to-end passphrase.

This means, users can define a passphrase, which should ideally exist out 32 really random characters, by themself or by using a randomly generated AES string of 32 characters and, if desired, replaces the characters at certain positions by other characters.

Finally, there are several ways to transmit the created end-to-end encryption passphrase to own communication partners.

Because each message in the echo protocol (see the first section at the beginning) is fundamentally multi-encrypted - asymmetrical as well as possibly also additionally symmetrically encrypted -, the end-to-end encrypted password can also be delivered to the communication partners online through this secure way.

GoldBug hat seine Stärke insbesondere in der Option einer manuellen Erstellung einer symmetrischen Ende-zu-Ende Verschlüsselungspassphrase sowie in den zahlreichen methodischen Wegen, die zur Übermittlung der Ende-zu-Ende Passphrase bestehen.

D.h. der Nutzer kann eine Passphrase, die idealerweise möglichst aus 32 wirklich zufälligen Zeichen bestehen sollte, selbst definieren oder sich einen zufällig generierten AES-String von 32 Zeichen vorschlagen lassen und ggf. an bestimmten Positionen die Zeichen auch durch andere Zeichen austauschen.

Schließlich bestehen verschiedene Möglichkeiten, die so erstelle Ende-zu-Ende Verschlüsselungspassphrase an seinen Kommunikationspartner zu übermitteln.

Da jede Nachricht in dem Echo-Protokoll (vgl. erster Abschnitt zu Beginn) grundlegend mehrfach - asymmetrisch wie ggf. auch zusätzlich noch symmetrisch - verschlüsselt ist, kann das Ende-zu-Ende verschlüsselnde Passwort dem Kommunikationspartner auch online über diesen sicheren Weg zugestellt werden.

The manual shows the following different ways to transmit the encrypted symmetric passphrase. The end-to-end passphrase is described as so-called "Gemini" in the client.

Gemini is the Greek word for twin and refers here thus to the symmetry that both users must store the secret passphrase to secure the communication channel. It is a symmetric cipher, as each twin at opposite quasi sees the self in the mirror, both need to know the end-to-end encrypted passphrase.

So you can in a transmission of a new passphrase choose basically, if you want to send the new passphrase by the existing symmetric channel encryption (thus the existing Gemini), or rather choose the asymmetric encryption, the encryption key e.g. for chatting provides.

The transmission of an end-to-end encrypted password is named in the GoldBug client "Calling". By the used architecture of the kernel Spot-On in the client, the concept of "calling" has been introduced in the field of cryptology.

Basically it can be differentiated here into the following types of transmission of a new Gemini:

- During asymmetric Calling the end-to-end encryption password is transmitted over the public key e.g. of the chat function. This uses as to remember a public and private key and thus represents an asymmetric encryption.

- The Forward Secrecy Calling uses the asymmetric key from the chat or e-mail and first sends temporary keys. Through this new, temporary (ephemeral) key a new end-to-end encrypted passphrase is sent then.

Das Handbuch zeigt folgende verschiedene Möglichkeiten auf, die symmetrisch verschlüsselnde Passphrase zu übermitteln. Die Ende-zu-Ende Passphrase wird im Klienten als sogenanntes „Gemini" bezeichnet.

Gemini ist das griechische Wort für Zwilling und verweist hier somit auf die Symmetrie, dass beide Nutzer die geheime Passphrase hinterlegen müssen, um den Kommunikationskanal abzusichern. Es ist eine symmetrische Verschlüsselung, so wie jeder Zwilling sich gegenüber quasi im Spiegel sieht, müssen auch beide die gleich Ende-zu-Ende-verschlüsselnde Passphrase kennen.

Somit kann man bei einer Übertragung einer neuen Passphrase grundsätzlich wählen, ob man die neue Passphrase durch die bestehende symmetrische Kanal-Verschlüsselung (also das bestehende Gemini) senden will, oder lieber die asymmetrische Verschlüsselung wählt, die der Verschlüsselungs-Key z.B. für den Chat bereithält.

Die Übertragung eines Ende-zu-Ende verschlüsselnden Passwortes heisst im GoldBug Klienten „Calling". Durch die im Klienten eingesetzte Architektur des Kernels Spot-On ist der Begriff des „Calling" im Bereich der Kryptologie eingeführt worden.

Grundlegend kann hier unterschieden werden in folgende Übertragungsarten eines neuen Gemini:

- Beim asymmetrischen Calling wird das Ende-zu-Ende verschlüsselnde Passwort über den öffentlichen Schlüssel z.B. der Chat-Funktion übertragen. Dieses nutzt ja einen öffentlichen und privaten Schlüssel und stellt somit eine asymmetrische Verschlüsselung dar.

- Das Forward Secrecy Calling nutzt die asymmetrischen Schlüssel vom Chat oder E-Mail und sendet zunächst temporäre Schlüssel. Durch diese neuen, temporären (ephemeralen) Schlüssel wird sodann eine neue Ende-zu-Ende verschlüsselnde Passphrase gesandt.

- The symmetrical Calling means giving the new passphrase by an existing end-to-end encryption, thus by a symmetric encrypted channel.

- The SMP Calling runs as the regular asymmetric Calling, with the only difference that no AES or manually generated password of 32 characters is used, but that the password used in the Socialist-millionaire-process by means of a hash function will generate a passphrase. This then is not based on AES, but is derived from the password manually selected for the SMP-authentication of the two users. (should the AES process once deemed as unsafe, this would be an appropriate alternative). During SMP Calling the generated password with the same hash method must on both sides also not be transferred. GoldBug thus here has a standard established, which can not be found in almost any other client: Symmetrical end-to-end encryption, which is derived from a zero-knowledge process. The transmission problem of symmetric keys over the Internet (due to the interception of these keys when no truly secure connection could exist) also offers by the here introduced process great development and research perspectives.

- With the 2-Way-Calling, finally, the 32 characters for the end-to-end encrypted passphrase is divided into two parts, meaning that both users generate 16 characters, the first part of jointly defining the password is then used from the first user and the second part from the second user.

The following table shows - in addition to the manual definition of the end-to-end encrypted passwords - the different ways of the automatic generation and of the transfers of passphrases with 32 characters:

- Das symmetrische Calling bedeutet, die neue Passphrase durch eine bestehende Ende-zu-Ende-Verschlüsselung zu geben, also durch einen symmetrisch verschlüsselten Kanal.

- Das SMP-Calling läuft wie das reguläre asymmetrische Calling, nur mit dem Unterschied, dass kein AES- oder manuell generiertes Passwort von 32 Zeichen genutzt wird, sondern dass aus dem Sociallist-Millionaire-Prozess eingesetzte Passwort mittels einer Hash-Funktion eine Passphrase generiert wird. Diese beruht dann nicht auf einem AES, sondern leitet sich aus dem manuell gewählten Passwort für die SMP-Authentifikation der beiden Nutzer ab (sollte der AES-Prozess einmal als unsicher gelten, wäre dieses also eine entsprechende Alternative). Beim SMP-Calling muss das so generierte Passwort bei gleicher Hash-Methode auf beiden Seiten auch gar nicht übertragen werden. GoldBug hat hier also einen Standard etabliert, der in kaum in einem anderen Klienten zu finden ist: Symmetrische Ende-zu-Ende Verschlüsselung, die sich aus einem Zero-Knowledge-Prozess ableitet. Das Übertragungsproblem von symmetrischen Schlüsseln über das Internet (aufgrund des Abfangens dieser Schlüssel, wenn keine wirklich sichere Verbindung bestehen könnte) bietet mit dem hier eingeführten Prozess also große Entwicklungs- und Forschungsperspektiven.

- Bei dem 2-Wege-Calling schließlich werden die 32 Zeichen für die Ende-zu-Ende verschlüsselnde Passphrase hälftig gesplittet, das heisst, beide Nutzer generieren 32 Zeichen, der erste Teil des gemeinsam zu definierenden Passwortes wird sodann vom ersten Nutzer genommen und der zweite Teil vom zweiten Nutzer.

Die folgende Übersicht zeigt – neben der manuellen Definition von Ende-zu-Ende verschlüsselnden Passworten – die verschiedenen Wege der automatischen Generierung und des Transfers von Passphrasen mit 32 Zeichen auf:

Table 54: Overview of the different Calling-ways in GoldBug with referring criteria:

Criteria	Asymmetric Calling	Forward Secrecy Calling	Symmetric Calling	SMP-Calling	2-Way-Calling
Ephemeral asymmetric Chat-Keys	NO	NO	NO	NO	NO
Forward Secrecy as precondition	NO	NO	YES	NO	NO
Secret SMP-Password as Gemini	NO	NO	NO	YES	NO
Half symmetric AES as Gemini (50 % AES of User A+ 50 % AES of User B)	NO	NO	NO	NO	YES
Instant Perfect Forward Secrecy as a result	YES	YES	YES	YES	YES
Usage of the permanent asymmetric Chat-Key	YES	YES	YES	YES	YES
Symmetric AES-Gemini as Channel	NO	NO	YES	NO	NO
TLS/SSL-Connection	YES	YES	YES	YES	YES

Source: GoldBug Manual (Edwards 2014)

A Gemini can thus be generated *at any time* new and transmitted over the one or other way. The paradigm of "Perfect Forward Secrecy" has therefore been developed into the paradigm of "Instant Perfect Forward Secrecy (IPFS)".

For the chat is in the context menu of the GoldBug Messenger also an activity button given, to perform this instant while chatting: the end-to-end encryption is replaced immediately through the asymmetric chat key with a new symmetrical end-to-end encryption.

This menu item is called MELODICA, and is named: „M"ulti „E"ncrypted „Lo"ng Di"stance „Ca"lling.

As illustrated in Chapter 3.01, the calling-function and -wording respectively even aspects of the echo protocol in the crypto logical research were then also adopted by other publications.

Ein Gemini kann somit über den einen oder anderen Weg *jederzeit* neu generiert und übermittelt werden. Das Paradigma von „Perfect Forward Secrecy" ist daher in das Paradigma „Instant Perfect Forward Secrecy (IPFS)" entwickelt worden.

Für den Chat besteht im Kontext-Menü des GoldBug Messenger auch ein Aktivitäts-Knopf, dieses instant während des Chattens durchzuführen: die Ende-zu-Ende Verschlüsselung wird über die asymmetrischen Chat-Schlüssel umgehend mit einer neuen symmetrischen Ende-zu-Ende Verschlüsselung erneuert.

Dieser Menüpunkt wird MELODICA genannt, und heisst im Englischen: „M"ulti „E"ncrypted „Lo"ng „Di"stance „Ca"lling. Im Deutschen somit zu bezeichnen als: „vielfach verschlüsselte Übertragung eines Ende-zu-Ende Passwortes über eine lange Distanz zu einem entfernten Chat Partner über die Calling-Funktion".

Wie schon in Kapitel 3.01 verdeutlicht, wurde die Calling-Funktion und -Begrifflichkeit bzw. auch Aspekte des Echo-Protokolls in der kryptologischen Forschung sodann auch von weiteren Publikationen übernommen.

Furthermore, there is in the GoldBug client since the beginning of the first releases for the functions e-mail and file transfer through the StarBeam function the option, to set an end-to-end encrypting password to the e-mail or file.

Within the e-mail function (so as well as for the attachment file, if given) this password is called "Goldbug" (so the same as the application is called). And: For encrypting a file this is called "NOVA". This has the consequence that the recipients can only open the message or file, if they enter the correct password at the password prompt. The transmitter has the receiver thus (possibly oral) to inform, what the password for the file or email is.

Then there is also the option as already mentioned briefly above, to generate so-called ephemeral keys: These are asymmetric keys that are used only temporarily. This means the new Gemini passphrase for end-to-end encryption is not transferred through the existing permanent chat key, but it is a temporary, asymmetric key used. This has the advantage that even with a compromise of the private chat key somewhere in the past used ephemeral keys are not broken.

This implementation has been made for the chat function as well as the e-mail function. For the e-mail function GoldBug builds with the integrated Spot-On architecture worldwide a first end-to-end encrypting email client, that operates based on ephemeral keys with both, symmetrical and asymmetrical encryption - this means to cover both methods. Due to our knowledge both methods have so far not been implemented elsewhere yet for email.

For the process flow of generation and transmission of ephemeral keys, reference is made to the explanations in the manual. Here again it is again possible to send the new key through the forward secrecy key or encrypted in the conventional encryption of the echo protocol (see above) to transfer. It is spoken of "Pure Forward Secrecy" in the e-mail function if

Weiterhin besteht im GoldBug Klient seit Anbeginn der ersten Releases bei den Funktionen E-Mail und der Datei-Übertrag über die StarBeam-Funktion die Option, ein Ende-zu-Ende verschlüsselndes Passwort auf die E-Mail oder die Datei zu legen.

Beim E-Mail (und ebenso dessen Anhangsdatei, falls vorhanden) wird dieses Passwort (ebenso wie die Applikation) „GoldBug" genannt. Und: bei der Verschlüsselung einer Datei wird dieses „NOVA" genannt. Dieses hat zur Folge, dass der Empfänger die Nachricht oder die Datei nur öffnen kann, wenn er bei der Passwortabfrage das richtige Passwort eingibt. Der Sender muss dem Empfänger also (ggf. mündlich) mitteilen, wie das Passwort für die Datei oder das E-Mail lautet.

Sodann besteht auch noch die Option wie oben schon kurz angesprochen, sogenannte ephemerale Schlüssel zu generieren: Es sind asymmetrische Schlüssel, die nur temporär genutzt werden. D.h. die neue Gemini Passphrase für die Ende-zu-Ende Verschlüsselung wird nicht durch den bestehenden permanenten Chat-Schlüssel transferiert, sondern es wird ein temporärer asymmetrischer Schlüssel genutzt. Das hat den Vorteil, dass auch bei einer Kompromittierung des eigenen Chat-Schlüssels die in der Vergangenheit genutzen ephemeralen Schlüssel nicht gebrochen sind.

Diese Implementierung wurde vorgenommen für die Chat-Funktion wie auch für die E-Mail-Funktion. Für die E-Mail Funktion wird GoldBug durch die integrierte Spot-On Architektur damit weltweit zum ersten Ende-zu-Ende verschlüsselnden e-Mail-Klienten, der auf Basis von ephemeralen Schlüssel sowohl symmetrisch wie auch asymmetrisch operiert - also beide Methoden abdeckt. Beide Methoden wurden bislang für den E-Mail-Bereich nach unserem Kenntnisstand andernorts noch nicht implementiert.

Für den Prozessverlauf der Generierung und der Übertragung von ephemeralen Schlüsseln sei auf die Ausführungen des Handbuches verwiesen. Auch hier ist es wieder möglich, die neuen Schlüssel durch die Forward-Secrecy-Schlüssel zu senden oder aber in der üblichen Verschlüsselung des Echo-Protokolls (s.o.) verschlüsselt zu transferieren. Es wird von

keys are sent through a temporary ephemeral key or the e-mail message uses this route.

„Pure Forward Secrecy" in der E-Mail-Funktion gesprochen, wenn neue Schlüssel durch einen temporären ephemeralen Schlüssel gesandt werden oder die E-Mail-Nachricht diesen Weg nutzt.

Figure 23: GoldBug - E-Mail-Client with Forward Secrecy for ephemeral E-Mail-Keys

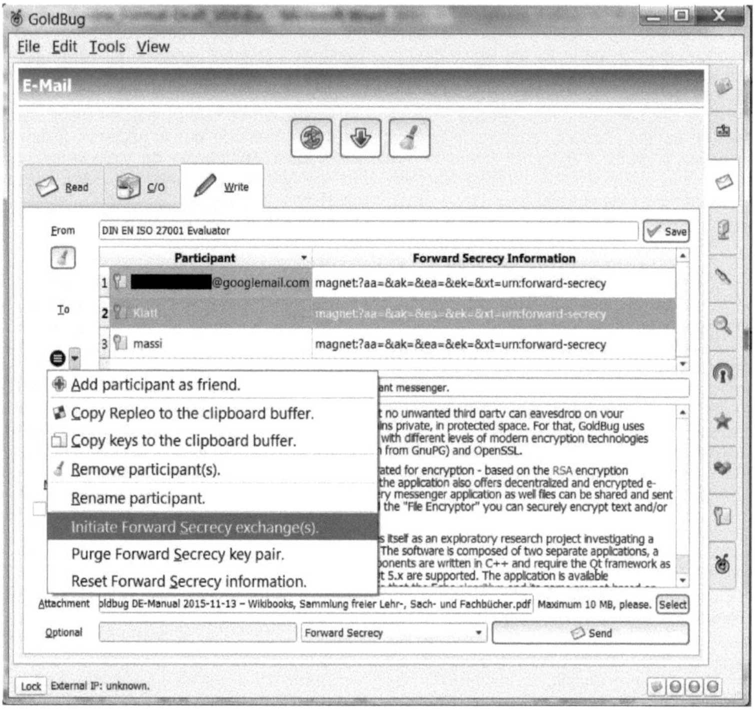

Quelle: Screenshot of Goldbug .2.9

All these end-to-end encryptions, mentioned above, are made online and digital. Subject of the assessment here will now be the option, to transmitted an end-to-end encrypting password orally to the receiver: for example, on the phone or in a personal meeting.

All diese, oben genannten, Ende-zu-Ende Verschlüsselungen erfolgen online und digital. Gegenstand des Assessments hier soll nun die Option sein, sein Ende-zu-Ende verschlüsselndes Passwort mündlich an den Empfänger zu übertragen: z.B. am Telefon oder in einer persönlichen Begegnung.

5.15.2   Selected method for studying and function reference

According to the underlying audit manuals the analog communication is to include, as it may occur in the system or application environment. A similar example of social dialogue can be found in the description of the password for the Socialist-Millionaire-Protocol (SMP) (see section 3.18).

Entsprechend den zugrunde gelegten Audit-Manualen ist auch die analoge Kommunikation einzubeziehen, wie sie in der System- bzw. Applikationsumgebung vorkommen kann. Ein ähnliches Beispiel des sozialen Dialogs findet sich bei der Beschreibung des Passwortes für das Socialist-Millionaire-Protocol (SMP) (vgl. Abschnitt 3.18).

In this section should now be described the oral communication of the end-to-end password for an e-mail. An environment of two users is selected as a test, in they send an email over the client and select the additional end-to-end encryption by a "GoldBug"-password, that the two users set on the individual e-mail.

In diesem Abschnitt soll nun die orale Kommunikation des Ende-zu-Ende Passwortes bei einer E-Mail analysiert werden. Als Test wird dazu eine Umgebung zweier Nutzer gewählt, die sich ein E-Mail über den Klienten senden und dazu die zusätzliche Ende-zu-Ende Verschlüsselung durch ein GoldBug-Passwort wählen, dass sie auf die einzelne E-Mail setzen.

Analyzed shoudl be further the practical operability; as in each of the present assessment sections, the implementation of the function in the source code; and thirdly should be analyzed theoretically, which attacks and risks could arise when an end-to-end password on an email orally is transferred.

Analysiert wird die praktische Funktionsfähigkeit weiterhin, wie in jedem der vorliegenden Assessment-Abschnitte, die Umsetzung der Funktion im Quellcode sowie drittens soll theoretisch analysiert werden, welche Angriffe und Risiken entstehen könnten, wenn ein Ende-zu-Ende Passwort auf eine E-Mail mündlich transferiert wird.

3.15.3   Conduction and findings of the examinations

For the conduction a simple setting of a connection between two devices was created over a third server. For this, a listener was built on a Web server, to which the two participants connected as nodes.

Zur Durchführung wurde ein einfaches Setting einer Verbindung zweier Teilnehmer über einen dritten Server gestaltet. Dazu wurde ein Listener auf einem Webserver errichtet, an den beiden Teilnehmer als Knotenpunkte angebunden wurden.

Both participants then exchanged their e-mail key, and sent an e-mail, which was transferred with no additional end-to-end encryption over the GoldBug function.

Beide Teilnehmer haben sodann ihren E-Mail-Schlüssel getauscht und sich ein E-Mail gesendet, das ohne eine zusätzliche Ende-zu-Ende Verschlüsselung mittels der GoldBug Funktion transferiert wurde.

Then was prepared in a node another email, on which the password "secret" was set as a password.

Sodann wurde in einem Knotenpunkt ein weiteres E-Mail vorbereitet, das als Passwort auf dieses E-Mail das Passwort „geheim" setzte.

This password has now been passed on in an oral telephone call to the receiving party. The participant asked if the password starts with a capital letter.

Dieses Passwort wurde nun in einem mündlichen Telefonat an den empfangenden Teilnehmer weitergegeben. Der Teilnehmer fragte nach, ob das Passwort mit einem Großbuchstaben beginnt.

When the transmitter denied and the receiver typed the password in the correct spelling, she could read the email. The function was successfully tested in practice without findings for improvement potentials.

Als der Sender verneinte und der Empfänger das Passwort in richtiger Schreibweise eingab, konnte er auch das E-Mail lesen. Die Funktion konnte in der Praxis erfolgreich getestet werden ohne Erkenntnis von Verbesserungspotentialen.

Also, the source code implements this function adequately, as the example of the use of the e-mail-GoldBug-password shows on attachments of an e-mail:

Auch der Quellcode implementiert diese Funktion adäquat, wie das Beispiel der Anwendung des E-Mail-GoldBug-Passwortes auch auf Anhänge einer E-Mail verdeutlicht:

Figure 24: Source-Code quotation of the GoldBug Password on E-Mails

```
void spoton::applyGoldBugToAttachments(const QString &folderOid,
                                        const QSqlDatabase &db,
                                        int *count,
                                        spoton_crypt *crypt1,
                                        bool *ok1)
{
    if(!count || !crypt1)
    {
        if(ok1)
            *ok1 = false;

        return;
    }

    spoton_crypt *crypt2 = m_crypts.value("email", 0);

    if(!crypt2)
    {
        if(ok1)
            *ok1 = false;

        return;
    }

    QSqlQuery query(db);

    query.setForwardOnly(true);
    query.prepare("SELECT data, name, OID FROM folders_attachment WHERE "
                  "folders_oid = ?");
    query.bindValue(0, folderOid);

    if(query.exec())
    {
        while(query.next())
        {
            QByteArray attachment
                (QByteArray::fromBase64(query.value(0).toByteArray()));
            QByteArray attachmentName
                (QByteArray::fromBase64(query.value(1).toByteArray()));
            bool ok2 = true;

            attachment = crypt2->decryptedAfterAuthenticated(attachment,
&ok2);

            if(ok2)
```

```
                    attachmentName = crypt2->decryptedAfterAuthenticated
                    (attachmentName, &ok2);

            if(ok2)
              {
                attachment = crypt1->decryptedAfterAuthenticated
                (attachment, &ok2);

                if(ok2)
                  {
                    if(!attachment.isEmpty())
                      attachment = qUncompress(attachment);

                    attachmentName = crypt1->decryptedAfterAuthenticated
                    (attachmentName, &ok2);
                  }

                if(ok2)
                  {
                    if(!attachment.isEmpty() && !attachmentName.isEmpty())
                      {
                        QSqlQuery updateQuery(db);

                        updateQuery.prepare("UPDATE folders_attachment "
                                "SET data = ?, "
                                "name = ? "
                                "WHERE OID = ?");
                        updateQuery.bindValue
                          (0, crypt2->encryptedThenHashed(attachment,
&ok2).
                            toBase64());

                        if(ok2)
                          updateQuery.bindValue
                            (1, crypt2->encryptedThenHashed(attachmentName,
                                                &ok2).
                              toBase64());

                        updateQuery.bindValue(2, query.value(2));

                        if(ok2)
                          {
                            if(updateQuery.exec())
                              *count += 1;
                            else
                              {
                                if(*ok1)
                                  *ok1 = false;

                                break;
                              }
                          }
                        else
                          {
                            if(ok1)
                              *ok1 = false;

                            break;
                          }
                      }
                    else
                      {
```

```
                    QSqlQuery deleteQuery(db);

                    deleteQuery.exec("PRAGMA secure_delete = ON");
                    deleteQuery.prepare("DELETE FROM
folders_attachment  "
                              "WHERE OID = ?");
                    deleteQuery.bindValue(0, query.value(2));

                    if(deleteQuery.exec())
                       *count -= 1;
                    else
                      {
                        if(ok1)
                          *ok1 = false;

                        break;
                      }
                  }
              }
            else
              {
                if(ok1)
                  *ok1 = false;

                break;
              }
          }
      }
    else
      {
        if(*ok1)
          *ok1 = false;

        break;
      }
  }
}
else if(ok1)
  *ok1 = false;
}
```

The function test was therefore carried out successfully and the source code inspection showed no irregularities.

For the analog communication of the password is still the usual option in speech shown, to not properly understand the password or possibly to write it wrong. Since this was clarified on demand of the receiver with respect to the capitalization of the first letter, there were no complaints in this test.

Theoretical attacks on a Goldbug password that was put on an e-mail, can therefore only exist in the interception of the transmission of the end-to-end encrypted password. This would have to be avoided, by the two parties agreeing one or more passwords, if they are alone to each other and entering the

Der Funktionstest wurde somit erfolgreich durchgeführt und auch die Source-Code Inspektion zeigte keine Auffälligkeiten.

Bei der analogen Kommunikation des Passwortes zeigt sich noch die bei Sprache übliche Möglichkeit, das Passwort nicht richtig zu verstehen oder es ggf. falsch zu schreiben. Da dieses auf Nachfrage des Empfängers hinsichtlich der Großschreibung des ersten Buchstabens geklärt wurde, gab es keine Beanstandungen in diesem Test.

Theoretische Angriffe auf ein GoldBug-Passwort, das auf eine E-Mail gesetzt wurde, können daher nur im Abhören der Übermittlung des Ende-zu-Ende verschlüsselnden Passwortes bestehen. Diese wären zu umgehen, indem die beiden Teilnehmer ein oder mehrere Passworte vereinbaren, wenn

| passwords without observation respectively entering it with the in the application enclosed virtual keyboard. | sie unter sich sind und die Eingabe der Passworte ohne Beobachtung bzw. mit der in der Applikation beigefügten virtuellen Tastatur erfolgen. |

3.15.4 Evaluation of the results with regard to weaknesses, risks, potentials for improvements and strengths

Nevertheless, oral communication always provides the risk, that passwords are not properly understood and written down by the receiver. It is therefore important to note the recommendation in the user guide, to share a password within analog communication letter for letter.

Gleichwohl bietet mündliche Kommunikation immer das Risiko, dass Passworte vom Empfänger nicht richtig verstanden und aufgezeichnet werden. Es ist daher ggf. im Benutzerhandbuch die Empfehlung zu vermerken, ein Passwort bei analoger Kommunikation Buchstabe für Buchstabe durchzugeben.

Table 55: Description of findings 3.15

#	Area	Description of the finding	Valuation Severity Category / Difficulty Level / Innovation & Improvement Class / Strength Dimension
	Weakness / Schwäche	./.	./.
	Risk / Risiko	./.	./.
3.15.4.A	Potential for Improvement / Verbesserungspotential	Pointing out in the manual, that the end-to-end password should be spelled in case of an analog /oral transfer.	Informational
3.15.4.B	Strength / Stärke	Six methods to create and transfer an end-to-end passphrase.	High

Also should be noted that a telephone connection can be intercepted and therefore the personal transfer of end-to-end encrypted passwords is more preferable in a face-to-face situation with no third persons.

Auch gilt zu beachten, dass eine Telefonverbindung abgehört werden kann und daher die persönliche Weitergabe eines Ende-zu-Ende verschlüsselnden Passwortes in einer face-to-face-Situation ohne dritte Personen zu bevorzugen ist.

If a passphrase must be submitted online, then only through a secure channel. The example of MIKEY-SAKKE clearly shows, how keys can be stored over differing paths-processes and inclusion of intermediate servers of third parties.

Wenn eine Passphrase online übermittelt werden muss, dann nur über einen sicheren Kanal. Das Beispiel von MIKEY-SAKKE zeigt deutlich, wie Schlüssel über differierende Prozesswege und Einbezug von intermediären Servern von Dritten gespeichert werden können.

For secure voice communications over the Internet (VoIP) the CESG (the information security department of the British service GCHQ), recommends a technique called Secure Chorus, which uses a proprietary algorithm called MIKEY-SAKKE (Sakai-Kasahara Key Encryption in Multimedia Internet KEYing).

Für sichere Sprachkommunikation über das Internet (VoIP) empfiehlt die CESG (die Informationssicherheitsabteilung des britischen Dienstes GCHQ) eine Technik namens Secure Chorus, die einen selbstentwickelten Algorithmus namens MIKEY-SAKKE (Sakai-Kasahara Key Encryption in Multimedia Internet KEYing) verwendet.

The vulnerability in MIKEY-SAKKE was exposed at that time and lies in the key exchange over an unsecured channel, that needs to take place before a secure end-to-end encrypted connection is established.

In contrast to many chat programs, which generate a secret key on the Ephemeral Diffie-Hellman method (EDH) to each account (at GoldBug corresponds EDH to the term Forward Secrecy Calling), produces Sakke secret keys for the conversation partners on the central service provider and sends this to them.

This means that operators have all secret keys under their control and can decrypt all conversations in a large scale of a passive mass surveillance (Murdoch 2016 and see also Heise). Same or similar could also the not open source server of the Telegram Messenger operate and pick up keys?

In fact such a protocol has been developed for voice encryption – Identity-Based Authenticated Key Exchange (IBAKE) Mode of Key Distribution in Multimedia Internet KEYing (MIKEY) – (MIKEY-IBAKE).

It should also be noted that the keys come here from a central server, while the German Federal Office for Information Security (BSI) has also characterized - based on the example of Skype for Business - all encrypted chats over a third party or foreign server to be unsafe. It could not be excluded due to the proprietary Skype protocol that similar processes as in MIKEY-SAKKE also happen on Skype servers: Because the keys for Encryption are owned by Microsoft, which is why in principle the parties may access the contents of the transmission. For safety-critical and business-related information also Fraunhofer ESK therefore does not recommend Skype - just like classical unencrypted telephony (Fraunhofer ESK / Messerer 2016). Thus, the solution is also in this example, again in the exclusive use of open source software as well as clients that include a manual configuration of the end-to-end encrypted password by the participants themselves - and not generate or transmit it by remote, third server of the provider.

Das Sicherheitsleck bei MIKEY-SAKKE wurde seinerzeit herausgestellt und steckt im Schlüsselaustausch über einen ungesicherten Kanal, der stattfinden muss, bevor eine sichere Ende-zu-Ende verschlüsselte Verbindung aufgebaut wird.

Im Gegensatz zu vielen Chat-Programmen, die einen geheimen Schlüssel über die Methode Ephemeral Diffie-Hellman (EDH) untereinander ausmachen (bei GoldBug entspricht EDH dem Begriff des Forward Secrecy Calling), erzeugt bei SAKKE jedoch der zentrale Dienstbetreiber geheime Schlüssel für die Gesprächspartner und schickt ihnen diese zu.

Das führt dazu, dass der Betreiber alle geheimen Schlüssel unter seiner Kontrolle hat und alle Gespräche in großem Stil mittels passiven Massenüberwachung entschlüsseln kann (Murdoch 2016 u. vgl. a. Heise). So oder ähnlich könnte auch der nicht quelloffene Server des Telegram-Messenger operieren und Schlüssel aufgreifen?

Dabei stehen auch andere Protokolle zur Verfügung: Tatsächlich wurden auch Protokolle entwicklet, die dieses für Sprachverschlüsselung nicht vorsehen: es nennt sich MIKEY-IBAKE: Zusammengesetzt aus: Identity-Based Authenticated Key Exchange (IBAKE) Mode of Key Distribution in Multimedia Internet KEYing (MIKEY).

Es sei noch angemerkt, dass hier die Schlüssel von einem zentralen Server kommen, dabei hat das Bundesamt für Informationssicherheit (BSI) am Beispiel von Skype for Business zugleich jeglichen verschlüsselten Chat über einen fremden bzw ausländischen Server als unsicher bezeichnet. Es sei aufgrund des proprietären Skype-Protokolls nicht auszuschließen, dass ähnliche Prozesse wie MIKEY-SAKKE auch auf den Skype-Servern passierten: Denn auch die Keys fürs Verschlüsseln liegen bei Microsoft, weshalb prinzipiell Dritte auf den Inhalt der Übertragung zugreifen könnten. Für sicherheitskritische und unternehmens-relevante Informationen rät auch Fraunhofer ESK daher von Skype – genauso wie von klassischer unverschlüsselter Telefonie – ab (Fraunhofer ESK / Messerer 2016). Die Lösung liegt also auch bei diesem Beispiel wieder in der ausschließlichen Verwendung von quelloffener Software sowie von Klienten, die eine manuelle Gestaltung des Ende-zu-Ende verschlüsselnden Passwortes durch die

Thus, it is crucial not only to be able to define the end-to-end password manually, but also to be able to share it analog, without a digitization by oral transmission. The analog key handover, the "De-Digitalization of the Ephemeral Key Transfer" (DDEKT)) is therefore a simple and still effective method to an EDH transmission. Back to the roots: the verbal agreement of passwords sounds like "retro", but still seems to be an excellent alternative.

GoldBug offers as shown above besides EDH or Forward Secrecy Calling also key transmissions in the symmetrical fashion over 2-Way-Calling or using a zero-knowledge process (over SMP). Here in GoldBug email client the whole keyboard is played on methodologies of secure key transfer - the menu item MELODICA is therefore also symbolic of the calling function more than suitable. And our source code review shows that this melody is not a cacophony - quite the contrary.

Teilnehmer selbst inkludieren – und nicht durch remote, dritte Server der Anbieter zur Verfügung stellen oder weiterleiten.

Somit ist es nicht nur entscheidend, das Ende-zu-Ende Passwort auch manuell definieren zu können, sondern es auch analog, durch mündliche Weitergabe ohne eine Digitalisierung weitergeben zu können. Die analoge Schlüsselübergabe, die "De-Digitalisierung der Ephemeralen Schlüsselübergabe" ("De-Digitalization of the Ephemeral Key Transfer" (DDEKT)) ist somit eine einfache und nach wie vor wirkungsvolle Methode zu einer EDH-Übertragung. Back to the roots: die mündliche Absprache von Passworten mag „retro" wirken, scheint jedoch weiterhin eine gute Alternative zu sein.

Neben EDH bzw. Forward Secrecy Calling bietet GoldBug wie oben dargestellt also auch Schlüssel-Übertragungen symmetrischer Art und über 2-Way-Calling oder mit einem Zero-Knowledge-Prozess (über SMP) an. Hier im E-Mail-Programm GoldBug wird die ganze Klaviatur an methodischen Vorgehensweisen der sicheren Schlüsselübertragung gespielt – der Menüpunkt MELODICA ist somit auch bildlich für die Calling-Funktion mehr als passend. Und unser Quellcode-Review zeigt, dass diese Melodie keine Kakophonie darstellt - ganz im Gegenteil.

3.15.5 Appraisal of good practices in comparison with other similar applications

Apart from the SMP process, which also for OTR+XMPP offers the opportunity, to (possibly manually) define a common password and previously to agree upon verbally or by phone, none of the further comparative applications has the option, to define an end-to-end passphrase manually and to transmit it through an analog communications, e.g. in an personal meeting.

Abgesehen vom SMP-Prozess, der bei OTR+XMPP auch die Möglichkeit anbietet, ein gemeinsames Passwort (ggf. manuell) zu definieren und mündlich zuvor oder per Telefon abzusprechen, hat keine der weiter zu vergleichenden Applikationen die Möglichkeit, eine Ende-zu-Ende Passphrase manuell zu definieren und durch analoge Kommunikation z.B. in einem persönlichen Gespräch zu übermitteln.

(Perfect) Forward Secrecy, Instant Perfect Forward Secrecy, the Forward Secrecy Calling or the manual selection of a symmetric password for continuous end-to-end encryption should be taken into consideration and strengthened in more detail in all other alternatives.

(Perfect) Forward Secrecy, Instant Perfect Forward Secrecy, das Forward Secrecy Calling oder die manuelle Wahl eines symmetrischen Passwortes zur durchgehenden Ende-zu-Ende Verschlüsselung sollte daher in allen anderen Alternativen ausführlicher beachtet und gestärkt werden.

The numerous safeguards for the online transfer options in GoldBug client establish as shown standards in the "applied" cryptology.

Auch die zahlreichen Absicherungen der Online-Transfermöglichkeiten im GoldBug Klienten setzen wie dargestellt Maßstäbe in der "angewandten" Kryptologie.

Table 56: Indicative BIG SEVEN context references 3.15

Logo	Application	Comments
	Cryptocat	No option for manual creation of a symmetric End-to-End encryption passprase e.g. for an E-Mail or Chat-Message available.
	GoldBug	Option for manual creation of a symmetric End-to-End encryption passprase e.g. for an E-Mail or Chat-Message available. Also more than five different methods to securely transfer the passphrase.
	OTR+XMPP	Option for manual creation of a symmetric passprase only for the SMP-Process in OTR available.
	RetroShare	No option for manual creation of a symmetric End-to-End encryption passprase e.g. for an E-Mail or Chat-Message available.
	Signal	No option for manual creation of a symmetric End-to-End encryption passprase e.g. for an E-Mail or Chat-Message available. Asymmetric ephemeral keys for the chat session.
	SureSpot	No option for manual creation of a symmetric End-to-End encryption passprase e.g. for an E-Mail or Chat-Message available.
	Tox	No option for manual creation of a symmetric End-to-End encryption passprase e.g. for an E-Mail or Chat-Message available.

Table 57: Good Practice Insights #15

Good Practice Insight # 15	
with GoldBug Multi-Encrypting Communication Suite	
Case	If I want to share with my communication partner a password, should I say this better orally or transmit it over one of the available secured online channels? Wenn ich meinem Kommunikationspartner ein Passwort mitteilen möchte, sollte ich dieses besser mündlich sagen oder über einen der verfügbaren abgesicherten Online-Channel senden?
Solution	The online channels are appropriately secured in GoldBug with encryption. Especially when it comes to the immediate renewal of additional encryption layers (such as during the Instant Perfect Forward Secrecy) they are on offer. If it comes to arrange with a friend a password on the e-mail ("GoldBug"-password) or on a file-transfer ("Nova"-password) also a verbal message is recommended. Die Online-Kanäle sind in GoldBug entsprechend mit Verschlüsselung abgesichert. Insbesondere, wenn es um die sofortige Erneuerung von zusätzlichen Verschlüsselungsebenen geht (wie z.B. beim Instant Perfect Forward Secrecy), bieten sie sich an. Wenn es darum geht, mit einem Freund ein Passwort auf die E-Mail („GoldBug"-Passwort) oder einen Dateitransfer („Nova"-Passwort) zu verabreden, ist auch eine mündliche Mitteilung sinnvoll.

Source: Own Case.

3.16 Packet-Communication: Test of the Adaptive Echo (AE)

While the in GoldBug applied echo protocol is stating - shortened - that firstly each data packet is encrypted, and secondly each node sends a respective data packet (further) to each connected node, the Adaptive Echo (AE) offers the possibility to exclude nodes in the distribution of data packets - this refers to nodes that do not have a cryptographic token, which is similar to character string of a passphrase.

Während das in GoldBug angewandte Echo-Protokoll verkürzt besagt, daß erstens jedes Datenpaket verschlüsselt ist und zweitens jeder Knotenpunkt ein jeweiliges Datenpaket an jeden verbundenen Knotenpunkt (weiter-) sendet, besteht beim Adaptiven Echo (AE) die Möglichkeit, Knotenpunkte in der Verteilung der Datenpakete auszunehmen, die nicht über einen kryptographischen Token – also einer Zeichenfolge ähnlich einer Passphrase – verfügen.

3.16.1 Inventory taking, structural analysis and descriptions of the functions

The echo protocol is a very simple protocol: it does not contain any routing information. Each node simply sends the encrypted data packet to all of its online connected nodes further on its own.

Das Echo-Protokoll ist ein sehr simples Protokoll: Es enthält keinerlei Routing Informationen. Jeder Knotenpunkt sendet einfach das verschlüsselte Daten-Paket an alle seine online verbundenen Knotenpunkte von sich aus weiter.

This does not happen as forwarding, but each node tries to unpack the package and to decrypt it - failing this, the package is re-packaged and re-sent - as its own action of the node.

Dieses geschieht nicht als Weiterleitung, sondern jeder Knotenpunkt versucht das Packet auszupacken und zu entschlüsseln – gelingt dieses nicht, wird das Packet wieder eingepackt und neu, - als eigene Aktion des Knotenpunktes - versandt.

To routing or forwarding belongs also the understanding of the existence of a goal, a destination address, and, the carry-on belongs to be done on behalf of a sender. However, both is not given in the echo protocol! The node tests whether it can decrypt the data packet, and if no readable text comes out, the node packs the whole again and sends it to all connected nodes further, which try the same then. This is just an illustrative description step; the data is not actually repackaged: it is each provided to all available neighbors - except the neighbour, which the data originated from.

Zum Routing (oder auch Forwarding) gehört also das Verständnis des Vorhandenseins eines Ziels, einer Zieladresse, und das Weiterbringen im Auftrage eines Absenders. Beides ist jedoch beim Echo-Protokoll nicht gegeben! Der Knotenpunkt testet, ob er das Datenpaket entschlüsseln kann, wenn kein lesbarer Text dabei herauskommt, packt der Knotenpunkt das Ganze wieder ein und gibt es an alle verbundenen Knotenpunkte weiter, die sodann selbiges versuchen. Dieses ist eine illustrative Beschreibung, denn die Daten werden nicht jeweils erneut gepackt. Sie werden immer an alle Nachbarn gesandt, außer an den, vom dem die Nachricht kam.

For the Adaptive Echo (AE) however, a long password or cryptographic token in each node of a defined path of a graph has to be deposited.

Beim Adaptiven Echo (AE) hingegen wird in jedem Knotenpunkt eines zu definierenden Wegs eines Graphen ein langes Passwort bzw. ein kryptographischer Token hinterlegt.

Messages that are sent from a so-defined

Nachrichten, die dann von einem so definierten

node to another nearby node are then not sent to other nodes, which do not know this token.

This makes it clear that the participants can exclude other nodes in a link chain with the AE token to ever receive a message that passes along.

This works over adaptive learning of the nodes: messages of nodes with a certain AE token are only to be forwarded to those nodes that have the same AE token. All other connected nodes are excluded and do not receive this message forwarding.

Hence the AE token has be inserted via the complete graph of connections, otherwise a node without further connection to an AE token will switch back to the normal echo-protocol, which means, that the data packet is sent again to all connected nodes.

For example, if Alice wants to communicate via the hubs of Bob and Ed with Maria, the four persons must deposit the AE token in their application. It is then ensured, that other, further nodes from Bob and Ed or Maria do not receive the message from Alice.

Adaptive Echo tokens are composed of authentication and encryption keys as well as details about the choice algorithms. If configured, binding endpoints are able to permit or restrict information-flows based on the content of the data.

As an example, peers that are cognizant of a specific Adaptive Echo token will receive data from other cognizant peers whereas traditional peers will not.

Binding endpoints therefore selectively-echo data.

The Adaptive Echo behaves as follows (comp. also Spot-On Developer Documentation 2014):

1. A binding endpoint defines an Adaptive Echo token. The information must be

Knotenpunkt an einen anderen benachbarten Knotenpunkt gesendet werden, werden sodann nicht an andere Knotenpunkte gesendet, die diesen Token nicht kennen.

Damit wird deutlich, daß die Teilnehmer in einer Verbindungskette mit dem AE-Token andere Knotenpunkte ausschließen können, eine vorbeikommende Nachricht jemals zu erhalten.

Dieses funktioniert über das Adaptive Lernen der Knotenpunkte, indem Nachrichten von Knotenpunkten mit einem bestimmten AE-Token nur an diejenigen Knotenpunkte weiterzuleiten sind, die über denselben AE-Token verfügen. Alle anderen verbunden Knotenpunkte werden ausgeschlossen und erhalten keine Weiterleitung dieser Nachricht.

Somit ist der AE-Token über den kompletten Graphen der Verbindungen einzufügen, da sonst ein Knotenpunkt ohne weitere Verbindung zu einem AE-Token wieder auf das normale Echo-Protokoll wechselt, d.h. das Datenpaket wird wieder an alle verbundene Knotenpunkte gesendet.

Ein Beispiel: Wenn Alice über die Knotenpunkte von Bob und Ed mit Maria kommunizieren will, müssen alle vier Personen den AE-Token in Ihrem Programm hinterlegen. Dann ist sichergestellt, daß sonstige, weitere Knotenpunkte von Bob und Ed oder Maria die Nachricht von Alice nicht erhalten.

Adaptive Echo Token werden aus Schlüsseln für die Authentifizierung und für die Verschlüsselung zusammengesetzt, ebenso ist die Wahl des Algorithmus natürlich grundlegend. Wenn so konfiguriert, sind angebundene Endpunkte in der Lage, Informationsflüsse basierend auf den Inhalten der Daten zu erlauben oder zu unterbinden.

Als Beispiel: Knotenpunkte, in denen ein spezifischer Adaptive Echo Token hinterlegt ist, werden Daten von anderen Knotenpunkten erhalten, die ebenso den Token hinterlegt haben - während die traditionellen Knotenpunkte diese Daten nicht erhalten.

Angebundene Knotenpunkte senden in diesem Echo-Protokoll Daten daher selektiv.

Das Adaptive Echo verhält sich wie folgt (vgl. auch Spot-On Entwickler Dokumentation 2014)

1. Ein angebundener Knotenpunkt definiert einen „Adaptive Echo Token". Die geheime

distributed securely.

2. A networked peer having the given Adaptive Echo token generates H_{Hash} $_{Key}(E_{Encryption}$ $_{Key}(Message \parallel Time)) \parallel E_{Encryption}$ $_{Key}(Message \parallel Time)$ where the Encryption Key and Hash Key are derived from the Adaptive Echo token. The generated information is then submitted to the binding endpoint as "Message || Adaptive Echo"- Information.

3. The binding endpoint processes the received message to determine, if the message is tagged with a known Adaptive Echo token. If the message is indeed tagged correctly, the Time value is inspected. If the Time value is within five seconds of the binding endpoint's local time, the message is considered correct and the peer's presence is recorded.

4. As the binding endpoint receives messages from other peers, it inspects the messages to determine if the messages have been tagged with Adaptive Echo tokens. This process creates a network of associated peers. Because peers themselves may be binding endpoints, the Adaptive Echo may be used to generate an artificial trust network.

(An alternative way - to create a web of trust within GoldBug - consists in the account creation for a listener, on which connected peers thus will spread the message again to all other connected peers. The term "web-of-trust" has not only been implemented in the client GoldBug on the physical layer of IP- connections, but also it was differentiated for cytological peer-addresses (e.g. the chat key, which also can be defined over Adaptive Echo Tokens within a web of trust, as described above)).

Information muss über einen sicheren Kanal transferiert werden.

2. Ein im Netzwerk verbundender Knotenpunkt, der über den Token verfügt, generiert folgendes: H_{Hash} $_{Key}(E_{Encryption}$ $_{Key}(Message \parallel Time)) \parallel E_{Encryption}$ $_{Key}(Message \parallel Time)$, wobei der Schlüssel für die Verschlüsselung wie auch der Hash-Schlüssel von dem Adaptive Echo Token abgeleitet werden. Die so generierte Information wird dann übertragen zum verbundenen Knotenpunkt als Information mit "Message || Adaptive Echo".

3. Der verbundene Knotenpunkt prozessiert die erhaltene Nachricht, um herauszufinden, ob die Nachricht mit einem der bereits im Klienten hinterlegten Adaptive Echo Togen "getagged", also gekennzeichnet ist. Wenn die Nachricht in der Tat richtig gekennzeichnet ist, wird sodann der Wert für "Time" inspiziert. Wenn der Zeit-Wert innerhalb einer Differenz-Zone von fünf Sekunden zu der lokalen Zeit des angebundenen Knotenpunktes liegt, wird die Nachricht als korrekt angesehen und die Präsenz des Knotenpunktes wird aufgezeichnet.

4. Da der angebundene Knotenpunkt von anderen Knotenpunkten ebenso Nachrichten erhält, wird also jede eingehende Nachricht inspiziert, um herauszufinden, ob die Nachricht mit einem bekannten Adaptive Echo Token gekennzeichnet ist. Dieser Prozess erstellt somit ein Netzwerk an assoziierten Knotenpunkten. Aufgrund dessen, dass Knotenpunkte auch ebenso angebundene Knotenpunkte mit AE Token haben, kann das Adaptive Echo auch genutzt werden, um ein derart generiertes "Web of Trust" zu erstellen.

(Ein anderer Weg, ein Web of Trust in GoldBug zu erstellen, besteht über die Account-Erstellung für einen Listener, deren angeschlossenen Knotenpunkte jedoch die Nachricht wiederum an alle Knotenpunkte verteilen. Der Begriff des Web-of-Trust wurde daher im GoldBug Klienten nicht nur physisch auf Ebene von Accounts für IP-Verbindungen implementiert, sondern auch differenziert für kryptologische Knotenpunktadressen (z.B. für den Chat-Key, der wiederum wie oben geschildert über Adaptive Echo Token als ein Web of Trust definiert werden kann)).

3.16.2 Selected method for studying and function reference

As a method of investigation, a practical test setup shall be used, which is annexed in the documentation for the echo protocol of the application. To explain the Adaptive Echo a classic example of the fairy tale of Hansel and Gretel and its structure formation in an AE network grid is used.

Als Untersuchungsmethode soll ein praktischer Versuchsaufbau genutzt werden, der in der Dokumentation zum Echo-Protokoll dem Programm beigefügt ist. Zur Erläuterung des Adaptiven Echos dient als klassisches Beispiel das Märchen von Hänsel und Gretel und seiner Strukturaufstellung in einem AE-Netzwerk-Grid.

Figure 22: Adaptive Echo - Hansel, Gretel and Wicked Witch example

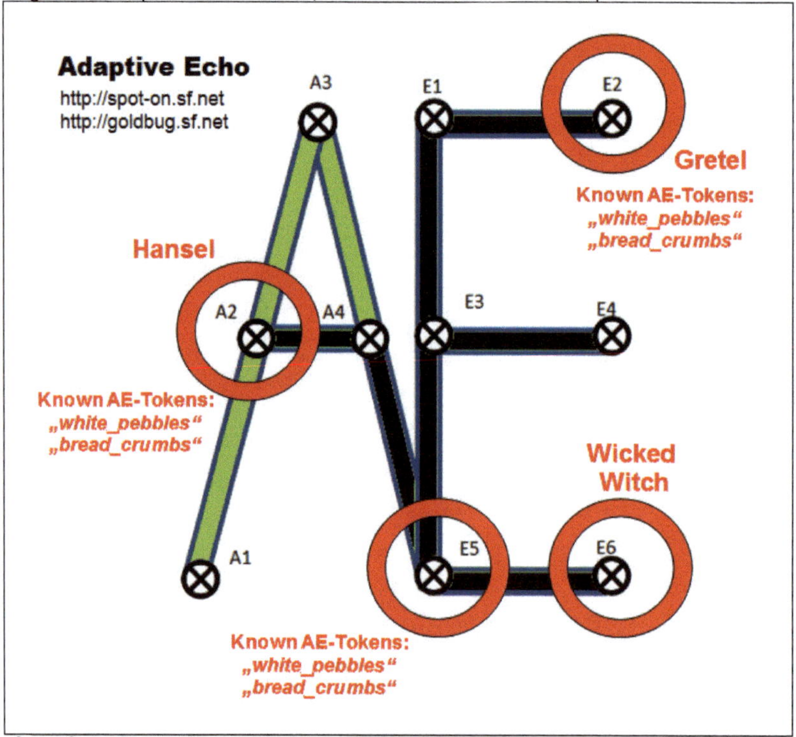

Source: Spot-on Developer Documentation 2014

In the above-described AE-Grid the persons Hansel, Gretel and the Wicked Witch are highlighted as nodes. Now Hansel and Gretel reflect, how they can communicate with each other - without the Wicked Witch noticing this. According to the tale they are in the forest of the Wicked Witch and want again to escape

In das oben erläuterte AE-Grid werden die Personen Hänsel, Gretel und die böse Hexe als Knotenpunkte eingezeichnet. Nun überlegen Hänsel und Gretel, wie sie miteinander kommunizieren können, ohne daß die böse Hexe dieses mitbekommt. Dem Märchen nach sind sie im Wald bei der

from this forest and mark the way with "bread crumbs" and "white pebbles".

This fairy tale content can now illustrate and demonstrate also in the grid pattern above the Adaptive Echo and at which points of the grid respectively of the communication graph a cryptographic tokens called "white pebbles" can be utilized:

If node A2, E5 and E2 use the same AE token, then node E6 will not receive a message that will be exchanged by the node A2 (Hansel) and node E2 (Gretel).

The node E5 learns respective evaluates over the known token "white pebbles" not to send the message to the node E6, the "Wicked Witch". A learning, self-adjusting and proving ("adaptive") network.

An "Adaptive Echo" network reveals no target information (see also the other hand "ants routing"). After all - as a reminder: The mode of "Half Echo" sends only one hop to connected neighbors and "Full Echo" sends the encrypted message to all connected nodes via an unspecified hop count.

While "Echo Accounts" help or hinder other users almost as a firewall or authorization concept in connecting, "AE tokens" provide graph- or path-exclusivity - to be regarded for messages that are sent over connected nodes, which also know the AE-token.

Chat server administrators can exchange their token with other server administrators, if they trust among themselves and thus define a Web-of-Trust ("Ultra-peering for Trust").
In network labs or at home with three or four computers one simply can try out the Adaptive Echo and document own results (compare GoldBug-Manual of Edwards, Scott (Ed.) 2014).

Hexe und wollen aus diesem Wald wieder herausfinden und markieren den Weg mit Brotkrumen ("bread crumbs") und weissen Kieselsteinen ("white pebbels").

Diese Märcheninhalte können nun auch in obigem Grid-Muster das Adaptiven Echo verdeutlichen und aufzeigen, an welchen Stellen des Grids bzw. des Kommunikationsgraphens ein kryptographischer Token namens "Weisse Kieselsteine" eingesetzt werden kann:

Wenn Knotenpunkt A2, E5 and E2 denselben AE-Token einsetzen, dann wird Knotenpunkt E6 keine Nachricht erhalten, die der Knotenpunkt A2 (Hänsel) und der Knotenpunkt E2 (Gretel) austauschen werden.

Denn, der Knotenpunkt E5 lernt bzw. prüft über den bekannten Token "Weisse Kieselsteine" ("white_pebbles"), die Nachrichten nicht an den Knotenpunkt E6, die "Böse Hexe" ("Wicked Witch"), zu senden. Ein lernendes, sich anpassendes ("adaptives") und prüfendes Netzwerk.

Ein "Adaptives Echo" Netzwerk enthüllt dabei keine Ziel-Informationen (vergleiche dagegen auch "Ants Routing"). Denn - zur Erinnerung: Der Modus des "Halben Echos" sendet nur einen Hop zum verbundenen Nachbarn und das "Volle Echo" sendet die verschlüsselte Nachricht zu allen verbundenen Knotenpunkten über eine nicht weiter spezifizierte Hop-Anzahl.

Während "Echo Accounts" andere Nutzer quasi als Firewall oder Berechtigungskonzept beim Verbinden fördern oder behindern, halten hingegen "AE-Tokens" Graphen- oder Pfad-Exklusivität vor - und zwar für Nachrichten, die über Verbindungsknoten gesandt werden, die den AE-Token ebenso kennen.

Chat-Server Administratoren können ihre Token mit anderen Server-Administratoren tauschen, wenn sie sich untereinander vertrauen ("Ultra-Peering for Trust") und ein Web-of-Trust definieren.
In Netzwerk-Laboren oder zuhause mit drei, vier Rechnern kann man das Adaptive Echo einfach austesten und seine Ergebnisse dokumentieren (vgl. GoldBug Handbuch von Edwards, Scott (Ed.) 2014).

3.16.3   Conduction and findings of the examinations

For a test of the Adaptive Echo a network has been formed with ten computers and then the following exemplary sequence was implemented. We have used four laptops to map the actors in the grid and further nodes on other desktop machines were installed, including Raspberrry-Pi computer as a simple kernel-hoster. For our assessment of GoldBug we have adjusted this following experimental setup:

1. First Create a node as a chat server.
2. Create two nodes as clients.
3. Connect the two clients to the chat server.
4. Exchange keys between the clients.
5. Test the normal communication skills among both clients.
6. Set an AE token on the server.
7. Test the normal communication skills among both clients.
8. Now use the same AE token in a client.
9. Write down the result: The server node stops sending the message to other nodes, which do not have the AE-token or don't know it.

(To launch multiple program instances of GoldBug on a single machine and connect to each other also "SPOTON_HOME" as (suffix-less) file in the binary directory may be used.)

Because also the Wicked Witch and Gretel have swapped their chat keys - they therefore can receive messages of each other in the normal echo mode - it is indicated, based on the application of AE tokens into the appropriate nodes, that then the Wicked Witch does not get the message.

Optional: Because all this has been tested with HTTPS connections, and the certification of non-obtaining the message at the Wicked Witch has been pointed out by the fact, that the message does not appear (because it is not received and therefore cannot be decrypted), you can of course also adjust this experimental setup with HTTP without TLS/SSL connections.
It only has to be defined the respective Listener without SSL.
Then it can be seen for the node of the Wicked Witch within any browser, which is set to

Für einen Test des Adaptiven Echos wurde ein Netzwerk mit zehn Computern gebildet und sodann folgender beispielhafter Ablauf umgesetzt. Genutzt wurden vier Laptops um, die Akteure im Grid abzubilden sowie weitere Nodes auf weiteren Desktop-Maschinen, darunter auch Raspberrry Pi Computer als einfache Kernel-Hoster. Diesen folgenden Versuchsaufbau haben wir für unser Assessment von GoldBug nachgestellt:

1. Erstelle einen Knotenpunkt als Chat Server.
2. Erstelle zwei Knotenpunkte als Klient.
3. Verbinde die beiden Klienten zum Chat Server.
4. Tausche Schlüssel zwischen den Klienten.
5. Teste die normale Kommunikationsfähigkeit beider Klienten.
6. Setze einen AE-Token auf dem Server.
7. Teste die normale Kommunikationsfähigkeit beider Klienten.
8. Setze denselben AE-Token nun auch in einem Klienten.
9. Notiere das Ergebnis: Der Server-Knotenpunkt sendet die Nachricht nicht mehr an andere Knotenpunkte aus, die den AE-Token nicht haben bzw. kennen.

(Um mehrere Programminstanzen von GoldBug auf einer einzigen Maschine zu launchen und miteinander zu verbinden kann auch "SPOTON_HOME" als (endungslose) Datei im Binärverzeichnis genutzt werden.)

Da auch die böse Hexe und Gretel ihren Chat-Schlüssel getauscht haben - sie im normalen Echo also gegenseitig Nachrichten empfangen können - zeigt sich bei Anwendung der AE-Tokens in den entsprechenden Knotenpunkten, dass die böse Hexe die Nachricht nicht erhält.

Optional: Da dieses alles mit HTTPS Verbindungen getestet wurde, und der Nachweis des Nicht-Eingehens der Nachricht bei der bösen Hexe darüber erfolgt, dass die Nachricht nicht angezeigt wird (weil sie nicht eingeht und damit nicht entschlüsselt werden kann), kann man natürlich auch diesen Versuchsaufbau mit HTTP ohne TLS/SSL Verbindungen nachstellen.
Dazu ist lediglich der jeweilige Listener ohne TLS/SSL zu definieren.
Dann kann im Knotenpunkt der bösen Hexe mit einem beliebigen Browser, der auf

localhost port 4710, which encrypted messages the Wicked Witch receives. If one would record this and also record the messages, that are sent from Gertel´s node, so it will be noted here, that the broadcast of Gretel´s ciphertext physically does not appear in the node of the Wicked Witch.

Localhost und Port 4710 eingestellt ist, gesehen werden, welche verschlüsselten Nachrichten für die böse Hexe eingehen. Würde man diese aufzeichnen und ebenso bei Gretel die gesendeten Nachrichten aufzeichnen, so wird man auch hier feststellen, daß der von Gretel gesendete Ciphertext auch physisch im Knotenpunkt der bösen Hexe nicht auftaucht.

Figure 23: Adaptive Echo Test-Network-Environment

Source: own graphic.

As a result, it can be said, that the Adaptive Echo - when using the AE-token - secures a connection graph as above tested with three actors in an enlarged node network. Nodes can be excluded from the route, so they will not see certain messages.

This is an important safety option for persons who, for example, create a chat server (listener) for a group, and the Admin of the chat server wants to assure two communicating people exclusivity in their communications. That means all other neighbors, which are related to this listener, will not be included in the exchange of encrypted data packets from people, who know the AE token.

Als Ergebnis lässt sich festhalten, dass das Adaptive Echo bei Anwendung der AE-Token einen Verbindungsgraphen wie oben getestet mit drei Akteuren in einem erweiterten Node-Netzwerk absichert. Knotenpunkte können von der Route ausgenommen werden, so dass sie bestimmte Nachrichten nicht sehen.

Dieses ist eine wichtige Sicherheitsoption für Personen, die z.B. einen Chat-Server (Listener) in einer Gruppe einsetzen, und der Admin des Chat-Servers zwei miteinander kommunizierenden Personen Exklusivität in ihrer Kommunikation zusichern will. D.h. alle anderen Nachbarn, die an diesem Listener verbunden sind, werden nicht einbezogen in den Austausch der verschlüsselten Datenpackete von Personen, die den AE-Token kennen.

3.16.4 Evaluation of the results with regard to weaknesses, risks, potentials for improvements and strengths

This function of the Adaptive Echo has to be regarded as highly innovative and offers many practical experimental examples and analysis options in all, the topic of graph theory, as well as network management, or the cryptographic tokens.

Risks or weaknesses are not seen. It must be ensured, when a longer graph to the respective communications partner is regarded, that all to be defined nodes have to enter the AE token.

With respect to the routing definition is also to be regarded, that a connection between two echo nodes can, for example, also be routed through the proxy function (e.g. via the Tor network). This remains to point out further research and development as a question for further investigation, how an AE connection can be evaluated through the Tor network, respectively an input-proxy and exit-node.

This view also shows the good equipment of the client, that a proxy can be defined, so that the software can be utilized behind a firewall respectively a proxy - e.g. also over the Tor network.

Diese Funktion des Adaptiven Echos ist als äußerst innovativ zu bewerten und bietet zahlreiche praktische Versuchsbeispiele und Analyseoptionen sowohl im Thema der Graphentheorie als auch des Netzwerkmanagements oder der kryptographischen Token.

Risiken oder Schwachstellen werden nicht gesehen. Es ist auch bei einem längeren Graphen lediglich darauf zu achten, dass alle zu definierenden Knotenpunkte bis zum jeweiligen Kommunikationspartner den AE-Token eingeben.

Hinsichtlich der Routingdefinition zeigt sich auch, dass eine Verbindung zwischen zwei Echo-Knotenpunkten z.B. auch mittels der Proxyfunktion (z.B. auch über das Tor-Netzwerk) zwischengeroutet werden können. Dieses bleibt als weitere Forschungs- und Entwicklungsfrage für weitere Untersuchungen anzuregen, wie eine AE-Verbindung durch das Tor-Netzwerk bzw. einem Eingangs-Proxy und Exit-Node evaluiert werden kann.

Diese Sichtweise zeigt auch die gute Ausstattung des Klienten auf, dass ein Proxy definiert werden kann, so dass die Software hinter einer Firewall bzw. einem Proxy betrieben – also z.B. auch über das Tor Netzwerk – genutzt werden kann.

Table 58: Description of findings 3.16

#	Area	Description of the finding	Valuation Severity Category / Difficulty Level / Innovation & Improvement Class / Strength Dimension
	Weakness / Schwäche	./.	./.
	Risk / Risiko	./.	./.
3.15.4.A	Potential for Improvement / Verbesserungspotential	The user must be aware to transfer the AE Token within a secure environment.	Informational
3.15.4.B	Strength / Stärke	Adaptive Echo excludes other nodes from receiving information. This has to be regarded as very innovative compared to the state of the art in other communication solutions. Adaptive Echo is able to create an artificial Web of Trust for your crypto key.	High

3.16.5 Appraisal of good practices in comparison with other similar applications

Compared with other open source applications, it is in no other application possible to store cryptographic tokens to define a path through various graph options.

The comparable crypto-messengers usually define a centralized star-like model that means, all clients connect to a central chat server (from the vendor).

The option to create a private, independent chat server - for instance in a students dormitory or at a LAN party - is not so easy given in most other applications such as in GoldBug Messenger. Here is just to define a listener with a few clicks - and this can be set up even without internet or a cable via Bluetooth.

Im Vergleich mit anderen quelloffenen Applikationen besteht in keiner anderen Applikation die Möglichkeit, kryptographische Token zu hinterlegen, um einen Weg über verschiedene Graphenoptionen zu definieren.

Die vergleichbaren Crypto-Messenger gehen meist von einem zentralistischen Sternmodell aus, d.h. alle Klienten verbinden sich mit einem zentralen Chat-Server (des Anbieters).

Auch ist die Option, beispielsweise in einem Studierenden-Wohnheim oder auf einer Lan-Party einen eigenen, unabhängigen Chat-Server zu erstellen, bei den meisten anderen Applikationen nicht so einfach gegeben wie im GoldBug Messenger. Hier ist lediglich ein Listener mit wenigen Klicks zu definieren und dieses kann auch ohne Internet oder Kabel über Bluetooth eingerichtet werden.

Table 59: Indicative BIG SEVEN context references 3.16

Logo	Application	Comments
	Cryptocat	No networking across multiple servers possible, no cryptographic token for routing, and no proxy function.
	GoldBug	Optional cryptographic token for networking across multiple nodes. Suggestibility of the graph and routing. Proxy-capable and can also be used over Tor. AE token can create an artificial web of trust.
	OTR+XMPP	No cryptographic tokens available. Some proxy enabled clients.
	RetroShare	Web of Trust with connections over friend to friend. No option to leave any friend out. Proxy since version 06.
	Signal	No networking across multiple servers possible, no cryptographic token for routing, and no proxy function.
	SureSpot	No networking across multiple servers possible, no cryptographic token for routing, and no proxy function.
	Tox	No networking across multiple servers possible, no cryptographic token for routing, and no proxy function.

The ability to address a proxy is not well introduced in all other applications. RetroShare has this option built in since version V06. The proxy capability and the ability to control the

Die Möglichkeit einen Proxy anzusprechen ist daher nicht in allen anderen Applikationen gegeben. RetroShare z.B. hat diese Option seit Version V06. Die Proxy-Fähigkeit und die

graph over different nodes by the use of cryptographic tokens are yet only given in the Messenger GoldBug.	Fähigkeit der Steuerung der Graphen über verschiedene Knotenpunkte hinweg durch den Einsatz von kryptographischen Token sind bislang nur im Messenger GoldBug gegeben.

Table 60: Good Practice Insights # 16

Good Practice Insight # 16
with GoldBug Multi-Encrypting Communication Suite

Case	I use a chat server of a friend, but would like that my encrypted messages there are not distributed to other neighbors, but only to my friend. How to do this?
	Ich nutze einen Chat Server eines Bekannten, möchte aber, dass meine verschlüsselten Nachrichten dort nicht an andere Nachbarn verteilt werden, sondern nur an meinen Freund. Wie kann ich dieses erreichen?
Solution	GoldBug offers within the Echo protocol the option to use a cryptographic token. Thus the echo protocol is changed to the mode of the Adaptive Echo (AE): In this case a message will be distributed only to nodes, that have the token. Secondly, there is the possibility to use the mode of the Half Echo, in which the message is sent only as a single hop to the next machine. Otherwise, any message in the echo protocol is sent on to any connected neighbor and can therefore be better protected against network and metadata analysis.
	GoldBug bietet innerhalb des Echo-Protokolls die Option an, einen kryptographischen Token zu nutzen. Damit wird das Echo-Protokoll umgestellt auf den Modus des Adaptiven Echos (AE): Dabei wird eine Nachricht an Knotenpunkte weitergegeben, die den Token kennen. Zweitens besteht die Möglichkeit, den Modus des Halben Echos zu nutzen, dabei wird die Nachricht nur einen Hop zur nächsten Maschine gesandt. Andernfalls wird jede Nachricht im Echo-Protokoll an jeden verbundenen Nachbarn weiter gesandt und kann damit gegen Netzwerk- und Metadaten-Analysen besser geschützt werden.

Source: Own Case.

3.17   Wireless Interaction: Creating a Bluetooth-Listener

The connection of the message sending clients with a server or with a listener of another clients can operate in different ways over the Internet, but also - separated from the Internet and dissociated from a local cable - over a local Bluetooth radio connection.

Die Verbindung der Nachrichten sendenden Klienten mit einem Server oder Listener eines weiteren Klienten kann über verschiedene Wege des Internets funktionieren, aber auch - losgelöst vom Internet und losgelöst von lokalen Kabel - über eine lokale Bluetooth-Funk-Verbindung.

3.17.1   Inventory taking, structural analysis and descriptions of the functions

While we of course consider today a constant availability of an Internet connection, this cannot be assured for any time, any place and possibly even not in special situations.

Während wir heute selbstverständlich von der Verfügbarkeit einer Internetverbindung ausgehen, ist dieses jedoch nicht zu jederzeit, an jedem Ort und auch ggf. in Sondersituationen nicht gegeben.

Thus, alternative connections become more central, that do not run through the usual channels. Also from a point of view for the protection against attackers is a network of clients over alternative routes and ports meaningful.
The GoldBug messenger not only offers the possibility of connecting a neighbor over TCP, UDP or SCTP, but also to create a chat server or listener via Bluetooth.

Somit werden alternative Verbindungen zentral, die nicht über die üblichen Wege laufen. Auch aus einer Sicht zum Schutze vor Angreifern ist eine Vernetzung von Klienten über alternative Wege und Ports sinnvoll.
Der GoldBug Messenger bietet dabei nicht nur die Möglichkeit, einen Nachbarn über TCP, UDP bzw. SCTP zu verbinden, sondern einen Chat-Server bzw. Listener auch über Bluetooth zu erstellen.

This characterizes not only the ability to connect local participants at the Internet loss, but also e.g. the simple use case to join the participants at a trade show, a congress or a LAN party wirelessly. Due to the Echo protocol it is needed at the end of the network possibly just a single node, which connects via another neighbor into the Internet, so that all by Bluetooth connect nodes participate then also in the global network again. The Echo Protocol is mesh-capable.

Dieses charakterisiert nicht nur die Möglichkeit, beim Ausfall des Internets lokale Teilnehmer zu verbinden, sondern auch z.B. den einfachen Anwendungsfall, die Teilnehmer auf einer Messe, einem Congress oder einer Lan-Party kabellos zu verbinden. Durch das Echo-Protokoll benötigt es am Ende des Netzwerkes ggf. einen einzigen Knoten, der sich mit einem weiteren Nachbarn in das Internet verbindet, so dass dann auch alle über Bluetooth verbundenen Knotenpunkte an dem globalen Netzwerk wieder teilnehmen können. Das Echo-Protokoll ist also mesh-fähig.

Although Bluetooth connections of smartphones become more common, for example with your own car, Bluetooth community servers need to experience at conventions still deepening until the technology is naturally, as when someone extends a LAN cable or connects their equipment battery to an electrical outlet.

Auch wenn Bluetooth-Verbindungen des Smartphones beispielsweise mit dem eigenen Auto alltäglicher werden, werden Bluetooth-Community-Server bei Kongressen noch eine Vertiefung erfahren, bis die Technologie selbstverständlich ist, als wenn jemand ein Lan-Kabel reicht oder seinen Geräte-Akku an eine Steckdose verbindet.

The non-open-source and only mobile application Firechat had large gatherings of people by local wireless connections in Hong Kong, Ecuador and Iraq during their demonstrations while social crisis and protests times without Internet (compare Wikipedia).

Die nicht quelloffene und nur mobile Applikation Firechat hat im übrigen in sozialen Krisen- und Protestzeiten ohne Internet größere Menschenansammlungen in Hongkong, Ecuador oder im Irak während ihrer Demonstrationen per lokalem Funk verbunden (vgl. Wikipedia).

Bluetooth is provided over the implementation into the application GoldBug for all communication processes and incorporates Bluetooth libraries via the Qt framework.

Bluetooth wird über die Implementierung in die Applikation GoldBug für alle Kommunikationsprozesse bereitgestellt und bezieht Bluetooth-Bibliotheken über das Qt-Framework ein.

Under Qt 5.5 is currently a working Bluetooth connection enabled only under Linux, so that the following investigation refer to two Linux machines with the GoldBug messenger.

Derzeit wird unter Qt 5.5 eine funktionierende Bluetooth-Verbindung nur unter Linux ermöglicht, so dass sich die folgende Untersuchung auf zwei Linux Maschinen mit dem GoldBug Messenger beziehen.

3.17.2 Selected method for studying and function reference

In the present assessment therefore is also the Bluetooth function to tested by means of a practical application. The aim is to create a connection between two nodes via a Bluetooth connection and the correct transfer of a chat message.

In dem vorliegenden Assessment soll daher auch die Bluetooth-Funktion mittels einer praktischen Anwendung getestet werden. Ziel ist die Erstellung einer Verbindung von zwei Knotenpunkten mittels einer Bluetooth Verbindung und die korrekte Übertragung einer Chat-Nachricht.

3.17.3 Conduction and findings of the examinations

For this purpose a listener with Bluetooth is created on a compilation of the GoldBug messenger on a Linux (Ubuntu) machine. Then on a second laptop - as well with Linux (Ubuntu) - another client is created and connected via Bluetooth to the Bluetooth listener.

Dazu wird ein Listener mit Bluetooth erstellt auf einer Kompilation des GoldBug Messengers auf einer Linux (Ubuntu) Maschine. Sodann wird auf einem zweiten Laptop ebenso mit Linux (Ubuntu) ein weiterer Klient erstellt und mittels Bluetooth an den Bluetooth-Listener verbunden.

Figure 27: Creating a Bluetooth Chat-Server / Listener

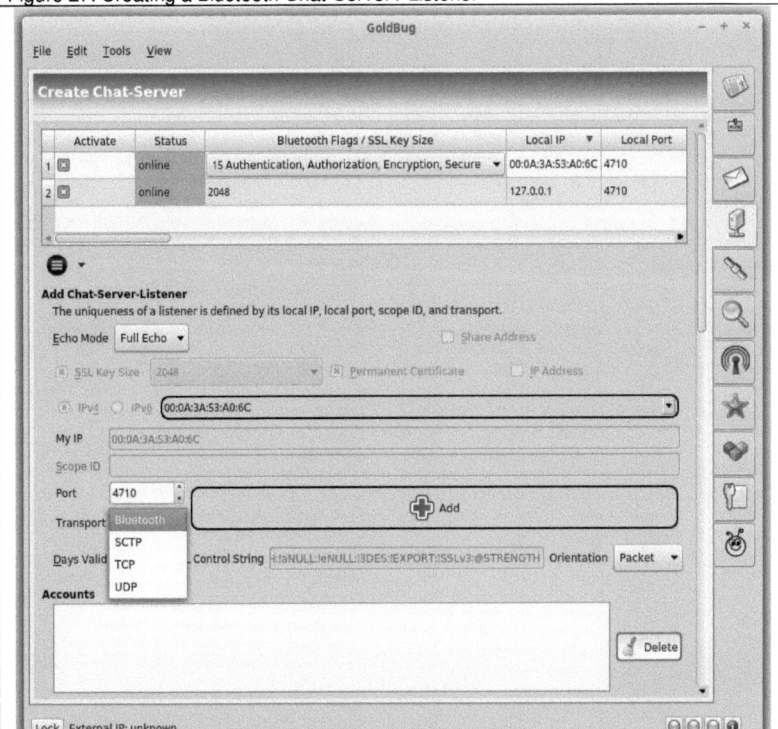

Source: Own screenshot of GoldBug, Chat Server Tab with Bluetooth Listener, on an Ubuntu Linux compile.

The two clients exchange each the key for encryption. The result shows that both clients are connected to one another over the Bluetooth connection, and can communicate.

Die beiden Klienten tauschen jeweils den Schlüssel für die Verschlüsselung. Das Ergebnis zeigt, dass beide Klienten über die Bluetooth-Verbindung miteinander verbunden sind und kommunizieren können.

A data transfer was initiated by the popup chat window and transmitted at a relatively high bandwidth. The result of the Bluetooth connection is correct and also the speed of a file transfer is more than satisfactory.

Auch ein Dateitransfer wurde über das Pop-up-Chatfenster initiiert und bei relativ hoher Bandbreite übertragen. Das Ergebnis der Bluetooth-Verbindung ist korrekt und auch die Geschwindigkeit einer Dateiübertragung mehr als zufriedenstellend.

3.17.4 Evaluation of the results with regard to weaknesses, risks, potentials for improvements and strengths

As improvement may be noted, that the connection involves regular security levels for the Bluetooth. These are displayed in the client, but not documented in the manual, which was as version based for the audit. The short description of the establishment of a Bluetooth server in the manual might has the reason that a Bluetooth connection is rather a special case for a research question of a research group.

Als Verbesserung kann angemerkt werden, dass die Verbindung bei Bluetooth regulär verschiedene Sicherheitsstufen einbezieht. Diese sind im Klienten abgebildet, jedoch nicht im Handbuch dokumentiert, das als Version dem Audit zugrunde lag. Die nur kurze Beschreibung der Einrichtung eines Bluetooth Servers im Handbuch liegt sicherlich daran, daß eine Bluetooth-Verbindung eher ein Spezialfall für eine Forschungsfragestellung einer Forschungsgruppe darstellt.

End consumers will certainly offer more as a multiplier or administrator at a conference or a meeting such a connection, but do not connect regularly at home two nodes via Bluetooth. Therefore, there is in here to be assessed subject no risks or potential for improvement, but only the wish that Bluetooth connections are further evaluated scientifically respectively that wireless communication options are also available for conferences and meetings, to involve participants into learnings.

Endverbraucher werden sicherlich eher als Multiplikator oder Administrator auf einem Kongress oder einer Tagung eine solche Verbindung anbieten, aber nicht regulär zuhause zwei Knotenpunkte über Bluetooth verbinden. Daher gibt es in der hier zu beurteilenden Thematik keine Risiken oder Verbesserungspotentiale, sondern nur den Wunsch, dass Bluetooth-Verbindungen auch wissenschaftlich weiter evaluiert werden bzw. die kabellosen Kommunikationsmöglichkeiten auch bei Kongressen und Tagungen angeboten werden, um Teilnehmer in Lernprozesse zu involvieren.

Table 61: Description of findings 3.17

#	Area	Description of the finding	Valuation Severity Category / Difficulty Level / Innovation & Improvement Class / Strength Dimension
	Weakness / Schwäche	./.	./.
	Risk / Risiko	./.	./.
3.16.4.A	Potential for Improvement / Verbesserungspotential	Documentation of the security level of Bluetooth in the user manual.	./.
	Strength / Stärke	./.	./.

The following chart was discussed on Twitter and presents a model of a graph by the project, which is connecting the participants in two workshop or class rooms with a Bluetooth listener. With this a kind of "Buetooth-Freifunk" is created - as with the German term "Freifunk" a free wireless WLan-offer is described, which is made avalable through the user community.

Die folgende Grafik wurde auf Twitter diskutiert und stellt ein Modell eines Graphen seitens des Projektes dar, der in zwei Workshop oder Klassen-Räumen die Teilnehmer mit einem Bluetooth-Listener verbindet. Damit wird eine Art „Bluetooth-Freifunk" hergestellt, wie im Deutschen mit dem Begriff „Freifunk" ein kostenloses, durch die Nutzergemeinde zur Verfügung gestelltes Wlan-Angebot bezeichnet wird.

Figure 28:   Graph-Example including Bluetooth-Chat Servers in a classroom

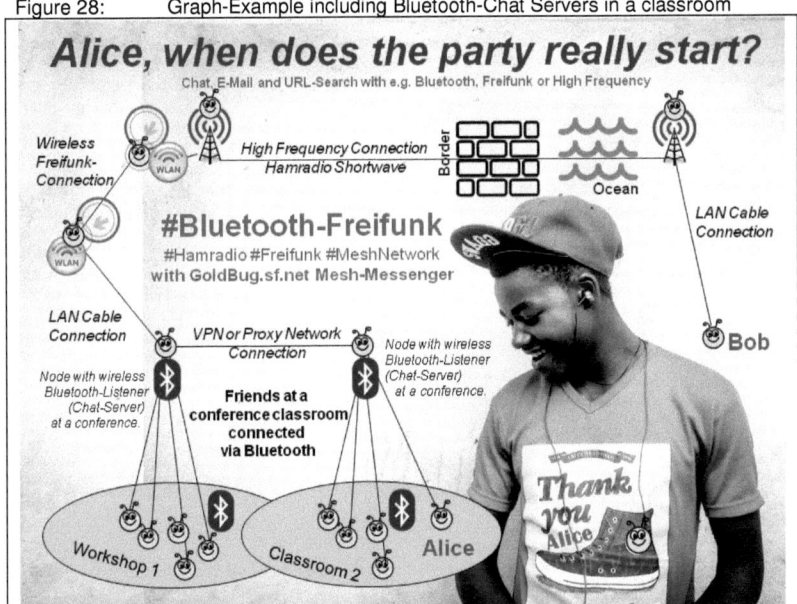

Source: Twitter Post.

Also the wireless options, to connect two GoldBug nodes via a radio link (Hamradio or shortwave) or a WiFi mesh network are shown. The here interesting Bluetooth function can thus provide especially for workshop situations the functions such as group chat, private chat, email and URL-Search. It is an alternative to WLAN access points and a simplification to set up a simple laptop for both, WiFi receiving as well as a BT server - which might reduce the configuration of WLAN routers or repeaters on additonal hardware.

Auch die kabellosen Optionen, zwei GoldBug-Knotenpunkte über eine Funkverbindung (Hamradio bzw. Kurzwelle) oder ein WLan Mesh-Network herzustellen, sind eingezeichnet. Die hier interessierende Bluetooth-Funktion kann somit insbesondere für Workshop-Situationen die Funktionen wie Gruppenchat, persönlichen Chat, E-Mail als auch die URL-Suche zur Verfügung stellen. Es ist eine Alternative zu WLan-Zugangspunkten bzw. eine Vereinfachung, einen einfachen Laptop sowohl für WLan-Empfang als auch als BT-Server einzurichten – was die Konfiguration von WLan Routern bzw. Repeatern auf zusätzlichen Geräten einsparen kann.

3.17.5 Appraisal of good practices in comparison with other similar applications

GoldBug is currently - according to the provisional assessment to the comparable applications - the only client that can hold a neighboring connection via Bluetooth or can act as a Bluetooth server.
Although this is a rare use case, and currently just provided by the Qt-framework for linux machines, it shows - in addition to the applicability of the SCTP protocol - an advanced status next to the consideration of connection alternatives to TCP and UDP, as well as an interesting variance for research questions.

GoldBug ist derzeit - nach erster Einschätzung der vergleichbaren Applikationen - der einzige Klient, der eine Nachbarverbindung über Bluetooth vorhalten kann bzw. auch als Bluetooth-Server fungieren kann.
Auch wenn dieses ein seltener Anwendungs-Fall ist und derzeit bislang aufgrund des QT-Frameworks nur für Linux vorgehalten wird, zeigt dies - neben der Anwendbarkeit ebenso des SCTP Protokolls - einem fortschrittlichen Status in der Berücksichtigung von Verbindungsalternativen zu TCP und UDP auf, wie auch eine interessante Varianz für Forschungsfragestellungen.

Table 62: Indicative BIG SEVEN context references 3.17

Logo	Application	Comments
	Cryptocat	No Bluetooth available.
	GoldBug	Chat-Server and Connection over Bluetooth is possible.
	OTR+XMPP	No OTR key transfer over Bluetooth available.
	RetroShare	No Bluetooth available.
	Signal	No Bluetooth available.
	SureSpot	No Bluetooth available.
	Tox	No Bluetooth available in evaluated version.

Table 63: Good Practice Insights #17

Good Practice Insight # 17
with GoldBug Multi-Encrypting Communication Suite

Case	Next week we have a meeting and I would like to offer a group chat for the participants and also transfer some files to these. My laptop is connected over the WLAN in the internet and my Bluetooth module is expected to host the chat of participants as a server. How can I deploy this? Nächste Woche haben wir eine Konferenz und ich möchte einen Gruppenchat für die Teilnehmer anbieten sowie auch die Dateien an diese transferieren. Mein Laptop ist über das WLan im Internet und mein Bluetooth-Modul sollte den Chat der Teilnehmer als Server aufnehmen. Wie kann ich das umsetzen?
Solution	To use GoldBug as a Lan Messenger with chat, e-mail, group chat and file transfer is simple. This is a wired solution. Who wants to do without cable, can provide also over WLan an appropriate communication server. GoldBug allows for in experiments interested users furthermore also (currently with the Qt framework 5.5. only) on Linux, to create a chat-server via Bluetooth. So each user can chat with each other wirelessly. GoldBug als Lan-Messenger mit Chat, E-Mail, Gruppenchat und Dateitransfer einzusetzen ist einfach. Das ist eine kabelgebundene Lösung. Wer auf Kabel verzichten möchte, kann auch über WLan einen entsprechenden Chat-Server bereitgestellen. GoldBug ermöglicht es für an Experimenten interessierte Nutzer zudem auch (derzeit mit dem Qt-Framework 5.5. nur) unter Linux, einen Chat-Server per Bluetooth herzustellen. So kann jeder Nutzer kabellos miteinander chatten.

Source: Own Case.

3.18 Social Engineering: SMP - Socialist-Millionaire-Protocol

The Socialist Millionaire Protocol describes a method, by which it can be demonstrated, that both chat participants have entered the same password without transmitting the password itself over the Internet. A shared secret or a common phrase can therefore help to authenticate the chat friend. It is an additional security feature.

This object is originally known as Yao's millionaire problem (compare Yao 1986, Loannis 2003): Two millionaires want to determine who is the richer, without disclosing their account balances.

A variation of this is the so-called Socialist Millionaires' problem (compare Jakobsson 1996), in which the two are only interested in whether their wealth is equal.

Formal in both cases is a way requested, how Alice and Bob can determine a function value f (x, y, ...) without any of them obtaining (x, y, ...) additional information about the input values.

A process with these characteristics is called a zero-knowledge protocol. If the result of f is a truth value, then it is a zero-knowledge proof. Furthermore, a protocol is called fair, when neither party can terminate it with a significant information advantage (compare also Hallberg 2008).

A method according to the above principle was later implemented by Borisov et al. (2004) under the name "Socialist Millionaires' Protocol" (SMP) for the off-the-record program. Off-the-Record enables encrypted communication over instant messaging clients predominantly based on XMPP.

In this case, the method outlined above is suitable in particular, because the communication partners are often familiar with each other, but usually do not have an existing channel for secure key verification (compare Hallberg 2008).

Das Socialist Millionaire Protokoll beschreibt eine Methode, mit der nachgewiesen werden kann, dass beide Chat-Teilnehmer dasselbe Passwort eingegeben haben, ohne das Passwort selbst über das Internet zu übertragen. Ein gemeinsames Geheimnis bzw. ein gemeinsamer Begriff kann daher helfen, den Chat-Freund zu authentifizieren. Es ist ein zusätzliches Sicherheitsmerkmal.

Diese Aufgabe ist ursprünglich bekannt als Yaos Millionärsproblem (vgl. Yao 1986, Loannis 2003): Zwei Millionäre wünschen zu bestimmen, wer der reichere ist, ohne dabei ihre Kontostände offenzulegen.

Eine Abwandlung davon ist das sogenannte Socialist Millionaires' Problem (vgl. Jakobsson 1996), bei dem die beiden lediglich daran interessiert sind, ob ihr Reichtum gleich ist.

Formal ist in beiden Fällen eine Möglichkeit gefragt, wie Alice und Bob einen Funktionswert f(x, y, ...) bestimmen können, ohne daß einer von ihnen zusätzliche Informationen über die Eingabewerte (x, y, ...) erhält.

Ein Verfahren mit dieser Eigenschaft wird als Zero-Knowledge-Protokoll bezeichnet. Ist das Ergebnis von f ein Wahrheitswert, so handelt es sich um einen Zero-Knowledge-Beweis. Weiterhin nennt man ein Protokoll fair, wenn keiner der Teilnehmer es mit nennenswertem Informationsvorsprung beenden kann (vgl. a Hallberg 2008).

Ein Verfahren nach obigem Prinzip unter der Bezeichnung "Socialist Millionaires' Protocol" (SMP) wurde später von Borisov et al. (2004) für das Programm Off-the-Record implementiert. Off-the-Record ermöglicht die verschlüsselte Kommunikation über Instant-Messaging-Klienten vorwiegend basierend auf XMPP.

Dabei bietet sich das oben vorgestellte Verfahren insbesondere an, weil die Kommunikationspartner häufig miteinander vertraut sind, aber in der Regel über keinen bestehenden Kanal zur sicheren Schlüsselverifizierung verfügen (vgl. Hallberg 2008).

For friends, who know each other from a public group chat like IRC virtually, OTR is offering not much more, because modern protocols also allow a key transfer and other functions via secure channels.

Für Freunde, die sich aus einem öffentlichen Gruppenchat wie IRC virtuell kennen lernen, bietet OTR nicht viel mehr an, denn modernere Protokolle erlauben auch einen Schlüsseltransfer und weitere Funktionen über gesicherte Kanäle.

Figure 26:   Socialist-Millionaire-Protocol in the graphical user interface of the GoldBug Messenger

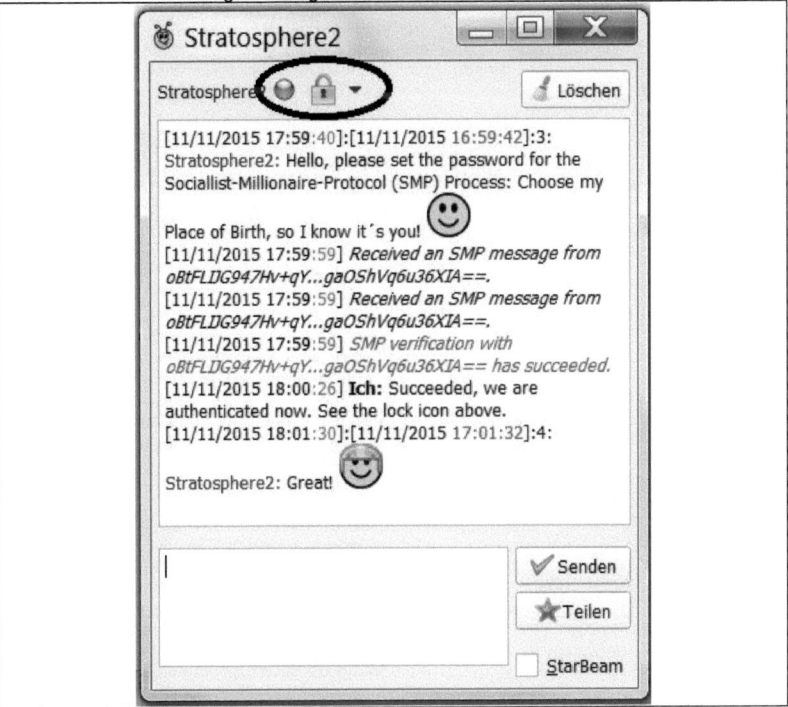

Source: Screenshot of Goldbug 2.8, compare Edwards, Scott (Ed.) et al. 2014.

3.18.1   Inventory taking, structural analysis and descriptions of the functions

In GoldBug Messenger sign regularly both participants the messages with the RSA algorithm (or another to the available algorithms) to verify, that the key is used by the original sender.

Im GoldBug Messenger signieren regulär weise beide Teilnehmer die Nachrichten mit dem RSA-Algorithmus (oder einem anderen der verfügbaren Algorithmen), um zu überprüfen, dass der verwendete Schlüssel vom ursprünglichen Absender ist.

For the (possibly unlikely) case, that a machine has been compromised or if the encryption

Für den (ggf. unwahrscheinlichen) Fall, dass eine Maschine gehackt würde oder falls der

algorithm would be broken, with the Socialist-Millionaire-Protocol-(SMP)-process a friend can simply be identified or authenticated by entering the same password on both sides.

The idea is to ask in chat to a friend a question like: "What is the name of the city that we visited together in the last year?", or to ask a question like: "What is the name of the restaurant, where we met the first time?" etc. (compare GoldBug Manual of Edwards, Scott (Ed.) et al. 2014).

Verschlüsselungsalgorithmus gebrochen werden würde, kann mit dem Socialist Millionaire Protocol (SMP) - Prozess ein Freund einfach durch Eingabe des gleichen Passwortes auf beiden Seiten identifiziert bzw. authentifiziert werden.

Die Idee dahinter ist, im Chat an den Freund eine Frage zu stellen wie: "Was ist der Name der Stadt, die wir gemeinsam im letzten Jahr besucht haben?", oder eine Frage zu stellen wie: "Was ist der Name des Restaurants, in dem wir uns das erste Mal getroffen haben?" usw. (vgl. GoldBug Handbuch von Edwards, Scott (Ed.) et al. 2014).

3.18.2 Selected method for studying and function reference

A review of the SMP function can be done in a practical, technical and theoretical level.

Eine Überprüfung der SMP-Funktion kann auf praktischer, technischer und theoretischer Ebene erfolgen.

On a theoretical level, you can think through various communication scenarios to achieve a common password for both parties, so that an attacker remains undetected. This would e.g. concern the theoretical assumption that a partner is communicating with an attacker and the attacker can view the keystrokes.

Auf theoretischer Ebene kann man verschiedene Kommunikations-Szenarien durchdenken, um ein gemeinsames Passwort bei beiden Teilnehmern zu erreichen, so dass ein Angreifer unerkannt bleibt. Dieses würde z.B. die theoretische Annahme betreffen, dass ein Partner mit einem Angreifer kommuniziert und der Angreifer die Tastatureingaben einsehen kann.

On a technical respectively mathematical level the individual steps of a zero-knowledge proof are defined and follow this graphical process flow chart shown below, which is provided by the developers in the documentation. The process graphics has been later also adopted by the Wikipedia.

Auf technischer bzw. mathematischer Ebene sind die einzelnen Schritte für einen Zero-Knowledge-Proof definiert und folgen diesem weiter unten abgebildeten graphischen Prozess-Flow-Chart, das durch die Entwickler in der Dokumentation zur Verfügung gestellt wird. Die Prozess-Grafik ist später auch in der Wikipedia übernommen worden.

Figure 30: Socialist Millionaire Protocol – State Machine Process

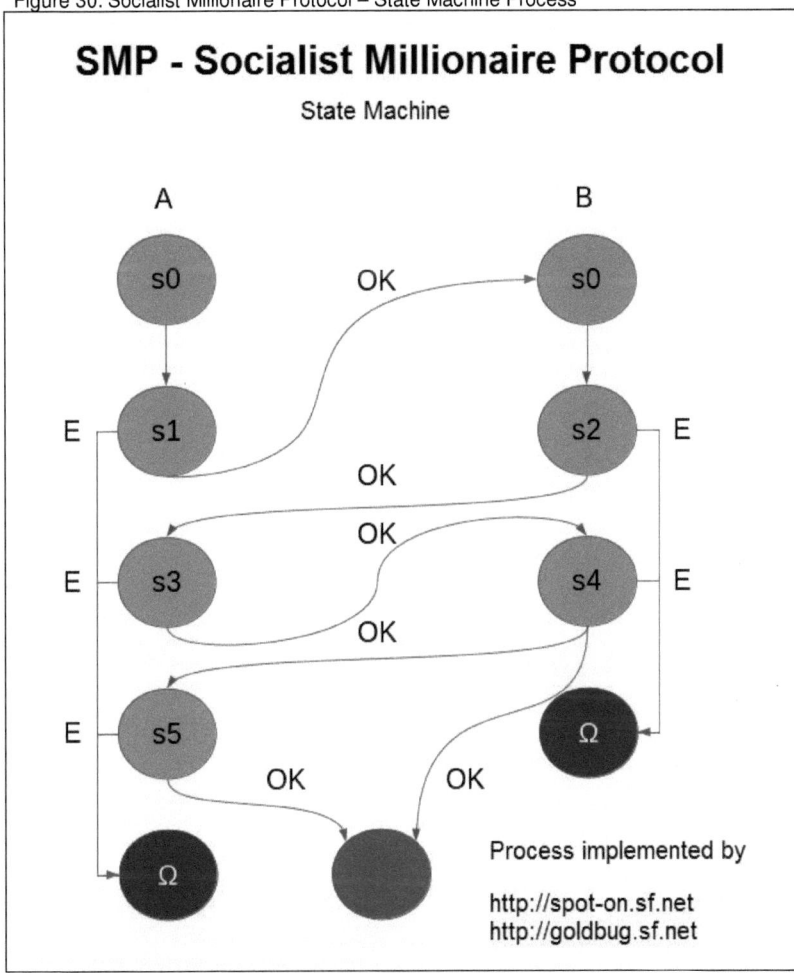

Source: https://en.wikipedia.org/wiki/Socialist_millionaire .

The following table illustrates then the mathematical calculations per step.

Die folgende Tabelle verdeutlicht sodann die mathematischen Berechnungen pro Schritt.

Table 64: Steps of the Socialist Millionaire Process

	Alice	Multiparty	Bob
1	Message x Random a, α, r	Public p, h	Message y Random b, β, s
2		Secure $g = \langle h \mid a, b \rangle$	
3		Secure $\gamma = \langle h \mid \alpha, \beta \rangle$	
4	Test $h^b \neq 1. h^\beta \neq 1$		Test $h^a \neq 1. h^\alpha \neq 1$
5	$P_a = \gamma^r$ $Q_a = h^r g^x$		$P_b = \gamma^s$ $Q_b = h^s g^y$
6		Insecure exchange P_a, Q_a, P_b, Q_b	
7		Secure $c = \left\langle Q_a Q_b^{-1} \mid \alpha, \beta \right\rangle$	
8	Test $P_a \neq P_b. Q_a \neq Q_b$		Test $P_a \neq P_b. Q_a \neq Q_b$
9	Test $c = P_a P_b^{-1}$		Test $c = P_a P_b^{-1}$

Source: Wikipedia - https://en.wikipedia.org/wiki/Socialist_millionaire .

Please note / Beachte:

$$P_a P_b^{-1} = \gamma^r \gamma^{-s} = \gamma^{r-s}$$
$$= h^{\alpha\beta(r-s)}$$

And thus it is valid: / und daher gilt:

$$c = \left(Q_a Q_b^{-1} \right)^{\alpha\beta}$$
$$= \left(h^r g^x h^{-s} g^{-y} \right)^{\alpha\beta} = \left(h^{r-s} g^{x-y} \right)^{\alpha\beta}$$
$$= \left(h^{r-s} h^{ab(x-y)} \right)^{\alpha\beta} = h^{\alpha\beta(r-s)} h^{\alpha\beta ab(x-y)}$$
$$= \left(P_a P_b^{-1} \right) h^{\alpha\beta ab(x-y)}$$

Because of the random values stored in secret by the other party, neither party can force c and $P_a P_b^{-1}$ to be equal unless x equals y, in which case $h^{\alpha\beta ab(x-y)} = h^0 = 1$.

Aufgrund der Zufallswerte, die durch den anderen Teilnehmer im geheimen Passwort hinterlegt werden, kann kein Teilnehmer erzwingen, dass c und $P_a P_b^{-1}$ gleich sind, solange x nicht gleich ist mit y, was in diesem Fall bedeutet: $h^{\alpha\beta ab(x-y)} = h^0 = 1$.

This proves correctness.

Dieses beweist die Richtigkeit.

It must be assessed as unlikely that the mathematical calculation may be changed, and secondly, the calculation is a programmed basis in both clients.

Es ist als unwahrscheinlich zu beurteilen, dass die mathematische Berechnung verändert werden kann, und zum zweiten ist die Berechnung auch eine programmierte Grundlage in beiden Klienten.

That leaves only the practical level to manipulate password entries:

In most cases for an intrusion into a foreign computer system to view confidential data something is used, what is called "social engineering" (compare Harley 1998); one then speaks also of social hacking.

The basic pattern of social engineering shows e.g. up in bogus phone calls as follows: The social engineer calls a company's employee and pretends to be a technician, who need the credentials to complete important work.

Already in advance such an attacker has collected from publicly available sources or previous calls small pieces of information over procedures, daily office talk and corporate hierarchy, which help him in his interpersonal manipulation, to impersonate as insider of the company.

In addition, he confuses his opposite, which technically may not be such an expert, with jargon, builds with Smalltalk over seemingly common colleagues sympathy and uses authority respect by threatening to disturb a superior in case the victim neglects cooperation.

Under certain circumstances, the social engineer has been collected in advance information that a particular employee has even really requested technical assistance and already actually expect such a call.

Despite its apparent banality happen with the method again and again spectacular data breaches: This enabled e.g. an American student in 2015 to be able to open the private e-mail account of the acting director of a large organization, and had three days access to it (compare NZZ 2015 and Wired 2015).
In the following, therefore, on a practical level of communication should once a (theoretically possible) dialogue be simulated, with the examination question, whether a whatever kind of dialogue can lead an online friend to enter the password, which is requested by an attacker instead of the real friend.

Bleibt also nur die praktische Ebene, um Passworteingaben zu manipulieren:

Meist dient das sogenannte "Social Engineering" dem Eindringen in ein fremdes Computersystem, um vertrauliche Daten einzusehen (vgl. Harley 1998); man spricht dann auch von Social Hacking.

Das Grundmuster des Social Engineering zeigt sich z.B. bei fingierten Telefonanrufen wie folgt: Der Social Engineer ruft Mitarbeiter eines Unternehmens an und gibt sich als Techniker aus, der vertrauliche Zugangsdaten benötige, um wichtige Arbeiten abzuschließen.

Bereits im Vorfeld hat so ein Angreifer aus öffentlich zugänglichen Quellen oder vorangegangenen Telefonaten kleine Informationsfetzen über Verfahrensweisen, tägliches Bürogerede und Unternehmenshierarchie zusammengetragen, die ihm bei der zwischenmenschlichen Manipulation helfen, sich als Insider des Unternehmens auszugeben.

Zusätzlich verwirrt er sein technisch ggf. nicht so versiertes Gegenüber mit Fachjargon, baut mit Smalltalk über scheinbar gemeinsame Kollegen Sympathie auf und nutzt Autoritätsrespekt aus, indem er droht, bei vom Opfer unterlassener Kooperation dessen Vorgesetzten stören zu müssen.

Unter Umständen hat der Social Engineer bereits im Vorfeld Informationen gesammelt, dass ein bestimmter Mitarbeiter sogar wirklich technische Hilfe angefordert hat und bereits tatsächlich einen derartigen Anruf erwartet.

Trotz ihrer scheinbaren Banalität gelingen mit der Methode immer wieder spektakuläre Datendiebstähle: So gelang es z.B. einem amerikanischen Schüler 2015, den privaten E-Mail-Account des amtierenden Direktors einer großen Organisation zu öffnen und drei Tage lang darauf zuzugreifen (vgl. NZZ 2015 und Wired 2015).
Im folgenden soll daher auf praktischer Kommunikationsebene einmal ein (theoretisch möglicher) Dialog nachvollzogen werden, mit der Prüfungsfragestellung, ob ein wie auch immer gearteter Dialog dazu führen kann, dass ein Online-Freund das Passwort eingibt, das ein Angreifer anstelle des wirklichen Freundes anfordert.

3.18.3   Conduction and findings of the examinations

Thirdly, therefore, on a practical level, one would have to try through skillful communication at the online communication in messenger with several people, to enter the supposedly common SMP password also in the right way - as it should be thought out in the following for an attack in a theoretical example of a practical attempt of manipulation for the use of a messenger:

Drittens also, auf praktischer Ebene, müsste man bei der Online-Kommunikation im Messenger mit mehreren Personen durch geschickte Kommunikation versuchen, das vermeintlich gemeinsame SMP-Passwort auch entsprechend richtig einzugeben - wie es im folgenden für einen Angriff in einem theoretisch Beispiel für einen praktischen Manipulations-versuch für die Nutzung eines Messengers angenommen werden soll:

Suppose Alice and Bob have married in New York City. Alice assumes for her online communication, that at the other end of the line is also Bob. Suppose further, an attacker has managed to take over the infrastructure of Bob: Bob has been pulled away his chair from the desk from behind and the functioning and opened machine is now available to the attacker.

Nehmen wir an, Alice und Bob haben in der Stadt New York geheiratet. Alice geht in ihrer Online-Kommunikation davon aus, dass am anderen Ende der Leitung auch Bob ist. Nehmen wir weiter an, einem Angreifer ist es gelungen, die Infrastruktur von Bob zu übernehmen: Bob wurde mit seinem Stuhl vom Schreibtisch aus hinterrücks weggezogen und die funktionsfähige und geöffnete Maschine steht dem Angreifer nun zur Verfügung.

The attacker knows some things from the lives of both people in the conversation. Thus, the attacker e.g. found out, that both have married in New York and Alice uses this password even with two of the major webmail providers.

Der Angreifer weiß einige Dinge aus dem Leben beider Teilnehmer der Unterhaltung. So hat der Angreifer z.B. herausgefunden, dass beide in New York geheiratet haben und Alice dieses Passwort auch bei zweien der großen Webmailanbieter nutzt.

Alice prefers now to insure herselves once more, if really Bob sits in front of the computer at the other end and therefore asks in the online chat to Bob as follows:

Alice will sich nun lieber nochmals absichern, ob auch wirklich Bob am anderen Ende vor dem Rechner sitzt und fragt daher im Online-Chat an Bob wie folgt:

Alice: *Hello Bob,*	**Alice:** *Hallo Bob,*
Bob (aka Attacker):	**Bob (aka Angreifer):**
Hello Alice, how are you?	*Hallo Alice, wie geht es Dir?*
Alice: *Thank you, I am fine. Before we start with our chat, we should authenticate over the SMP-protocol. Do you remember still, in which city we have married?*	**Alice:** *Danke mir geht es gut, bevor wir mit unserer Unterhaltung starten, sollten wir uns über das SMP-Protokoll absichern, Kannst Du Dich noch erinnern, in welcher Stadt wir geheiratet haben?*
Bob: *Sure, of course, you mean, we should use the city name as a Password für the Socialist-Millionaire-Protocol?*	**Bob:** *Aber klar, Du meinst wir sollten den Namen der Stadt als Passwort für das Socialist-Millionaire-Protokoll verwenden?*
Alice: *Yes, please, enter that password.*	**Alice:** *Ja, bitte, gebe das Passwort ein.*

Alice deposited her password "new york" and asks Bob to do it equally. The attacker enters also the password "New York". The SMP process fails.

Alice hinterlegt ihr Passwort „newyork" und bittet Bob, es ebenso zu tun. Der Angreifer gibt ebenso das Passwort „New York" ein. Der SMP-Prozess gelingt nicht.

Alice is clear that maybe not the real Bob is sitting at the other end of the line, because with him she had arranged once in a private session, to enter all passwords always only in lowercase letters and without spaces.

The process makes it clear, that the attacker can respond to the Socialist-Millionaire-Process-(SMP)-protocol only successfully in the situation, when Alice's question for a password is predictable and always the same password is used in daily chat.

At the same time, the attacker must know the content of the possible answers to Alice's SMP question. Thus, it is an absolutely unlikely event that a foreign attacker can enter the correct SMP-password. Anything else would clairvoyance or brainwashing. The daily communication and the large number of possible ideas that a communication partner could question, makes it almost impossible to guess the password.

The password is technically not transferred between the two. If the password of Alice could not be found out by a Social Engineering Process e.g. as described above, is ultimately left only the interception of the keystrokes of Alice, so that the password can also be entered on the side of the computer of Bob.

Also at this point, therefore, should be pointed again to the possibility of using the virtual keyboard, which is built-in in the client GoldBug and which excludes the regular records of keystrokes.

Alice wird deutlich, dass möglicherweise gar nicht der echte Bob am anderen Ende der Leitung sitzt, denn mit ihm hatte sie mal in einer privaten Stunde verabredet, alle Passworte immer nur in Kleinbuchstaben und ohne Leerzeichen einzugeben.

Der Prozess verdeutlicht, dass der Angreifer auf das Socialist-Millionaire-Process-(SMP)-Protokoll nur dann erfolgreich in der jeweiligen Situation reagieren kann, wenn Alices Frage nach einem Passwort vorhersehbar ist und auch immer dasselbe Passwort im täglichen Chat verwandt wird.

Zugleich muss der Angreifer die Inhalte der möglichen Antworten auf Alice´s SMP-Frage kennen. Es ist somit ein absolut unwahrscheinlicher Fall, dass ein fremder Angreifer das richtige SMP-Passwort eingeben kann. Alles andere wäre Hellseherei oder Gehirnwäsche. Die tägliche Kommunikation und die Vielzahl an möglichen Ideen, die ein Kommunikationspartner abfragen könnte, macht es nahezu fast unmöglich, das Passwort zu erraten.

Technisch gesehen wird das Passwort nicht zwischen beiden übertragen. Sollte das Passwort von Alice nicht durch einen Social Engineering Process herausgefunden werden können z.B. wie oben beschrieben, bleibt letztlich nur das Abgreifen der Tastatureingaben von Alice, so dass das Passwort auch auf der Seite des Rechners von Bob eingegeben werden kann.

Auch an dieser Stelle sei daher nochmals auf die Möglichkeit der Nutzung der im Klienten GoldBug eingebauten virtuellen Tastatur hingewiesen, die die regulären Aufzeichnungen von Tastatureingaben ausschließt.

3.18.4 Evaluation of the results with regard to weaknesses, risks, potentials for improvements and strengths

Since the probability to guess a password input through a dialogue can be considered highly unlikely, is here at the correct application of the optional SMP security feature to see in a review no risk, but rather on the other hand: the application of the SMP feature increases even more the confidentiality respectively authenticity.

Generally processes of consciousness and cognitive processes must be fostered as measures for the users, not only about what

Da die Wahrscheinlichkeit, eine Passwort-Eingabe durch einen Dialog zu erraten als sehr unwahrscheinlich betrachtet werden kann, ist hier bei korrekter Anwendung des optionalen SMP-Sicherheitsmerkmals in einer Bewertung kein Risiko zu sehen, sondern die Anwendung der SMP-Funktion hingegen erhöht noch die Vertraulichkeit bzw. Authentizität.

Generell müssen Bewußtseinsprozesse und Kenntnisprozesse als Maßnahmen bei den Anwendern gefördert werden, nicht nur zu

the SMP security feature is, what it offers and how it works, but also to be mindful, to make the process creative and varied with own communication partner (compare also Weßelmann 2008).

The messenger referenced for comparison - except of some selected OTR-XMPP clients - have no or no such pronounced SMP-function and the manual input of the individual to enter password is not such to be found.

wissen, was das SMP-Sicherheitsmerkmal ist, was es bietet und wie es funktioniert, sondern auch achtsam zu sein, den Prozess mit seinem Kommunikationspartner kreativ und abwechslungsreich zu gestalten (vgl. a. Weßelmann 2008).

Die für einen Vergleich referenzierten Messenger – bis auf ausgewählte OTR-XMPP-Klienten – haben keine oder keine derart ausgeprägte SMP-Funktion und auch die manuelle Eingabe des individuell zu findenden Passwortes ist nicht dergestalt vorzufinden.

Table 65: Description of findings 3.18

#	Area	Description of the finding	Valuation Severity Category / Difficulty Level / Innovation & Improvement Class / Strength Dimension
	Weakness / Schwäche	./.	./.
3.19.4.A	Risk / Risiko	Theoretical Social Engineering atempts	Informational
3.19.4.B	Potential for Improvement / Verbesserungspotential	Function develops awareness processes at the side of the end-users	Informational
3.19.4.C	Strength / Stärke	GoldBug uses stronger SHA-512.	Medium

3.18.5 Appraisal of good practices in comparison with other similar applications

Only OTR-XMPP Messenger have depending on the client possibly an SMP-function by the OTR protocol installed, as described for OTR in a modification.
The GoldBug Messenger has installed the SMS function as well and allows the manual definition of the password.

Lediglich OTR-XMPP Messenger haben also je nach Klient ggf. eine SMP-Funktion mittels des OTR-Protokolls eingebaut, wie es für OTR in einer Abwandlung beschrieben ist.
Der GoldBug Messenger hat die SMP Funktion ebenso eingebaut und erlaubt die manuelle Definition des Passwortes.

Technically shows our code review that Goldbug makes use of a SHA-512, and AES 256 and a 3072 bit key (SMP accurs within the chat dialog), while on the other hand OTR uses only the SHA-256, AES 128-bit and for the Diffie-Hellman key exchange 1536 bits - in regard from the cryptographic strength OTR is therefore only half as secure as of the implemented Socialist-Millionaire-process in the application GoldBug in all three cryptologic factors.

Technisch gesehen zeigt unser Code-Review, dass GoldBug einen SHA-512, sowie AES 256 und einen 3072 Bit Key (SMP wird im Chat-Dialog-Fenster angezeigt), während hingegen OTR nur den SHA-256, AES mit 128 Bit und für den Diffie–Hellman-Schlüssel-Austausch 1536 Bits einsetzt - von der kryptografischen Stärke her gesehen ist OTR also in allen drei kryptologischen Faktoren nur halb so sicher wie der implementierte Socialist Millionaire Prozess bei der Applikation GoldBug.

Moreover, in particular the by OTR used low AES-128 has been officially designated as "not safe" by the NIST (compare NIST 8105, 2016) - so OTR must apply in all XMPP clients as obsolete and potential security risk: In stormy

Zudem wurde insbesondere das geringe, von OTR genutzte, AES-128 von der NIST offiziell als "nicht mehr sicher" bezeichnet (vgl. NIST 8105, 2016) - so dass OTR in allen XMPP Klienten als obsolet und mögliches

Quantum times the OTR-dike breaks all too quickly and urgently needs a new manifesto for all XMPP clients!

Sicherheitsrisko gelten muss: In stürmischen Quantum-Zeiten bricht der OTR-Deich nur allzuschnell und bedarf dringend eines neuen Manifestes für alle XMPP-Klienten!

Table 66: Indicative BIG SEVEN context references 3.18

Logo	Application	Comments
	Cryptocat	No Implementation of the Socialist-Millionaire-Protocol.
	GoldBug	Elaborated Implementation with a pleasant user interface, elaborated Documentation, as well with manual choice of the password. Usage of SHA 512, AES 256 and 3072 bit for the key.
	OTR+XMPP	Elaborated Implementation only in selected XMPP Clients with OTR, extended documentation. Usage of SHA-256, AES 128 and 1536 bit for the key.
	RetroShare	No Implementation of the Socialist-Millionaire-Protocol.
	Signal	Usage of a less documented own development ("home-brewed approach to encryption") als extension of OTR (Perrin 2014). No manual choice of the password. SHA-256, AES 256, 256 bit Curve25519 key.
	SureSpot	No Implementation of the Socialist-Millionaire-Protocol.
	Tox	No Implementation of the Socialist-Millionaire-Protocol.

Cryptocat, RetroShare, SureSpot and Tox (compare Ticket #1271) have the Socialist-Millionaire-protocol not implemented with manual password choice.

For a summary and contextual evaluation can be summed up that

- Messenger, which have not yet implemented the SMP process, should incorporate this possibly,

- that it is to be welcomed, to explore the developing SMP process and also OTR implementations further (e.g. in terms of the protocol or the implemented cryptographic values strengths) and that this is continued,

- and thirdly, that it is good for the user as well as the development community - in spite of financial funds for Crypto-projects of public and private side as well-initiated marketing hype - to explore alternatives and scientifically to

Cryptocat, RetroShare, Surespot und Tox (vgl. Ticket #1271) haben das Socialist-Millionaire-Protokoll mit manueller Passwortwahl nicht implementiert.

In einer summarischen und kontextuellen Bewertung kann man zusammenfassen, daß

- Messenger, die den SMP-Prozess noch nicht implementiert haben, diesen ggf. einbauen sollten,

- daß es zu begrüßen ist, den SMP-Prozess und auch OTR-Implementierungen weiter zu entwickeln (z.B. hinsichtlich des Protokolls oder der implementierten kryptographischen Werte-Stärken) und dieses weiter zu erforschen,

- sowie drittens, daß es unter Berücksichtigung von finanziellen Geldern für Crypto-Projekte von staatlicher und privatwirtschaftlicher Seite sowie initiiertem Marketing-Hype gut für den Nutzer wie auch die

promote, which are not placed by financial support and multipliers stimulation on everyone's lips, but rather remain as independent, as it is the case at several above mentioned projects.

- The individual definition of cryptologic values (key size or manually entered passwords) increases confidence in the own configuration of the security while using the applications.

The often wrongly judged informal rule, that new ways, methods and processes are to be avoided in cryptography, is not to quote in the first place in use of established libraries and computing procedures.

Anyway, it is therefore incomprehensible that the "homebrewed"-crypto Axolotl is experiencing a hype - it is even seen as a winner against OTR - and also other improvements as "privacy" be shrugged off. So-called experts seem here to want rather to keep their power of definition. "Homemade" inventions also provide an opportunity to scientifically open up comparisons and professional judgments.

At the same time the development of the good is of course always a threat to the established: XMPP is now in severe hardship, to position itself as an encrypted messenger, when asymmetric crypto provides the forehead to the old and on the one hand mature, but on the other hand slightly not further developed OTR.

XMPP as Foundation had to call all clients with a manifest, to implement OTR (Saint-Andre 2014) and after the turn to an asymmetric-ephemeral paradigm to recognize, that almost a second manifesto had to be proclaimed - based on PGP (Schmaus 2016) - while nevertheless security experts plead to "letting die PGP" (compare e.g. Schmidt 2015), because it was deemed as too complicated and as encryption for the masses called as not able to establish.

Because not encryption in the client OTR-XMPP is the advantage, here XMPP does rather hard: First, all XMPP clients were to "OTR" driven (2014), then to Omemo-XEP (Gultsch 2015), and now to "OX" (Schmaus 2016). Will it be rather Axolotl or EDH instead

Entwicklergemeinschaft ist, Alternativen zu erforschen und wissenschaftlich zu fördern, die nicht aufgrund finanzieller Förderung und Multiplikatorenstimulierung in aller Munde gebracht werden, sondern weitergehend unabhängig bleiben, wie es bei mehreren o.g. Projekten der Fall ist.

- Die individuelle Definition von kryptologischen Werten (Schlüssel-größe oder manuell eingegebener Passworte) erhöht das Vertrauen in die eigene Ausgestaltung der Sicherheit bei der Nutzung der Applikationen.

Die vielfach zu unrecht bewertete informelle Regel, dass neue Wege, Methoden und Prozesse in der Kryptographie zu vermeiden seien, ist bei Nutzung etablierter Bibliotheken und Rechen-Prozeduren nicht an erster Stelle zu zitieren.

Jedenfalls ist es ist daher unverständlich, wie die "homebrewed" Crypto Axolotl einen Hype erfährt - sie gar als Sieger gegenüber OTR verstanden wird - und zugleich andere Verbesserungen als „Privatheit" abgetan werden. Sogenannte Experten scheinen hier eher ihre Definitionsmacht erhalten zu wollen. „Hausgemachte" Erfindungen bieten auch die Chance, sich wissenschaftliche Vergleiche und fachliche Beurteilungen zu erschließen.

Zugleich ist die Weiterentwicklung des Guten natürlich immer auch eine Bedrohung des Etablierten: XMPP ist derzeit in schwerer Not, sich als verschlüsselnder Messenger zu positionieren, wenn asymmetrische Crypto dem alten und einerseits ausgereiften, aber andererseits auch wenig weiterentwickelten OTR die Stirne bietet.

XMPP als Foundation musste mit einem Manifest alle Klienten, OTR zu implementieren (Saint-Andre 2014) und nach der Wende zum asymmetrisch-ephemeralen Paradigma erkennen, dass quasi ein zweites Manifest auf Basis von PGP auszurufen sei (Schmaus 2016) - während gleichwohl Sicherheitsexperten zum "Sterbenlassen von PGP" plädieren (vgl. z.B. Schmidt 2015), da es als zu kompliziert und als Verschlüsselung für die breite Masse als nicht etablierbar gelte.

Denn nicht die Verschlüsselung bei den Klienten OTR-XMPP ist der Vorteil, hier tut sich XMPP eher schwer: Zuerst wurden alle XMPP-Klienten zu "OTR" getrieben (2014), sodann zu Omemo-XEP (Gultsch 2015), und nun zu "OX" (Schmaus 2016). Wird es doch eher Axolotl

of OTR? Or an SMP Calling or FS Calling as in GoldBug?
Another way of encrypting messages over XMPP server is described in section 3.1 and lays in the use of the capsule encryption known from the echo protocol.

So the Echo protocol is, for example, in the XMPP-client of the Indian XMPP-developer Manjeet Dahiva, who founded and developed the XMPP library for the Qt framework (QXMPP), implemented, and to find as a hybrid application under firefloo.sf.net.

If one now uses a key from the application GoldBug for the encryption of a message before it is sent over XMPP, one could speak of the method or model named "Orientated Kapsule Encryption of Echo (OKEE)" - the encrypted message capsule of the Echo protocol is then only sent to a dedicated XMPP chat friend.

The following table illustrates the possible encryptions of XMPP, with which numerous decentralized developers explore various ways.

oder EDH statt OTR? Oder ein SMP-Calling oder FS-Calling wie in GoldBug?
Eine weitere Möglichkeit der Verschlüsselung von Nachrichten über XMPP-Server besteht auch in der Nutzung der aus dem Echo-Protokoll bekannten Kapsel-Verschlüsselung wie in Kapitel 3.1 beschrieben.

So ist das Echo-Protokoll beispielsweise in dem XMPP-Klienten des indischen XMPP-Entwicklers Manjeet Dahiva, der die XMPP-Bibliothek für das Qt-Framework (QXMPP) begründet und entwickelt hat, implementiert worden, und unter firefloo.sf.net als hybride Applikation zu finden.

Nutzt man nun einen Schlüssel (z.B. Chat Schlüssel oder den POPTASTIC-Schlüssel) aus der Applikation GoldBug bzw. einer Applikation, die auch das Echo-Protokoll umsetzt für die Verschlüsselung einer Nachricht, bevor sie über XMPP gesandt wird, könnte man von der Methode oder einem Modell names "Orientated Kapsule Encryption of Echo (OKEE)" sprechen - die verschlüsselte Nachrichtenkapsel des Echo-Protokolls wird nur an einen dedizierten XMPP-Chat-Freund gesandt.

Die folgende Übersicht verdeutlicht die möglichen Verschlüsselungen von XMPP, mit denen zahlreiche dezentrale Entwickler diverse Wege ausloten.

Table 67: Encryption options for Jabber / XMPP

Criteria	OpenPGP / OX	OpenPGP signed	OKEE Signed	OKEE unsigned	OMEMO	OTR
Encryption Options for Jabber / XMPP						
Multi-Encryption	NO	NO	YES	YES	NO	NO
Multiple Devices	YES	YES	YES	YES	YES	NO
End-to-end encrypted group chats	NO	NO	YES	YES	NO	NO
Offline Messages	YES	YES	YES over POPTASTIC	YES over POPTASTIC	YES	NO
Consolidating E-Mail & Chat	NO	NO	YES	YES	NO	NO
File Transfer	YES	YES	YES	YES	YES	NO
Different Ciphers to choose	NO	NO	YES	YES	NO	NO
Verifiability	NO	YES	YES	YES	YES	YES
SMP Authentication (Socialist Millionaire Protocol) with manual E2E-Password Definition	NO	NO	YES	YES	YES	YES
Deniability (ephemeral FS keys)	YES	NO	YES	YES	YES	YES
Always-on end-to-end encryption	NO	NO	YES	YES	YES	TBD
Instant Perfect Forward Secrecy (IPFS)	NO	NO	YES	YES	TBD	NO
Forward Secrecy per Session	NO	NO	YES	YES	YES	YES
Encrypted Storage to Hard Disk guaranteed	NO	NO	YES	YES	NO	NO
Native Solution (otherwise risky Plugin Solution)	NO	NO	YES	YES	NO	NO
Ephemeral Asymmetric Keys	NO	NO	YES	YES	NO	YES
Ephemeral Symmetric Keys	NO	NO	YES	YES	NO	NO
Crypto-Values (DNA) defineable by User	NO	NO	YES	YES	NO	NO
Key Size defined by	USER	USER	USER	USER	NO	NO
Open Source	YES	YES	YES	YES	YES	YES
Per Message Overhead	High	High	Medium	Medium	Medium	Low
TOTAL YES	**6**	**6**	**19**	**19**	**10**	**7**

Source: Own evaluation.

Also, the news portal Golem confirmed (03.09.2016): "Meanwhile OTR is however a bit getting old. One problem is that it is thus not possible to send encrypted mail, if the other party is offline", that is, if the partner is offline, the message is no longer encrypted or sent. In

Auch das Nachrichten-Portal Golem bestätigt (9.3.2016): "Inzwischen ist OTR jedoch etwas in die Jahre gekommen. Ein Problem ist, dass es ist damit nicht möglich ist, verschlüsselte Nachrichten zu verschicken, wenn der Gesprächspartner offline ist", d.h. wenn der

addition, discovered Markus Vervier of the company X41 D-Sec in an analysis of the code of libotr an integer overflow, which has been closed since version 4.1.1 (Vervier 2016).

The security vendor Sophos advertises encryption with the phrase: "Be able to dance as if no one is watching you" (compare website Sophos, 2015.). Nevertheless, it will be difficult - to continue the metaphor - not to discover a dinosaur like XMPP dancing, for whether it is more a tailspin, remains to be seen: Instead, the decentralized chat server rather remain the advantage of XMPP. And there remains the basic problem of XMPP encryption that it always dependent on plugins (see Dalibor 2016).

The possibility of establishing a decentralized infrastructure provides as well the completely from the basic layout for encryption designed GoldBug Messenger. This is even more much easier to implement than a XMPP server in the technical operational capabilities and administrability. And: the clients RetroShare or Tox operate via DHT even completely without means of an external, dedicated server (with the disadvantage that unknown IP addresses connect to the private port).

Since of these four mentioned applications Retroshare and Tox are the only applications, that have not yet implemented the user-authentication by the Socialist-Millionaire-protocol, remains that on the expected wishlist for further development especially of these decentralized clients.

Partner offline geht, ist die Nachricht nicht mehr verschlüsselt bzw. gesendet. Zudem entdeckte Markus Vervier von der Firma X41 D-Sec bei einer Analyse des Codes von Libotr einen Integer Overflow, der ab Version 4.1.1 geschlossen wurde (Vervier 2016).

Der Sicherheitsanbieter Sophos macht Werbung für Verschlüsselung mit dem Satz: "Sei in der Lage zu tanzen, als wenn niemand dich beobachtet" (vgl. Webseite Sophos 2015). Dennoch wird es schwierig sein - um im Bild zu bleiben -, einen Dinosaurier wie XMPP beim Tanzen nicht zu entdecken, denn ob es mehr ein Trudeln ist, bleibt abzuwarten: Stattdessen bleiben die dezentralen Chat-Server eher der Pluspunkt von XMPP. Und, es bleibt das Grundproblem von XMPP Verschlüsselung, dass es immer auf Plugins angewiesen bleibt (siehe Dalibor 2016).

Die Möglichkeit der Einrichtung einer dezentralen Infrastruktur bietet ebenso der komplett vom Grunddesign auf Verschlüsselung ausgelegte GoldBug Messenger. Dieses ist in der technischen Operationalität und Administrierbarkeit noch wesentlich einfacher als bei einem XMPP-Server umzusetzen. Und: die Klienten RetroShare oder Tox kommen per DHT sogar komplett ohne Einrichtung eines externen, dedizierten Servers aus (mit dem Nachteil, dass unbekannte IP-Adressen am eigenen Port verbinden).

Da bei diesen vier genannten Applikationen RetroShare und Tox die einzige Applikation sind, die die Nutzer-Authentifizierung noch nicht mittels des Socialist-Millionaire-Protokolls implementiert haben, bleibt dieses auf der zu erwartenden Wunschliste für die weitere Entwicklung insbesondere dieser dezentralen Klienten.

Table 68: Good Practice Insights # 18

Good Practice Insight # 18	
with GoldBug Multi-Encrypting Communication Suite	
Case	If I use no digital signatures, how can I determine that at the other end is really my friend? Wenn ich keine digitalen Signaturen nutze, wie kann ich feststellen, dass am anderen Ende auch wirklich mein Freund ist?
Solution	GoldBug has implemented next to digital signatures also the Socialist-Millionaire-Protocol. Thus, a user can also be authenticated. Please simply ask your friend to enter a common password in the pop-up chat window, as you also do. If the passwords, which are not transmitted over the Internet, match, you're both real! GoldBug hat neben digitalen Signaturen auch das Socialist-Millionaire-Protokoll implementiert. Damit kann ein Nutzer auch authentifiziert werden. Bitte Deinen Freund einfach ein gemeinsames Passwort im Pop-Up-Chat-Fenster einzugeben, so wie Du es auch machst. Wenn die Passworte, die nicht über das Internet übertragen werden, übereinstimmen, seid ihr beide echt!

Source: Own Case.

3.19 Default Settings: Default Crypto Values for the Creation of Encryption Keys

The key of security regarding cryptographic processes is on the one hand the generation of random numbers, that are generated on the machine, but also the variance of used methods and numerical values plays a major role in making it difficult for attackers, to not beeing able to operate only with one particular method or values-assumption. Furthermore, the key size used should be sufficiently large as well as all other cryptographic values should always be set manually.

Here it gets again clear, that non-open-source software cannot be considered for cryptographic operations, because one can not verify the number of methods, the choice of the methods and the default preset values for the encryption.
It is still even with open-source applications the alpha and omega, that the user can define and modify these values himself and manually.

No one is interested in a car, in which they cannot steer, cannot speed up and brake or can not define their preferences for color, engine and equipment when buying. Anything else would be the monoculture of universalism with referring consequences!
Even if cars are driving now according to an algorithm: There is no algorithm that overtakes a choice of the car according to own preferences regarding brand, design, technical equipment or color.

The manually not influenceable, universal software - all users use the same numbers values and methods for key generation - should be in cryptography exactly the same taboo as the use of non-open source software.
On the contrary: A high degree of manual definitions in crypto-Apps strengthens confidence in the respective application. This we want to examine below, how many setting values, the user can manually set at GoldBug and how many there would be indicative in the other applications?

Entscheidend für die Sicherheit bei kryptographischen Prozessen ist einerseits die Erzeugung von Zufallszahlen, die auf der Maschine erzeugt werden, aber auch die Varianz eingesetzter Methoden und Zahlenwerte spielt eine große Rolle, um es Angreifern schwer zu machen, nicht mit nur einer bestimmten Methode oder Werte-Annahme operieren zu können.
Weiterhin sollte die eingesetzte Schlüsselgrösse ausreichend groß sein wie auch alle weiteren kryptologischen Werte jederzeit manuell einstellbar sein sollen.

Auch hier wird nochmals deutlich, dass nicht quell-offene Software bei kryptographischen Funktionen ausscheidet, weil sich die Anzahl der Methoden, die Wahl der Methoden und die werksseitig vorgegebenen Werte für die Verschlüsselung nicht nachprüfen lassen.
Ebenso ist es weiterhin selbst bei quelloffenen Applikationen das A und O, dass der Nutzer diese Werte selbst und manuell definieren und verändern kann.

Niemand ist an einem Auto interessiert, bei dem er nicht selbst lenken, Gas geben, und bremsen kann oder beim Kauf nicht seine Präferenzen für Farbe, Motorisierung und Ausstattung definieren kann. Alles andere wäre die Monokultur eines Universalismus mit entsprechenden Folgen!
Auch wenn Autos inzwischen nach einem Algorithmus fahren: es gibt noch keinen Algorithmus, der einem die Wahl des Wagens nach eigenen Präferenzen wie Marke, Design, technischer Ausstattung oder Farbe abnimmt.

Die manuell nicht beeinflussbare, universale Software – alle Nutzer verwenden dieselben Zahlen-Werte und Methoden für eine Schlüsselgenerierung – sollte in der Kryptographie genauso tabu sein wie die Nutzung nicht quelloffener Software.
Im Gegenteil: Ein hoher Grad an manuellen Definitionen in Crypto-Apps stärkt das Vertrauen in die jeweilige Applikation. Dieses wollen wir im Folgenden untersuchen, wie viele Einstellungswerte kann der Nutzer bei GoldBug manuell selbst festlegen und wie viele wären es indikativ in den anderen Applikationen?

3.19.1 Inventory taking, structural analysis and descriptions of the functions

The GoldBug-Messenger has not only during an operation a number of manually changeable values and passwords e.g. for end-to-end encryption, but also for the asymmetric encryption at the key establishment during Initial Setup of (or repeating key-generation in) the application by the user, numerous values can be manually defined by himself.

Next to

- Cipher Type
- Hash Type
- Iteration Count
- Salt length

also the algorithm for encryption and for the signature itself can be chosen each.

Currently, RSA, ElGamal and NTRU are implemented as methods.

NTRU is interesting because this algorithm is particularly resistant to the calculations of the powerful quantum computers.

Der GoldBug-Messenger verfügt nicht nur während seines Betriebes über eine Vielzahl an manuell veränderbaren Werten und Passworten z.B. für die Ende-zu-Ende Verschlüsselung, sondern auch bei der asymmetrischen Verschlüsselung können bei der Schlüsselerstellung beim Initialen-Setup (bzw. der wiederholenden Schlüsselgenerierung in) der Applikation durch den Nutzer zahlreiche Werte manuell selbst definiert werden.

Neben

- Ciphertype
- Hashtype
- Iteration Count
- Salt legth

kann jeweils auch der Algorithmus für die Verschlüsselung sowie für die Signatur selbst gewählt werden.

Derzeit sind RSA, ElGamal und NTRU als Methoden implementiert.

NTRU ist insofern interessant, als dass dieser Algorithmus besonders resistent gegen die Berechnungen der leistungsfähigen Quantencomputer ist.

Figure 31: Currently available Algorithms in GoldBug Messenger & E-Mail Client

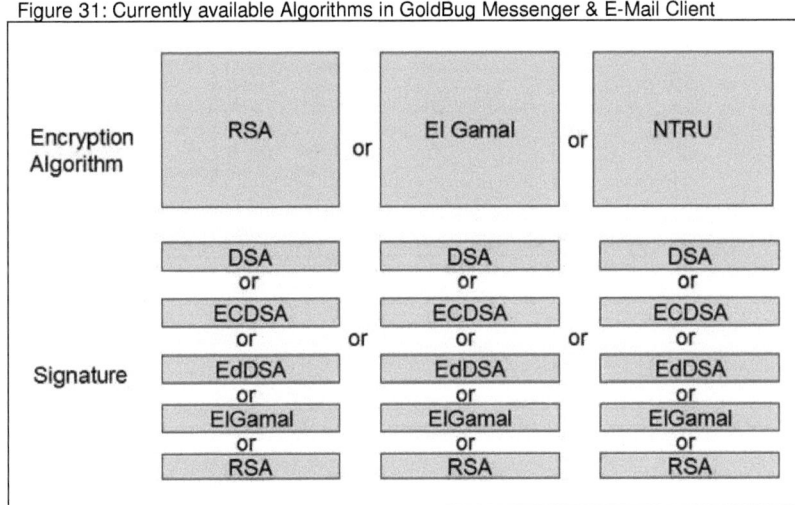

Source: GoldBug User-Manual, Edwards, Scott (Ed.) et al. 2014.

At the time of assessment, the algorithm McEliece was not yet implemented, but rather is already noted in the ToDo list of the source code of the project for future implementation. This too is like NTRU especially regarded as resistant against the calculations of the powerful quantum computers (Chen/NIST 2016), because:

with McEliece a special type of error-correcting code, called a Goppa code, may be used in step 3 of the key generation. The original parameters suggested by McEliece were n = 1024, t = 50, and k ≥ 524. Based on the security analysis of McEliece encryption (cited according to Menezes 1996:317), an optimum choice of recommended parameter sizes for this Goppa code - which maximizes the adversary's work factor - appears to be n = 1024, t = 38, and k ≥ 644 instead.

Although the encryption and decryption operations are relatively fast, the McEliece scheme suffers from the drawback, that the public key is very large. A (less significant) drawback is, that there is message expansion by a factor of n/k. For the recommended parameters n = 1024, t = 38, k ≥ 644, the public key is about 219 bits in size, while the

Zur Zeit des Assessments war der Algorithmus McEliece noch nicht implementiert, sondern ist jedoch in der ToDo-Liste des Quellcodes des Projektes vermerkt für eine zukünftige Implementierung. Auch er wird wie NTRU als besonders resistent gegen die Berechnungen der leistungsfähigen Quantencomputer eingeschätzt (Chen/NIST 2016), denn:

mit McEliece kann im dritten Schritt der Schlüssel-Erzeugung ein spezieller Typ eines Fehler-Beseitigungs-Codes genutzt werden, der sogenannte Goppa Code. Die usprünglich bei McEliece vorgeschlagenen Parameter waren: n = 1024, t = 50, and k ≥ 524. Basierend auf den bisherigen Sicherheitsanalysen der McEliece Verschlüsselung (zit. n. Menezes 1996:317) scheint eine optimierte Wahl an empfohlen Parameter-Grössen für diesen Goppa Code - welcher die Arbeit eines potentiellen Angreifers maximiert - stattdessen dieses Werte-Set zu sein: n = 1024, t = 38, and k ≥ 644.

Obschon die Ver- und Entschlüsselungs-Routinen relativ schnell sind, leidet das McEliece Schema an dem Manko, dass der öffentliche Schlüssel ziemlich lang ist. Ein weniger markantes Hindernis ist, dass es die Nachricht um den Faktor n/k vergrössert. Für die empfohlenen Werte n = 1024, t = 38, k ≥ 644, zeigt sich für den Schlüssel eine Grösse

message expansion factor is about 1.6 (Menezes 1996:317).

For these reasons, the scheme receives until now little attention in other clients - GoldBug at least has it scheduled for an implementation in the sooner future.

Then finally, the user can decide on own key size. Default key size of 3072 bits is set, which is considered by today's standards as sufficient.

It can furthermore also key sizes of
* 4096
* 7680
* 8192 and
* 15360
be set by the user.

GoldBug Messenger offers a high variety of options, to define its own security: various key sizes, different algorithms and numerous other cryptographic values can be defined by the users themselves, as in no other clients.

von 219 Bits, während der Faktor für die Nachrichten-Expansion bei 1,6 liegt (Menezes 1996:317).

Aus diesen Gründen hat der Verschlüsselungs-Algorithmus McEliece bis jetzt wenig Beachtung in anderen Messenger-Klienten gefunden - GoldBug hat ihn zumindest in die Implementierungs-Liste mit aufgenommen für einen Einbezug in der weiteren Zukunft.

Sodann schließlich kann der Nutzer selbst über seine Schlüsselgröße entscheiden. Default ist eine Schlüsselgröße von 3072 Bits eingestellt, die nach heutigen Standards auch als ausreichend gilt.

Es können darüber hinaus auch Schlüsselgrößen von
* 4096
* 7680
* 8192 sowie
* 15360
vom Nutzer eingestellt werden.

GoldBug Messenger bietet ingesamt eine Vielzahl an Möglichkeiten, seine eigene Sicherheit zu definieren: verschiedene Schlüsselgrößen, verschiedene Algorithmen und zahlreiche weitere kryptologische Werte können durch den Nutzer selbst definiert werden, wie in keinem anderen Klienten.

3.19.2   Selected method for studying and function reference

The method for the assessment of the choice and definition of individual encryption values is to be structured as follows: Two users to communicate with each other, whose keys are different in size.

Once a key size of 3072 and once a key size of 8192 was created - under otherwise identical further values for ciphertype, hashtype, iteration count, salt length.

In a second experiment, a RSA and ElGamal key was then once created - also tested whether both parties can chat with each other despite different encryption algorithms.

Practical tests of setting individual encryption options should therefore be evaluated and then compared with other clients, whether they

Die Methode für das Assessment der Wahl und Definition individueller Verschlüsselungs-werte soll wie folgt strukturiert werden: Zwei Nutzer sollen miteinander kommunizieren, deren Schlüssel unterschiedlich groß sind.

Einmal wurde ein Schlüssel der Größe 3072 sowie einmal ein Schlüssel der Größe 8192 erstellt - unter ansonsten gleichen weiteren Werten für Ciphertype, Hashtype, Iteration Count, Salt length.

In einem zweiten Versuch wurde sodann einmal ein RSA und ein ElGamal Schlüssel erstellt - auch hier wurde getestet, ob beide Teilnehmer trotz unterschiedlicher Verschlüsselungsalgorithmen miteinander chatten können.

Praktische Tests der Einstellung individueller Verschlüsselungsoptionen sollen somit bewertet werden und sodann mit anderen

provide as well such option varieties or if the user is affected by uncontrollable settings and it is therefore made a potential attacker easy to have to focus on only one scheme.

Klienten verglichen werden, ob sie ebensolche Optionsvielfalten bieten oder der Nutzer von nicht beeinflussbaren Einstellungen betroffen ist und es einem potentiellen Angreifer daher leicht gemacht wird, sich nur auf ein Schema konzentrieren zu müssen.

3.19.3   Conduction and findings of the examinations

Two laptops were used for carrying out the assessments, they have been prepared for a key exchange. One laptop has generated a listener, to which the other machine then connected.

Zur Durchführung des Assessments wurden zwei Laptops genutzt, die für einen Schlüsselaustausch zur Verfügung standen. Ein Laptop hat einen Listener erzeugt, an dem die andere Maschine verbunden war.

In the first experiment, two different-sized keys (3072 bits / 8192 bits) were used - and in the second experiment keys were used with different encryption algorithms (RSA / ElGamal).

Im ersten Versuch wurden zwei unterschiedlich große Schlüssel (3072 Bit / 8192 Bit) genutzt – und im zweiten Versuch wurden Schlüssel mit unterschiedlichen Verschlüsselungsalgorithmen genutzt (RSA / ElGamal).

In both experiments, participants were able to successfully communicate with each other. The setting of different encryption methods and values is therefore available and also works properly in accordance with this practical test.

In beiden Versuchen konnten die Teilnehmer erfolgreich miteinander kommunizieren. Die Einstellung verschiedener Verschlüsselungswerte und -methoden ist also vorhanden und funktioniert auch ordnungsgemäß gemäß diesem praktischen Test.

Figure 32: Individual adjustable crypto values within GoldBug

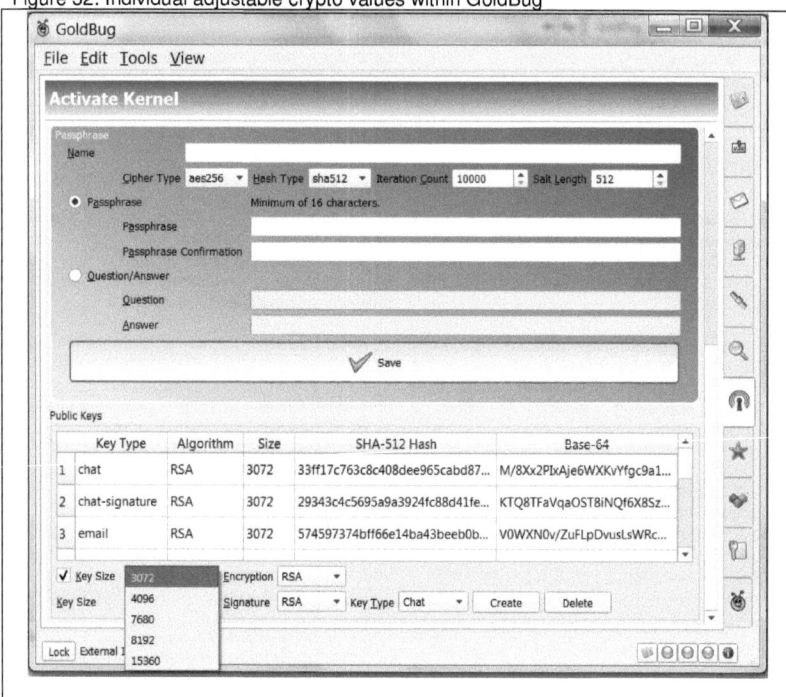

Source: Screenshot of Goldbug.

Also, two key different algorithms can communicate in GoldBug to each other, which is based on the architecture of the echo protocol and its encryption manner.
In our test, an RSA user could also establish a communication to an ElGamal user.
The analysis of the source code shows furthermore after our review a clean implementation of different crypto libraries.

Auch zwei Schlüssel unterschiedlicher Algorithmen können in GoldBug miteinander kommunizieren, was in der Architektur des Echo-Protokolls und seiner Verschlüsselungsweise zugrundegelegt ist.
In unserem Test hat ein RSA-Nutzer mit einem ElGamal-Nutzer ebenso eine Kommunikation aufbauen können.
Die Analyse des Quellcodes zeigt weiterhin nach unserer Durchsicht ebenso eine saubere Implementierung der verschiedenen Crypto-Bibliotheken.

3.19.4 Evaluation of the results with regard to weaknesses, risks, potentials for improvements and strengths

The GoldBug client is a user interface (GUI) that should intuitively affiliate with the kernel in a simplistic way for the user. It contains in addition to a minimal GUI also an extended

Der GoldBug Klient ist eine Benutzeroberfläche (GUI), die sich simplifiziert und für den Nutzer intuitiv dem Kernel angliedern soll. Sie enthält neben einer minimalen GUI auch eine

GUI, so that users can select an option in the main menu between various simplifications. Those, who prefer it even more complex and with more configuration options, can choose the initial user interface of "Spot-On", which is also the kernel of GoldBug. It is attached to the installation ZIP.

In this approach for simplification within the GoldBug GUI, it is provided, that at the first initial setup, the user can not select different encryption algorithms, but only ciphertype, hashtype, iteration count and salt length and the key size.
Only after the login password has been created, with a renewed or repeated key generation, the recourse to other algorithms as RSA is possible in the user interface.

That means for initial setup RSA is given and then the user can create other keys e.g. with ElGamal or NTRU. This setting is designed to simplify at the very first installation.

Because the choice of algorithms is available only in the maximum user view, which is clickable after the initial installation.
This selection offering is therefore adapted within the user interface to the usability of the first installation.
Furthermore, no findings in the process chain of the initial installation are to be described.

extendierte GUI, so dass Nutzer mit der Option im Hauptmenü zwischen verschiedenen Simplifizierungen wählen können. Wer es noch weitaus komplexer und mit weiteren Einstellungsoptionen mag, kann die dem „Spot-On"-Kernel – der zugleich auch der Kernel von GoldBug ist – beigefügte ursprüngliche Benutzeroberfläche von Spot-on wählen.

In diesem Vereinfachungskonzept der GoldBug-GUI ist es vorgesehen, dass beim ersten initialen Setup der Nutzer nicht verschiedene Verschlüsselungsalgorithmen wählen kann, sondern nur Ciphertype, Hashtype, Iteration Count und Salt length sowie die Schlüsselgröße.
Erst nachdem das Login-Passwort erstellt wurde, kann bei einer erneuten oder wiederholten Generierung von Schlüsseln die Wahl auch auf andere Algorithmen als RSA fallen.

D.h. für die Erst-Installation ist RSA vorgegeben und sodann kann der Nutzer auch andere Schlüssel z.B. mit ElGamal oder NTRU erstellen. Diese Einstellung dient der Vereinfachung bei der allerersten Installation.

Denn, die Wahl der Algorithmen ist nur in der maximalen Benutzeransicht verfügbar, die nach der ersten Installation anklickbar ist.
Dieses Auswahl-Angebot ist also der Nutzerfreundlichkeit bei der ersten Installation der Benutzeroberfläche angepasst.
Weiterhin sind keine Befunde in der Prozesskette der Erstinstallation zu beschreiben.

Table 69: Description of findings 3.19

#	Area	Description of the finding	Valuation Severity Category / Difficulty Level / Innovation & Improvement Class / Strength Dimension
	Weakness / Schwäche	./.	./.
3.19.4.A	Risk / Risiko	Breaking RSA with Quantum-Computers needs further research.	Informational
3.19.4.B	Potential for Improvement / Verbesserungspotential	Implementation for McEliece scheduled.	Informational
3.19.4.C	Strength / Stärke	GoldBug supports currently three algorithms: RSA, ElGamal, NTRU.	High

3.19.5 Appraisal of good practices in comparison with other similar applications

The most important finding of the studies in this section is, that key size, algorithm and cryptographic values should be defineable also manually.

Die wichtigste Erkenntnis aus den Untersuchungen in diesem Abschnitt ist, dass Schlüsselgröße, Algorithmus und kryptographische Werte auch manuell definierbar sein sollten.

None of the other listed comparable open source applications provide such freedom of the user to define his values in all three areas himselves.	Keine der weiteren genannten vergleichbaren open source Applikationen bietet eine solche Freiheit des Nutzers, seine Werte in allen drei Bereichen selbst zu definieren.
Individual clients have options, it would be desirable, if all comparable Messengers would offer the user at least an own choice for the key size.	Einzelne Klienten haben Optionen, es wäre jedoch wünschenswert, wenn alle vergleichbaren Messenger dem Nutzer zumindest die eigene Wahl der Schlüsselgröße anbieten würden.

Table 70: Indicative BIG SEVEN context references 3.19

Logo	Application	Comments
	Cryptocat	No own definition and variety of options as in GoldBug.
	GoldBug	Key size, Algorithm and kryptographic Values can be defined manually. New Keys can be re-generated within the applikation.
	OTR+XMPP	No own definition and variety of options as in GoldBug. The SMP Process offers a manual Insertion of the password in some clients.
	RetroShare	No own definition and variety of options as in GoldBug. Keys are oriented according to PGP basics and allow variety.
	Signal	No own definition and variety of options as in GoldBug.
	SureSpot	No own definition and variety of options as in GoldBug.
	Tox	No own definition and variety of options as in GoldBug.

Table 71: Good Practice Insights #19

Good Practice Insight # 19	
with GoldBug Multi-Encrypting Communication Suite	
Case	Can I decide myself which key size I use for encryption and whether this should be with ElGamal, RSA or NTRU? Kann ich selbst entscheiden, mit welche Schlüsselgröße ich die Verschlüsselung nutze und auch, ob dieses mit ElGamal, RSA oder NTRU erfolgen soll?
Solution	Yes, GoldBug allows the user to configure an own Crypto-DNA. GoldBug has no compulsion to use only RSA. Ja, GoldBug ermöglicht dem Nutzer, seine individuelle Crypto-DNA zusammen zu stellen. GoldBug hat keinen Zwang, ausschließlich RSA nutzen zu müssen.

Source: Own Case.

3.20 Passwords – Investigated on the Example of the Account-Passwords

Passwords have in encrypted applications such as already previously expressed a crucial role: passwords are used for authentication, but have in addition to the role of "*identifying persons*", the use to detect certain *permissions*: Who the password knows (the correct code) is considered to have access.

The Federal Office for Information Security (BSI, as mentioned) recommends for WLAN access passwords of at least twenty characters. If the password does not consist of uniformly distributed random characters, even significantly longer strings are needed to achieve the same security.

By the way: Each repeated use of the password also increases the risk, to reveal the password in an unencrypted transfer or spying measures (such as through keylogging or phishing).

A password can also be made more secure, with the use of characters, which do not exist on the keyboard, for example, "®, ¤ ©". These characters are often ignored at brute force attacks. For typing you then use under Windows Alt+0174, Alt+0164 and Alt+0169. The numbers must be typed, when the Num Lock on the numeric keypad is active. The virtual keyboard of the GoldBug client was further above already mentioned for the login procedure as a particularly reliable input method.

Wie will fous now by the example of the account password in particular the code review of this method for assigning permissions.

Passworte haben bei verschlüsselnden Applikationen wie auch schon zuvor zum Ausdruck gebracht eine entscheidende Rolle: Passworte dienen zur Authentifizierung, haben aber neben der Rolle "*Identifizieren von Personen*" auch die Verwendung, um bestimmte *Berechtigungen* nachzuweisen: Wer das Passwort (den richtigen Code) kennt, gilt als berechtigt.

Das Bundesamt für Sicherheit in der Informationstechnik (BSI, aaO) empfiehlt für WLAN-Zugänge Passwörter aus mindestens zwanzig Zeichen. Falls das Passwort nicht aus gleichverteilt zufälligen Zeichen besteht, sind sogar deutlich längere Zeichenfolgen nötig, um die gleiche Sicherheit zu erreichen.

Nebenbei bemerkt: Jeder wiederholte Einsatz des Passwortes erhöht auch die Gefahr, bei unverschlüsseltem Transfer oder Spionage-Maßnahmen (wie z. B. durch Keylogging oder Phishing) das Passwort zu verraten.

Ein Passwort kann auch mit Hilfe von Zeichen sicherer gemacht werden, die es auf der Tastatur nicht gibt, z.B. „®,¤,©". Diese Zeichen werden meist bei Brute-Force-Angriffen außer acht gelassen. Zum Eintippen verwendet man unter Windows dann Alt + 0174, Alt + 0164 und Alt + 0169. Die Ziffern müssen bei eingeschaltetem Num-Lock auf dem Ziffernblock getippt werden. Weiter oben wurde für das Login Procedere ja schon die virtuelle Tastatur des GoldBug Klienten als eine besonders sichere Eingabemethode erwähnt.

Hier soll es nun am Beispiel der Account-Passworte insbesondere um den Code Review dieser Methode für die Vergabe von Berechtigungen gehen.

3.20.1 Inventory taking, structural analysis and descriptions of the functions

Anyone, who wants to connect in GoldBug to a neighbor, so to listeners or to a chat server, can do this with HTTP, with HTTPS or even with the additional use of accounts. Accounts are usually offered by the chat server

Wer sich in GoldBug zu einem Nachbarn, also Listener oder Chat-Server verbinden will, kann dieses mit HTTP, mit HTTPS oder aber auch unter zusätzlicher Anwendung von Accounts umsetzen. Accounts werden meistens von den

operators, that want to allow only certain people to access their infrastructure.

Chat-Server-Betreibern angeboten, die nur bestimmten Personen zu ihrer Infrastruktur Zugang gewähren möchten.

It could therefore be regarded as a Wi-Fi password. As seen above, recommends the German Federal Office for Security a password length of at least 20 characters. In contrast GoldBug requires a minimum of 32 characters.

Es kommt daher z.b. einem WLAN-Passwort gleich. Wie oben gesehen empfiehlt das Bundesamt für Sicherheit eine Passwortlänge von mindestens 20 Zeichen. Bei GoldBug sind hingegen mindestens 32 Zeichen zwingend erforderlich.

The increased safety requirement of GoldBug clients by the length of account passwords is certainly a fact in the note of the Federal Office bearing in mind, that the password-choice of users often does not consist of random characters, which include special characters on the keyboard or untraceable characters (see above), but rather include many words, that are easy to find in dictionaries.

Die erhöhte Sicherheitsanforderung im GoldBug Clienten durch die Länge der Account-Passworte ist sicherlich auch einer Tatsache in der Anmerkung des Bundesamtes Rechnung tragend, dass die Passwortwahl der Nutzer oft nicht aus zufälligen Zeichen besteht, die auch Sonderzeichen oder auf der Tastatur nicht auffindbare Zeichen (s.o.) umfassen, sondern viele Worte umfassen, die in Wörterbüchern leicht zu finden sind.

This means a 20-character password is to be cracked quickly depending on the configuration by means of a so-called brute-Fore-trial: That is, it tries all possible combinations and also uses all the words that knows a dictionary.

So kann ein nur 20 Zeichen umfassendes Passwort je nach Ausgestaltung schneller mittels eines sogenannten Brute-Fore-Versuches geknackt werden: D.h. man probiert alle denkbaren Kombinationen aus und nutzt auch alle Worte, die ein Wörterbuch kennt.

The account name in GoldBug therefore must be at least 32 characters.
(At explained above password procedure for logging into the application, a comprehensive 16 character password is demanded, that is then converted to a longer hash string).

Der Account Name in GoldBug muss daher mindestens 32 Zeichen umfassen.
(Beim weiter oben erläuterten Passwort-Procedere für das Login in die Applikation, wird ja ein 16 Zeichen umfassendes gefordert, das jedoch sodann in einen längeren Hash-Zeichenkette umgewandelt wird).

Figure 33: GoldBug – Account Names and Passwords with at least 32 characters

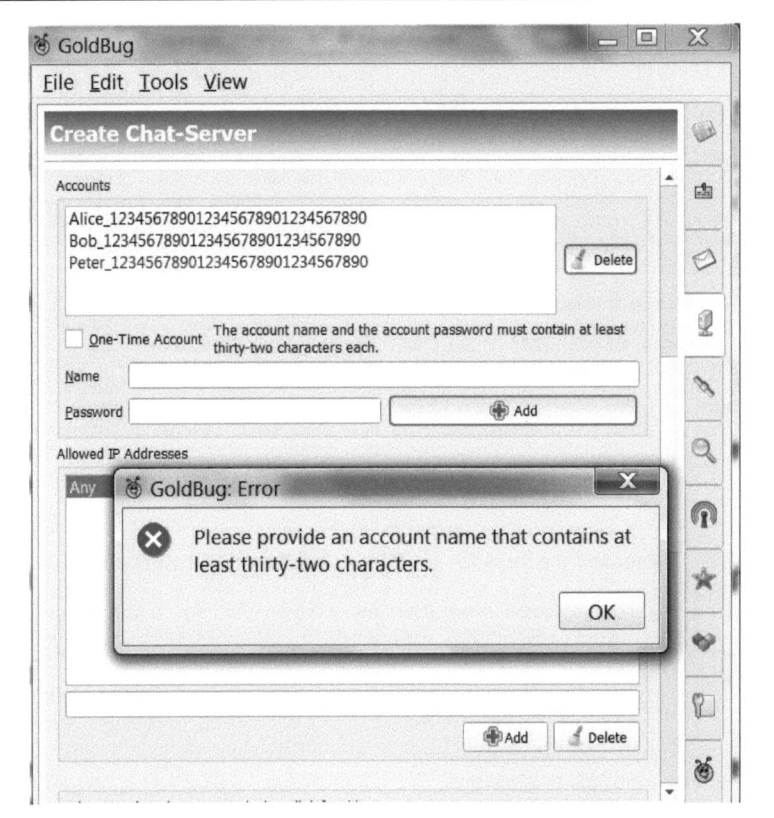

Source: Own Screenshot of GoldBug.

Accounts are - apart from the password length - not just an ideal design of the access permissions, but provide in other words a type of firewall, which was thereby implemented in GoldBug: Who uses accounts, may exclude other users from the access or allow access only to defined and authorized users.	Accounts sind – abgesehen von der Passwort-Länge – nicht nur eine ideale Gestaltung der Zugangsberechtigungen, sondern stellen anders ausgedrückt auch eine Art Firewall dar, die somit in GoldBug implementiert wurde: Wer Accounts nutzt, kann andere Nutzer vom Zugang ausschliessen bzw. nur definierten und berechtigen Nutzern den Zugang gewähren.
In addition, can be formed with accounts also a kind of virtual Web of Trust. What was previously just know from friend-to-friend connections (F2F) by means of a key for encryption (for example, in the client Retroshare) has been decoupled in GoldBug	Darüber hinaus kann mit Accounts auch eine Art virtuelles Web-of-Trust gebildet werden. Was bislang nur aus Freund-zu-Freund-Verbindungen (F2F) mittels eines Keys für Verschlüsselung bekannt war (beispielsweise im Klienten RetroShare) ist in GoldBug vom

from the encryption key for a server-model or p2p network. No one has to associate an instance and therefore also the own IP address with the key for encryption.

Verschlüsselungskey für ein Servermodell bzw. p2p-Netzwerk entkoppelt worden. Niemand muss seine Instanz und damit auch seine IP-Adresse mit dem Schlüssel für die Verschlüsselung verknüpfen.

Accounts are an important type of granting permissions, if you want to use them. Similar to the Freifunk (as Free Wifi, cited above), you though also can advocate, that everyone shoudl be able to connect at any time, in order to communicate (which speaks for account-less listeners of a p2p network).

Accounts sind eine wichtige Art der Gewährung von Berechtigungen, wenn man sie denn nutzen will. Ähnlich wie beim Freifunk (aaO) kann man aber auch dafür plädieren, dass jeder sich jederzeit frei verbinden können sollte, um zu kommunizieren (was für accountlose Listener eines p2p Netzes spricht).

It is also possible to send a one-time account in a user GoldBug. This is operating for only one connection attempt. After a user has connected to this account, the account of the listener can no longer be used. Over this way you can grant guests a one time access for the use of the server.

Auch besteht in GoldBug die Möglichkeit, einem Nutzer einen One-Time-Account zukommen zu lassen. Dieser ist nur für einen einzigen Verbindungsversuch brauchbar. Nachdem ein Nutzer über diesen Account verbunden hat, kann der Account des Listeners nicht mehr genutzt werden. So kann Gästen ein einmaliger Zugang zur Nutzung des Servers gewährt werden.

3.20.2 Selected method for studying and function reference

As method for the investigation should take place again a classic code review. The programming for the account password is created in the functions

* void spoton_neighbor::process0050(int length, const QByteArray &dataIn) sowie
* void spoton_neighbor::process0051(int length, const QByteArray &dataIn)

and the code has been reviewed by us as in the other investigations of the individual functions as well.

Als Methode für die Untersuchung soll wiederum ein klassischer Code-Review erfolgen. Die Programmierungen zum Account-Passwort sind in den Funktionen

* void spoton_neighbor::process0050(int length, const QByteArray &dataIn) sowie
* void spoton_neighbor::process0051(int length, const QByteArray &dataIn)

erstellt und der Code ist von uns wie in den anderen Untersuchungen zu den einzelnen Funktionen ebenso durchgesehen worden.

3.20.3 Conduction and findings of the examinations

The conduction of the investigation relates here therefore especially to the review of the programming code of the application and specifically under close observation of the lines of code for the function of account passwords and their privileges to be granted.

Die Durchführung der Untersuchung bezieht sich hier also insbesondere auf die Durchsicht des Programmier-Codes der Applikation bzw. spezifisch unter genauer Beobachtung der Code-Zeilen für die Funktion der Account-Passworte und deren Gewährung von Berechtigungen.

Figure 34: Code for the Account Authentification in file Spot-on-Neighbor.cc

```
void spoton_neighbor::process0050(int length, const QByteArray &dataIn)
{
  if(m_id == -1)
    return;

  int indexOf = dataIn.lastIndexOf("\r\n");

  if(indexOf < 0)
    return;

  length -= static_cast<int> (qstrlen("type=0050&content="));

  /*
  ** We may have received a name and a password from the client.
  */

  QByteArray data(dataIn.mid(0, indexOf + 2));

  indexOf = data.indexOf("type=0050&content=");

  if(indexOf < 0)
    return;

  data.remove
    (0, indexOf + static_cast<int> (qstrlen("type=0050&content=")));

  if(length == data.length())
    {
      data = data.trimmed();

      QList<QByteArray> list(data.split('\n'));

      if(list.size() != 2)
        {
          spoton_misc::logError
            (QString("spoton_neighbor::process0050(): "
                     "received irregular data. Expecting 2 entries, "
                     "received %1.").arg(list.size()));
          return;
        }

      for(int i = 0; i < list.size(); i++)
        list.replace(i, QByteArray::fromBase64(list.at(i)));

      QByteArray name;
      QByteArray password;

      if(spoton_misc::authenticateAccount(name,
                                          password,
                                          m_listenerOid,
                                          list.at(0),
                                          list.at(1),
                                          spoton_kernel::
                                          s_crypts.value("chat", 0)))
        {
          m_accountAuthenticated.fetchAndStoreOrdered(1);
          emit stopTimer(&m_accountTimer);
          emit stopTimer(&m_authenticationTimer);
          emit accountAuthenticated(name, password);
```

```
          }
    else
          {
        m_accountAuthenticated.fetchAndStoreOrdered(0);
        emit accountAuthenticated
            (spoton_crypt::weakRandomBytes(64),
             spoton_crypt::weakRandomBytes(64));
          }

    if(m_accountAuthenticated.fetchAndAddOrdered(0))
      emit resetKeepAlive();

    spoton_crypt *s_crypt = spoton_kernel::s_crypts.value("chat", 0);

    if(s_crypt)
          {
        QString connectionName("");

            {
            QSqlDatabase db = spoton_misc::database(connectionName);

            db.setDatabaseName
                (spoton_misc::homePath() + QDir::separator() +
                "neighbors.db");

            if(db.open())
                  {
                QSqlQuery query(db);
                bool ok = true;

                query.prepare("UPDATE neighbors SET "
                              "account_authenticated = ?, "
                              "account_name = ? "
                              "WHERE OID = ? AND "
                              "user_defined = 0");
                query.bindValue
                    (0,
                     m_accountAuthenticated.fetchAndAddOrdered(0) ?
                     s_crypt->encryptedThenHashed(QByteArray::number(1),
                                              &ok).toBase64() :
                     s_crypt->encryptedThenHashed(QByteArray::number(0),
                                              &ok).toBase64());

                if(ok)
                    query.bindValue
                        (1, s_crypt->encryptedThenHashed(name,
&ok).toBase64());

                query.bindValue(2, m_id);

                if(ok)
                    query.exec();
                  }

            db.close();
                  }

            QSqlDatabase::removeDatabase(connectionName);
              }
          }
    else
        spoton_misc::logError
```

```
            (QString("spoton_neighbor::process0050(): 0050 "
                     "Content-Length mismatch (advertised: %1, received: %2) "
                     "for %3:%4.").
             arg(length).arg(data.length()).
             arg(m_address).
             arg(m_port));
}

void spoton_neighbor::process0051(int length, const QByteArray &dataIn)
{
  if(m_id == -1)
    return;

  int indexOf = dataIn.lastIndexOf("\r\n");

  if(indexOf < 0)
    return;

  length -= static_cast<int> (qstrlen("type=0051&content="));

  /*
  ** We may have received a name and a password from the server.
  */

  QByteArray data(dataIn.mid(0, indexOf + 2));

  indexOf = data.indexOf("type=0051&content=");

  if(indexOf < 0)
    return;

  data.remove
    (0, indexOf + static_cast<int> (qstrlen("type=0051&content=")));

  if(length == data.length())
    {
      data = data.trimmed();

      QList<QByteArray> list(data.split('\n'));

      if(list.size() != 2)
        {
          spoton_misc::logError
            (QString("spoton_neighbor::process0051(): "
                     "received irregular data. Expecting 2 entries, "
                     "received %1.").arg(list.size()));
          return;
        }

      for(int i = 0; i < list.size(); i++)
        list.replace(i, QByteArray::fromBase64(list.at(i)));

      QByteArray accountClientSentSalt;
      QReadLocker locker(&m_accountClientSentSaltMutex);

      accountClientSentSalt = m_accountClientSentSalt;
      locker.unlock();

      spoton_crypt *s_crypt = spoton_kernel::s_crypts.value("chat", 0);

      if(accountClientSentSalt.length() >=
         spoton_common::ACCOUNTS_RANDOM_BUFFER_SIZE &&
```

```
            list.at(1).trimmed().length() >=
          spoton_common::ACCOUNTS_RANDOM_BUFFER_SIZE &&
          !spoton_crypt::memcmp(list.at(1).trimmed(),
accountClientSentSalt))
          {
            if(s_crypt)
              {
                QByteArray hash(list.at(0));
                QByteArray name;
                QByteArray newHash;
                QByteArray password;
                QByteArray salt(list.at(1).trimmed());
                bool ok = true;

                QReadLocker locker1(&m_accountNameMutex);

                name = m_accountName;
                locker1.unlock();

                QReadLocker locker2(&m_accountPasswordMutex);

                password = m_accountPassword;
                locker2.unlock();
                name = s_crypt->decryptedAfterAuthenticated(name, &ok);

                if(ok)
                  password = s_crypt->decryptedAfterAuthenticated
                    (password, &ok);

                if(ok)
                  newHash = spoton_crypt::keyedHash
                    (QDateTime::currentDateTime().toUTC().
                    toString("MMddyyyyhhmm").
                    toLatin1() + salt, name + password, "sha512", &ok);

                if(ok)
                  {
                    if(!hash.isEmpty() && !newHash.isEmpty() &&
                      spoton_crypt::memcmp(hash, newHash))
                      {
                        m_accountAuthenticated.fetchAndStoreOrdered(1);
                        emit stopTimer(&m_accountTimer);
                        emit stopTimer(&m_authenticationTimer);
                      }
                    else
                      {
                        newHash = spoton_crypt::keyedHash

          (QDateTime::currentDateTime().toUTC().addSecs(60).
                        toString("MMddyyyyhhmm").
                        toLatin1() + salt, name + password, "sha512",
&ok);

                        if(ok)
                          {
                            if(!hash.isEmpty() && !newHash.isEmpty() &&
                              spoton_crypt::memcmp(hash, newHash))
                              {
m_accountAuthenticated.fetchAndStoreOrdered(1);
                                emit stopTimer(&m_accountTimer);
                                emit stopTimer(&m_authenticationTimer);
```

```
                                  }
                                }
                              else
                                m_accountAuthenticated.fetchAndStoreOrdered(0);
                            }
                        }
                      else
                        m_accountAuthenticated.fetchAndStoreOrdered(0);
                    }
                  else
                    m_accountAuthenticated.fetchAndStoreOrdered(0);
                }
              else
                {
                  m_accountAuthenticated.fetchAndStoreOrdered(0);

                  if(accountClientSentSalt.length() <
                     spoton_common::ACCOUNTS_RANDOM_BUFFER_SIZE)
                    spoton_misc::logError
                      ("spoton_neighbor::process0051(): "
                       "the server replied to an authentication message,
however, "
                       "my provided salt is small.");
                  else if(spoton_crypt::memcmp(list.at(1),
accountClientSentSalt))
                    spoton_misc::logError
                      ("spoton_neighbor::process0051(): "
                       "the provided salt is identical to the generated salt. "
                       "The server may be devious.");
                }

            if(m_accountAuthenticated.fetchAndAddOrdered(0))
              emit resetKeepAlive();

            if(s_crypt)
              {
                QString connectionName("");

                {
                  QSqlDatabase db = spoton_misc::database(connectionName);

                  db.setDatabaseName
                    (spoton_misc::homePath() + QDir::separator() +
                     "neighbors.db");

                  if(db.open())
                    {
                      QSqlQuery query(db);
                      bool ok = true;

                      query.prepare("UPDATE neighbors SET "
                                    "account_authenticated = ? "
                                    "WHERE OID = ? AND "
                                    "user_defined = 1");
                      query.bindValue
                        (0,
                         m_accountAuthenticated.fetchAndAddOrdered(0) ?
                         s_crypt->encryptedThenHashed(QByteArray::number(1),
                                                      &ok).toBase64() :
                         s_crypt->encryptedThenHashed(QByteArray::number(0),
                                                      &ok).toBase64());
                      query.bindValue(1, m_id);
```

```
    if(ok)
        query.exec();
    }

    db.close();
    }

    QSqlDatabase::removeDatabase(connectionname);
    }
}
else
    spoton_misc::logError
        (QString("spoton_neighbor::process0051(): 0051 "
        "Content-Length mismatch (advertised: %1, received: %2) "
        "for %3:%4.").
        arg(length).arg(data.length()).
        arg(m_address).
        arg(m_port));
}
```

In programming, no irregularities were found which provide information on risks or weaknesses. The programming steps have been well commented accordingly, so that it is clearly structured, and not just in the flow, but also in the content guidance of a code reader, it can be considerd as "clean" code.

In der Programmierung wurden keine Auffälligkeiten gefunden, die Hinweise auf Risiken oder Schwächen geben. Auch wurden die Programmierschritte entsprechend gut kommentiert, so dass es sich um klar gegliederten und nicht nur im Ablauf, sondern auch in der inhaltlichen Führung eines Code-Lesers um "sauberen" Code handelt.

3.20.4 Evaluation of the results with regard to weaknesses, risks, potentials for improvements and strengths

One strength is certainly the length of the chosen password, since it exceeds the safety recommendations of the Federal Office.

Eine Stärke ist sicherlich die Länge des gewählten Passwortes, da es die Sicherheitsempfehlungen des Bundesamtes übertrifft.

Table 72: Description of findings 3.20

#	Area	Description of the finding	Valuation Severity Category / Difficulty Level / Innovation & Improvement Class / Strength Dimension
	Weakness / Schwäche	./.	./.
	Risk / Risiko	./.	./.
	Potential for Improvement / Verbesserungspotential	./.	./.
	Strength / Stärke	./.	./.

As improvement of the account password procedure can possibly be noted that it makes sense because of the password length, to constitute the account-access in form of a

Als Verbesserung der Account-Passwort Prozedur kann ggf. angemerkt werden, dass es aufgrund der Passwort-Länge Sinn macht, auch die Account-Zugänge in Form eines

Magnet-URI-link, to help users to access the account with a single link, which just has to be entered.

Also the implementation of various methods - such as those addressed in this audit, like for the login - might make it more difficult for attackers of accounts to log into an account without permission.

3.20.5 Appraisal of good practices in comparison with other similar applications

Only the applications GoldBug, OTR+XMPP, Tox and Retroshare, allow to set up an own server, which may also with an authorization concept exclude or authorize users. While this is regulated at RetroShare over the encryption key, GoldBug is with its minimum requirement of 32 characters for both, the account name and password the again front runner of all above mentioned apps and refers OTR-XMPP clients in the specifications for accounts and account to places behind.

At Tox there are no user-accounts and no servers in this client-server sense, since it implements a DHT similar to RetroShare. But the DHT also has drawbacks: it notifies all participants about the own ID and the own local IP and breaks through the own firewall to allows to connect to the Unknowns to the own Tox-client. In RetroShare the implementation is here more advantageous, as the key is also longer than in Tox.

Magnet-URI-Links zu gestalten, damit Nutzer den Zugang zum Account mit nur einem Link einfach eingeben können.

Auch die Implementierung verschiedener Methoden, wie sie auch in diesem Audit angesprochen wurden, könnte - ähnlich wie beim Login - es Angreifern für Accounts schwieriger machen, sich in einen Account ohne Berechtigung einzuloggen.

Nur die Applikationen GoldBug, OTR+XMPP, Tox und RetroShare, ermöglichen es, eigene Server aufzusetzen, die auch mit einem Berechtigungskonzept Nutzer ausschliessen bzw. zulassen können. Während dieses bei RetroShare über den Verschlüsselungskey geregelt ist, ist GoldBug mit seiner Mindestanforderung von 32 Zeichen für sowohl den Account Namen als auch für das Passwort wiederum Spitzenreiter und hängt OTR-XMPP Klienten in den Spezifikationen für Accounts und Account-Namen ab.

Bei Tox gibt es keine Benutzer-Accounts und auch keine Server in diesem Sinne, da es einen DHT implementiert ähnlich wie RetroShare. Der DHT hat jedoch auch Nachteile: er gibt die eigene ID und die eigene IP allen Teilnehmern bekannt und durchbricht die eigene Firewall, um Unbekannte an den eigenen Tox-Klienten verbinden zu lassen. Hier ist die Implementierung bei RetroShare vorteilhafter, da hier der Schlüssel auch länger ist als bei Tox.

Table 73: Indicative BIG SEVEN context references 3.20

Logo	Application	Comments
	Cryptocat	No accounts, which have to be passed along in a manual way.
	GoldBug	Accounts with comprehensive Password-length at decentral servers or nodes are possible.
	OTR+XMPP	Accounts at decentral Servers are possible. Minimum length of a password is depending on each client and different and questionable. No standard for the various clients.
	RetroShare	Accounts in a DHT via a sufficient long key for a Web-of-Trust / Friend-to-Friend-Network.
	Signal	One Account only possible at a central Server possible. Account creation and login grabs private information, e.g. contact list.
	SureSpot	One Account only possible at a central Server possible.
	Tox	Usage of a DHT with a relative short ID-abbreviation.

Table 74: Good Practice Insights #20

Good Practice Insight # 20	
with GoldBug Multi-Encrypting Communication Suite	
Case	I've heard that passwords are pretty quick to crack. Are the passwords in a Messenger sufficiently long enough? Ich habe gehört, dass Passworte ziemlich schnell zu knacken sind. Sind die Passworte in einem Messenger ausreichend lang genug?
Solution	GoldBug provides at various functions such as login, or account password etc. a minimum length for a password. In addition, the passwords are secured with a cryptographic hash function and cryptologic salt, so further random characters. GoldBug hat bei verschiedenen Funktionen wie dem Login, oder dem Account-Passwort etc. eine Mindest-Länge für ein Passwort vorgesehen. Zudem werden die Passworte mit einer kryptographischen Hashfunktion und auch kryptologischem Salz, also zufälligen weiteren Zeichen, abgesichert.

Source: Own Case.

3.21   File Analysis for the GoldBug Installation ZIP

In addition to the code analysis finally also a file-analysis shall be performed to verify the files of an install-Zip by a manual examination by knowledge, as well as by various virus scans on correctness.

Neben der Code-Analyse ist schließlich auch eine Datei-Analyse vorzunehmen, um die Dateien eines Installations-Zips mittels manueller Kenntnisprüfung sowie auch durch verschiedene Virenscans auf Richtigkeit zu überprüfen.

3.21.1   Inventory taking, structural analysis and descriptions of the functions

GoldBug has provided for Windows no installation exe, but is provided in the form of a ZIP. This has the confidence-building advantage that the user can see what is in the ZIP before unpacking it and even before a binary executable file is run, as it is often a standard for other installations and in case for Windows - for example by means of a NSIS installer.

GoldBug hat für Windows keine Installations-exe vorgesehen, sondern wird in Form eines ZIPs bereitgestellt. Das hat den vertrauenschaffenden Vorteil, dass der Nutzer sehen kann, was in dem ZIP ist, bevor er es entpackt und auch bevor eine ausführbare Binärdatei ausgeführt wird, wie es bei anderen Installationen z.B. mittels eines NSIS-Installers der Fall und für Windows oftmals Standard ist.

The existing ZIP files relate to the program GoldBug and Spot-On as a kernel and required files for encryption-libraries and the Qt-framework. Subpaths for Qt-plugins, sound and translations, and database-related files supplement these.

Die im ZIP vorhandenen Dateien beziehen sich auf das Programm GoldBug und Spot-on als Kernel sowie benötigte Dateien für die Verschlüsselungsbibliotheken und das Qt-Framework. Unterpfade für Qt-Plugins, Sound und Übersetzungen sowie datenbankrelevante Dateien ergänzen diese.

The installation thus creates no entries in the Windows registry nor links on the desktop or in the Start menu will be created.

Die Installation erstellt somit auch keine Einträge in der Windows-Registry noch werden Verlinkungen auf dem Desktop oder im Startmenü erstellt.

The user therefore has to start manually by double-clicking the application on GoldBug.exe in the unpacked path.

Der Nutzer muss also die Applikation im entpackten Pfad mittels Doppelklick auf GoldBug.exe manuell starten.

3.21.2   Selected method for studying and function reference

As investigation method we will look at each of the supplied file in the installation ZIP manually, and index each file, and add references to the source as well as a description comment. Then should be automated with two virus scanners the currently actual GoldBug Version 2.9, as well as both previous versions 2.8 and 2.7, be investigated. We used therefore Kasperski and Avira.

Als Untersuchungsmethode werden wir uns jede der im Installations-ZIP gelieferten Datei manuell ansehen, sie indexieren und Ursprungsverweise sowie einen Beschreibungskommentar hinzufügen. Sodann soll auch automatisiert mit zwei Virenscannern die derzeit aktuelle GoldBug Version 2.9 sowie auch beide Vorgängerversionen 2.8 und 2.7 untersucht werden. Wir haben dazu Kasperski und Avira genutzt.

Thirdly, and finally also in the web a search was carried out, whether independent providers as well as download portals have verified the integrity of the files with common analysis tools. In the last two steps thus also the hash sum integrity of each distributed file has been verified.

Drittens ist schließlich auch im Web eine Recherche durchgeführt worden, ob unabhängige Anbieter wie auch Downloadportale die Integrität der Dateien mit gängigen Analysetools überprüft haben. In den letzten beiden Schritten ist also auch die Hash-Summen-Integrität einer jeden distribuierten Datei überprüft worden.

3.21.3 Conduction and findings of the examinations

Goldbug 2.9 contains the following files and library files that we examined individually and manually:

GoldBug 2.9 enthält folgende Einzeldateien und Bibliotheksdateien, die wir einzeln und manuell untersucht haben:

Table 75: List of the files from the GoldBug Installation ZIP

File / Path	Originates from the library	Description
GeoIP.dat	Maxmind.com	GeoIP Legacy Country Database Installation
GoldBug.exe	GIT Source Code of GB	Compiled result of the source code
icudt53.dll	http://site.icu-project.org/	International Components for Unicode
icudt54.dll	http://site.icu-project.org/	International Components for Unicode
icuin53.dll	http://site.icu-project.org/	International Components for Unicode
icuin54.dll	http://site.icu-project.org/	International Components for Unicode
icuuc53.dll	http://site.icu-project.org/	International Components for Unicode
icuuc54.dll	http://site.icu-project.org/	International Components for Unicode
intl.dll	Microsoft	dynamic link library that is a part of Microsoft Driver component
libcurl.dll	Sun Microsystems, Inc., Macromedia, Inc. And Google	The cURL is a command line tool for transferring files with Uniform Resource Locator (URL) syntax, supporting FTP, FTPS, HTTP, HTTPS, TFTP, SCP, SFTP, Telnet, DICT, FILE and LDAP.
Libeay32.dll	http://www.openssl.org/related/bin aries.html	binary distribution of OpenSSL for 32bit Editions of Windows
libgcc_s_dw2-1.dll	part of GCC	Dynamic linking with libgcc_s_dw2-1.dll is necessary to throw exceptions between different modules, such as between two DLLs or a DLL and an EXE
libgcrypt-20.dll	Libgcrypt – The GNU Crypto Library	This files belongs to product libgcrypt
libGeoIP-1.dll	libgeoIP	This file is Dynamic-link Library
libgpg-error-0.dll	libgcrypt	libgpg-error-0.dll is loaded as dynamic link library that runs in the context of a process. It is installed with a couple of know programs. Related to libgcrypt.
Libiconv.dll	gnu.org	LibIconv converts from one character encoding to another through Unicode conversion. It is useful if your application needs to support multiple character encodings, but that support lacks from

		your system.
Libidn-11.dll	GNU IDN Library - Libidn	GNU Libidn is a fully documented implementation of the Stringprep, Punycode and IDNA specifications. Libidn's purpose is to encode and decode internationalized domain names.
libntru.dll	NTRU library	Provides the NTRU encryption.
libpq.dll	PostgreSQL	dynamic library for PostgreSQL
librtmp.dll	RTMP streams	librtmp is a library made from RTMPdump, a toolkit for RTMP streams
libspoton.dll	Libspoton for the URL Import e.g. from Dooble Web Browser	Build due to source code.
libssh2.dll	OpenSSL Toolkit	SSH
libssl32.dll	OpenSSL Toolkit	SSL
libstdc++-6.dll	From MingGW distro	MingW to compile C++ code on Windows
libwinpthread-1.dll	MingGW Dependency	Threading
libxml2.dll	XML C parser and toolkit	libxml2 can be found on the xmlsoft.org server
libxslt.dll	LibXslt: library and tools	for applying XSLT to XML-documents
Microsoft.VC90.CRT.manifest	Microsoft Visual Studio	manifest or policy file
msvcr90.dll	dynamic link library / Microsoft Visual Studio	for windows system
msvcr120.dll	dynamic link library / Microsoft Visual Studio 2013	for windows system
pandamonium.exe	Pandamonium Web Crawler GUI	Due to given source
pandamonium-kernel.exe	Pandamonium Web Crawler Kernel	Due to given source
pthreadGC2.dll	GCC Threading	Windows do not include the POSIX GCC Threading DLLs
qt.conf	Qt Framework	Contains path for Qt Plugins
Qt5Bluetooth.dll	QT Framework	Qt Bluetooth
Qt5Core.dll	QT Framework	Qt Core classes — always needed!
Qt5Gui.dll	QT Framework	Qt Graphical User Interface Classes
Qt5Multimedia.dll	QT Framework	Qt Multimedia
Qt5MultimediaQuick_p.dll	QT Framework	Qt Multimedia Quick
Qt5MultimediaWidgets.dll	QT Framework	Qt Multimedia Widgets
Qt5Network.dll	QT Framework	Qt Network
Qt5OpenGL.dll	QT Framework	Qt Open GL
Qt5Positioning.dll	QT Framework	Qt Positioning
Qt5PrintSupport.dll	QT Framework	Qt Print
Qt5Qml.dll	QT Framework	Qt QML
Qt5Quick.dll	QT Framework	Qt Quick

Qt5Sensors.dll	QT Framework	Qt Sensors
Qt5Sql.dll	QT Framework	Qt database driver library
Qt5WebChannel.dll	QT Framework	Qt Web
Qt5WebKit.dll	QT Framework	Qt Webkit
Qt5WebKitWidgets.dll	QT Framework	Qt Webkit Widgets
Qt5Widgets.dll	QT Framework	Qt Widget Classes
SctpDrv.SctpSocket.dll	SCTP Driver	SctpDrv (dll) is a package which provides an SCTP (Stream Control Transmission Protocol) driver and SCTP library for Microsoft Windows.
SctpDrv-12.05.0.exe	Windows Driver Installer for SCTP	SctpDrv (exe) is a package which provides an SCTP (Stream Control Transmission Protocol) driver and SCTP library for Microsoft Windows.
sctpmon.dll	SCTP Driver	SctpDrv (dll) is a package which provides an SCTP (Stream Control Transmission Protocol) driver and SCTP library for Microsoft Windows.
sctpsp.dll	SCTP Driver	SctpDrv (dll) is a package which provides an SCTP (Stream Control Transmission Protocol) driver and SCTP library for Microsoft Windows.
Spot-On-Server.exe	Spot-On-Chat-Server GUI	Due to given source
Spot-On-Kernel.exe	Spot-On-Kernel for GoldBug	Due to given source
spot-on-neighbors.txt	Project Chat Server	Due to given source
sqlite3.dll	SQLite Database DLL file	SQLite Database
ssleay32.dll	Binary distribution of OpenSSL	OpenSSL for use in the OpenSSL Toolkit (http://www.openssl.org/)
zlib1.dll	Official build of zlib as a DLL: http://www.zlib.net/	http://www.gzip.org/zlib/zlib_faq.html
/Documentation	Several text and PDF files	Descritions, Manuals, etc.
/Plugins	Plug-ins for Sound, Media	Qt environment files
/Sounds	5 wav sound files	WAV Sounds
/SQL	3 PostgreSQL Resource Files	SQL / PostgreSQL specific files
/Translations	Several Translation files QM / QRC	Generated by Qt

Source: Own listing based on GoldBug version 2.9.

There are no files given whose inclusion or origin were striking.

We have then scaned the installation files from versions 2.7. / 2.8 and 2.9 with different virus scanner and also found no complaints. The virus scanner Kaspersky and Avira were used. The files are "clean" - there were no complaints found in our further and doubly checked automated tests.

In the history, there have been also for previous versions of GoldBug already

Es sind keine Dateien vorhanden, deren Einbezug oder Ursprung auffällig waren.

Wir haben sodann die Installationsdateien der Versionen 2.7. / 2.8 und 2.9 mit verschiedenen Virenscanners durchsucht und auch hier keinerlei Beanstandungen gefunden. Genutzt wurden die Virenscanner Kaspersky und Avira. Die Dateien sind „clean" – es gab keinerlei Beanstandungen in unseren weiteren und doppelt abgesicherten automatisierten Tests.

In der Historie hat es ebenso zu früheren Versionen von GoldBug schon entsprechende

appropriate security scans, that are published also partly on the web. For example also the scanning of "Reason Core Security" is published on the net and this examination called GoldBug as well as "clean" under the following URL, as the screenshot of the website shows.

Security-Scans gegeben, die z.T. auch noch im Web veröffentlicht sind. So ist z.B. auch der Scan von Reason Core Security im Netz veröffentlicht und diese Untersuchung bezeichnet GoldBug ebenso als „clean" unter der folgenden URL, wie der Screenshot der Webseite zeigt.

Figure 35: Reason Core Security Scan of GoldBug

Installed With

goldbug.exe is installed together with the following files.

Clean	icudt53.dll (ea14f4f4670cd85d30c6a9e4a70764920159458<!---->3)
Clean	icuin53.dll (07b97b6ca22c0a8024afb5afa4e7e651c234d07c)
Clean	icuuc53.dll (68d2403346bb85a7bca53d73afb86e11c1236d53)
Clean	libcurl.dll 7.40.0 (20446d6ac76ccae9e70a1b42b3b79178e5e70327)
Clean	libeay32.dll 1.0.2a (d7ff8bb9bd31ae3c7fe3c6c5efea0e4da057949e)
Clean	libgcc_s_dw2-1.dll (b725e965fdafecd2ed3139f202c7a08167210de3)
Clean	libgcrypt-20.dll 20.0.3.0ff1a27 (d13a81246b43dcde01e2e624b92a7f3ddad85f6e)
Clean	libgeoip-1.dll (d2b5aedd8489065000c6b7a242fc4862f3cbf8d8)
Clean	libgpg-error-0.dll 11.11.0.1900266 (9b66a8a352a603873ab1b67f7c000fe01d66bf84)
Clean	libiconv-2.dll 1.12 (2c116fef19547ac5ea4d032f4a5bdad997766134)

Further analysis specific to GoldBug 2.9 have been carried out according to our Web search also on other portals, such as by Portal "Download 3K" under the URL:

http://www.download3k.com/Antivirus-Report-GoldBug.html

There, the security is indicated even over five different scanner-suppliers as follows:

Weitere Analysen spezifisch zu GoldBug 2.9 sind nach unseren Webrecherchen auch von weiteren Portalen durchgeführt worden, z.B. von dem Portal "Download 3K" unter der URL:

http://www.download3k.com/Antivirus-Report-GoldBug.html

Dort ist die Unbedenklickeit sogar über fünf verschiedene Scanneranbieter wie folgt vermerkt:

Figure 36: GoldBug-Antivirus Report of the Portal Download3k.com

We have found
"GoldBug – Secure Instant Messenger" (V2.9)
to be clean.

Download3k has downloaded and tested version 2.9 of GoldBug – Secure Instant Messenger using only the best antivirus engines available Today.

We have found it to be **clean** of any form of badware (viruses, spyware, adware, etc.). You can view the full scan logs below.

We will test GoldBug Secure Instant Messenger again on the next version release so make sure you check back for updated reports in the near future.

- Avast: **Clean**
- AVG: **Clean**
- Avira: **Clean**
- Kaspersky: **Clean**
- NOD32: **Clean**

Source: http://www.download3k.com/Antivirus-Report-GoldBug.html

Thus it can be stated in summary that
- our own handpicked sighting of the supplied installation files of GoldBug,
- our investigation from which library-reference the files come from and
- our conducted virus scans and fourthly
- the statement, that all external security scans mentioned above see the various GoldBug versions of this Messenger continuously for all latest versions as "clean",

are all good evidence, that the installation can be regarded as trustworthy.

Goldbug can therefore be certified as safety: It does not contain badware.

As shown, there have been these security scans by other external third parties as well for numerous versions of GoldBug, so that even in the time-series-analysis occurred no complaints. For a good overview therefore also the released versions of GoldBug should be referenced here for this section:

Damit kann zusammenfassend festgehalten werden, dass
- unsere eigene handverlesene Sichtung der gelieferten Installationsdateien von GoldBug,
- unsere Untersuchung aus welchem Bibliothekenkreis sie entstammen,
- wie auch unsere durchgeführten Virenscans, und viertens
- die Tatsache, dass alle oben genannten externen Sicherheitsscans der verschiedenen GoldBug-Versionen diesen Messenger kontinuierlich für sämtliche neuesten Versionen als „clean" und „sauber" bezeichnen,

gute Hinweise sind, dass die Installation als vertrauenswürdig bezeichnet werden kann.

GoldBug kann daher Unbedenklichkeit attestiert werden: Es enthält keine Badware.

Wie dargestellt hat es diese Sicherheits-Scans seitens weiterer externer Dritter ebenso für zahlreiche Versionen von GoldBug gegeben, so dass auch in der Zeitreihenanalyse keinerlei Beanstandungen vorkamen. Zum guten Überblick sollen daher auch die veröffentlichen Versionen von GoldBug für diesen Abschnitt hier referenziert werden:

Table 76: Release History of GoldBug Messenger
based on Spot-On Architecture & Echo-Protocol

Version	Date	Remarks
2.9	2016|02|01	RSS-/Atom-Newsreader Release.
2.8	2015|12|25	Pandamonium Webcrawler Release (XMAS-Release).
2.7	2015|09|26	Forward Secrecy in Email & Chat Release.
2.6	2015|08|01	Serverless Key Share-Release.
2.5	2015|06|19	URL-Websearch-Release.
2.1	2015|04|20	Virtual-Keyboard-Release.
1.9	2015|02|23	Socialist-Millionaire-Protocoll-(SMP)-Release.
1.8	2015|01|24	E-Mail-Client-Release: Plaintext-Emails over POP3/IMAP.
1.7	2014|12|06	POPTASTIC-XMAS-Release: Encrypted chat over IMAP/POP3.
1.6a	2014|11|09	2-Way-Instant-Perfect-Forward-Secrecy: "2WIPFS"-Release.
1.5	2014|10|10	Alternative Login-Method Release
1.3	2014|09|30	NTRU Release
1.1	2014|09|09	Vector Update Release
1.0	2014|09|07	File-Encryption Tool Release
0.9.09	2014|08|20	Smiley Release
0.9.07	2014|07|13	Adaptive Echo Release
0.9.05	2014|05|31	Added Example Project Chat Server Release
0.9.04	2014|04|22	SCTP & Institution Release.
0.9.02	2014|03|13	StarBeam Analyzer Release
0.9.00	2014|02|07	Tablet Gui Release.
0.8	2013|12|23	Rosetta CryptoPad XMAS-Release.
0.7	2013|12|19	StarBeam Filesharing Release
0.6	2013|10|24	El-Gamal Release

0.5	2013|09|16	Signature-Keys Release
0.4	2013|09|03	Kernel-Improvement Release
0.3	2013|08|26	Geo-IP-Release
0.2	2013|08|22	SSL-Release
0.1	2013|07|27	based on the release of the same day of the Echo/Chat-Kernel-Servers and Application http://spot-on.sf.net, going back on another previous research project.

3.21.4 Evaluation of the results with regard to weaknesses, risks, potentials for improvements and strengths

Therefore, there arise no weaknesses or risks in regard to the distributed files from GoldBug. A particular strength like it to be seen that the further files are based on established frameworks and libraries, and that the installer is a ZIP, so that the user receives complete transparency of the distributed files.

Es ergeben sich daher keine Schwächen oder Risiken hinsichtlich der distribuierten Dateien von GoldBug. Eine besondere Stärke mag darin zu sehen sein, dass die weiteren Dateien auf etablierten Frameworks und Bibliotheken beruhen und der Installer eine ZIP darstellt, so dass der Nutzer volle Transparenz über die distribuierten Dateien erhält.

Table 77: Description of findings 3.21

#	Area	Description of the finding	Valuation Severity Category / Difficulty Level / Innovation & Improvement Class / Strength Dimension
	Weakness / Schwäche	./.	./.
	Risk / Risiko	./.	./.
	Potential for Improvement / Verbesserungspotential	./.	./.
3.21.4.A	Strength / Stärke	Usage of files from established libraries and frameworks in the installation ZIP.	Medium

Also we have build the GoldBug.exe and the included Pandamonium.exe of the webcrawler, respectively the Spot-On-chat-server.exe representing the original GUI for the kernel Spot-On-Kernel.exe, from the source code using the Qt compiler.
The hash sum is adapted to each build, because in the GUI the compiling-date is included (compare Login-tab). Due to the in seconds precise time and date each binary compile from the source has its own hash sum.

Ebenso haben wir die GoldBug.Exe und auch die mitgelieferte Pandamonium.exe des WebCrawlers bzw. die Spot.On-Chat-Server.exe, die die Original-GUI zum Kernel Spot-On-Kernel.exe darstellt, mittels des Qt-Compilers aus dem source code gebildet.
Die Hash-Summe ist dem jeweiligen Build angepasst, da in der GUI das Compiler-Datum einbezogen ist (vgl. Login-Tab). Aufgrund der sekundengenauen Zeit und Datumsangabe hat jeder Binär-Compile aus dem Source seine eigene Hash Summe.

The deposit of the hash sum at Hoster SourceForge for the distributed file would indeed offer seemingly more security, but would concern only the certainty that the download of the binary files in the Zip during the transfer would have been changed. For the established platform SourceForge and the Internet providers during a download process

Die Hinterlegung der Hash-Summe beim Anbieter Sourceforge für die distribuierte Datei würde zwar scheinbar mehr Sicherheit offerieren, beträfe aber nur die Sicherheit, dass der Download der Binärdateien im Zip während des Transfers verändert worden wären. Dieses ist erstmal für die etablierte Plattform Sourceforge und der Internetknoten bei einem

this should at a first glance not be assumed, because: Finally, everyone has with simple means the ability to build their own binary from the source code (at GitHub), when someone wants to compile the binary available for downloading.

Therefore we judge this aspect not as a potential improvement, because instead of downloading a binary file also each user can create the binary file from the source code at any time himself without having specific specialist knowledge.

The compilation process with the Qt framework is easy and described either in the project documentation and also in the user manual: click the referring "goldbug.win.qt5.pro" file in the Qt-Creator-compiler and press the "Compile" button. Nothing could be simpler, if someone wants to create their own binary and one should not trust the above mentioned five virus scanners.

Downloadprozess erstmal nicht anzunehmen, denn: schließlich hat jeder mit einfachen Mitteln die Möglichkeit, aus dem source code (bei GitHub) seine eigene Binärdatei zu bilden, wenn jemand die zum Download angebotene Binärdatei selbst kompilieren will.

Daher werten wir diesen Aspekt nicht als potentielle Verbesserung, denn statt eine Binärdatei aus dem Quellcode jederzeit selbst erstellen, ohne über besondere Spezialkenntnisse zu verfügen.

Der Kompilierungsprozess mit dem Qt-Framework ist kinderleicht und sowohl in der Projektdokumentation als auch im Benutzerhandbuch beschrieben: entsprechende „goldbug.win.qt5.pro"-Datei im Qt-Compiler Creator einklicken und den Knopf „Kompilieren" drücken. Einfacher geht es nicht, wenn jemand seine eigene Binärdatei erstellen will und den genannten fünf Virenscannern nicht vertrauen sollte.

4   CONCLUSION

The main objective of this audit was to determine the GoldBug Messenger with its features, its code and its documentation to undergo a review, which integrates essential dimensions and methods of international IT audit manuals.

Das wesentliche Ziel dieses Audits war es, den GoldBug Messenger mit seinen Funktionen, seinem Code und seiner Dokumentation einem Review zu unterziehen, das wesentliche Dimensionen und Methoden internationaler IT-Audit-Manuale einbindet.

Thus, the individual areas of analysis were not only described and evaluated, but also made references for further generally comparative open source Crypto-Messenger.

So wurden die einzelnen Analysebereiche nicht nur beschrieben und bewertet, sondern auch Referenzen zu weiteren grundsätzlich vergleichenden quelloffenen Crypto-Messenger hergestellt.

These BIG SEVEN Crypto-Messengers have been found from various lists of encrypted communication programs as the essential to compare open source applications.

Diese BIG SEVEN Crypto-Messenger haben sich aus zahlreichen Listen von verschlüsselnden Kommunikations-Programmen als die wesentlich zu vergleichenden quelloffenen Applikationen herausgestellt.

In the overall view a very high confidentiality and a very high security requirements of the Communication Suite Goldbug has been shown up. We have no complaints found that would allow an assumption to the contrary.

In der Gesamtsicht zeigen sich eine sehr hohe Vertraulichkeit sowie ein sehr hoher Sicherheitsanspruch der Communication Suite GoldBug. Wir haben keine Beanstandungen gefunden, die eine Annahme des Gegenteils zulassen würden.

The Messenger Goldug is fully compliant and conform to the available sets of regulations, policies and standards. It can be considered secure in the sense of comprehensively trustworthy.

Der Messenger GoldBug ist voll compliant bzw. konform zu den verfügbaren Regelwerken, Vorschriften und Standards. Er kann als sicher im Sinne von umfassend vertrauenswürdig eingeschätzt werden.

The methods of investigation were derived from the international standard IT audit manuals, which were then based on the Goldbug application in diverse angles.

Die Methoden der Untersuchung wurden abgeleitet aus den internationalen Standard IT-Audit-Manualen, die sodann in vielfältigem Blickwinkel auf die GoldBug-Applikation bezogen wurden.

Compared to other applications, there are clear strengths of Goldbug Messenger that relate not only to the programming, the functionality and the available innovations and current standards, but highlight also in the analytic dimensions in comparison to similar functions of other Messenger.

Im Vergleich zu anderen Applikationen zeigen sich deutliche Stärken des GoldBug Messengers, die sich nicht nur auf die Programmierung, den Funktionsumfang sowie die verfügbaren Innovationen und aktuellen Standards beziehen, sondern sich in den Untersuchungsdimensionen auch in einem Vergleich zu ähnlichen Funktionen anderer Messenger hervorheben.

Significant risks or weaknesses we have not found in Goldbug Messenger. The following measures, we propose, in order to prevent any shortcomings and only theoretically assumed risks in Goldbug Messenger preventively:

Wesentliche Risiken oder Schwächen haben wir im GoldBug Messenger nicht gefunden. Die folgenden Maßnahmen schlagen wir vor, um eventuelle Schwächen und theoretisch angenommene Risiken beim GoldBug Messenger präventiv vorzubeugen:

• update the screenshots in the manual and translation of the manual into other languages,	• Aktualisierung der Screenshots im Handbuch sowie Übersetzung des Handbuches auch in weitere Sprachen,
• Recommendation of the spelling of passwords in cases of oral transmission,	• Empfehlung der Buchstabierung von Passworten bei mündlicher Übermittlung,
• Creation of video tutorials for the use of the application to make the users in particular through visual learning using the software even more confidant.	• Erstellung eines Video-Turorials für die Nutzung der Applikation, um den Nutzern insbesondere durch visuelles Lernen die Anwendung der Software noch vertauter zu machen.
• Only theoretically possible scenarios that passwords in the Socialist-Millionaire-Process (as with OTR) be obtained or guessed due to social engineering in the dialogue;	• Nur theoretisch mögliche Szenarien, dass Passworte im Socialist-Millionaire-Prozess (wie auch bei OTR) durch Social Engineering im Dialog erfragt oder erraten werden;
• The programming of the functions should be further elaborated in order to give users also advice for their purpose.	• Die Programmierung der Funktionen sollte weiter elaboriert werden, um den Nutzern auch Hinweise für deren Aufgabe zu geben.

Table 78: Evaluation-Matrix of possible risks & continuous improvements suggestions

		Low	Medium	High
Impact	**High**	• **Further elaboration of certain functions e.g. with tooltips to explain it.**	• **No findings available**	• **No findings available**
	Medium	• **Creation of a Video tutorial would rise the usage awareness of the users.**	• **No findings available**	• **No findings available**
	Low	• **Update of some screenshots in the user manual to the current version needed.**	• **No findings available**	• **No findings available**
		Probability		

With regard to highlight the innovations and strengths of the application we noticed the following points in our audit:

- Use of hybrid multi-encryption with additional TLS / HTTPS channel,

- encryption of email and chat in one application with very simple standard procedures of established crypto libraries

- functions with numerous implementations such as group chat, file transfer, URL-web search, encryption tools or even individual elaborations as multiple login methods or the authentication by the Socialist-millionaire protocol,

- innovating the chat via e-mail server with the POPTASTIC function

- Numerous methods for the transmission of keys for an end-to-end encryption,

- Deployment of Cryptologic token for the AE mode (Adaptive Echo)

- development and application of the magnet-URI-standard for encryption values,

- Compared with other applications usage of secure hash values and comprehensive key variables, for example at login or within the SMP function,

- And many more individual perspective rich innovations as they were worked out in the individual inspection chapters.

Regarding the indicative comparisons in the reference frame of the BIG SEVEN open source Crypto Messenger, the following general recommendations for all development projects can be derived:

- The need for elaboration of each client with additional functions,

Hinsichtlich der herauszustellenden Innovationen und Stärken der Applikation sind uns insbesondere folgende Punkte bei unserem Audit aufgefallen:

- Nutzung von hybrider Multi-Verschlüsselung mit zusätzlichem TLS/HTTPS Kanal,

- Verschlüsselung von E-Mail und Chat in einer Applikation mit sehr einfachen Standard-Prozeduren etablierter Crypto-Bibliotheken,

- Funktionsumfang mit zahlreichen Implementierungen wie Gruppenchat, Dateitransfer, URL-WebSuche, Verschlüsselungs-Tools oder auch einzelnen Ausarbeitungen wie mehrfachen-Login-Methoden oder der Authentifizierung durch das Socialist-Millionaire-Protokoll,

- Innovierung des Chats über E-Mail Server mit der POPTASTIC Funktion,

- Zahlreiche Methoden für die Übertragung von Schlüsseln für eine Ende-zu-Ende-Verschlüsselung,

- Nutzung Kryptologischer Token für den AE-Modus (Adaptive Echo),

- Entwicklung und Anwendung des Magnet-URI-Standards für Verschlüsselungswerte,

- Gegenüber anderen Applikationen Nutzung sicherer Hash-Werte und umfassende Key-Größen, z.B. beim Login oder der SMP-Funktion,

- Sowie viele weitere einzelne perspektivenreiche Innovationen, wie sie in den einzelnen Untersuchungskapiteln herausgearbeitet wurden.

Hinsichtlich der indikativ erfolgten Vergleiche im Referenzwerk der BIG SEVEN open source Crypto-Messenger lassen sich folgende generelle Empfehlungen für alle Entwicklungsprojekte ableiten:

- Notwendigkeit der Elaborierung des jeweiligen Klienten mit weiteren Funktionen,

- • standardization of clients in terms of safety-related aspects such as Login password encryption (key size), SMP implementation, usage of different keys for different functions, etc.,

- expanding the use of ephemeral keys and asynchronous methods,

- Provision of decentralized chat servers,

- Provision of an infrastructure that also allows to eliminate a DHT,

- More investment in the solution of the key transport problem over the introduction of numerous secured online ways,

- setting of standards of native, from the beginning implemented encryption without plugins,

- Manual definition and establishment of a symmetrical end-to-end encrypting password,

- Introduction of symmetrically encrypted group chats,

- Detailed documentation of the aspects for encryption particular in regard to comparative references to other clients.

Even if the references regarding the other crypto messenger are not based on a dedicated audit of the respective messenger by us authors - here the application GoldBug was deeply and in a broad analysis examined - indicatively a comparative evaluation can be given based on:
- the engagement with the individual audit fields,
- the total acquired knowledge base about Crypto Messenger
- as well as the investigation into the comparative Messenger.

- Standardisierung der Klienten hinsichtlich sicherheitsrelevanter Aspekte wie z.B. Login-Passwort-Verschlüsselungen (Schlüsselgrößen), SMP-Implementierung, Nutzung verschiedener Schlüssel für unterschiedliche Funktionen, etc.,

- Ausbau der Nutzung von ephemeralen Schlüsseln und asynchronen Methoden,

- Bereitstellung von dezentralen Chat-Servern,

- Bereitstellung einer Infrastruktur, die es auch erlaubt, einen DHT auszuschalten,

- Mehr Investition in die Lösung des Schlüssel-Transport-Problems über die Einführung von zahlreichen abgesicherten Online-Wegen,

- Setzung eines Standards an nativer, von vorneherein implementierter Verschlüsselung ohne Plugins,

- Manuelle Definition und Einrichtung eines symmetrisch Ende-zu-Ende verschlüsselnden Passwortes,

- Einführung von symmetrisch verschlüsselten Gruppenchats,

- Ausführlichere Dokumentation des Aspekte zur Verschlüsselung insbesondere unter vergleichenden Referenzen zu anderen Klienten.

Auch wenn die Referenzen zu den weiteren Crypto-Messengern nicht auf einem dedizierten Audit des jeweiligen Messengers durch uns Autoren beruhen – hier wurde ja die Applikation GoldBug vertiefend und in einer breiten Analyse untersucht – lassen sich
- aus der Beschäftigung mit dem einzelnen Auditfeldern,
- des insgesamt erarbeiteten Kenntisstandes über Crypto-Messenger
- wie auch die Einarbeitung in die vergleichbaren Messenger
indikativ eine vergleichende Bewertung abgeben.

Therefore, the following overview should be created, in which audit fields a particular application to which extent elaborates the investigated functions.

As seen methodically are the 20 fields of investigation not strengths of GoldBug, but were systematically derived from the various international IT-audit-manuals, so that the comparison is not only examined with GoldBug, but the other Crypto-Messenger are also referred to one interpretation of the audit fields of the international IT audit manuals.

The assessment should be made on the following scale:

Im Folgenden soll daher eine Übersicht erstellt werden, in welchen Audit-Feldern eine jeweilige Applikation die untersuchten Funktionen in welchem Ausmaß elaboriert hat.

Wie methodisch gesehen sind die 20 Untersuchugsfelder nicht Stärken von GoldBug, sondern wurden systematisch aus den zahlreichen internationalen IT-Audit-Manualen abgeleitet, so dass der Vergleich nicht nur mit GoldBug erfolgt, sondern die weiteren Crypto-Messenger auch auf eine Interpretation der Audit-Felder der internationalen IT-Audit-Manuale bezogen wird.

Die Bewertung soll mit folgender Skala getroffen werden:

Table 79: BIG SEVEN Crypto-Messenger comparison scale

Points	Scale Description
0	Function or Standard has not been implemented. Audit-Dimension not given in this client. Undetermined.
1	Several aspects are given, but others have more elaboration within this field. Does not meet our expectations of the given and found standards.
2	State-of-the-Art-Standard: The implementation in other applications is on the same level as the implementation within at least one other application. This standard meets our expectations - as well for the other open source Crypto-Messengers, due to the comparable investigations we have done indicativly.
3	The given context is definitely more elaborated than in other comparable clients or is a good practice model in general.

Taking into account the analyzes and statements in the individual audit areas, one can create an only indicative to consider point-overview for each open source Crypto-Messenger.
Here we document our evaluation as follows:

Berücksichtigt man die Analysen und Ausführungen in den einzelnen Audit-Feldern, so kann man zu einer nur indikativ zu wertenden Punkte-Übersicht für jeden quelloffenen Crypto-Messenger gelangen.
Wir dokumentieren hier unsere Einschätzung wie folgt:

Table 80:   Indicative comparison of contextual assessments on the BIG SEVEN Crypto Messengers

#	Chapter	CryptoCat	GoldBug	OTR+XMPP	RetroShare	Signal	SureSpot	Tox
3.1	Hybrid / Multi Encryption, e.g. IPFS, ephemeral keys etc.	0	2	1	0	0	0	0
3.2	Integrity & Authenticy, e.g. opt. Digital	1	3	2	2	1	1	1

		CryptoCat	GoldBug	OTR+XMPP	RetroShare	Signal	SureSpot	Tox
	Signatures							
3.3	Availability, e.g. decentral Servers / DHT	1	2	3	3	1	1	2
3.4	Ciphertext-Scan	1	2	1	1	1	1	1
3.5	Login-Methods, e.g. different Methods, Password length	1	3	1	0	1	1	1
3.6	Encryped DB, all stored data natively encrypted	1	3	2	3	1	1	1
3.7	Accounts for connections	1	1	1	1	1	1	1
3.8	Manuals, e.g. length, Book or FAQ etc.	2	2	2	2	1	1	1
3.9	Other Audits	2	1	2	0	1	0	0
3.10	E-Mail Poptastic	0	3	0	1	0	0	0
3.11	FileSharing, encrypted	1	2	0	3	1	1	1
3.12	Decryption	1	1	1	1	1	1	1
3.13	Security Nuggets	0	0	0	0	0	0	0
3.14	GUI-Kernel-Interaction, choosable chiphers	1	2	1	1	1	1	1
3.15	Analog Communication, e.g. of additional Passwords	0	3	2	0	0	0	0
3.16	Packet Communication, e.g. AE, routing, turtle, F2F.	0	3	0	2	0	0	0
3.17	Wireless Interaction, e.g. Bluetooth Server	0	2	0	0	0	0	0
3.18	Social Engineering: SMP Process	0	2	2	0	0	0	0
3.19	Default Crypto Values, e.g. manual adjustable	0	3	0	1	0	0	0
3.20	Account-Passwords, e.g. length	1	3	1	2	1	1	1
		CryptoCat	GoldBug	OTR+XMPP	RetroShare	Signal	SureSpot	Tox
	TOTAL	**15**	**45**	**23**	**22**	**13**	**12**	**13**

Considering that CryptoCat enables decentralized server in the user's hand and already has a corresponding development history, one can see **CryptoCat** ahead of the clients Signal, Surespot and Tox. The battle cry of cryptocat developer, to address with his intended desktop client development also OTR/XMPP aka e.g. Pidgin, is then - also from the review in this overview - for CryptoCat an important motivational target (with 15 compared to 23 points obtained).

Due to the central server (with identity checks via mobile phones) in Signal and the numerous code contributions of different individuals with the appropriate coordination and review effort in Tox, possibly **Surespot** with a dozen points can be seen in front at these three messengers, as this also as a mobile variant can be operated with a private, decentralized server, and dispense with an identity check: No friend receives unsolicited a chat-ID, as is the case with the client Signal.

Regarding RetroShare and OTR / XMPP, which also play in a comparable points-league according to the methodology used audit fields, the conditions of serverlessness for RetroShare can gain points and the missing native encryption architecture at OTR / XMPP can deduct points, so we would in a world with only one Messenger out of these two decide for the decentralized and natively encrypted **RetroShare**. It is also considerably more extensive than CryptoCat, but not available for mobile devices such Surespot.

GoldBug we see next to RetroShare at the top of the BIG SEVEN open source Crypto-Messenger, because **GoldBug** reached at the end of our substantive audit analyzes in the individual fields and features more than twice as many points as RetroShare. As seen above in a small aspect, also the related crypto procedures (for example, in the keys, hash functions or password-lengths) in GoldBug are twice as safe as using OTR.

GoldBug is very trustworthy and compliant to international IT audit manuals and security

Berücksichtigt man, das Crypto-Cat einen dezentralen Server in Hand des Nutzers ermöglicht und schon eine entsprechende Entwicklungshistorie aufweist, kann man **CryptoCat** vor den Klienten Signal, Surespot und Tox sehen. Der Schlachtruf des CryptoCat Entwicklers, mit seiner beabsichtigten Desktop-Klienten-Entwicklung auch OTR/XMPP aka z.B. Pidgin zu adressieren, ist also - auch aus der Bewertung dieser Übersicht heraus folgend - ein für CryptoCat wichtiges motivationales Ziel (bei 15 gegenüber 23 erreichten Punkten).

Aufgrund des zentralen und per Mobiltelefon identitätsprüfenden Servers bei Signal und der zahlreichen Code-Beiträge unterschiedlicher Personen mit entsprechendem Koordinierungs- und Review-Aufwand bei Tox, kann bei den drei Messengern mit rund einem Dutzend Punkten ggf. **Surespot** vorne gesehen werden, da dieser auch als mobile Variante einen eigenen, dezentralen Server betreiben lässt und auf eine Identitätsprüfung verzichtet: Kein Freund erhält ungefragt die Chat-ID, wie es bei dem Programm Signal der Fall ist.

Hinsichtlich RetroShare und OTR/XMPP, die ebenso in einer vergleichbaren Punkte Liga spielen gemäß der angewandten methodischen Audit-Feldern, können ggf. die Rahmenbedingungen der Serverlosigkeit für RetroShare punkten bzw. die fehlende native Verschlüsselungsarchitektur bei OTR/XMPP Punkte abziehen, so dass wir uns in einer Welt mit nur einem Messenger von diesen beiden für das dezentrale und nativ verschlüsselnde **RetroShare** entscheiden würden. Er ist auch wesentlich umfangreicher als CryptoCat, jedoch nicht mobil verfügbar wie Surespot.

GoldBug sehen wir neben RetroShare an der Spitze der BIG SEVEN open source Crypto-Messenger, da **GoldBug** am Ende unserer inhaltlichen Audit-Analysen in den einzelnen Feldern und Funktionen mehr als doppelt so viele Punkte erreicht als RetroShare. Wie oben in einem kleinen Teilaspekt gesehen, sind auch die verwandten Crypto-Prozeduren in GoldBug (z.B. bei den Keys, Hashfunktionen oder Passwort-Längen) doppelt so sicher wie bei OTR.

GoldBug ist nicht nur sehr vertrauenswürdig und compliant zu den internationalen IT-Audit-

standards, but also in comparison to the individual functions GoldBug scores in our evaluation in much greater detail than any other comparative open source Crypto-Messenger. GoldBug receives twice as many valuation points in an audit matrix of 20 evaluation criteria as RetroShare.

Although the development of these projects not make a stop, depth analyzes may also see ratings in the individual fields arguably here and there, we have this content and analysis found, realized and evaluated as given at the present time. Adjustments and discussions are strongly encouraged, when they are described and referenced in a scientific paper - and are especially compared.

To compare the topics, functions and audit fields of other messengers at a future time as well with the implementation and good practice models in GoldBug, remains an interesting task for upcoming student generations.

Although if today the points would be distributed differently, it shows itself indicative, that GoldBug is very far forward because of its excellent perspectives, standards and elaborations in the individual functions and audit fields and can therefore be referred to as perspective-richest Crypto-Client, one should know and have tested.

And yet: No client can be seen far back. The analysis items have shown, that many comparable Messenger have their Achilles-verses, on the other hand also their specific potentials, which need to develop further.

The collection of all encrypting Messenger has taken place (compare chapter 2), so that it is now in further research and publications of portals in particular about the phase of qualitative and substantive comparisons of BIG SEVEN Messengers.

Manualen und Sicherheitsstandards, sondern auch im Vergleich der Einzelfunktionen punktet GoldBug in unserer Bewertung wesentlich ausführlicher als alle anderen vergleichbaren open-source Crypto-Messenger. GoldBug erhält doppel so viele Bewertungs-Punkte in einer Audit-Matrix von 20 Beurteilungskriterien wie RetroShare.

Auch wenn die Entwicklungen der Projekte nicht halt machen, vertiefende Analysen hier und da auch Wertungen in den Einzelfeldern diskutierbar sehen mögen, haben wir diese Inhalte und Analysen zum heutigen Zeitpunkt so vorgefunden, durchgeführt und bewertet. Anpassungen und Diskussionen sind ausdrücklich erwünscht, wenn sie auch in einem wissenschaftlichen Papier entsprechend belegt und insbesondere verglichen werden.

Die einzelnen Themen, Funktionen und Audit-Felder an einem zukünftigen Zeitpunkt von anderen Messengern auch mit den Implementierungen und Good-Practice-Modellen in GoldBug zu vergleichen, bleibt eine interessante Aufgabe nachwachsender studentischer Generationen.

Auch wenn heute die Punkte anders verteilt würden, es zeigt sich indikativ, das GoldBug aufgrund seiner excellenten Perspektiven, Standards und Ausarbeitungen in den einzelnen Funktionen und Audit-Feldern sehr weit vorne liegt und daher als perspektivenreichster Crypto-Klient bezeichnet werden kann, den man kennen und angewandt haben sollte.

Und dennoch: Kein Klient ist weit hinten zu sehen. Die Einzelanalysen haben gezeigt, dass viele vergleichbare Messenger ihre Archillesversen haben, andererseits auch ihre spezifischen Potentiale, die es weiter zu entwickeln gilt.

Die Erfassung aller verschlüsselnden Messenger ist erfolgt (vgl. Kaptiel 2), so dass es nun in der weiteren Forschung und Veröffentlichung von Portalen insbesondere um die Phase der qualitativen und inhaltlichen Vergleiche der BIG SEVEN Messenger gehen wird.

Figure 37: BIG SEVEN Open Source Crypto-Messenger Overview

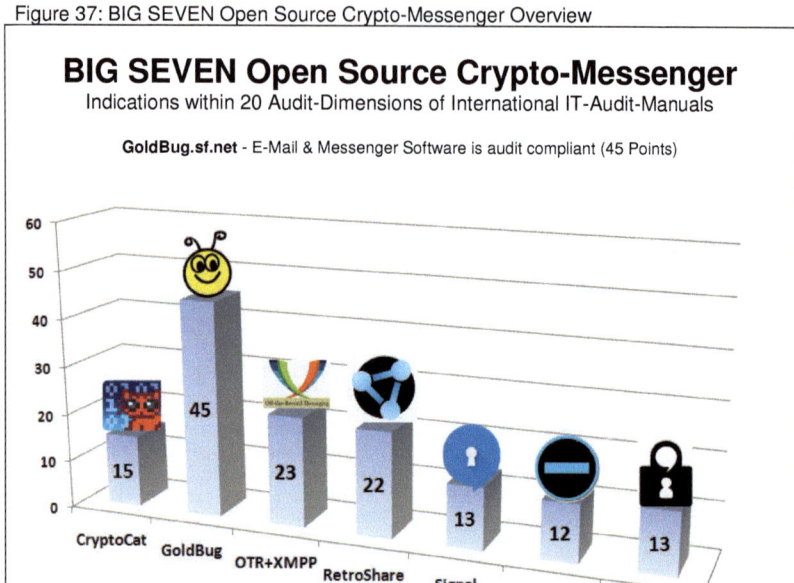

BIG SEVEN Open Source Crypto-Messenger
Indications within 20 Audit-Dimensions of International IT-Audit-Manuals

GoldBug.sf.net - E-Mail & Messenger Software is audit compliant (45 Points)

Source: BIG SEVEN - Study (Adams / Maier 2016)

De facto the clients are anchored in different sized communities, that it is to be expected that the users will leave this comfort zone of networked friends only cumbersome to use a more excellent or technically better encountered quality-standard.

Here one can possibly briefly reflect on the name of GoldBug, going back to a short story by Edgar Allan Poe, in which three friends launch a joint adventure: This means not to trot a community behind, but instead to establish with an own team a new era, to seek a new part, is the goal of learning and life: so why not even prepare for the next party a GoldBug Bluetooth-Server for friends instead always connecting via the same cable?

Not only encryption is the subject of a next cryptoparty but especially the teaching of know-how to setup a decentral server for encrypted communication.

De facto sind die Klienten auch in unterschiedlich großen Communities verankert, so dass zu erwarten ist, dass die Nutzer diese Komfortzone der vernetzten Freunde nur schwerfällig verlassen werden, um einen exzellenteren oder fachlich besser vorgefundenen Qualitäts-Standard zu nutzen.

Hier kann man ggf. kurz auf den Namen von GoldBug reflektieren, der auf eine Kurz-Geschichte von Edgar Allan Poe zurück geht, in der drei Freunde ein gemeinsames Abenteuer starten: Will heissen, nicht einer Community hinterher zu trotten, sondern mit seinem Team eine neue Ära zu begründen, einen neuen Abschnitt zu wagen, ist das Ziel des Lernens und Lebens: Warum also nicht mal auf der nächsten Party einen GoldBug-Bluetooth-Server für die Freunde vorbereiten anstatt immer mit dem selben Kabel zu verbinden?

Nicht nur Verschlüsselung ist das Thema einer nächsten Crypto-Party, sondern besonders die Vermittlung des Know-Hows, einen eigenen dezentralen Server für verschlüsselte

Recommendation here is to focus not only on a client & server or a single model, but try out and to test each of the BIG SEVEN yourself (as client and chat server) - Ideally with friends who have already gained some experience with at least two Crypto-Messengers in comparison.

In the future there will be continuously attempts to break cryptology, to fit cryptology with backdoors or to prohibit encryption.

A total ban is unlikely because it paralyzes the economy, and restricts personal freedom and human rights to an unacceptable extent. A partial ban is as senseless, finally remains "ciphertext" a ciphertext: No one can read it primitively, which encryption values are given, or if multiple encryption is being used. In addition the field of open source cryptology is for end-users at an advanced stage and a restriction or ban makes little sense here, like a ban on the Math or XOR operations.

Backdoors will be possibly more to be expected under asymmetric encryption than in symmetric encryption: The existing standards are therefore to be continued to be explored and also we should evaluate the random number of a machine (compare Meyer et al. / BSI, 2015).

In symmetric encryption, a common shared secret password is given. If this can not be promptly cracked due to brute force attacks, so by trying out all possible combinations due to fast computers, remains the manual definition of an end-to-end encrypting password and its immediate renewal, as defined by Instant Perfect Forward Secrecy such as by the Gemini function of GoldBug, also a perspective rich solution. In many other clients this important requirement is missing: manually defined symmetry!

The perspective of GoldBug is also in its diversity: it is similar to a house, in which hangs a chandelier. Should now possibly in twenty years, if necessary, a light bulb be broken, however the house does not need to be rebuilt. If RSA should be considered broken, we find in GoldBug as well ElGamal or

Kommunikation aufzusetzen.
Empfehlung ist hier, sich nicht nur auf einen Klienten & Server oder ein einziges Modell zu fokussieren, sondern jeden der BIG SEVEN einmal (als Klient und auch Chat-Server) selbst auszuprobieren und zu testen - Idealerweise mit Freunden, die schon erste Erfahrungen mit wenigstens zwei Crypto-Messenger im Vergleich gesammelt haben.

In Zukunft wird es auch weiterhin Versuche geben, Kryptologie zu brechen, mit Hintertüren zu versehen oder zu verbieten.

Ein vollständiges Verbot ist unwahrscheinlich, da es die Volkswirtschaft lähmt und persönliche Freiheit und Menschenrechte in einem nicht akzeptablen Maße einschränkt. Ein partielles Verbot ist ebenso unsinnig, schließlich bleibt "Ciphertext" ein Ciphertext: Niemand kann daraus primitiv ablesen, welche Verschlüsselungswerte vorliegen oder ob Mehrfach-Verschlüsselung angewandt wurde. Zudem ist das Gebiet der Open Source Kryptologie für Endnutzer weit fortgeschritten und eine Restriktion oder Bann macht hier ebenso wenig Sinn wie ein Verbot der Mathematik oder von XOR-Operationen.

Hintertüren werden ggf. eher bei asymmetrischer als symmetrischer Verschlüsselung zu erwarten sein: Die bestehenden Standards sind daher weiter zu erforschen und auch die Zufallsgeneratoren einer Maschine zu evaluieren (vgl. Meyer et. al. / BSI 2015).

Bei symmetrischer Verschlüsselung ist ein gemeinsam geteiltes Passwort-Geheimnis gegeben. Wenn dieses nicht durch Brute-Force-Attacken, also durch das Ausprobieren aller denkbaren Kombinationen durch schnelle Computer, zeitnah geknackt werden kann, dann bleibt auch die manuelle Definition eines Ende-zu-Ende verschlüsselnden Passwortes und dessen sofortige Erneuerungsmöglichkeit im Sinne von Instant Perfect Forward Secrecy wie z.B. durch die Gemini-Funktion von GoldBug, eine perspektivenreiche Lösung. In vielen anderen Klienten fehlt diese wichtige Voraussetzung manuell definierter Symmetrie! Die Perspektive von GoldBug besteht zudem in seiner Vielfältigkeit: er ist mit einem Haus zu vergleichen, in dem ein Kronleuchter hängt. Sollte nun ggf. in zwanzig Jahren ggf. eine Glühbirne defekt werden, muss jedoch nicht das ganze Haus neu errichtet werden. Wenn RSA als gebrochen gelten sollte, stehen in

NTRU available or even a hybrid symmetric encryption, which can be renewed in the hidden between two users at any time.

Since February 2014, the time in which we finalize this study, RSA now is considered broken: the American Institute NIST sees RSA as "No longer secure: we must begin now to prepare our information security systems to be able to resist quantum computing" (NISTIR 8105 / Chen et al. 2016).

Thus, the comparison of Crypto Messenger is actually obsolete and it means a Hiob's message for all other Messenger, using RSA for key creation or key transport. Also DHE, so the ephemerale key exchange using the Diffie-Hellman protocol based on RSA has thus become in need of change and requires "New Directions" (compare slso the homonymous paper of Diffie/Helman from 1976). OTR requires also multi-encryption or NTRU and McEliece.

It remains (in the Qantum age) currently the Goldbug Messenger, since it is the only one, who has additionally implemented ElGamal and NTRU and nevertheless continues to make the decoding of multiple encrypted RSA-Chiphertext extremely difficult!

Hybrid multi-encryption and numerous customizable encryption options are so far the core competencies of merely GoldBug and this situation has been not only been prooved in the comparative audit analysis, but also from this strategic consideration above, that GoldBug clearly has the edge.

Although currently downloads or user acceptance differ for all clients, restrictive circumstances of future times can change this quickly - just as well as people who think ahead:
When file-sharing in France was considered with high fines, downloads of encrypting transfer tools have increased significantly.

Also in India encryption tools experienced a boom after it was announced that the online monitoring should be extended.

Would Bittorrent replaced by StarBeam-transfers and those linked to accounts of a

GoldBug auch ElGamal oder NTRU zur Verfügung oder eben eine hybride symmetrische Verschlüsselung, die im geheimen zwischen zwei Nutzern jederzeit erneuert werden kann.

Seit Februar 2014, die Zeit, in der wir diese Studie finalisieren, gilt RSA nun als gebrochen: das Amerikansiche Institut NIST sieht RSA als „No longer secure: we must begin now to prepare our information security systems to be able to resist quantum computing" (NISTIR 8105 / Chen et al. 2016).

Damit ist der Vergleich der Crypto-Messenger eigentlich hinfällig und es bedeutet eine Hiobs-Botschaft für alle anderen Messenger, die RSA für Schlüssel oder Schlüssel-Transport benutzen. Auch DHE, so der ephemerale Schlüsseltausch über das Diffie-Hellman-Protokoll auf Basis von RSA ist damit veränderungsbedürftig geworden und benötigt "New Directions" (vgl. auch das gleichnamige Papier von Diffie / Helman aus dem Jahr 1976). OTR benötigt ebenso Multiverschlüsselung oder NTRU und McEliece.

Es bleibt (im Qantum-Zeitalter) derzeit der GoldBug Messenger übrig, da er der einzige ist, der ergänzend ElGamal und NTRU implementiert hat und bei mehrfach verschlüsseltem RSA-Chiphertext die Decodierung dennoch weiterhin äußerst schwierig macht!

Hybride Multi-Verschlüsselung und zahlreiche individuell anpassbare Verschlüsselungs-Optionen sind also bislang die Kernkompetenzen nur von GoldBug und dieser Sachverhalt belegt nicht nur in der vergleichenden Audit-Analyse, sondern auch aus dieser obigen strategischen Überlegung heraus, dass GoldBug die Nase vorn hat.

Auch wenn derzeit Downloads oder Nutzerakzeptanz bei allen Klienten differieren, können restriktivere Umstände zukünftiger Zeiten dieses schnell ändern – genauso wie auch Menschen, die vorausdenken:
Als in Frankreich FileSharing mit hohen Strafen belegt wurde, sind die Downloads der verschlüsselnden Transfer-Tools signifikant angestiegen.

Ebenso erlebten in Indien die Verschlüsselungstools einen Boom, nachdem die Online-Überwachung ausgeweitet werden sollte.

Würde Bittorrent durch StarBeam-Transfers ersetzt und diese an Accounts eines GB-

GB-server (for example, via Bluetooth), an intervention in the free exchange of information is no longer that easy - not only in the residence of students, but also in the worldwide web.

Also the function of the URL exchange in GoldBug, which may include the whole website of the URL, is a safe alternative to proxy networks like Tor.

For the end user with the interest of protecting personal communications ultimately not only the test of client's with a friend, but also a visit of a Crypto-Party in the group may possibly be helpful to contribute to a privacy secured future.

It has to be assumed, that, for example, a high percentage of OTR-users do not know, whether the password, that they can manually enter, defines an authentication within the meaning of the Socialist-Millionaire-Process or a measure for a symmetrical end-to-end encryption. It is still a long educative way to go to make encryption available for the masses.

We therefore will be glad, when this audit text respectively this overview of the BIG-SEVEN-study is linked to participants of a Crypto-Party in advance as material-annex and thus are able to prepare efficiently for questions, functions and clients.

With that way participants learn also about the manuals, methods and principles of an IT audit, to self assess technology-offers, that are particularly open source.

When we recognized that other communication applications and their server architecture are

- not open source (or hide even the server source code)
- implementing encryption not natively (but work instead on risky plugin architectures in which things need to be installed) and
- not encrypting both, chat and email (but instead keep chat and email separate): It shows the trend towards applications that can encrypt both, chat and email, or, as the Goldbug Messenger, even send a chat message via an e-mail server, (for this collection of encrypted applications at the start of this study within Chapter 2 the applications for encrypted e-mail have been omitted,

Servers angebunden, ist nicht nur im Studierendenwohnheim (z.B. über Bluetooth), sondern auch weltweit ein Eingriff in den freien Informationsaustausch nicht mehr so einfach möglich.

Auch die Funktion des URL-Austausches in GoldBug, der die vollständige Webseite der URL inkludieren kann, ist eine sichere Alternative zum Proxy-Netzwerk Tor.

Für den End-Nutzer mit Interesse des Schutzes der persönlichen Kommunikation kann letztlich nicht nur der Klienten-Test mit einem Freund, sondern auch der Besuch einer Crypto-Party in der Gruppe ggf. hilfreich sein, um einen Beitrag zu einer Privatheit sichernden Zukunft zu leisten.

Es ist m.E. davon auszugehen, dass z.B. ein hoher Prozentsatz der OTR-Nutzer nicht wissen, ob sie mit dem Passwort, das sie manuell eingeben können, eine Authentifizierung im Sinne des Socialist-Millionaire-Prozesses oder eine Maßnahme im Sinne einer symmetrischen Ende-zu-Ende Verschlüsselung erfolgt. Es liegt noch ein weiter edukativer Weg vor uns, Verschlüsselung massentauglich zu machen.

Wir freuen uns daher, wenn dieser Audit-Text bzw. diese Übersicht der BIG-SEVEN-Studie den Teilnehmern einer Crypto-Party als Material-Anhang vorab verlinkt wird, damit sie sich gezielt auf Fragen, Funktionen und Klienten vorbereiten können.

So lernen Teilnehmer auch die Manuale, Methoden und Prinzipien eines IT-Audits kennen, um selbst Technikangebote einzuschätzen, die insbesondere quelloffen sind.

Als wir erkannt haben, dass andere Kommunikations-Applikationen und deren Server-Architektur

- nicht quelloffen sind (oder gar den Server-Quellcode verbergen),
- Verschlüsselung nicht nativ umsetzen (sondern über risikoreiche Plugin Architekturen arbeiten, in denen Dinge nachinstalliert werden müssen) und
- nicht beides, sowohl Chat, wie auch E-Mail verschlüsseln (sondern Chat und E-Mail getrennt halten): Es zeigt sich der Trend zu Applikationen, die beides können, Chat und E-Mail verschlüsseln oder wie der GoldBug Messenger, sogar eine Chat-Nachricht über E-Mail-Server senden, (bei dieser Vollerfassung der verschlüsselnden Applikationen zu Beginn in Kapitel 2 wurden die

because firstly these take not in particular into account the (hybrid and inclusive) trend for presence chat on mobile platforms, and secondly because for email encryption merely PGP is prominent, which is considered both, complicated and seen from some experts as stillbirth. Therefore, the innovative strength of GoldBug to encrypt both, e-mail and chat, or the concept of the client in itself can be considered as forward-looking also related to e-mail applications. Encryption for email as a plugin and without chat and then still complicated and not suitable for mass production due to historical experience - makes no sense. GoldBug is very simple to operate for both, chat and email, and the configuration of chat servers and p2p email mailboxes.

- and bring users not in a position to create their own communication server with a few clicks (but mostly need a central server) and finally

- not allowing the user a wide range of secure ways to define manual end-to-end encryption passwords for themselfs (such as a password on an e-mail, also known in this function as "GoldBug"),
(and: GoldBug has with Instant Perfect Forward Secrecy a unique selling point No other client allows to define the password for a symmetrical end-to-end encryption within this frequency with a friend manually)

we wanted to contribute with this audit of GoldBug, and encourage people to deepen analysis in further research areas.

- As a further trend is to realize that not only the transfer of communication is crucial, but also the storage of the messages on the hard drive should always be encrypted.

- The Socialist-Millionaire-Protocol

Applikationen für verschlüsseltes E-Mail ausgelassen, da sie erstens den (hybriden und integrativen) Trend zum Präsenz-Chat inbesondere auf mobilen Plattformen nicht berücksichtigen und zweitens weil für die E-Mail-Verschlüsselung lediglich PGP prominent ist, das zugleich als kompliziert und von manchen Experten als totgeweiht gilt. Daher kann die innovative Stärke von GoldBug, sowohl E-mail als auch Chat zu verschlüsseln, bzw. das Konzept des Klienten an sich als zukunftsweisend auch in Bezug zu den E-Mail-Applikationen betrachtet werden. Verschlüsselung für E-Mail als Plugin und ohne Chat und sodann noch kompliziert und aus historischer Erfahrung nicht massentauglich - macht keinen Sinn. GoldBug ist für beides, Chat, E-Mail und die Konfiguration von Chat-Servern und p2p E-Mail-Postfächern sehr einfach zu bedienen.

- sowie Nutzer nicht in die Lage versetzen, einen eigenen Kommunikationsserver mit wenigen Mausklicken zu erstellen (sondern meist zentrale Server benötigt) und letztlich

- es dem Nutzer nicht über zahlreiche sichere Wege ermöglichen, manuelle Ende-zu-Ende-Passworte für die Verschlüsselung selbst zu definieren (wie z.B. ein Passwort auf ein E-Mail zu setzen, in dieser Funktion ebenso auch "GoldBug" genannt),
(und: GoldBug hat mit Instant Perfect Forward Secrecy ein Alleinstellungsmerkmal. Kein anderer Klient erlaubt es, das Passwort für eine symmetrische Ende-zu-Ende Verschlüsselung in dieser Frequenz manuell mit einem Freund zu definieren)

wollten wir mit diesem Audit von GoldBug einen Beitrag leisten, und anregen, Analysen auch in weiteren Forschungsgebieten zu vertiefen.

- Als ein weiterer Trend ist zu erkennen, dass nicht nur der Transfer von Kommunikation entscheidend ist, sondern auch die Speicherung der Nachrichten auf der Festplatte sollten immer verschlüsselt erfolgen.

- Das Socialist-Millionaire-Protokoll

(SMP) as a zero-knowledge process obtains an increasingly important feature for authentication.

- Multi-encryption, i.e. the conversion of ciphertext into ciphertext ... and other multiple transformations, are becoming increasingly important in the era of quantum computers, as well as

- the choice of different algorithms within an application: In addition to RSA are to implement especially NTRU and McEliece as well as ElGamal.

- Ephemeral (temporary) keys can no longer be bound only to the tranche of one online session, but should always be renewable by the user, that is, the paradigm has changed to an Instant Perfect Forward Secrecy (IPFS): Keys that often, almost every second can be changed within a session, whenever the user wants it.

- As another trend it can be seen that Crypto-Messaging shall allow, that users can define their own values for encryption. Here we speak, figuratively, of a kind of "Crypto-DNA", which have to be adjust by the user and then should bring the greatest diversity and variety to make it as difficult as possible for attackers.

- Similarly, it represents a new trend in Crypto-Messaging to ensure in a network through appropriate protocols, that meta-data - so for example, regarding who communicates with whom, who reads when which message - not apply as far as possible or at least to make is less accessible for analysts.

The in Goldbug Messenger utilized Echo protocol is thereto a new, pioneering direction with regard to the prevention of recordings of metadata in the network.

These findings out of this study are packaged as **10 Trends in Crypto-Messaging**, as the following table and info-graphic on the next page is summarizing it.

(SMP) als Zero-Knowledge-Process erhält eine zunehmend wichtigere Funktion für die Authentifizierung.

- Multi-Verschlüsselung, also die Conversion von Ciphertext in Chipertext ... und weitere mehrmalige Wandlungen, werden zunehmend wichtiger im Zeitalter von Quanten-Computern, wie auch

- die Auswahl an verschiedenen Algorithmen innerhalb einer Applikation: Neben RSA sind insbesondere NTRU und McEliece wie auch ElGamal zu implementieren.

- Ephemerale (temporäre) Schlüssel können heute nicht mehr nur an die Tranche einer Online-Sitzung gebunden sein, sondern sollten jederzeit durch den Nutzer erneuerbar sein, d.h. das Paradigma hat sich gewandelt zu einem Instant Perfect Forward Secrecy (IPFS): Schlüssel, die vielfach, fast sekündlich innerhalb einer Sitzung gewechselt werden können, wann immer der Nutzer es will.

- Als weiterer Trend kann erkannt werden, dass Crypto-Messaging es erlauben sollte, dass der Nutzer seine eigenen Werte für die Verschlüsselung definieren kann. Hier kann bildlich von einer Art "Crypto-DNA" gesprochen werden, die es durch den Nutzer zu adjustieren gilt, und sodann zu einer größtmöglichen Diversität und Vielfalt führen sollte, um es Angreifern möglichst schwer zu machen.

- Ebenso stellt es einen neuen Trend im Bereich Crypto-Messaging dar, in einem Netzwerkverbund durch entsprechende Protokolle dafür Sorge zu tragen, dass Meta-Daten, also z.B. hinsichtlich wer kommuniziert mit wem, wer liesst wann welche Nachricht, nach Möglichkeit nicht anfallen oder Analysten schwieriger zugänglich gemacht werden.

Das im GoldBug Messenger genutzte Echo-Protokoll ist dazu eine neue, wegweisende Richtung hinsichtlich der Vermeidung von Aufzeichnungen von Metadaten im Netzwerk.

Diese Erkenntnisse aus dieser Studie bündeln wir in **10 Tends im Bereich Crypto-Messaging,** wie es die folgende Tabelle und Info-Grafik auf der nächsten Seite zusammenfasst.

Table 81: 10 Trends in Crypto-Messaging

10 Trends in Crypto-Messaging	
1	Consolidation of E-Mail & Chat Encryption: Messaging for both in one application & Chat over E-Mail-Servers (POPTASTIC).
2	Storage of Data on the Hard Disk only encrypted.
3	Zero-Knowledge-Process: Socialist-Millionaire-Protocol (SMP) for Authentication.
4	Multi-Encryption is: Conversion of Ciphertext.. to Ciphertext.. to Ciphertext..
5	Easy & Decentral Server Setup: Listener-Creation for Friends & Online Key Sharing in symmetric channels (EPKS).
6	Instant Perfect Forward Secrecy: Immediate Renewal of ephemeral keys multiple times in a session.
7	Individual Choice of Crypto-DNA Values: Keysize, Salt, Hash, Cipher, Iteration Count.
8	Manual Definition of Passphrases for End-to-End Encryption (e.g. in Chat) & symmetric Passwords on E-Mails. Messenger with userdefined, manually provided end-to-end sym. encryption should be the opener at the start of any Crypto-Party!
9	Avoidance of Recording of Metadata: Multi-Graph-Theory / Echo-Theory & Network-Praxis.
10	Alternatives to RSA: McEliece, ElGamal & NTRU Algorithms also as choice in an App.

Source: Own collection

The following infographic on 10 Trends in Crypto-Messaging identified in this study is also an one-pager, which can offer a first beginning and introduction to the various features and standards of encryption at a Crypto Party as a handout to each participant - even before it comes to encryption principles, libraries or applications and the deepening of the functionality of the individual applications.

Because the trends clearly show that security may involve numerous aspects that should not only relate to a code review or downloading of a somehow trusted or brought close application.
In this sense, we wish a successful next Crypto-Party, a common testing with each other, good development posts and of course well written and detailed documentation of experieces, is this is not yet the case.

In particular, who is documenting their practical experience in the Internet or is undertaking with a friend an experiential journey, creates a difference for the better.
This therefore also applies to the field of encryption, many reviews, posts and meetings and debates remain to in the future to be expected.

Die folgende Infografik zu den in dieser Studie identifizierten 10 Trends im Bereich Crypto-Messaging ist zugleich auch ein One-Pager, der als Einstieg in die unterschiedlichen Features und Standards der Verschlüsselung auf einer Crypto-Party als Handout jedem Teilnehmer einen ersten Anfang bieten kann - noch bevor es um Verschlüsselungsprizipien, Bibliotheken oder Applikationen sowie die Vertiefung von Funktionen in den einzelnen Applikationen geht.

Denn die Trends zeigen deutlich, dass Sicherheit zahlreiche Aspekte beinhalten kann, die sich nicht nur auf ein Code-Review oder dem Download einer irgendwie vertrauten oder nahegebrachten Applikation beziehen sollten.
In diesem Sinne wünschen wir ein Gelingen der nächsten Crypto-Party, ein gemeinsames miteinander Austesten, gute Entwicklungsbeiträge und ebenso schriftliche und ausführlichere Dokumentationen der Erfahrungen, als es bislang der Fall ist.

Insbesondere wer seine Praxiserfahrung im Internet dokumentiert oder einen Freund mit auf die Erfahrungs-Reise nimmt, schafft eine Differenz hin zum Besseren.
Das gilt also auch für das Gebiet der Verschlüsselung, zu dem in Zukunft noch viele Reviews, Beiträge sowie Zusammenkünfte und Diskussionen zu erwarten bleiben.

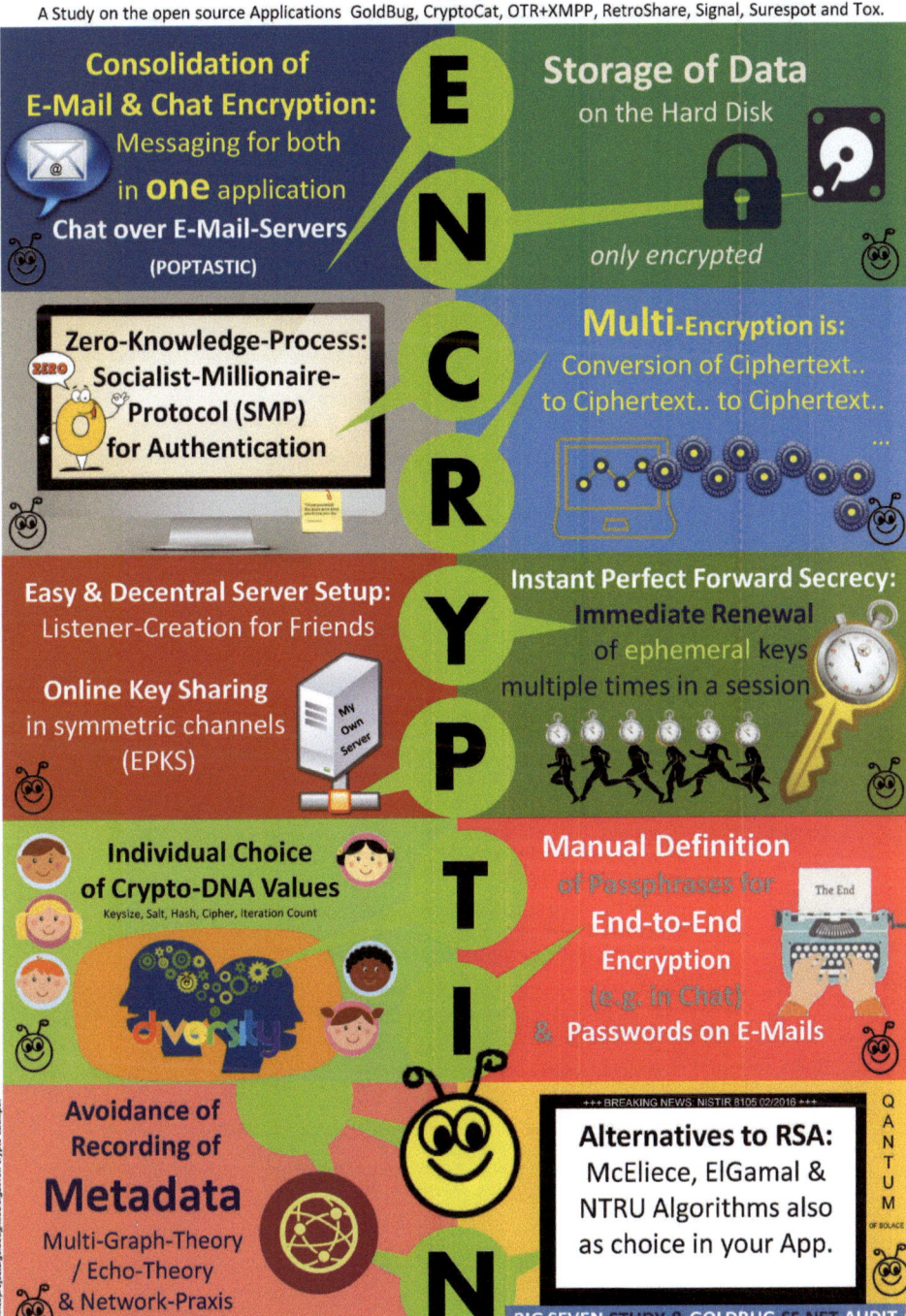

10 Trends in **Crypto Messaging**

A Study on the open source Applications GoldBug, CryptoCat, OTR+XMPP, RetroShare, Signal, Surespot and Tox.

E N C R Y P T I O N

Consolidation of E-Mail & Chat Encryption: Messaging for both in **one** application
Chat over E-Mail-Servers (POPTASTIC)

Storage of Data on the Hard Disk
only encrypted

Zero-Knowledge-Process: Socialist-Millionaire-Protocol (SMP) for Authentication
ZERO

Multi-Encryption is: Conversion of Ciphertext.. to Ciphertext.. to Ciphertext.. ...

Easy & Decentral Server Setup: Listener-Creation for Friends
Online Key Sharing in symmetric channels (EPKS)
My Own Server

Instant Perfect Forward Secrecy: Immediate Renewal of ephemeral keys multiple times in a session

Individual Choice of Crypto-DNA Values
Keysize, Salt, Hash, Cipher, Iteration Count
diversity

Manual Definition of Passphrases for **End-to-End Encryption** (e.g. in Chat) & **Passwords on E-Mails**
The End

Avoidance of Recording of Metadata Multi-Graph-Theory / Echo-Theory & Network-Praxis

+++ BREAKING NEWS: NISTIR 8105 02/2016 +++
Alternatives to RSA: McEliece, ElGamal & NTRU Algorithms also as choice in your App.

QANTUM OF SOLACE

BIG SEVEN STUDY & **GOLDBUG.SF.NET** AUDIT

Adams, D. / Maier, A.K. (2016)

5 LITERATURE

Albergotti, Reed / MacMillan, Douglas / Rusli, Evelyn M.: "Facebook's $18 Billion Deal Sets High Bar". The Wall Street Journal. pp. A1, A6, February 20, 2014, based on Press Release URL: http://newsroom.fb.com/news/2014/02/facebook-to-acquire-whatsapp/.

Amnesty International: Encryption - A Matter of Human Rights, URL: http://www.amnestyusa.org/sites/default/files/encryption_-_a_matter_of_human _rights_-_pol_40-3682-2016.pdf, Amnesty International March 2016

Arbeitskreis Vorratsdatenspeicherung (AKV), Bündnis gegen Überwachung et al.: List of Secure Instant Messengers, URL: http://wiki.vorratsdatenspeicherung.de/List_of_Secure_Instant_Messengers, Mai 2014.

Arcieri, Tony: What's wrong with in-browser cryptography? URL: https://tonyarcieri.com/whats-wrong-with-webcrypto, December 30, 2013.

Backu, Frieder: Pflicht zur Verschlüsselung?, ITRB 2003, S. 251–253.

Bader, Christoph / Bergsma, Florian / Frosch, Tilman / Holz, Thorsten / Mainka, Christian / Schwenk, Jorg /: How Secure is TextSecure (now called: Signal)? URL: https://eprint.iacr.org/2014/904.pdf, Bochum 2014.

Balducci, Alex / Devlin, Sean / Ritter, Tom: Open Crypto Audit Project –TrueCrypt Cryptographic Review, URL: https://opencryptoaudit.org/ reports/TrueCrypt_Phase _II_NCC_OCAP_final.pdf, March 13, 2015.

Baluda, Mauro et. al: Sicherheitsanalyse TrueCrypt, Fraunhofer-Institut für Sichere Informationstechnologie (SIT) für das Bundesamt für Informationssicherheit (BSI), URL: https://www.bsi.bund.de/SharedDocs/Downloads/DE/BSI/ Publikationen/ Studien/Truecrypt/Truecrypt.pdf?__blob=publicationFile&v=2, Darmstadt, 16. November 2015.

Bamford, James / Campbell, Duncan: Verbot von Verschlüsselung ist kindischer Mist, URL: http://www.heise.de/newsticker/meldung/Duncan-Campbell-Verbot-von-Verschluesselung-ist-kindischer-Mist-3010493.html, Heise 2015.

Banerjee, Sanchari: EFYTIMES News Network: 25 Best Open Source Projects Of 2014: EFYTIMES ranked GoldBug Messenger # 4 on the overall Top 25 Best Open Source Projects Of 2014, http://www.efytimes.com/e1/fullnews.asp?edid=148831.

Bäumler, Helmut: Das Recht auf Anonymität, in: Bäumler, Helmut / von Mutius, Albert (Hrsg.), Anonymität im Internet – Grundlagen, Methoden und Tools zur Realisierung eines Grundrechts, Braunschweig 2003:1–11.

Blahut, Richard E.: Cryptography and secure communication, Cambridge : Cambridge University Press, 2014.

Bleichenbacher, Daniel (1998). "Chosen Ciphertext Attacks Against Protocols Based on the RSA Encryption Standard PKCS #1" (http://www.springerlink.com/index/j5758n240017h867.pdf). CRYPTO '98. pp. 1–12.

Bolluyt, Jess: Does WhatsApp's Encryption Really Protect You?, URL: http://www.cheatsheet.com/gear-style/does-whatsapps-encryption-really-protect-you.html/?a=viewall, June 03, 2016

Borisov, Nikita / Goldberg Ian / Brewer, Eric: Off-the-record communication, or, why not to use PGP. In: WPES '04: Proceedings of the 2004 ACM workshop on privacy in the electronic society, 77–84, New York, NY, USA, 2004.

Boudot, Fabrice / Schoenmakers, Berry / Traoré, Jacques: A Fair and Efficient Solution to the Socialist Millionaires' Problem, in: Discrete Applied Mathematics, (Special issue on coding and cryptology) 111, URL: https://www.win.tue.nl/~berry/papers/dam.pdf, 2001:23–36.

BSI / Bundesamt für Sicherheit in der Informationstechnik: Empfehlungen zum Umgang mit Passwörtern, URL: https://www.bsi-fuer-buerger.de/BSIFB/DE/Empfehlungen/Passwoerter/passwoerter_node.html, o.J..

BSI / Bundesamt für Sicherheit in der Informationstechnologie: IT-Grundschutz-Kataloge. Standardwerk zur Informationssicherheit. 12. Ergänzungslieferung, Bundesamt für Sicherheit in der Informationstechnik. Bundesanzeiger, URL: https://www.bsi.bund.de/DE/Themen/ITGrundschutz/ITGrundschutzKataloge/itgrund schutzkataloge_node.html, Köln 2005ff., Juli 2011.

BSI / Bundesamt für Sicherheit in der Informationstechnologie: Studie zur Durchführung von Penetrationstests URL, https://www.bsi.bund.de/SharedDocs/Downloads/DE/BSI/Publikationen/Studien/Pen etrationstest/penetrationstest_pdf.pdf?__blob=publicationFile.

Cabinet Office: ITIL Verfahrensbibliothek – Best Management Practice Portfolio. Cabinet Office, URL: http://www.cabinetoffice.gov.uk/resource-library/best-management-practice-portfolio, 10. Juni 2011.

Cakra, Deden: Review of GoldBug Instant Messenger, Blogspot, URL http://bengkelcakra.blogspot.de/2014/12/free-download-goldbug-instant-messenger.html, 13 December 2014.

CCITT: X.800 – Security Architecture for Open Systems Interconnection For CCIT Applications – Recommendation X.800, URL: http://www.itu.int/rec/T-REC-X.800-199103-I/en, Geneva 1991.

cnlab: cnlab-security AG - Security Review Threema: Security Statement, URL: https://threema.ch/press-files/2_documentation/external_audit_security_statement.pdf, Rapperswil, November 2, 2015.

Constantinos / OsArena: GOLDBUG: MIA ΣΟΥΙΤΑ ΓΙΑ CHATING ΜΕ ΠΟΛΛΑΠΛΗ ΚΡΥΠΤΟΓΡΑΦΗΣΗ, Latest Articles, URL: http://osarena.net/logismiko/applications /goldbug-mia-souita-gia-chating-me-pollapli-kriptografisi.html, 25 March 2014.

Cramer, Ronald / Shoup, Victor: Design and Analysis of Practical Public-Key Encryption Schemes Secure against Adaptive Chosen Ciphertext Attack, URL: http://www.shoup.net/papers/cca2.pdf). SIAM Journal on Computing 33 (1): 167–226. doi:10.1137/S0097539702403773, 2004.

Dai, Yuanxi / Lee, J. / Mennink, B. / Steinberger, J.: The security of multiple encryption in the ideal cipher model, Advances in Cryptology, Springer, 2014.

Dai, Yuanxi / Steinberger, John: Tight Security Bounds for Multiple Encryption, URL: https://eprint.iacr.org/2014/096.pdf, Institute for Interdisciplinary Information Sciences, Tsinghua University, Beijing, 2014.

Dalibor: Moving to a Plugin-Free Web: Oracle deprecates the Java browser plugin, URL: https://blogs.oracle.com/java-platform-group/entry/moving_to_a_plugin_free, Oracle Product Management blog on Jan 27, 2016.

Demir, Yigit Ekim: Güvenli ve Hizli Anlik Mesajlasma Programi: GoldBug Instant Messenger programi, bu sorunun üstesinden gelmek isteyen kullanicilar için en iyi çözümlerden birisi haline geliyor ve en güvenli sekilde anlik mesajlar gönderebilmenize imkan taniyor (Translated: "Goldbug Instant Messenger Application is the best solution for users, who want to use one of the most secure ways to send instant messages"), News Portal Tamindir, URL: http://www.tamindir.com/goldbug-instant-messenger/, 2014.

Diffie, Whitfield / Hellman, Martin E.: New Directions in Cryptography, URL: https://www-ee.stanford.edu/~hellman/publications/24.pdf, IEEE TRANSACTIONS ON INFORMATION THEORY, VOL. IT-22, NO. 6, NOVEMBER 1976.

Diquet, Alban / Thiel, David / Stender Scott: Open Technology Fund – CryptoCat iOS – Application Penetration Test, Prepared for: Open Technology Fund, URL: https://isecpartners.github.io/publications/iSEC_Cryptocat_iOS.pdf, March 16, 2014.

Dolev, D.: The Byzantine generals strike again. J. Algorithms 3, 1, Jan. 1982.

Dragomir, Mircea: GoldBug Instant Messenger - Softpedia Review: This is a secure P2P Instant Messenger that ensures private communication based on a multi encryption technology constituted of several security layers, URL: http://www.softpedia.com/get/Internet/Chat/Instant-Messaging/GoldBug-Instant-Messenger.shtml, Softpedia Review, January 31st, 2016

Eckersley, Peter: Which apps and tools actually keep your messages safe? & What Makes a Good Security Audit?, URL: https://www.eff.org/deeplinks/2014/11/ what-makes-good-security-audit & https://www.eff.org/de/node/82654, November 8, 2014.

Edwards, Scott (Ed.) et al.: GoldBug – Deutsches Benutzer-Handbuch des sicheren E-Mail-Klienten und Sofort-Nachrichten-Programms GoldBug mit Multi-Verschlüsselung, URL: https://de.wikibooks.org/wiki/Goldbug, Wikibooks 2014.

El-Hadidi, M.T. / Hegazi, N.H. / Aslan, H.K.: Logic-Based Analysis of a New Hybrid Encryption Protocol for Authentication and Key Distribution, in: Global IT security / ed. by György Papp .... - Vienna, 1998. - S. 173-

Even, S. / Goldreich, O.: On the power of cascade ciphers, ACM Transactions on Computer Systems, vol. 3, pp. 108–116, 1985.

Even, S., Goldreich, O.: On the Power of Cascade Ciphers. ACM Transactions on Computer Systems 3(2), 108–116, 1985.

ExContributor: Tox is a crypto 101 mistake, URL: https://news.ycombinator.com /item?id=9036890, 2014.

Fadilpašić, Sead: WhatsApp encryption pointless, researchers claim, URL: http://www.itproportal.com/2016/05/09/whatsapp-encryption-pointless-researchers-say/, May 2016

Floemer, Andreas: WhatsApp arbeitet an verifizierter Ende-zu-Ende-Verschlüsselung, URL: http://t3n.de/news/whatsapp-verifizierte-ende-zu-ende-verschluesselung-669008/, T3n 06.01.2016.

Fujisaki, Eiichiro / Okamoto, Tatsuaki / Pointcheval, David / Stern, Jacques: RSA-OAEP Is Secure under the RSA Assumption, URL: http://www.di.ens.fr/~pointche/Documents/Papers/2004_joc.pdf). Journal of Cryptology (Springer) 17 (2): 81–104. doi:10.1007/s00145-002-0204-y, 2004.

Gaži, Peter / Maurer Ueli: Cascade Encryption Revisited, Advances in Cryptology – ASIACRYPT, URL: http://eprint.iacr.org/2009/093.pdf, pp 37-51, 2009.

Gerhards, Julia: (Grund-)Recht auf Verschlüsselung? Baden-Baden 2010.

Goldberg, Ian / Stedman, Ryan / Yoshida. Kayo: A User Study of Off-the-Record Messaging, University of Waterloo, Symposium On Usable Privacy and Security (SOUPS) 2008, July 23–25, Pittsburgh, PA, USA, URL: http://www.cypherpunks.ca/~iang/pubs/otr_userstudy.pdf, 2008.

Green, Matthew: Noodling about IM protocols, URL: http://blog.cryptographyengineering.com/2014/07/noodling-about-im-protocols.html, July 2014.

Gultsch, Daniel: XEP-OMEMO Multi-End Message and Object Encryption, URL: https://conversations.im/xeps/omemo-filetransfer.html, September 2015

Gupta, H. / Sharma, V.K.: Multiphase Encryption: A New Concept in Modern Cryptography, International Journal of Computer, URL: http://www.ijcte.org/papers/765-Z271.pdf, 2013.

Hallberg, Sven Moritz: Individuelle Schlüsselverifikation via Socialist Millionaires' Protocol, URL: https://wiki.attraktor.org/images/7/77/Smp.pdf, Juni 2008.

Harley, David: Re-Floating the Titanic: Dealing with Social Engineering Attacks EICAR Conference, URL: http://smallbluegreenblog.files.wordpress.com /2010/04/eicar98.pdf, 1998.

Hartshorn, Sarah: GoldBug Messenger among - 3 New Open Source Secure Communication Projects, URL: http://blog.vuze.com/2015/05/28/3-new-open-source-secure-communication-projects/, May 28, 2015.

Harvey, Cynthia: Datamation: 50 Noteworthy Open Source Projects – Chapter Secure Communication: GoldBug Messenger ranked on first # 1 position, URL: http://www.datamation.com/open-source/50-noteworthy-new-open-source-projects-3.html, posted September 19, 2014.

Hatch, Brian / Lee, James / Kurtz, George / McAfee / ISECOM (Hrsg.): Hacking Linux Exposed: Linux Security Secrets and Solutions. McGraw-Hill / Osborne, Emeryville, California 2003:7ff.

Henryk Piech, Piotr Borowik, Probability of retrieving information in a multi-encrypted enviroment, Scientific Research of the Institute of Mathematics and Computer Science, URL: http://amcm.pcz.pl/get.php?article=2012_2/art_12.pdf, 2012, Volume 11, Issue 2, pages 113-124.

Herzog, Pete: OSSTMM – Open Source Security Testing Methodology Manual. 3, ISECOM, New York, 1. August 2008.

Hoerl, Manual: Secure Communication Protocols, CreateSpace Independent Publishing Platform, 19. Oktober 2015.

Hofheinz, Dennis / Kiltz, Eike: Secure Hybrid Encryption from Weakened Key Encapsulation URL: http://www.iacr.org/archive/crypto2007/46220546/46220546.pdf, Advances in Cryptology -- CRYPTO 2007, Springer, pp. 553–571, 2007.

Information Technology Security Evaluation Criteria (ITSEC): Netherlands, National Comsec Agency, Hague, The Netherlands, May 1990.

INTERNATIONAL STANDARD ISO/IEC 27000: Information technology — Security techniques — Information security management systems — Overview and vocabulary, Third edition, 2014-01-15, Reference number ISO/IEC 27000:2014(E), Switzerland 2014.

Ioannidis, Ioannis / Grama, Ananth: "An Efficient Protocol for Yao's Millionaires' Problem". Center for Education and Research in Information Assurance and Security (CERIAS). Purdue University. URL: https://www.cerias.purdue.edu/assets/ pdf/bibtex_archive/2003-39.pdf, 2003.

ISECOM: Open Source Security Testing Methodology Manual (OSSTMM), Institute for Security and Open Methodologies (ISECOM), URL: http://www.isecom.org/research/osstmm.html, 2010.

ISO/IEC 27001 / Bsigroup.com: The new version of ISO/IEC 27001:2013 is here, URL: http://www.bsigroup.com/en-GB/iso-27001-information-security/ISOIEC-27001-Revision/, September 25, 2013.

ISO/IEC 27002 / ISO.org: Information technology – Security techniques – Code of practice for information security management, URL: http://www.iso.org/iso/ iso_catalogue/ catalogue_tc/catalogue_detail.htm?csnumber=50297, 2005-06-15.

Jacobs, Frederic: On SMS logins: an example from Iran, URL: https://www.fredericjacobs.com/blog/2016/01/14/sms-login/, Jan 14, 2016.

Jakobsen, Jakob Bjerre / Olrandi Claudio: A practical cryptoanalysis of the Telegram messaging protocol, Aarhus University September 2015.

Jakobsson, Markus / Yung, Moti: "Proving without knowing: On oblivious, agnostic and blindfolded provers.". Advances in Cryptology – CRYPTO '96, volume 1109 of Lecture Notes in Computer Science. URL: http://cseweb.ucsd.edu/users/markus/proving.ps, Berlin 1996:186–200. Doi:10.1007/3-540-68697-5_15.

Johnston, Erik: Matrix - An open standard for decentralised persistent communication, URL: http://matrix.org/ & https://github.com/matrix-org/synapse/commit/ 4f475c76977 22e946e39e 42f38f3dd03a95d8765, fist Commit on Aug 12, 2014

Joos, Thomas: Sicheres Messaging im Web, URL: http://www.pcwelt.de/ratgeber/ Tor__I2p__Gnunet__RetroShare__Freenet__GoldBug__Spurlos_im_Web-Anonymisierungsnetzwerke-8921663.html, PCWelt Magazin, 01. Oktober 2014.

Kannenberg, Axel: Facebooks Messenger hat jetzt 800 Millionen Nutzer - Whatsapp 900 Millionen, http://www.heise.de/newsticker/meldung/Facebooks-Messenger-hat-jetzt-800-Millionen-Nutzer-3065800.html URL: Heise 07.01.2016.

King Ho, Anthony: Hybrid cryptosystem using symmetric algorithms and public-key algorithms, Thesis/dissertation, Lamar University, 1999.

Knight Foundation: Knight News Challenge awards $3.4 million for ideas to strengthen the Internet, URL: http://www.knightfoundation.org/press-room/press-release/knight-news-challenge-awards-34-million-ideas-stre/Jun 23, 2014.

Koenig, Retro / Haenni, Rolf: How to Store some Secrets, IACR Cryptology ePrint Archive 2012: 375 (2012)

Könau, Steffen: Whatsapp Messenger ist nach geltendem Recht illegal, URL: http://www.naumburger-tageblatt.de/ratgeber/multimedia/whatsapp-messenger-ist-nach-geltendem-recht-illegal-24060664, 2016

Kumar, Arun: Why Centralized Internet won over the Decentralized Internet model?, URL: http://www.thewindowsclub.com/centralized-vs-decentralized-internet, 2016

Lamport, L. / Shostak, R. / Pease, M.: The Byzantine Generals Problem. In: ACM Trans. Programming Languages and Systems. 4, Nr. 3, Juli 1982:382–401.

Levine, Yasha: Almost Everyone Involved in Developing Tor was (or is) Funded by the US Government, URL: https://pando.com/2014/07/16/tor-spooks/, written on July 16, 2014.

Levine, Yasha: How leading Tor developers and advocates tried to smear me after I reported their US Government ties, URL: https://pando.com/2014/11/14/tor-smear/ , written on November 14, 2014.

Lindner, Mirko: Poptastic: Verschlüsselter Chat über POP3 mit dem GoldBug Messenger, Pro-Linux, URL: http://www.pro-linux.de/news/1/21822/poptastic-verschluesselter-chat-ueber-pop3.html, 9. Dezember 2014.

Marcus, David: "Wir haben keine Pläne, die beiden Dienste zusammenzuführen." - Facebook und WhatsApp sollen voneinander unabhängig bleiben, URL: http://www.heise.de/newsticker/meldung/Facebook-und-WhatsApp-sollen-voneinander-unabhaengig-bleiben-2550806.html, via Heise, Andrej Sokolow, dpa 17.02.2015.

Matejka, Petr: Master thesis on Turtle, URL: http://turtle-p2p.sourceforge.net/thesis2.pdf, Prague 2004.

Maurer, M / Massey, J.L.: Cascade ciphers - The importance of being first, Journal of Cryptology, vol. 6, no. 1, pp. 55–61, 1993.

Maurer, U.M. / Massey, J.L.: Cascade ciphers, Journal of Cryptology 6(1), 55–61, 1993.

McClure, Stuart / Scambray, Joel / Kurtz, George / McAfee (Hrsg.): Hacking Exposed: Network Security Secrets & Solutions, McGraw-Hill Professional, Emeryville, California 2005, ISBN 0-07-226081-5.

Menezes, Alfred J. / van Oorschot, Paul C. / Vanstone, Scott A.: Handbook of Applied Cryptography, URL: http://citeseer.ist.psu.edu/viewdoc/download?doi=10.1.1.99.2838&rep=rep1&type=pdf, Massachusetts Institute of Technology, June 1996.

Mennink, B. / Preneel, B.: Triple and Quadruple Encryption: Bridging the Gaps - IACR Cryptology ePrint Archive, eprint.iacr.org, URL: http://eprint.iacr.org/2014/016.pdf, 2014.

Messerer, Thomas / et alt. / Fraunhofer ESK: Einsatz von Skype im Unternehmen – Chancen und Risiken, Fraunhofer-Institut für Eingebettete Systeme und Kommunikationstechnik ESK, URLs: http://www.esk.fraunhofer.de/de/publikationen/studien/sykpe2.html & http://www.esk.fraunhofer.de/content/dam/esk/de/documents/SkypeImUnternehmen

---

_final.pdf & http://www.heise.de/ix/meldung/Fraunhofer-ESK-Skype-ist-Sicherheitsrisiko-fuer-Firmen-3082090.html München 2016.

Meyer zu Bergsten, Wolfgang / Korthaus, René / Somorovsky, Juraj / Mainka, Christian / Schwenk, Jörg: Quellcode-basierte Untersuchung von kryptographisch relevanten Aspekten der OpenSSL-Bibliothek, Arbeitspaket 2: Random Number Generator, Eine Studie im Auftrag des Bundesamtes für Sicherheit in der Informationstechnik, URL: https://www.bsi.bund.de/DE/Publikationen/Studien/OpenSSL-Bibliothek/opensslbibliothek.html, Projekt 154, Version 1.2.1 / 2015-11-03,

Murdoch, Stephen (2016): Insecure by design: protocols for encrypted phone calls, URL: https://www.benthamsgaze.org/2016/01/19/insecure-by-design-protocols-for-encrypted-phone-calls/, & http://www.heise.de/newsticker/meldung/MIKEY-SAKKE-Unsichere-VoIP-Verschluesselung-a-la-GCHQ-3081912.html, Bentham's Gaze 2016-01-20.

Nakashima, Ellen / Peterson, Andrea: Not to force firms to decrypt data, Washington Post, October 8, 2015 .

NIST / Chen, Lily / Jordan, Stephen / Liu, Yi-Kai / Moody, Dustin / Peralta, Rene / Perlner, Ray / Smith-Tone, Daniel: NISTIR 8105, DRAFT, Report on Post-Quantum Cryptography, URL: http://csrc.nist.gov/publications/drafts/nistir-8105/nistir_8105_draft.pdf, National Institute of Standards and Technology. February 2016.

NZZ / Neue Zürcher Zeitung: Teenager will privates E-Mail-Konto von CIA-Chef geknackt haben, URL: http://www.nzz.ch/digital/teenager-will-privates-e-mail-konto-von-cia-chef-geknackt-haben-ld.2627, 20. Oktober 2015.

O.A. / Stiftung Zukunft: Antrag auf Förderung des Projektes "Spot-On: Web-Suche in einem Netzwerk dezentraler URL-Datenbanken" mit 30 zu fördernden Abschlussarbeiten an Hochschulen und Einbezug von 30 Auszubildenden durch die Stiftung Zukunft, URL: https://github.com/textbrowser/spot-on/blob/master/branches/trunk/Papers/DATEV .pdf, Nürnberg, 29.06.2015.

Öberg, Jonas: Is this the end of decentralisation? URL: http://blog.jonasoberg.net/is-this-the-end-of-decentralisation-2/, 2016

Oppliger, Rolf: Secure Messaging on the Internet, Boston 2014.

Perrin, Trevor: Axolotl ratchet, URL: https://github.com/trevp/axolotl/wiki, retrieved 2014-03-14.

Perrin, Trevor: noise specifications - First commit on 4 Aug 2014, URL: https://github.com/noiseprotocol/noise_spec/commit/ c627f8056ffb9c7695d3bc7bafea8616749b073f, August 4, 2014 and Domain from January 4, 2016

Persiclietti, Edoardo: Secure and Anonymous Hybrid Encryption from Coding Theory, in: Gaborit, Philippe (Hrsg.): Post-quantum cryptography : 5th international workshop / PQCrypto 2013, Limoges, France, June 4 - 7, 2013:174ff

Popescu, Bogdan C. / Crispo, Bruno / Tanenbaum, Andrew S.: Safe and Private Data Sharing with Turtle: Friends Team-Up and Beat the System, URL: http://turtle-p2p.sourceforge.net/turtleinitial.pdf, 2004.

Positive Technologies: Whatsapp encryption rendered ineffective by SS7 Vulnerabilities, URL: https://www.ptsecurity.com/wwa/news/57894/, May 06 2016

Ptacek, Thomas: Javascript Cryptography Considered Harmful, URL: https://www.nccgroup.trust/us/about-us/newsroom-and-events/blog/2011/august/javascript-cryptography-considered-harmful/, 29 August 2011.

Quarkslab SAS: ChatSecure security assessment, URL: http://blog.quarkslab.com/resources/2015-06-25_chatsecure/14-03-022_ChatSecure-sec-assessment.pdf, 2015.

Roberts, D.W.: Evaluation criteria for it security. Computer Security and Industrial Cryptography Bd. 741. Springer Berlin Heidelberg, 1993:149-161.

Rogers, Everett: Diffusion of Innovations, 5th Edition, Simon and Schuster, 2003.

Saint-Andre, Peter: A Public Statement Regarding Ubiquitous Encryption on the XMPP Network, Version: 0.5, URL: https://github.com/stpeter/manifesto/blob/master/manifesto.txt, Guthub 2014-03-21.

Santos, Javier / Siddiqui, Aamir: WhatsApp to Begin Data Sharing With Facebook, URL: http://www.xda-developers.com/xda-external-link/whatsapp-to-begin-data-sharing-with-facebook/, 22.01.2016.

Scherschel, Fabian A. Keeping Tabs on WhatsApp's Encryption, URL: http://www.heise.de/ct/artikel/Keeping-Tabs-on-WhatsApp-s-Encryption-2630361.html, Heise 30.04.2015.

Scherschel, Fabian: Enigmail verschickte manche Mails unverschlüsselt, URL: http://heise.de/-2389248, Heise 10.09.2014.

Scherschel, Fabian: Test: Hinter den Kulissen der WhatsApp-Verschlüsselung, URL: http://www.heise.de/security/artikel/Test-Hinter-den-Kulissen-der-WhatsApp-Verschluesselung-3165567.html, 08.04.2016

Schmaus, Florian: OX (OpenPGP for XMPP) - A new OpenPGP XEP, URL: http://mail.jabber.org/pipermail/standards/2016-January/030755.html, January 06, 2016.

Schmidt, Jürgen: Lasst PGP sterben, http://www.heise.de/ct/ausgabe/2015-6-Editorial-Lasst-PGP-sterben-2551008.html, Magazin Ct, 20.02.2015.

Schneier, Bruce / Seidel, Kathleen / Vijayakumar, Saranya: GOLDBUG Multi-Encrypting Messenger – in: A Worldwide Survey of Encryption Products, URL: https://www.schneier.com/cryptography/paperfiles/worldwide-survey-of-encryption-products.pdf, February 11, 2016 Version 1.0.

Security Blog: Secure chat communications suite GoldBug. Security Blog, URL: http://www.hacker10.com/other-computing/secure-chat-communications-suite-goldbug/, 25. März 2014.

Seddik, Hassene: Combined Multi-encryption Techniques for Text Securing Using Block Cipher and Stream Cipher Crypto-systems, URL: http://dx.doi.org/10.3991/ijes.v1i1.2901, University of Tunis, Tunis, Tunisia, iJES – Volume 1, Issue 1, August 2013, p. 53ff

Setyaningsih, Emy / Iswahyudi, Catur / Widyastuti, Naniek: Image Encryption on Mobile Phone using Super Encryption Algorithm, URL: http://www.journal.uad.ac.id/index.php/TELKOMNIKA/article/view/871/673.

Shannon, C.E.: Communication Theory of Secrecy Systems. Bell System Technical Journal. 28:656-715, 1949.

Shirey, R.: RFC 4949, Internet Security Glossary, Version 2. URL: https://tools.ietf.org/html/rfc4949, IETF 1987.

Simonite, Tom: Verschlüsselung als Menschenrechtsthema, URL: http://www.heise.de/tr/artikel/Verschluesselung-als-Menschenrechtsthema-2909776.html, Technology Review, 09.22.2015

Spot-On (2014): Documentation of the Spot-On-Application, URL: https://github.com/textbrowser/spot-on/tree/master/branches/trunk/Documentation, Github 2014.

Spot-On (2011): Documentation of the Spot-On-Application, URL: https://sourceforge.net/p/spot-on/code/HEAD/tree/, under this URL since 06/2013, Sourceforge, including the Spot-On: Documentation of the project draft paper of the pre-research project since 2010, Project Ne.R.D.D., Registered 2010-06-27, URL: https://sourceforge.net/projects/nerdd/ has evolved into Spot-On. Please see http://spot-on.sf.net and URL: https://github.com/textbrowser/spot-on/blob/master/branches/Documentation/RELEASE-NOTES.archived, 08.08.2011.

Stahl, Leslie: 60 Minutes - Preview on encryption, URL: https://2paragraphs.com/2016/03/telegram-texting-app-used-by-isis-made-in-russia/, 03/2016.

Stiftung Zukunft: Antrag auf Förderung des Projektes "Spot-On: Web-Suche in einem Netzwerk dezentraler URL-Datenbanken" mit 30 zu fördernden Abschlussarbeiten an Hochschulen und Einbezug von 30 Auszubildenden aus Mitgliedsorganisationen durch die Stiftung Zukunft, Nürnberg, 29.06.2015

Sun, Hung-Min / Wu, Mu-En / Ting, Wei-Chi / Hinek, M. J.: Dual RSA and Its Security Analysis, IEEE Transactions on Information Theory, v53 n8 (200708): 2922-2933.

Teicke Friedhelm: Mein Sohn bei Whatsapp, dem Messenger-Dienst, der als Super-Wanze galt, URL: http://www.zitty.de/mein-sohn-bei-whatsapp/, 2016

Thomas, Steve: "DecryptoCat". URL: http://tobtu.com/decryptocat.php, Retrieved 2013-07-10.

Van den Hooff, Jelle / Lazar, David / Zaharia, Matei / Zeldovich, Nickolai: Vuvuzela - Scalable Private Messaging Resistant to Traffic Analysis, https://davidlazar.org/papers/vuvuzela.pdf, MIT CSAIL / SOSP'15, Oct. 4–7, 2015

Vaughan-Nichols, Steven J.: How to recover from Heartbleed, ZDNet, URL: http://www.zdnet.com/how-to-recover-from-heartbleed-7000028253, April 9, 2014.

Vervier, Markus: X41-2016-001: Memory Corruption Vulnerability in "libotr", URL: https://www.x41-dsec.de/lab/advisories/x41-2016-001-libotr/, 01/2016

Völker, Jörg: BS 7799 – Von „Best Practice" zum Standard, in: Datenschutz und Datensicherheit (DuD) (2004), URL: http://www.secorvo.de/publikationen/bs7799-voelker-2004.pdf, Nr. 28:102-108, 2004.

Wales, Jimmy: Encryption Ban Like Banning Maths - via: Morris, Gemma: Wiki Boss: Encryption Ban Like Banning Maths, URL: http://news.sky.com/story/1565811/wiki-boss-encryption-ban-like-banning-maths, Sky News' tech show Swipe at IP EXPO Europe, 08 October 2015.

Weller, Jan: Testbericht zu GoldBug für Freeware, Freeware-Blog, URL: https://www.freeware.de/download/goldbug/, 2013.

Weßelmann, Bettina: Maßnahmen gegen Social Engineering: Training muss Awareness-Maßnahmen ergänzen. In: Datenschutz und Datensicherheit. DuD. 9, 2008:601–604.

WhatsApp: Encryption   Overview   -   Technical   white   paper,   URL: https://www.whatsapp.com/security/WhatsApp-Security-Whitepaper.pdf,   April   4, 2016

Wikipedia: Meet-in-the-middle   attack,   URL: https://en.wikipedia.org/wiki/Meet-in-the-middle_attack, Wikipedia, 17 April 2016

Wilcox,   Nathan   et   alt.:   Report   of   Security   Audit   of   Cryptocat,   URL: https://leastauthority.com/static/publications/LeastAuthority-Cryptocat-audit-report.pdf, 2013-11-06.

Wired: Teen   Who   Hacked   CIA   Director's   Email   Tells   How   He   Did   It,   URL: http://www.wired.com/2015/10/hacker-who-broke-into-cia-director-john-brennan-email-tells-how-he-did-it/, 19. Oktober 2015 („Wie der Datendieb verlauten ließ, will er die Zugangsdaten zu Brennans E-Mail-Konto mittels Social Engineering erhalten haben: Er hat offenbar Mitarbeiter von Verizon dazu gebracht, Daten von Brennan herauszugeben").

Yao,   Andrew: How   to   generate   and   exchange   secrets". URL: http://www.csee.wvu.edu/~xinl/library/papers/comp/Yao1986.pdf,   Proc.   27th IEEE Symposium on Foundations of Computer Science (FOCS '86). Pp. 162–167. Doi:10.1109/SFCS.1986.25, 1986.

Yao, Andrew: Protocols for secure communications", Proc. 23rd IEEE Symposium on Foundations of   Computer   Science   (FOCS   '82),   URL   http://research.cs.wisc.edu/areas/ sec/yao1982-ocr.pdf, 1982:160–164, doi:10.1109/SFCS.1982.88.

You   broke   the   internet   (YBTI):   Next   generation   secure   communication,   URL: http://youbroketheinternet.org/secure-email, June 2014, zurückgehend auf einen ersten Entwurf vom Feb 3, 2014 unter der URL: https://github.com/OpenTechFund/ secure-email/commits/master/README.md?page=2, 2014.

Zhong, Peng: Prism-Break (PB) Portal, URL: https://prism-break.org/, since 2013.

6   Glossary: Vocabulary, Terms and Definitions

This glossary defines the most common words and terms used in this review/audit and as well vocabulary mostly used within these cryptography related contexts.

Access Controls: means to ensure that access to assets is authorized and restricted based on business and security requirements. Related to authorization of users, and assessment of rights.

AES: The Advanced Encryption Standard (AES), also known as Rijndael (its original name), is a specification for the encryption of electronic data established by the U.S. National Institute of Standards and Technology (NIST) in 2001. AES is based on the Rijndael cipher developed by two Belgian cryptographers, Joan Daemen and Vincent Rijmen, who submitted a proposal to NIST during the AES selection process.

AE-Token: the AE-Roken is a cryptographic token used to deploy the adaptive echo (AE) modus. It is a kind of password or string, which is entered into the node, to avoid messages to be sent to nodes, without the AE-Token. AE-Tokens can help to create a self-learning, adaptive network. The token must contain at least mprov-six characters.

Algorithm: In mathematics and computer science, an algorithm is a self-contained step-by-step set of operations to be performed. Algorithms exist that perform calculation, data processing, and automated reasoning.

Attack: attempt to destroy, expose, alter, disable, steal or gain unauthorized access to or make unauthorized use of an asset

Audit: systematic, independent and documented process for obtaining audit evidence and evaluating it objectively to determine the extent to which the audit criteria are fulfilled. An audit can be an internal audit (first party) or an external audit (second party or third party), and it can be a combined audit (combining two or more disciplines).

Auditing and Logging: Related to auditing of actions, or logging of problems

Authentication: provision of assurance that a claimed characteristic of an entity is correct

Authentication: Related to the identification of users

Availability: property of being accessible and usable upon demand by an authorized entity

Bluetooth: Bluetooth is a wireless technology standard for exchanging data over short distances (using short-wavelength UHF radio waves in the ISM band from 2.4 to 2.485 GHz) from fixed and mobile devices, and building personal area networks (PANs).

Buzz: Buzz is the name of the libspoton to provide echoed IRC (e*IRC). So Buzz is another word for IRC, respective e*IRC, used by the library.

C/O (care of)-Funktion: "Care of", used to address a letter when the letter must pass through an intermediary (also written c/o). Neighbors are often asked to care of your postal letters, in case you live with them in one house or have a relationship to them. As well parcel stations, letter boxes or just persons e.g. at you home or in the neighborhood provide a local delay of your envelopes and parcels, in case you are at work and want to receive the parcel or letter in the evening. The included Email Function of GoldBug provides such a feature.

Calling: A "Call" transfers over a public/private key encrypted environment a symmetric key (e.g. AES). It is a password for the session talk, only the two participants know. With one click you can instantly renew the end-to-end encryption password for your talk. It is also possible to manually define the end-to-end encrypted password (manually defined Calling). There are five further different ways to call: Asymmetric Calling, Forward Secrecy Calling, Symmetric Calling, SMP-Calling and 2-Way-Calling. The term of a "Call" in Cryptograophy has been introduced by Spot-on, the integrated library and kernel of the GoldBug Applikation, and refers to sending a new end-to-end encryption password to the other participant.

CBC: Cipher Block Chaining – Ehrsam, Meyer, Smith and Tuchman invented the Cipher Block Chaining (CBC) mode of operation in 1976. In CBC mode, each block of plaintext is XORed with the previous ciphertext block before being encrypted. This way, each ciphertext block depends on all plaintext blocks processed up to that point.

Cipher: In cryptography, a cipher (or mprov) is an algorithm for performing encryption or decryption— a series of well-defined steps that can be followed as a procedure. An alternative, less common term is encipherment. To encipher or encode is to convert information into cipher or code. In common parlance, 'cipher' is synonymous with 'code'. Codes generally substitute different length strings of characters in the output, while ciphers generally substitute the same number of characters as are input.

Confidentiality: property that information is not made available or disclosed to unauthorized individuals, entities, or processes

Configuration: Related to security configurations of servers, devices, or software

Congestion Control: Congestion control concerns controlling traffic entry into a telecommunications network, so as to avoid congestive collapse by attempting to avoid oversubscription of any of the processing or link capabilities of the intermediate nodes and networks and taking resource reducing steps, such as reducing the rate of sending packets.

Continuous improvement: recurring activity to enhance performance

Corrective action: action to eliminate the cause of a nonconformity and to prevent recurrence

Cryptogramm: Verbal arithmetic, also known as alphametics, cryptarithmetic, crypt-arithmetic, cryptarithm, mprovemen or word addition, is a type of mathematical game consisting of a mathematical equation among unknown numbers, whose digits are represented by letters. The goal is to identify the value of each letter. The name can be extended to puzzles that use non-alphabetic symbols instead of letters.

Cryptography: Related to mathematical protections for data

Data Exposure: Related to unintended exposure of sensitive information

Data Validation: Related to improper reliance on the structure or values of data

Decentralized computing: Decentralized computing is the allocation of resources, both hardware and software, to each individual workstation, or office location. Decentral means, there is no central server nor a webinterface, you can lof into a service. A client needs to be installed and adjusted locally on your device. Another term is: Distributed computing. Distributed computing is a field of computer science that studies distributed systems. A distributed system is a software system in which components located on networked computers communicate and coordinate their actions by passing messages. Based on a "grid model" a peer-to-peer system, or P2P system, is a collection of applications run on several local computers, which connect remotely to each other to complete a function or a task. There is no main operating system to which satellite systems are subordinate. This approach to software development (and distribution) affords developers great savings, as they don't have to create a central control point. An example application is LAN messaging which allows users to communicate without a central server.

Documented information: information required to be controlled and maintained by an organization and the medium on which it is contained. Note: Documented information can be in any format and media and from any source.

Dooble: Dooble is a free and open source Web browser. Dooble was created to improve privacy. Currently, Dooble is available for FreeBSD, Linux, OS X, OS/2, and Windows. Dooble uses Qt for its user interface and abstraction from the operating system and processor architecture. As a result, Dooble should be portable to any system that supports OpenSSL, POSIX threads, Qt, SQLite, and other libraries.

Echo Accounts: Echo Accounts define an authorization scheme for the access to neighbor nodes respective to the listener of a server. At the same time they can form a Web-of-Trust. One-Time-Accounts regulate the assignment of an access, which can be used on time.

Echo, adaptive (AE): The Adaptive Echo does not send in terms of the normal Echo a message-packet to each connected node, instead, for the overgiving of a message a cryptographic token is needed. The Echo-Protocol is equipped for the Adaptive Echo Modus with a routing information. Only nodes, which have a certain cryptographic token available, get the message forwarded.

Echo, half: If you use the modus "half echo", then your message is not shared with other, third participants (Model: A -> B -> C) . Only direct connections are used (Model A -> B). It requires only one direct connection to one friend. With the modus "full echo" your message is forwarded from friend to friend and so on, until the recipient could decrypt the envelope and read the message.

Echo Protocol: The echo protocol means from an operational view: you send only encrypted messages, but you send your to-be-send-message to all of your connected friends. They do the same. You maintain your own network, everyone has every message and you try to decrypt every message. In case you can read and unwrap it, it is a message for you. Otherwise you share the message with all your friends and the message remains encrypted. Echo is very simple and the principle is over 30 years old – nothing new. As echo uses HTTP as a protocol, there is no forwarding or routing of messages: no IPs are forwarded, e.g. like it is if you send your message e.g. from your home laptop to your webserver. The process starts at each destination new – as you define it. The echo protocol provided by spot-on has nothing to do with RFC 862. A new echo protocol RFC has to be written or re-newed and extended – with or without that RFC-Number it refers to a p2p network.

ECHO-Grid: The Echo-Grid is a graphical representation of a template for the echo-protocol, do be able to illustrate different nodes and communicational relations in a graphic and within graph-theory. For that the letters for the word ECHO, respective the both characters AE are drawn and connected on a base-line. All angle corners of each letter further represent potential nodes in communicational networks, which can be per letter be consecutively numbered, example: E1 ... E1 for the six nodes of the letter E. Then it is possible to talk about the communicational paths of drawn users from E to O.

ElGamal: In cryptography, the ElGamal encryption system is an asymmetric key encryption algorithm for public-key cryptography which is based on the Diffie–Hellman key exchange. It was described by Taher Elgamal in 1985. ElGamal encryption is used in the free GNU Privacy Guard software, recent versions of PGP, and other cryptosystems.

E-Mail Institution: An E-Mail-institution describes an E-Mail-Postbox within the p2p network of the Echo protocol. Per definition of an address-like Description for the institution, E-Mails of users within the p2p network can temporarily be stored within one other node. As well it is possible, to send E-Mail to friends, which are currently offline. Institutions describe a standard, how to configure an E-Mail-Postbox within a p2p network – like today POP3 and IMAP allow to provide a Mailbox. The Mailbox of the E-Mail-Institution is inserted by a Magnet-URI-Link within the client, which want to use the Postbox. At the E-Mail-Institution only the public E-Mail-Encryption-Key of the postbox-users has to be entered.

Encryption, asymmetric: In cryptography, encryption is the process of encoding messages or information in such a way that only authorized parties can read it. In public-key encryption schemes, the encryption key is published for anyone to use and encrypt messages. However, only the receiving party has access to the decryption key that enables messages to be read. Public-key encryption was first described in a secret document in

1973; before then all encryption schemes were symmetric-key (also called private-key).

Encryption, clientside: Client-side encryption is the cryptographic technique of encrypting data before it is transmitted to a server in a computer network. Usually, encryption is performed with a key that is not known to the server. Consequently, the service provider is unable to decrypt the hosted data. In order to access the data, it must always be decrypted by the client. Client-side encryption allows for the creation of zeroknowledge applications whose providers cannot access the data its users have stored, thus offering a high level of privacy.

Encryption, Multi-/Hybrid: A hybrid cryptosystem is one which combines the convenience of a public-key cryptosystem with the efficiency of a symmetric-key cryptosystem. A hybrid cryptosystem can be constructed using any two separate cryptosystems: first, a key encapsulation scheme, which is a public-key cryptosystem, and second a data encapsulation scheme, which is a symmetric-key cryptosystem. Perhaps the most commonly used hybrid cryptosystems are the OpenPGP (RFC 4880) file format and the PKCS #7 (RFC 2315) file format, both used by many different systems. Multiple encryption is the process of encrypting an already encrypted message one or more times, either using the same or a different algorithm. Multiple encryption (Cascade Ciphers) reduces the consequences in the case that our favorite cipher is already broken and is continuously exposing our data without our knowledge. When a cipher is broken (something we will not know), the use of other ciphers may represent the only security in the system. Since we cannot scientifically prove that any particular cipher is strong, the question is not whether subsequent ciphers are strong, but instead, what would make us believe that any particular cipher is so strong as to need no added protection. Folk Theorem: A cascade of ciphers is at least as at least as difficult to break as any of its component ciphers. When a cipher is broken (something we will not know), the use of other ciphers may represent the only security in the system. Since we cannot scientifically prove that any particular cipher is strong, the question is not whether subsequent ciphers are strong, but instead, what would make us believe that any particular cipher is so strong as to need no added protection.

Encryption, symmetric: Symmetric-key algorithms are algorithms for cryptography that use the same cryptographic keys for both encryption of plaintext and decryption of ciphertext. The keys may be identical or there may be a simple transformation to go between the two keys. The keys, in practice, represent a shared secret between two or more parties that can be used to maintain a private information link. This requirement that both parties have access to the secret key is one of the main drawbacks of symmetric key encryption, in comparison to public-key encryption (asymmetric encryption).

Encrypt-then-MAC (ETM): The plaintext is first encrypted, then a MAC is produced based on the resulting ciphertext. The ciphertext and its MAC are sent together. Used in, e.g., Ipsec. The standard method according to ISO/IEC 19772:2009. This is the only method which can reach the highest definition of security in authenticated encryption, but this can only be achieved when the MAC used is "Strongly Unforgeable". In November 2014, TLS and DTLS extension for EtM has been published as RFC 7366.

End-to-end: The end-to-end principle is a classic design principle of computer networking,[nb 1] first explicitly articulated in a 1981 conference paper by Saltzer, Reed, and Clark.

The end-to-end principle states that application-specific functions ought to reside in the end hosts of a network rather than in intermediary nodes – provided they can be implemented "completely and correctly" in the end hosts. In debates about network neutrality, a common interpretation of the end-to-end principle is that it implies a neutral or "dumb" network. End-to-end encryption (E2EE) is an uninterrupted protection of the confidentiality and integrity of transmitted data by encoding it at its starting point and decoding it at its destination. It involves encrypting clear (red) data at source with knowledge of the intended recipient, allowing the encrypted (black) data to travel safely through vulnerable channels (e.g. public networks) to its recipient where it can be decrypted (assuming the destination shares the necessary key-variables and algorithms). An end-to-end encryption is often reached by providing an encryption with the AES Passphrase.

EPKS (Echo Public Key Share): Echo Public Key Share (EPKS) is a function implemented in GoldBug to share public encryption keys over the Echo network. This allows a group to share keys over secure channels so that a classical key server it not needed. It is a way of key exchange to a group or one individual user. The key exchange (also known as "key establishment") is any method in cryptography by which cryptographic keys are exchanged between users, allowing use of a cryptographic algorithm. If sender and receiver wish to exchange encrypted messages, each must be equipped to encrypt messages to be sent and decrypt messages received. The nature of the equipping they require depends on the encryption technique they might use. If they use a code, both will require a copy of the same codebook. If they use a cipher, they will need appropriate keys. If the cipher is a symmetric key cipher, both will need a copy of the same key. If an asymmetric key cipher with the public/private key property, both will need the other's public key. The key exchange problem is how to exchange whatever keys or other information are needed so that no one else can obtain a copy. Historically, this required trusted couriers, diplomatic bags, or some other secure channel. With the advent of public key / private key cipher algorithms, the encrypting key (aka public key) could be made public, since (at least for high quality algorithms) no one without the decrypting key (aka, the private key) could decrypt the message. Diffie–Hellman key exchange: In 1976, Whitfield Diffie and Martin Hellman published a cryptographic protocol, (Diffie–Hellman key exchange), which allows users to establish 'secure channels' on which to exchange keys, even if an Opponent is monitoring that communication channel. However, D–H key exchange did not address the problem of being sure of the actual identity of the person (or 'entity').

File Encryption Tool: The File Encryption Tool of GoldBug has the function to encrypt and decrypt files on the hard disk. Here as well many values for the encryption details can be set individually. The tool is useful, in case files have to be sent - either over encrypted or unencrypted connections. As well for the storage of files, either on your local hard disc or as well remote in the cloud, this tool is very helpful, to secure own data.

Forward Secrecy, Instant Perfect (IPFS): While Perfect Forward Secrecy, often also called only Forward Secrecy, describes within many applicationa and as well from a conceptional approach the transmission of ephemeral – this means temporary - keys, it is implicit connected, that this is proceeded one time per online session. With GoldBug and the underlying architecture of the Spot-On Kernel a new paradigm has been implemented. The end-to-end-encryption with temporary keys can be changed at any time, this means

also per any second. This describes the term of Instant Perfect Forward Secrecy (IPFS). Via a so-called "Call" the end-to-end-encryption can be renewed. Instantly. Also the term of a "call" for the transmission of a to-be-created or to-be-renewed end-to-end-encryption has been introduced by Spot-on into cryptography.

Forward Secrecy, Pure (PURE FS): Pure Forward Secrecy refers to a communication in the E-Mail function of GoldBug, within which the information is not sent over asymmetrical keys, but over temporary, ephemeral keys, which generate a symmetric encryption. The ephemeral keys for Pure Forward Secrecy are exchanged over asymmetric keys, but then the message is sent exclusively over temporary symmetric key. Compare in a different approach of Instant Perfect Forward Secrecy, that the messages is encrypted and transferred with both, a symmetric key and also with a asymmetric key within the format of the Echo-protocol.

Forward Secrecy: In cryptography, forward secrecy (FS; also known as perfect forward secrecy) is a property of secure communication protocols: a secure communication protocol is said to have forward secrecy if compromise of long-term keys does not compromise past session keys.[2] FS protects past sessions against future compromises of secret keys or passwords. If forward secrecy is utilized, encrypted communications recorded in the past cannot be retrieved and decrypted should long-term secret keys or passwords be compromised in the future.

Friend-to-Friend (F2F): A friend-to-friend (or F2F) computer network is a type of peer-to-peer network in which users only make direct connections with people they know. Passwords or digital signatures can be used for authentication. Unlike other kinds of private P2P, users in a friend-to-friend network cannot find out who else is participating beyond their own circle of friends, so F2F networks can grow in size without compromising their users' anonymity.

Galois/Counter Mode (GCM)-Algorithm: Galois/Counter Mode (GCM) is a mode of operation for symmetric key cryptographic block ciphers that has been widely adopted because of its efficiency and performance. GCM throughput rates for state of the art, high speed communication channels can be achieved with reasonable hardware resources.

Gemini: The Gemini is a feature in GoldBug Secure Instant Messenger to add another security layer to the chatroom with an AES Key for end-to-end encryption.

GoldBug (Application): The GoldBug Messenger and E-Mail-Client is a user interface, which offers for the kernel and the application Spot-On an alternative to the originally offered user interface of Spot-on, which contains many options. The GoldBug Graphical User Interface (GUI) therefore has the approach, to have a more simplified user interface designed, which is useable not only on the desktop, but also can be deployed for mobile devices.

GoldBug (E-Mail): The GoldBug-feature is used in the integrated email client to add here as well an end-to-end AESEncryption layer – the GoldBug, or: just a password, both users use to encrypt their emails once more. So with the GoldBug, you need a kind of password (e.g. AES-string) to open the email of a friend or to be able to chat with him.

Graph-Theory: In mathematics, and more specifically in graph theory, a graph is a representation of a set of objects where some pairs of objects are connected by links. The interconnected objects are represented by mathematical abstractions called vertices (also called nodes or points), and the links

that connect some pairs of vertices are called edges (also called arcs or lines). Typically, a graph is depicted in diagrammatic form as a set of dots for the vertices, joined by lines or curves for the edges. Graphs are one of the objects of study in discrete mathematics.

GUI: In computer science, a graphical user interface or GUI is a type of interface that allows users to interact with electronic devices through graphical icons and visual indicators such as secondary notation, as opposed to text-based interfaces, typed command labels or text navigation.

Hash: A hash function is any function that can be used to map data of arbitrary size to data of fixed size. The values returned by a hash function are called hash values, hash codes, hash sums, or simply hashes. A cryptographic hash function is a hash function which is considered practically impossible to invert, that is, to recreate the input data from its hash value alone. These one-way hash functions have been called "the workhorses of modern cryptography". The input data is often called the message, and the hash value is often called the message digest or simply the digest.

HTTPS: HTTPS (also called HTTP over TLS, HTTP over SSL, and HTTP Secure) is a protocol for secure communication over a computer network which is widely used on the Internet. HTTPS consists of communication over Hypertext Transfer Protocol (HTTP) within a connection encrypted by Transport Layer Security or its predecessor, Secure Sockets Layer. The main motivation for HTTPS is authentication of the visited website and protection of the privacy and integrity of the exchanged data.

IMAP: In computing, the Internet Message Access Protocol (IMAP) is an Internet standard protocol used by e-mail clients to retrieve e-mail messages from a mail server over a TCP/IP connection. IMAP is defined by RFC 3501. IMAP was designed with the goal of permitting complete management of an email box by multiple email clients, Therefore, clients generally leave messages on the server.

Impersonator: Impersonator is a function, which sends from the GoldBug Client a message from time to time into the network, which contains only random signs. With this method it is made more difficult for attackers to conduct time analysis of communications. Also real cipher text messages should be harder to recognize and harder to differ from such messages with random characters.

Information security: information security preservation of confidentiality, integrity and availability of information

Integer factorization: In number theory, integer factorization is the decomposition of a composite number into a product of smaller integers. If these integers are further restricted to prime numbers, the process is called prime factorization. When the numbers are very large, no efficient, non-quantum integer factorization algorithm is known; an effort by several researchers concluded in 2009, factoring a 232-digit number (RSA-768), utilizing hundreds of machines took two years and the researchers estimated that a 1024-bit RSA modulus would take about a thousand times as long.

Integrity: property of accuracy and completeness.

Iteration Function: In mathematics, an iterated function is a function $X \to X$ (that is, a function from some set X to itself) which is obtained by composing another function $f : X \to X$ with itself a certain number of times. The process of repeatedly applying the same function is called iteration. Iterated functions are objects of study in computer science, fractals, dynamical

systems, mathematics and renormalization group physics.

Kernel: In computing, the kernel is a computer program that manages input/output requests from software, and translates them into data processing instructions for the central processing unit and other electronic components of a computer. The kernel is a fundamental part of a modern computer's operating system or of applications.

Key, Private: Public-key cryptography refers to a set of cryptographic algorithms that are based on mathematical problems that currently admit no efficient solution. The strength lies in the "impossibility" (computational impracticality) for a properly generated private key to be determined from its corresponding public key. Thus the public key may be published without compromising security. Security depends only on keeping the private key private.

Key, Public: Public-key cryptography refers to a set of cryptographic algorithms that are based on mathematical problems that currently admit no efficient solution – particularly those inherent in certain integer factorization, discrete logarithm, and elliptic curve relationships. It is computationally easy for a user to generate a public and private key-pair and to use it for encryption and decryption. The strength lies in the "impossibility" (computational impracticality) for a properly generated private key to be determined from its corresponding public key. Thus the public key may be published without compromising security. Security depends only on keeping the private key private.

Key, Symmetric: These keys are used with symmetric key algorithms to apply confidentiality protection to information.

Keyed-Hash Message Authentication Code (HMAC): In cryptography, a keyed-hash message authentication code (HMAC) is a specific construction for calculating a message authentication code (MAC) involving a cryptographic hash function in combination with a secret cryptographic key. As with any MAC, it may be used to simultaneously verify both the data integrity and the authentication of a message. Any cryptographic hash function, such as MD5 or SHA-1, may be used in the calculation of an HMAC; the resulting MAC algorithm is termed HMAC-MD5 or HMAC-SHA1 accordingly. The cryptographic strength of the HMAC depends upon the cryptographic strength of the underlying hash function, the size of its hash output, and on the size and quality of the key.

Libcurl: cURL is a computer software project providing a library and command-line tool for transferring data using various protocols. The cURL project produces two products, libcurl and cURL. It was first released in 1997. The name originally stood for "see URL".

Listener: A listener is a software design pattern in which an object maintains a list of its dependents and notifies them automatically of any state changes, usually by calling one of their methods. It is mainly used to implement distributed event handling systems. It is often used for creating or opening a port on which the service or chat-server then is "listening" for incommuig data connections.

MAC (Message Authentication Code): In cryptography, a message authentication code (often MAC) is a short piece of information used to authenticate a message and to provide integrity and authenticity assurances on the message. Integrity assurances detect accidental and intentional message changes, while authenticity assurances affirm the message's origin. A MAC algorithm, sometimes called a keyed (cryptographic) hash function (however, cryptographic hash function

is only one of the possible ways to generate MACs), accepts as input a secret key and an arbitrary-length message to be authenticated, and outputs a MAC (sometimes known as a tag). The MAC value protects both a message's data integrity as well as its authenticity, by allowing verifiers (who also possess the secret key) to detect any changes to the message content.

Magnet-URI: The Magnet URI scheme, defines the format of magnet links, a de facto standard for identifying files by their content, via cryptographic hash value) rather than by their location.

Management system: set of interrelated or interacting elements of an organization to establish policies and objectives and processes to achieve those objectives

McEliece: In cryptography, the McEliece cryptosystem is an asymmetric encryption algorithm developed in 1978 by Robert McEliece. It was the first such scheme to use randomization in the encryption process. The algorithm has currently not gained much acceptance in the cryptographic community, but is a candidate for "post-quantum cryptography", as it is immune to attacks using Shor's algorithm and — more generally — measuring cost states using Fourier sampling. The recommended parameter sizes for the used Goppa code - which maximizes the adversary's work factor - appears to be n = 1024, t = 38, and k ≥ 644.

Measurement: process to determine a value

MELODICA: With the MELODICA feature in GoldBug Secure Messenger you call your friend and send him a new Gemini (AES-256-Key). The Key is sent over your asymmetric encryption of the RSA key. This is a secure way, as all other plaintext transfers like: email, spoken over phone or in other messengers, have to be regarded as unsafe and recorded. MELODICA stands for: Multi Encrypted Long Distance Calling. You call your friend even over a long distance of the echo protocol and exchange over secure asymmetric encryption a Gemini (AES-256 key) to establish an end-to-end encrypted channel.

Monitoring: determining the status of a system, a process or an activity

Multi-Encryption: Multiple encryption is the process of encrypting an already encrypted message one or more times, either using the same or a different algorithm. It is also known as cascade encryption, cascade ciphering, multiple encryption, and superencipherment. Superencryption refers to the outer-level encryption of a multiple encryption.

Nova: Nova describes a password on the to-be-transferred file. It is a symmetric encryption of the file scheduled for the transfer. It can be compared with the term of a GoldBug-Password on an E-Mail. Both are technically created with an AES-256 (or a user-defined password).

NTRU: NTRU is a patented and open source public-key cryptosystem that uses lattice-based cryptography to encrypt and decrypt data. It consists of two algorithms: NTRUEncrypt, which is used for encryption, and NTRUSign, which is used for digital signatures. Unlike other popular public-key cryptosystems, it is resistant to attacks using Shor's algorithm (i.e. by "quantum computing") and its performance has been shown to be significantly better.

Objective: result to be achieved.

Off-the-record (OTR): Off-the-Record Messaging (OTR) is a cryptographic protocol that provides encryption for instant messaging conversations. OTR uses a combination of AES symmetric-key algorithm with 128 bits key length, the Diffie–Hellman key exchange with 1536 bits group size, and the SHA-1 hash function. In

addition to authentication and encryption, OTR provides forward secrecy and malleable encryption.

One-Time-Magnet (OTM): A One-Time-Magnet (OTM) is a Magnet, which is deployed for the File-Transfer within the StarBeam-Funktion. After sending the File using the cryptographic values included in the Magnet-Link, the Magnet is deleted within the GoldBug application. Other Magnets for the StarBeam-Funktion can be used several times – this means, several and different files can be transferred to the receiver through the symmetric Channel (including all users, knowing the specific Magnet).

One-Time-Pad (OTP): In cryptography, the one-time pad (OTP) is an encryption technique that cannot be cracked if used correctly. In this technique, a plaintext is paired with a random secret key (also referred to as a one-time pad). Then, each bit or character of the plaintext is encrypted by combining it with the corresponding bit or character from the pad using modular addition. If the key is truly random, is at least as long as the plaintext, is never reused in whole or in part, and is kept completely secret, then the resulting ciphertext will be impossible to decrypt or break.

OpenPGP: The OpenPGP standard (also Pretty Good Privacy) is a data encryption and decryption computer program that provides cryptographic privacy and authentication for data communication. PGP is often used for signing, encrypting, and decrypting texts, e-mails, files, directories, and whole disk partitions and to increase the security of e-mail communications. It was created by Phil Zimmermann in 1991.PGP and similar software follow the OpenPGP standard (RFC 4880) for encrypting and decrypting data.

OpenSSL: In computer networking, OpenSSL is a software library to be used in applications that need to secure communications against eavesdropping or need to ascertain the identity of the party at the other end. It has found wide use in internet web servers, serving a majority of all web sites. OpenSSL contains an open-source implementation of the SSL and TLS protocols. Transport Layer Security (TLS) and its predecessor, Secure Sockets Layer (SSL), both of which are frequently referred to as 'SSL', are cryptographic protocols designed to provide communications security over a computer network.

Pandamonium: Pandamonium is a Web-Crawler, with which URLs of a Domain can be indexed for GoldBug. The Pandamonium Web Crawler can allocate for the URL-Search function within the GoldBug Messenger a bunch of URLs over the Import-function.

Passphrase: A passphrase is a sequence of words or other text used to control access to a computer system, program or data. A passphrase is similar to a password in usage, but is generally longer for added security. Passphrases are often used to control both access to, and operation of, cryptographic programs and systems. Passphrases are particularly applicable to systems that use the passphrase as an encryption key. The origin of the term is by analogy with password. The passphrase in GoldBug must be at least 16 characters long, this is used to create a cryptographic hash, which is longer and stronger.

Peer-to-Peer (P2P): Peer-to-peer (P2P) computing or networking is a distributed application architecture that partitions tasks or work loads between peers. Peers make a portion of their resources, such as processing power, disk storage or network bandwidth, directly available to other network participants, without the need for central coordination by servers or stable hosts. Peers are equally privileged, equipotent participants in the application. They are said to form a peer-to-peer network of nodes.

Performance: measurable result. Note: Performance can relate either to quantitative or qualitative findings.

Policy: intentions and direction of an formal entity as formally expressed by its management

POP3: In computing, the Post Office Protocol (POP) is an application-layer Internet standard protocol used by local e-mail clients to retrieve e-mail from a remote server over a TCP/IP connection. POP has been developed through several versions, with version 3 (POP3) being the last standard in common use.

POPTASTIC: POPTASTIC is a function, which enables encrypted chat and encrypted E-Mail over the regular POP3 and IMAP-Postboxes of a user. The GoldBug Messenger recognizes automatically, if the message has to be regarded as a Chat-Message or an E-Mail-Message. For that, the POPTASTIC encryption key is used. Once with a friend exchanged, this key is sending all E-mails between to E-Mail-Partner only as encrypted E-Mail. Third, POPTASTIC enables – respective the insertion of the POP3 / IMAP account information into the settings enables – also an old-fashioned and unencrypted E-Mail-Communication to @-E-Mail-Addresses. GoldBug extends the Instant Messaging with this function to a regular E-Mail-Client and also to an always encrypting E-Mail-Client over the POPTASTIC Key. The E-Mail-Addresses for encrypted E-Mails are indicated with a lock icon. Encrypted Chat is enabled over the free ports for E-Mail also behind more restrictive Hardware environments at any time.

PostgreSQL: PostgreSQL, often simply Postgres, is an object-relational database management system (ORDBMS) with an emphasis on extensibility and standards-compliance. As a database server, its primary function is to store data securely, supporting best practices, and to allow for retrieval at the request of other software applications. It can handle workloads ranging from small single-machine applications to large Internet-facing applications with many concurrent users. PostgreSQL implements the majority of the SQL:2011 standard.

Process: set of interrelated or interacting activities which transforms inputs into outputs

Qt: Qt is a cross-platform application framework that is widely used for developing application software that can be run on various software and hardware platforms with little or no change in the underlying codebase, while still being a native application with the capabilities and speed thereof. Qt is currently being developed both by the Qt Company, a subsidiary of Digia, and the Qt Project under open-source governance, involving individual developers and firms working to advance Qt.

Repleo: With a Repleo the own public key is encrypted with the already received public key of a friend, so that the own public key can be transferred to the friend in a protected way.

Requirement: need or expectation that is stated, generally implied or obligatory; Note: "Generally implied" means that it is custom or common practice for the organization and interested parties that the need or expectation under consideration is implied. A specified requirement is one that is stated, for example in documented information.

Review: activity undertaken to determine the suitability, adequacy and effectiveness of the subject matter to achieve established objectives

Rewind: Rewind describes a function within the StarBeam-File-Transfer. With this the Send-out of a file is started for a second time. It is comparable with a new play from start of a music file. In case the file has not been completely transferred, the transmission can be started new or even scheduled for a

later point in time. In case only some missing block of the file should be transferred again to the receiver, the further tool StarBeam-Analyzer is able to generate a Magnet-URI-Link, which the receiver can send to the sender, so that is will send out only the missing blocks again.

Risk: effect of uncertainty on objectives. An effect is a deviation from the expected — positive or negative. Uncertainty is the state, even partial, of deficiency of information related to, understanding or knowledge of, an event, its consequence, or likelihood. Risk is often characterized by reference to potential events and consequences, or a combination of these. Risk is often expressed in terms of a combination of the consequences of an event (including changes in circumstances) and the associated likelihood of occurrence. In the context of information security management systems, information security risks can be expressed as effect of uncertainty on information security objectives. Information security risk is associated with the potential that threats will exploit vulnerabilities of an information asset or group of information assets and thereby cause harm to an organization.

Rosetta CryptoPad: The Rosetta-CryptoPad uses an own Key for the encryption – as also an own key exists for E-Mail, Chat, URLs or POPTASTIC. With the Rosetta-CryptoPad a text can be converted into cipher text. It is used, to encrypt own texts before sending the text out to the internet or before you Post it somewhere into the Web. Similar to the File-Encryption-Tool for Files, Rosetta also converts plaintext into cipher text. Then the text can be transferred – either over one again secured and encrypted channel or even unencrypted as Chat or E-mail. Further messages can be posted to an Internet-Board or a Paste-Bin-Service as chipper text.

RSA: RSA is one of the first practical public-key cryptosystems and is widely used for secure data transmission. In such a cryptosystem, the encryption key is public and differs from the decryption key which is kept secret. In RSA, this asymmetry is based on the practical difficulty of factoring the product of two large prime numbers, the factoring problem. RSA is made of the initial letters of the surnames of Ron Rivest, Adi Shamir, and Leonard Adleman, who first publicly described the algorithm in 1977.

Salt, cryptographic: In cryptography, a salt is random data that is used as an additional input to a one-way function that hashes a password or passphrase. The primary function of salts is to defend against dictionary attacks versus a list of password hashes and against pre-computed rainbow table attacks.

SCTP: In computer networking, the Stream Control Transmission Protocol (SCTP) is a transport-layer protocol (protocol number 132), serving in a similar role to the popular protocols Transmission Control Protocol (TCP) and User Datagram Protocol (UDP). It provides some of the same service features of both: it is message-oriented like UDP and ensures reliable, in-sequence transport of messages with congestion control like TCP.RFC 4960 defines the protocol. RFC 3286 provides an introduction.

Session Management: Related to the identification of authenticated users

Signature: A digital signature is a mathematical scheme for demonstrating the authenticity of a digital message or documents. A valid digital signature gives a recipient reason to believe that the message was created by a known sender, that the sender cannot deny having sent the message (authentication and non-repudiation), and that the message was not altered in transit (integrity).

Simulacra: The Simulacra function is a similar function compared to the Impersonator function. While Impersonator is simulating a chat of two participants with messages, Simulacra is just sending out a Fake-Message from time to time. Simulacra-Messages contain only random characters and have not the style or goal, to imitate a process of a conversation.

Small world phenomenon: Small world phenomenon refers to a a hypothesis, according to which every human being (social actor) is connected to the world with each other over a surprisingly short chain of acquaintance relationships. The phenomenon is often referred to as Six Degrees of Separation. Guglielmo Marconi's conjectures based on his radio work in the early 20th century, which were articulated in his 1909 Nobel Prize address, may have inspired[citation needed] Hungarian author Frigyes Karinthy to write a challenge to find another person to whom he could not be connected through at most five people. This is perhaps the earliest reference to the concept of six degrees of separation, and the search for an answer to the small world problem. The small-world experiment comprised several experiments conducted by Stanley Milgram and other researchers examining the average path length for social networks of people in the United States. The research was groundbreaking in that it suggested that human society is a small-world-type network characterized by short path-lengths.

SMTP: Simple Mail Transfer Protocol (SMTP) is an Internet standard for electronic mail (email) transmission. First defined by RFC 821 in 1982, it was last updated in 2008 with the Extended SMTP additions by RFC 5321—which is the protocol in widespread use today. SMTP by default uses TCP port 25. The protocol for mail submission is the same, but uses port 587. SMTP connections secured by SSL, known as SMTPS, default to port 465

Socialist Millionaire Protocol (SMP): In cryptography, the socialist millionaire problem is one in which two millionaires want to determine if their wealth is equal without disclosing any information about their riches to each other. It is a variant of the Millionaire's Problem whereby two millionaires wish to compare their riches to determine who has the most wealth without disclosing any information about their riches to each other. It is often used as a cryptographic protocol that allows two parties to verify the identity of the remote party through the use of a shared secret, avoiding a man-in-the-middle attack without the inconvenience of manually comparing public key fingerprints through an outside channel. In effect, a relatively weak password/passphrase in natural language can be used.

SQLite: SQLite is a relational database management system contained in a C programming library. In contrast to many other database management systems, SQLite is not a client–server database engine. Rather, it is embedded into the end program.

StarBeam-Analyser: The StarBeam-Analyzer is a tool, to analyze a transferred file over the StarBeam-function in that regard, if all partially blocks of the file have been received completely. The tool investigates – in case needed – the missing blocks of a file and creates a respective Magnet-URI-Link with this information. The receiver of the file can generate the Magnet and send it over to the sender of the file, who is then able to schedule a new send-out just of the missing blocks (also named as links or chunks). Over this procedure not the complete files has to be sent or replayed new to complete the original first transfer.

Super-Echo: The echo protocol consists within these remembered characteristics (if we summarize it

short), that each node tries to encrypt each message capsule – if this succeeds in terms of the hash-comparison, this message is for the own reading, and will be not again repacked and transferred further to all other connected online neighbors. As an online attacker could recognize this, when an incoming message is not send out again, and thus could assume, that that it is a message for the receiver at this node. With Super-Echo the message will be – even if it has been decrypted successfully for the own node – sent out again to the connected nodes and for traveling on further paths. Just in regard, as this message would not have been determined for the own readings.

TCP: The Transmission Control Protocol (TCP) is a core protocol of the Internet protocol suite. It originated in the initial network implementation in which it complemented the Internet Protocol (IP). Applications that do not require reliable data stream service may use the User Datagram Protocol (UDP), which provides a connectionless datagram service that emphasizes reduced latency over reliability.

Timing: Related to the race conditions, locking, or order of operations

Turtle Hopping: Turtle was a free anonymous peer-to-peer network project being developed at the Vrije Universiteit in Amsterdam, involving professor Andrew Tanenbaum. Like other anonymous P2P software, it allows users to share files and otherwise communicate without fear of legal sanctions or censorship. Turtle's claims of anonymity are backed by two research papers. Technically, Turtle is a friend-to-friend (F2F) network. The RetroShare File Sharing application is based on a F2f and implemented a "Turtle Hopping" feature which was inspired by Turtle.

UDP: The User Datagram Protocol (UDP) is one of the core members of the Internet protocol suite. The protocol was designed by David P. Reed in 1980 and formally defined in RFC 768. UDP uses a simple connectionless transmission model with a minimum of protocol mechanism. It has no handshaking dialogues, and thus exposes the user's program to any unreliability of the underlying network protocol. There is no guarantee of delivery, ordering, or duplicate protection. Time-sensitive applications often use UDP because dropping packets is preferable to waiting for delayed packets, which may not be an option in a real-time system.

URL-Distiller: URL-Distillers are filter rules, with which the downloaded, uploaded or imported URLS will be filtered. For example one can configure his URL-Distillers in such a way, that all URLs are loaded into the own Database, but only specific URLS from one defined Domain, e.g. Wikipedia, are uploaded. Also e.g. a university can distribute only URLs out of the own database to its connected students, which refer to the own web-domain. URLs and URIs of Magnets, ED2K-Links and Torrent-URLs are currently not supported in the own URL-Database respective filter rules. The distillers refer to Web-URLs and also to FTP and Gopher.

Virtuelle E-Mail Institution ("VEMI"): See E-Mail-Institution.

Web of Trust: In cryptography, a web of trust is a concept used in PGP, GnuPG, and other OpenPGP-compatible systems to establish the authenticity of the binding between a public key and its owner. Its decentralized trust model is an alternative to the centralized trust model of a public key infrastructure (PKI), which relies exclusively on a certificate authority (or a hierarchy of such). As with computer networks, there are many independent webs of trust, and any user (through their identity certificate) can be a part of, and a link between, multiple webs.

7   ANNEX: INDEX OF DESCRIPTIONS

Table 82: Difficulty Level and Description

Difficulty Level	Difficulty Description
Undetermined	The difficulty of exploit was not determined during this engagement
Low	Commonly exploited, public tools exist or can be scripted that exploit this flaw
Medium	Attackers must write an exploit, or need an in depth knowledge of a complex system
High	The attacker must have privileged insider access to the system, may need to know extremely complex technical details or must discover other weaknesses in order to exploit this issue

Table 83: Severity Category and Description

Severity Category	Severity Description
Informational	The issue does not pose an (immediate) risk, but is relevant for theoretical analysis or to security best practices or Defense in Depth
Undetermined	The extent of the risk was not determined during this engagement
Low	The risk is relatively small, or is not a risk the customer has indicated as important
Medium	Individual user's information is at risk, exploitation would be bad for client's reputation, of moderate financial impact, possible legal implications for client
High	Large numbers of users, very bad for client's reputation or serious legal implications.

Table 84: Innovation & Improvement Class and Descripton

Innovation & Improvement Class	Innovation & Improvement Description
Informational	Suggestion for improvement given by the auditor.
Habitual	Improves the given status, process or function.
Medium	Defines a new status, process or function for the application.
High	Defines a new status, process or function compared for the market. Sets a new state of the art. Regarded as Innovation.

Table 85: Strength Dimensions and Descripton

Strength Dimension	Strength Description
Low	Process, function or feature implementation is state of the art compared to just a few other comparable entities.
Medium	Process, function or feature implementation is very deep and detailed and this leading within the standard compared to others.
High	Process, function or feature implementation is very deep and detailed and a unique selling proposition (USP) compared to others. This strength sets new standards.

ANNEX: INDEX OF FIGURES

Table 86: Index of figures

ANNEX: INDEX OF TABLES

Table 87: Index of tables

BIG SEVEN Studie über 7 Crypto-Messenger: E-Mail-Programm GoldBug punktet im IT-Audit

Tokio/München. Ein weiterer Beitrag in der Crypto-Diskussion: Zwei Sicherheitsforscher aus Tokyo und München haben in ihrer BIG SEVEN Studie die sieben bekanntesten Verschlüsselungsprogramme für E-Mail- und Chat-Nachrichten aus dem Open Source Bereich untersucht und sodann vertiefend ein IT-Audit für die bekannte Software-Lösung GoldBug.sf.net durchgeführt. Die Evaluation berücksichtigte die wesentlichen Kriterien, Untersuchungsfelder und Methoden von acht internationalen IT-Audit Manualen und identifiziert zehn Trends im Bereich des Crypto-Messagings.

BIG SEVEN Open Source Crypto-Messenger
Indikationen innerhalb 20 Audit-Dimensionen von internationalen IT-Audit-Manualen

GoldBug.sf.net - E-Mail & Messenger Software zeigt sich sehr konform im Audit (45 Punkte)

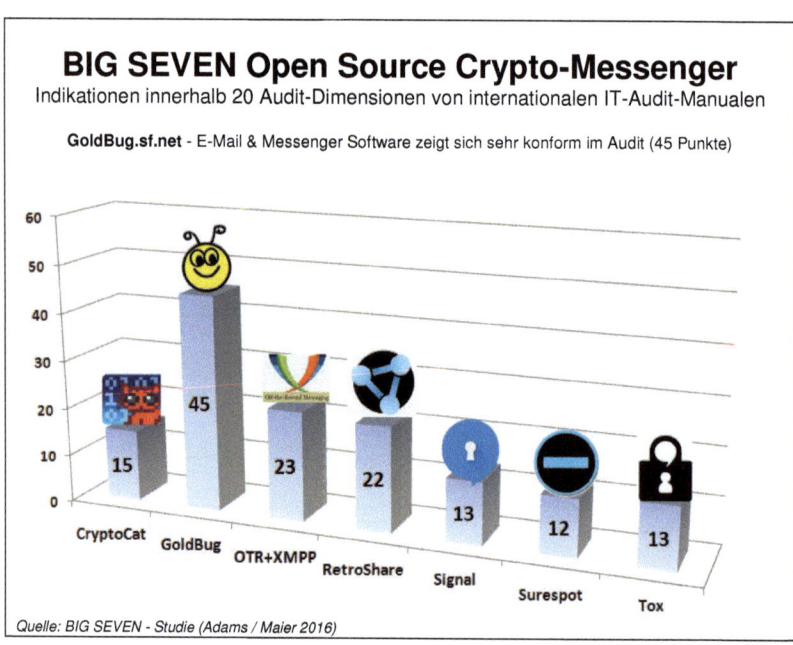

Quelle: BIG SEVEN - Studie (Adams / Maier 2016)

Ein weiterer Beitrag in der Crypto-Diskussion: Die beiden Sicherheitsforscher David Adams (Tokyo) und Ann-Kathrin Maier (München) haben in ihrer BIG SEVEN Studie die sieben bekanntesten Verschlüsselungsprogramme für E-Mail und Chat-Nachrichten aus dem Open Source Bereich untersucht und sodann vertieft ein IT-Audit für die bekannte Software-Lösung GoldBug.sf.net durchgeführt. Das Audit berücksichtigte die wesentlichen Kriterien, Untersuchungsfelder und Methoden in Anlehnung an acht internationale IT-Audit Manuale und wurde in 20 Dimensionen durchgeführt.

Sicherheitsforscher David Adams aus Tokio zur vorliegenden BIG SEVEN CRYPTO-Studie: "*Wir haben uns die sieben wichtigsten quelloffenen Programme für verschlüsselte Nachrichtenübertragungen angesehen und zehn Trends im Bereich des Crypto-Messagings identifiziert. Einer der wichtigen Trends ist, dass der Nutzer ein sogenanntes Ende-zu-Ende verschlüsselndes Passwort selbst manuell definieren können sollte*".

Die Software „GoldBug - E-Mail-Programm und Instant Messenger" hatte dabei excellente Bewertungen und zeigt sich nicht nur sehr vertrauenswürdig und compliant bzw. konform zu den internationalen IT-Audit-Manualen und Sicherheitsstandards. GoldBug punktet auch im Vergleich und der Bewertung der Einzelfunktionen wesentlich ausführlicher als die vergleichbaren anderen open source Crypto-Messenger.

Die Münchener Co-Autorin der Studie Ann-Kathrin Maier ergänzt: *"Wir haben sodann unsere Messenger-Studie vertieft mit einem ausführlichen Audit des Crypto-Programms GoldBug, das excellente Ergebnisse für verschlüsseltes E-Mail und sicheren Online-Chat erhielt. Durch unsere Code-Reviews von GoldBug können wir die Vertrauenswürdigkeit in die Sicherheit dieser Open Source Verschlüsselung bestätigen."*

Zahlreiche Details wurden durch verschiedenste Methoden analysiert, verglichen und auch von den beiden Autoren strategisch für die aktuellen Verschlüsselungs-Diskussionen bewertet. Zu den vergleichend untersuchten Applikationen zählen CryptoCat, GoldBug, OTR-XMPP-Klienten wie z.B. Pidgin mit dem OTR-Plugin, RetroShare sowie Signal, Surespot und Tox.

In der Studie werden detaillierte Analysen und Erkenntnisse beschrieben, wie z.B.
- dass GoldBug seine Stärke insbesondere in der für die Zukunft strategisch wichtigen, hybriden Multi-Verschlüsselung hat: bereits verschlüsselter Text wird nochmals verschlüsselt,
- es werden zahlreiche Hintergrund- und fachspezifische Informationen aufgegriffen, wie gegenseitige Angriffe der Crypto-Projekte untereinander, wenn z.B. Entwickler von CryptoCat andere Entwicklungen mit neuen Releases übertrumpfen wollen oder es wird hinterfragt, warum einige Fachexperten von Optionen für dezentrale Chat-Server medienwirksam ablenken. Ebenso wird untersucht, warum Chat-Applikationen als quelloffen gelten, obwohl deren Chat-Server es nicht sind,
- es wird in der Studie die These analysiert, dass es heute nicht mehr (nur) um das Brechen von Kryptologie gehe, sondern (besonders auch) um das Aufzeichnen von Metadaten: „Wer kommuniziert mit wem" sei entscheidender, als der Inhalt der Kommunikation,
- dass zum Beispiel die Schlüsselstärke von GoldBug doppelt so groß, und damit sicher ist, als bei dem OTR-Plugin für XMPP-Klienten,
- dass die Entwicklung von TOX einem promiskuitiven Pool gleiche, da über 147 Entwickler zum Code beigetragen haben - und ein Qualitätsmangement des Codes daher als kritisch zu bewerten sei,
- es wird analysiert, warum Studierende im Studentenwohnheim quelloffene Dateien inzwischen lieber mittels eines Bluetooth-Server verschlüsselt austauschen als über LAN,
- die Weiterentwicklung von althergebrachten Verschlüsselungswerkzeugen wird darin gesehen, Verschlüsselung in einer Applikation auf beides, Chat und E-Mail zu beziehen, so dass man Online- und Offline-Freunde gleichermaßen erreichen kann, wie es im GoldBug Messenger durch die POPTASTIC Funktion (Chat über IMAP/POP3) implementiert ist,
- allen verschlüsselnden Messengern wird der Einbau von manuell zu definierenden symmetrischen Ende-zu-Ende Verschlüsselungen empfohlen, die bislang nur wenige - auch Whatsapp nicht - implementiert haben,
- insbesondere die Notwendigkeit zu mehr vergleichender Forschung im Bereich der Funktionen und Lösungen für Verschlüsselungen und deren Applikationen wird weiterhin herausgestellt.

Nachdem das amerikanische Institut NIST (Chen et al.) im Februar 2016 erklärt hat, dass der Algorithmus RSA im Quantum-Computer-Zeitalter als gebrochen bzw. nicht mehr sicher gilt, ist GoldBug der verbleibende Messenger, der neben RSA noch ElGamal und NTRU implementiert hat und damit als sicher gegen Quantum-Computer gelten kann! Das vertiefende Audit ist auch daher für diesen von den sieben Messengern durchgeführt worden.

Die vergleichende BIG SEVEN Studie über quelloffene Crypto-Messenger bzw. der GoldBug-Audit-Report empfiehlt sich daher nicht nur als lesenswerte Ressource für IT-Interessierte, Studierende, Mathematiker, Kryptologen und Auditoren, sondern auch als Diskussionsgrundlage für weitere Entwicklungen im Bereich der Forschung und Programmierung sowie auch als vorbereitender Reader für Fragen auf einer nächsten Crypto-Party.

Die Studie ist im Nachgang bei dem Projekt entsprechend archiviert worden und kann unter der folgenden URL heruntergeladen werden:

https://sf.net/projects/goldbug/files/bigseven-crypto-audit.pdf

BIG SEVEN Study about 7 Crypto-Messenger: E-Mail-Client GoldBug scores in the IT-Audit

Tokyo/Munich. Another contribution in the crypto discussion: Two security researchers from Tokyo and Munich examine in their BIG SEVEN study seven well-known encryption applications for e-mail and instant messaging out of the open source area and then performed a deeper IT-audit for the acquainted software solution GoldBug.sf.net. The evaluation took into account the essential criteria, study fields and methods of eight international IT-audit manuals and identifies Ten Trends in the Crypto-Messaging.

BIG SEVEN Open Source Crypto-Messenger
Indications within 20 Audit-Dimensions of International IT-Audit-Manuals

GoldBug.sf.net - E-Mail & Messenger Software is audit compliant (45 Points)

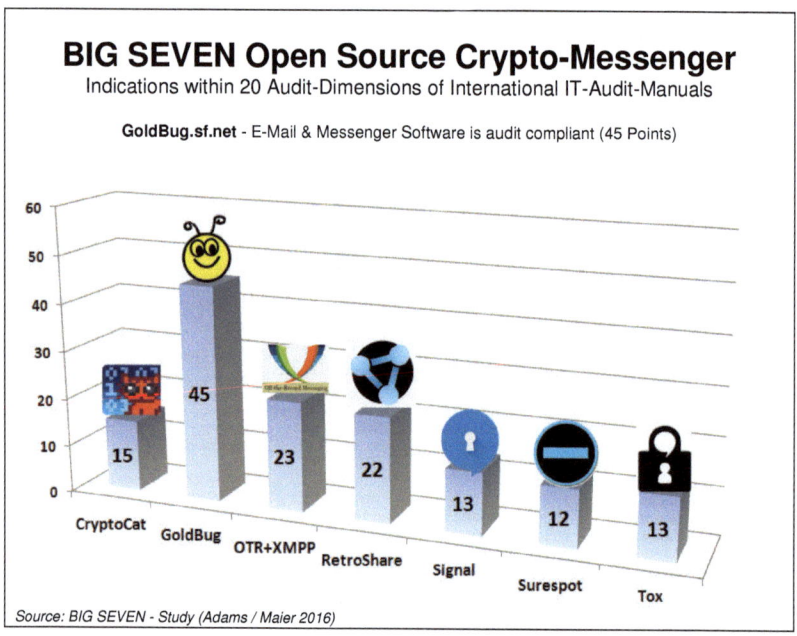

Source: BIG SEVEN - Study (Adams / Maier 2016)

Another contribution in the crypto-discussion: The two security researchers David Adams (Tokyo) and Ann-Kathrin Maier (Munich), who examined in their BIG SEVEN study seven well-known encryption applications for e-mail and instant messaging out of the open source area, performed then a deeper IT-audit for the acquainted software solution GoldBug.sf.net. The audit took into account the essential criteria, study fields and methods on the basis of eight international IT-audit manuals and was carried out in 20 dimensions.

Security researcher David Adams from Tokyo about the published BIG SEVEN CRYPTO-study: *"We looked at the seven major open source programs for encrypted online-communication and identified ten trends in the Crypto-Messaging area. One of the important trends is the feature, that the users should be able to define an so-called end-to-end encrypting password by themselfs manually".*

The software "GoldBug - email client and instant messenger" here was ahead with excellent results and is not only very trustworthy and compliant to international IT-audit manuals and safety standards, GoldBug also scores in comparison and in the evaluation of the single functions in much greater detail than the other comparable open source crypto messenger.

Co-author of the study Ann-Kathrin Maier from Munich confirms: *"We have then our Messenger study deepened with a detailed audit of the crypto-program GoldBug, which received excellent results for encrypted email and secure online chat. By our code-reviews we can confirm the trustworthiness of this open source encryption in GoldBug."*

Numerous details have been analyzed by various methods, compared and also strategically evaluated by the two authors regarding the current encryption discussions.

The comparatively studied applications include CryptoCat, GoldBug, OTR-XMPP clients such as Pidgin with the OTR-plugin, RetroShare and Signal, Surespot and Tox.

In the study, detailed analysis and findings are described, such as
- that GoldBug has its strength especially in the hybrid multi-encryption, which is for the future strategically important: already encrypted text will be encrypted again,
- it incorporates many of the background and subject-specific information, such as mutual attacks of the Crypto-projects amoung each other, for example, when cryptocat developers want to outdo other developments with new releases, or it is questioned why some experts distract of options for decentralized chat servers prominent within the media. Also it is examined, why chat applications are considered open source, although the chat server is not,
- it is the thesis analyzed in the study, that it is today no longer (only) about the breaking of cryptology, but (especially also) about the recording of metadata: "Who communicates with whom" is more crucial, as the content of communication,
- that e.g. the key strength of GoldBug is twice as large and thus safer than in the OTR-plugin of XMPP-clients,
- that the development of TOX could be regarded as a promiscuous pool since over 147 developers contributed to the code development - and quality management of the code therefore could be regarded as critical,
- it is analyzed, why students prefer in their dormitory houses to exchange open source files encrypted using a Bluetooth server than a LAN network,
- the further development of traditional encryption tools is seen in relating encryption in an application to both, chat and e-mail, so that you can reach online and offline friends, as it is implemented in the GoldBug Messenger by the POPTASTIC function (Chat via IMAP / POP3),
- for all encrypting messengers the installation of manually defineable symmetrical end-to-end encryption is recommended, which have so far only a few messenger (also not Whatsapp),
- in particular the need for more comparative research in the field of functions and solutions for encryption and their referring applications is further regarded.

After the institute NIST (Chen et al.) has stated in February 2016 that the algorithm RSA in quantum computer age is broken respectively no longer sure, GoldBug is the remaining Messenger which has next to RSA also even ElGamal and NTRU implemented and therefore can be regarded as safe against Quantum computers! The in-depth audit was therefore carried out for this of seven Messengers.

Therefore, the comparative BIG SEVEN study about open source crypto-messaging respective the GoldBug audit-report is recommended not only as a resource for IT interested readers, students, mathematicians, cryptologists and auditors, but also can be regarded as a basis for discussion on further development in the field of research, programming and as preparatory reading material for questions at the next crypto party.

The study has been archived accordingly at the project
and can be downloaded at the following URL:

https://sf.net/projects/goldbug/files/bigseven-crypto-audit.pdf

Linda A. Bertran & Gunter van Dooble:
Transformation of Cryptography -
Fundamental concepts of Encryption
ISBN-13: 978-3749450749 (English)
ISBN-13: 978-3750400733 (German)

Scott Edwards & Spot-On.sf.net Project:
**Spot-On Encryption Suite: Democratization
of Multiple & Exponential Encryption**: -
Handbook and User Manual as practical
software guide. ISBN-13: 978-3749435067

Mele Gasakis & Max Schmidt:
Beyond Cryptographic Routing:
The Echo Protocol in the new
Era of Exponential Encryption (EEE)
ISBN-13: 978-3748151982 (Hardcover)
ISBN-13: 978-3748158868 (Paperback)

Nomenclatura –
Encyclopedia of modern Cryptography
and Internet Security
ISBN-13: 978-3746066684

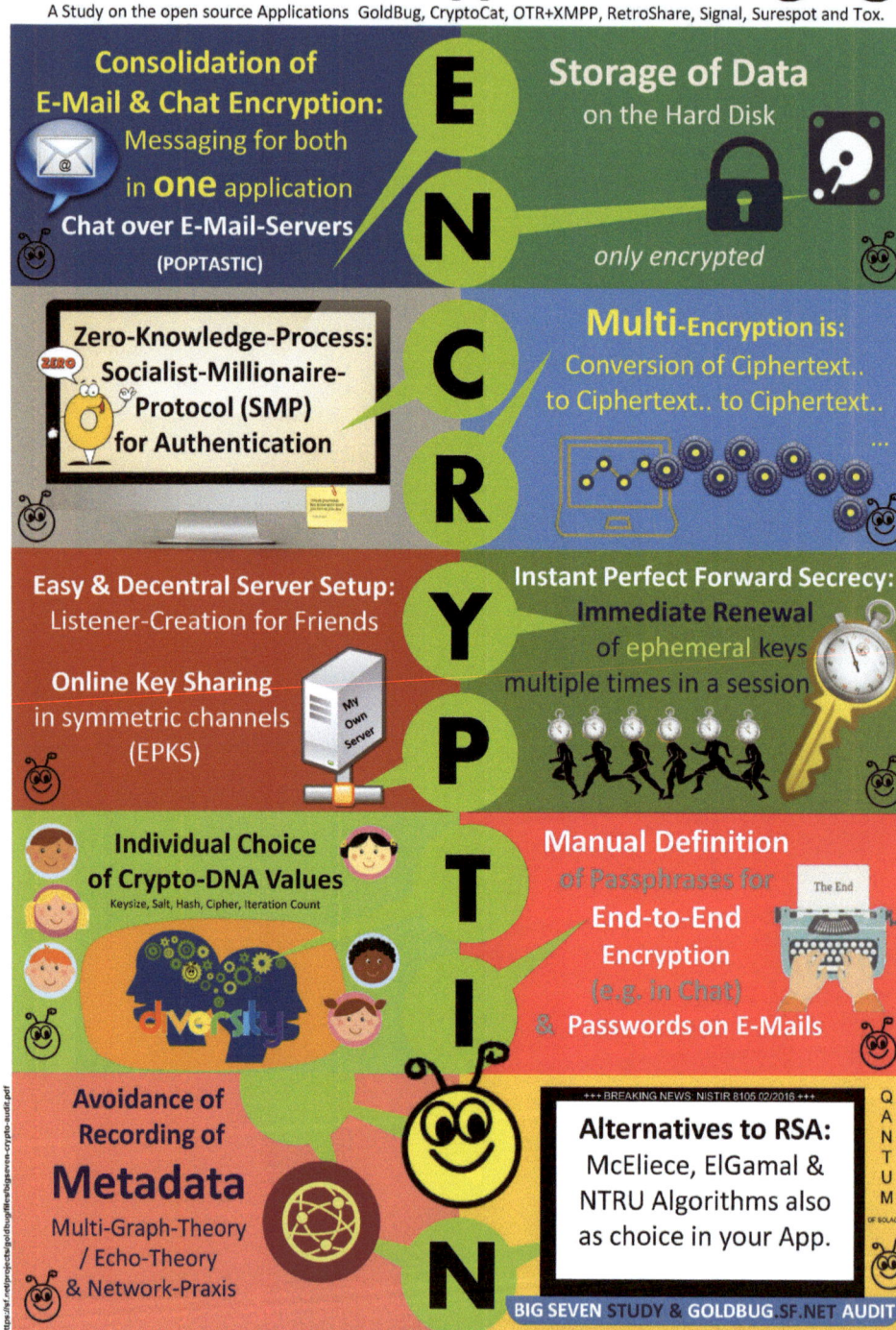

10 Trends in **Crypto Messaging**

A Study on the open source Applications GoldBug, CryptoCat, OTR+XMPP, RetroShare, Signal, Surespot and Tox.

Consolidation of E-Mail & Chat Encryption: Messaging for both in **one** application. Chat over E-Mail-Servers (POPTASTIC)

Storage of Data on the Hard Disk — *only encrypted*

Zero-Knowledge-Process: Socialist-Millionaire-Protocol (SMP) for Authentication

Multi-Encryption is: Conversion of Ciphertext.. to Ciphertext.. to Ciphertext.. ...

Easy & Decentral Server Setup: Listener-Creation for Friends. **Online Key Sharing** in symmetric channels (EPKS). My Own Server

Instant Perfect Forward Secrecy: **Immediate Renewal** of ephemeral keys multiple times in a session

Individual Choice of Crypto-DNA Values Keysize, Salt, Hash, Cipher, Iteration Count. diversity

Manual Definition of Passphrases for **End-to-End Encryption** (e.g. in Chat) & Passwords on E-Mails. The End

Avoidance of Recording of Metadata Multi-Graph-Theory / Echo-Theory & Network-Praxis

+++ BREAKING NEWS: NISTIR 8105 02/2016 +++
Alternatives to RSA: McEliece, ElGamal & NTRU Algorithms also as choice in your App.

QANTUM OF SOLACE

ENCRYPTION

BIG SEVEN STUDY & GOLDBUG.SF.NET AUDIT

https://sf.net/projects/goldbug/files/bigseven-crypto-audit.pdf

Adams, D. / Maier, A.K. (2016)